D1193266

THE POLITICS OF RETURN. INTERNATIONAL RETURN MIGRATION IN EUROPE

Proceedings of the First European Conference on International Return Migration

(Rome, November 11-14, 1981)

Edited by Daniel Kubat

1984

Centro Studi Emigrazione - Roma

Center for Migration Studies - New York

Copyright© 1983 by CSER

Centro Studi Emigrazione-Roma
Via Dandolo 58
00153 Roma (Italy)

Center for Migration Studies
209 Flagg Place
Staten Island, New York 10304 (USA)

ISBN 0-913256-68-4

PREFACE

Return migration, for a long time a rather neglected chapter in the study of migration processes and cycles, has been attracting increasing attention among scholars and researchers in the course of the last few years. The First European Conference on International Return Migration which took place in Rome from November 10 to 14, 1981, can be considered one major event which helped channel this rising interest in the subject and bring it into focus. Held under the auspices of the Research Committee on Migration of the International Sociological Association, the Conference availed itself of the organizational and scientific support of the Centro Studi Emigrazione in Rome and was attended by almost a hundred scholars and researchers from about 20 countries from all over the world.

The number of papers presented at the Conference and the numerous works specifically prepared for it, although not all of them were actually discussed, represent a rich and articulated analysis of return migration both in terms of the different content issues and of the different geographical areas covered.

It was soon apparent to the Organizing Committee that the material presented at the Conference should be gathered together since it represented, in its entirety, an extremely useful and up-to-date picture of international knowledge and debate concerning return migration. However, transforming the proceedings of the Conference into a homogeneous and compact publication was obviously to be anything but easy.

An Editorial Committee composed of F.P. Cerase, H.J. Hoffmann-Nowotny, D. Kubat, A. Richmond, G.F. Rosoli and S. Tomasi, was set up to discuss the matter. With the collaboration of the organizers of the single work sessions, a first-step revision of the papers was carried out. The second step, however, required actual editing and format homogeneization, an onerous and demanding task indeed, which Daniel Kubat accepted and, as the present volume, we believe, testifies, performed with excellence. To him, the Organizing Committee is exceedingly grateful.

The geographical dispersion of the authors of the papers and the many different languages they speak, have complicated matters, making communications somewhat less rapid and smooth than would have been desirable and demanding an unrelenting effort and constant collaboration from the staff of the Centro Studi Emigrazione which had, in the meantime, accepted responsibility for the publication of the book.

By the fall of 1983, most of the work had been completed and by the end of the year, Daniel Kubat, during a trip to Rome, had checked the galleys and made final revisions.

It is our hope that all those interested in return migration will indeed find this volume, concise and direct in style, a current and comprehensive perspective on return migration both in terms of scientific content and policy and operational proposals.

A final word of appreciation goes to the authors of the single papers; many of them may have suffered from the considerable revisions to their work but they all share with us the convinction that the overall result has more than warranted the process.

F.P. Cerase - G.F. Rosoli

ACKNOWLEDGEMENTS

Most of the papers in this volume are revised and often considerably shortened versions of the papers presented before *The First European Conference on International Return Migration*, held in Rome, November 10 through 14, 1981. The Conference was held under the auspices of the Research Committee on Migration of the International Sociological Association and of the Centro Studi Emigrazione in Rome.

Dr. Gianfausto Rosoli of the Centro Studi Emigrazione and Professor Franco Cerase, chairman of the Local Arrangement Committee for the Conference, not only took care of the Conference itself but guided the volume through the many stages of production. My indebtedness to them is deep.

Financial assistance for the Conference is gratefully acknowledged here as well, as it carried over into the preparation of this volume. The Ford Foundation, the Volkswagen Foundation, the Italian Consiglio Nazionale delle Ricerche, UNESCO and the ISA all gave generously.

In Waterloo, I found in Ursula Ortman a most dedicated and conscientious person. She handled all the revisions of the manuscripts. In Rome, Mary Paterson remained undaunted as language editor and compiler of the index. My thanks to her are boundless.

Again, the staff at the Centro in Rome, Gianfausto Rosoli, Graziano Tassello, Luigi Favero (cover design) and Maria Pia Lodi (typist) have produced the book swiftly once all the manuscripts arrived.

Last but not least, my sabbatical leave from the University of Waterloo enabled me to give my time to the volume. I found the close work with all the authors very rewarding and I thank them again.

Daniel Kubat

CONTENTS

Part II - Return migration and the host countries

Part III - Perspectives on return migration

A. Historical antecedents

INTRODUCTION

Daniel Kubat

> "At some future point in world civili-
> zation, it may well be discovered that
> right to free and open movements of
> people on the surface of the earth is
> fundamental to the structure of hu-
> man opportunity and is therefore
> basic in the same sense as free religion,
> speech and franchise".
> Roger Nett, ETHICS 81: 218

The standard disclaimer in the literature on migration and on return migration specifically that there is a pronounced dearth of writings on the matter cannot be made any more. There are now works on return migration both descriptive and analytic which make the field of return migration an established subdiscipline in the study of migration from whatever perspective, be it economics, geography, sociology or any social science hybrid. Part III, B of the present volume offers an inventory of the current literature on return migration.

The present volume adds to the current concern with return migration. The close to forty papers on the subject address return migration in Europe, especially in the present and the preceding decade and also offer excursions into the history of return migration to Europe. The central focus of the volume is however, what happens to the normally expected return flows when a variety of essentially restrictive measures are undertaken by the receiving countries to stem further in-migration and to encourage return. What happens is illustrated both on the national and local scale; other papers offer theoretical perspectives explaining return migration.

On the whole, it is argued through the individual papers, disparate as they may seem, that the relationship between a universalist philosophy of social security and both the number of people and their wealth is such that protecting the *status quo* cannot but ensue. Specifically, this applies to the movements of people where the international migration tends to flow into countries known both for their ample social security provisions and their history of abiding by rules of civility towards incoming foreigners. There, population pressures through in-migration tend to build up and when combined with economic dislocations produce conflict between an enlightened self-interest which has fostered in-migration in the first place and between a sheer self-interest which is isolationist. It seems that in the long run the enlightened self-interest will allow for cultural and economic diversification and lead to something akin to a flowering of a civilization, historical examples of which abound, the sheer self-interest tends to be predicated on the zero sum notion of finiteness of resources and a fixed division of the economic pie, thus precipitating an economic decline, again amply documented in history.

The jolt to the world economy resulting from the oil crisis of 1973 found its repercussions in the disruption of both international and the complementary return migration. In the case of international migration for the purpose of settlement, as was the peopling of the Americas and Oceania and other parts of the world during the past few centuries there remained the expectation that at least some of the settlers intended to return. Actually, many more did than was commonly held.

In any case, were one to think of migration as tied to the life cycle of migrants, settlement without return may be seen as a truncated migration cycle, along the lines of the argument which makes a "migratory chain" a logical parallel to the life cycle (OECD, 1978). The migratory chain is a chain of events in counterdistinction to "chain migration" where newly arrived migrants induce others from their former home neighborhood to follow (MacDonald and MacDonald, 1964). The migratory chain may be truncated for two main reasons: 1) inherent difficulty of return because of distance, cost or disruptions in the place of origin, physical or ideological, which make return unattractive; much of the settler migration would fall into this category. 2) The paradoxical situation where return is being either officially or at least informally encouraged but at a cost of forfeiting the option of in-migrating again; much of the present delay in international return migration in Europe falls into the second category.

The recent international migration in Europe represents an inflow of people seeking employment. The migrants hail mostly from the people-rich Mediterranean basin. Such international migration, when unimpeded by political controls normally includes fair return flows but whenever impeded, the expected return migration tends to diminish. In turn, the reluctance of in-migrants to return spawned *the politics of return* in the receiving countries, dictated by a sudden dearness of energy and the resulting economic slump and widespread unemployment making at least some of the foreign labor unneeded and even unwanted.

The irony of the situation is that very few sending countries really want their nationals back. There are, here and there, particularly in Yugoslavia and, to a lesser degree in Italy, explicit policies to encourage return and to aid with re-integration, but the realities of migration do not coincide with the wished for situation.

2

The Topics of discussion

There are three basic approaches by which the papers in this volume are arranged: (a) socio-demographic profiles of return migrants, their motivations, their needs and the circumstances of their return from the well of industrial nations in Northwest Europe to the Mediterranean basin, from Portugal and the Maghreb countries on the west to Turkey in the east. To these profiles are added microlevel vignettes of returnees from overseas both in the past and today, including return migrants to the Nordic countries, specifically to Finland; (b) policies stimulating return from particularly large, foreign labor employing countries, specifically France and Germany and the corresponding policies dealing with migrants returning to their home countries; finally, (c) a number of theoretical stances are presented each one offering an explanation of return migration, covering the present-day range of theoretical persuasions.

The papers as submitted were some 900 pages of typescript. The reduction in size was often at cost of omitting theoretical introductions and otherwise restructuring and reducing the papers; papers in French were rendered into English by the editor. Juxtaposed to the program of the Conference, reprinted in the Appendix, is the present organization of the papers which differs significantly from the sequence in which the papers were read at the Conference. The three orientations on basis of which the papers are grouped were outlined above. Other features of the Conference however cannot be fully captured by the present volume and deserve a mention. The organizers of the individual sessions had a free hand in selecting the papers. Several organizers have offered written remarks concerning their session from which appropriate passages are rendered here, together with the comments by the discussants.

There are, unfortunately, lacunae in the coverage of countries. Papers on labor importing countries like Switzerland or Austria or the three BENELUX countries are missed. Nonetheless, it may be presumed that return migrants do not differ much only because they are returning from a specific country, even though some differences may be appreciated.

The personal politics of return

The most extensive literature on return migration in Europe deals with the macro-economic questions. After all, the great labor migration after World War II into Northwest Europe was the result of the often conscious recruiting of labor. At first, countries with a history of labor out-migration, like Portugal or Spain or Italy were providing enough of spontaneous migrants. Later on, towards the end of the 1960's, the spontaneous labor intake was supplemented by organized labor recruiting, for instance from Greece and Turkey but also from the Maghreb region of Africa, from the latter particularly to France. It may be fair to say that migrants coming from a long standing migration tradi-

3

tion were also likely to become return migrants when the economy suffered a downturn, as was the case during the recession in 1966 and 1967, for instance, as documented for Germany to Spain (Mehrländer, 1979). The fact that such returns subsided after the oil crisis in 1973, when there was a virtual freeze on admitting foreign workers by most of the labor importing countries must be attributed to the thwarting of an essentially free movement whereby work and residence permits in hand became a scarce and irreplaceable commodity making a postponement of return desirable. This was just one example where administrative intervention hampers human behavior. Given the fact, for instance, that among the Portuguese migrants a culture of return was well ingrained (Brettel, 1979) there would not have been any need to thwart the migratory cycle. Similar point is made very clearly by Morokvasic in this volume.

Naturally, given the discrepancy in figures on migrants issued by the country of out-migration and the country of in-migration, returns are quite difficult to assess with any statistical accuracy (United Nations, 1979). As Rocha-Trindade (session organizer) commented about Portugal, "the emigrant himself has not always been interested in clarifying his position, declaring, for example, that his departure for his host country is temporary and that his return is permanent; or, saying neither one thing nor the other to either of the two countries concerned, so as to avoid irreversible options. In the minds of the majority of emigrants themselves the intention of returning to their own country has been present from the beginning, although the date for this return may never have been defined with sufficient precision, may vary in accordance with a complex set of variables and may for most migrants be a project that is continually postponed". Similar reluctance to state one's intentions to migrate can be found in Sweden despite its well run population register (Hesse-Biber, 1981).

These comments, well substantiated in the papers (Part I, B) make us somewhat more cautious when tackling macro-economic issues of migration and return. Similarly, Koula Kassimati (session organizer) observed the following about the human factor in return migration to the eastern Mediterranean: "Irrespective of the policy followed by the countries of origin to which the migrants return, the decision of the latter to stay or to go back lies within a general framework in which socio-economic elements dominate in both the recipient country and the country of origin. Confining ourselves to the personal-individual level, it has been found from a great number of surveys that repatriation is the dream of every migrant, but various objective conditions and subjective situations play their part in turning this into an "illusion of return", as shown specifically in the case of Turkish migrants in West Germany (Wilpert). The decision of these migrants to stay or to return cannot, in the final analysis, be attributed to voluntary options. The fundamental wish is to return to the home country; however, the initial length of stay is nearly always extended for a longer period and this in turn reinforces the wish to stay.

On the other hand, it is questionable whether the legal framework and the political morals can be considered sufficiently advantageous to the foreign worker in West Germany to contribute positively to the migrant's decision to stay in the recipient country. In other words, their future as well as that of their children seem uncertain in either country".

Whereas most of the countries of return make gestures to accomodate the returnees with only a modicum of enthusiasm, Yugoslavia is on record to actively seek the return of her nationals. Yugoslav policies are well documented in this volume (Part I, C). Kassimati, however, questioned the Yugoslav effort: "The question which arises here is to what extent the various policies which have been adopted from time to time in Yugoslavia conform with or are appropriate to the circumstances, that is to say the prospect of economic reintegration of the returnees and the policy of regional economic development". In Yugoslavia as elsewhere, return migrants seem to share one thing in common, namely, their length of stay abroad is inversely related to the chances of their return. "Certainly the most important point", Kassimati continued, "is the economic and professional reintegration of the returnees. All the empirical surveys agree that the returnees are to a large extent self-employed. Thus upon his return the migrant who was a factory worker in the recipient country becomes a petty-owner, opens a restaurant-cafe, becomes a taxi-driver, and thus only a small percentage of migrants return to agriculture and very few go into industry".

Such findings as those above should not be surprising. By now a classic, an American study of automobile workers in Detroit found that the American Dream for the assembly line workers was to go into business for themselves (Chinoy, 1955). After all, the assembly line workers were migrants whose non-industrial background would predispose them towards seeking self-employment in the same manner as the non-industrial background predisposes the foreign workers in Europe to seek self-employment after returning home.

The governmental politics of return

Whereas most of the literature on return migration centers on the countries of origin, studies of the impact of return migration of the host countries have not been frequent thus far. This volume contains analyses of aggregate data on return migration from France and from Germany juxtaposing the data to the prevailing policies. The studies on the migration exchange between Finland and Sweden (Part II) illustrate a parallel situation but on a smaller scale. Ursula Mehrlaender (session organizer) pointed out that while studies of return migration from France fare better than those dealing with return from Germany, there still is a paucity of such studies and, in particular not much concern is expressed about the issue. Return migration of foreigners from France and Germany has shown a rapid decline after 1974 (Lebon,

Körner). The respective policies of return as the cause for the decline are cited. While France has initiated specific return programs in form of vocational pretraining and direct cash grants to returnees, amplified eventually by the French-Algerian Agreement on return, Germany did not have any specific policies of return, with the exception of generous support for the workers' co-operatives in Turkey to attract Turkish workers from Germany. A more modest program was directed at the Greek workers (1). First, she asks "how realistic is the assumption of actual return of foreigners from the west European countries back home? My view is that the return home is an alternative to only a limited number of foreigners presently living abroad. Most of the foreigners have been living in their new countries for a long time and their civil and political rights have become clarified in their favor. They have brought their wives and children, their children go to school abroad, some of them acquire occupational training, most of the young foreigners already work in their new home country. Even though there are many social problems which have no instant solution, a slow process of integration has set in. The process of integration in the receiving country diminshes necessarily the need to return". Thus, the conclusions on Germany found in Körner have to be accepted, namely that measures to encourage return will work only when a comparative industrial development will have taken place in the countries of origin. There is support for this contention as migration between similarly developed regions is fairly easy and in effect circular, as it is more likely than not free. The case in point is the movement of nationals within the European Communities which are likely to be expanded in the foreseeable future, so as to include most of the present intra-European migrants.

For the time being, however, the problem of migrant workers or *Gastarbeiter* as they became known, remains. Hermann Korte (discussant) made the following points: "In the 1980's, the guest worker policy was an attempt by the West European countries to employ migrant workers as if they were seasonal workers but remaining for a period of at least two years. Today's problems that occur in connection with the efforts to encourage return migration are rooted in that policy. The social changes which have since emerged in the relationship between guest societies and the sending countries allow us to explain sociologically the relatively low rates of return".

"The recruitment of guest workers was predicated on the principle of rotation, that is a substitution of current foreign labor force by fresh, unspent and politically naive new workers. Körner calls this "come and go" or "buy and sell" phase in the history of international worker migration a phase of 'liberal circulation', a description I find wanting. More likely, one can view such a policy as 'imperialist' or 'colonialist' despite the apparent advantages for both the workers and their own countries. Lebon makes a similar mistake of not owning to an acknowledgement of profound changes in the nature of West European democracies since the 1960's where responsiveness to the rights of minority has become more profound and any administrative authoritarianism was doomed to failure".

6

"The sociological arguments can be formulated as follows: first of all, it should be assumed that an initially low but steadily increasing number of foreign workers will tend to stay in the country beyond the limit foreseen by the principle of rotation for reasons that employers may not wish to train new workers and that the present workers will wish to stay. Beyond such point, the workers will begin to be interested in their political and social rights. This process can assume an exponential character and it was actually accelerated by the various measures halting admission of new foreign workers into the receiving countries starting in 1973. An unanticipated consequence of the halt to in-migration was the end to the principle of worker rotation, bringing in turn a longer stay to the foreign workers in the country encouraging them to bring their families and increasing the workers' interest in their new country, politically and socially. Secondly, the dramatic democratization of the West European countries in fact as well as in their political make-up — a response to the popular movements of the 1960's — made the countries wary of disregard of human rights to all persons on their territory so that, with a few exceptions, no mass return of foreigners could have developed as instigated by the state".

"In other words the failure of the return migration policies such as there were can be attributed to the shift in the power relationship in favor of the previously powerless and not enfranchised foreign workers. The shift has been occurring during the last five years or so, that is after the major labor importing countries began policies curtailing inflow of new foreign labor and encouraging the present foreign labor force to return. As far as the Federal Republic of Germany is concerned, all recent developments indicate that the Republic is on her way to becoming a multicultural society offering new options and alternatives for foreigners to stay. Given the relative disadvantages facing them at home, more and more foreign workers are making a decision to stay where they are now".

"As far as the attempts of the politicians in Germany are concerned, many of them do not seem to be grasping the new political realities and have retained a philosophy of worker rotation when such politics do not seem to work and, besides, seem to sensitize the foreign workers to their political recourses leading them to asserting their rights in a better articulated fashion".

Be it as it may, the problem remains complex and to some degree dependent on the efforts of the original sending countries to attract their own nationals back. Perhaps the best example of that can be seen in the case of Sweden and Finland where the differences in industrial and social development have become diminished to such an extent that migration back and forth is easy. The two papers on the subject (Hammar, Sandlund) offer an illustration of possible future trends in return migration when the European Economic Community will have increased its membership and equalized the socioeconomic standing of its member states. At such time, a free flow of labor will perhaps also signify an increased return migration.

Explaining return

Even though our concern here is primarily with the recent international return migration in Europe for reasons that the large scale flows of population across borders present new problems and new challenges to all countries involved, a long view perspective may be gained by looking at return migration both in the past and over great distances. Four papers (Part III, A) cover both the past and the migration over a great distance in describing return migration to Europe from overseas.

Saskia Sassen-Koob (discussant) pointed out two aspects of overseas return migration which bear on the situation today. "The 'Ulster Custom' in Ireland, an unwritten law whereby tenants could sell their leases to incoming tenants, encouraged a free land market (t'Hart, 1981). Thus, access to land, the equivalent in the rural area to a job in the city would seem to be a significant factor in the destination of returnees. In the case of the Polish return migration during 1919-1923 that saw extremely high return levels, most were males in the prime working years with an average length of stay abroad between 5 and 10 years". Virtanen, by listing the characteristics of the Finnish return migrants, summarizes pretty much the *generalized* findings of the literature on return migration.

In this volume, we have thus a fair amount of information both aggregate and individual. We also have a fair survey of what kind of politics the respective governments pursue to solve some of the problem necessarily brought about by large population shifts which become out of step with economic development and change. In the final analysis, political decisions are taken with regard to perceived reactions of the constituencies but the correspondence is only indirect. In any case, the new Europe has again become a crucible of in-migrants and is likely to remain so.

Among the academicians, there still remain a number of approaches to explain migration and, in our case return migration. Again, the range of explanations follows pretty much the range of ideologies and they all are fairly represented in this volume (Part III, B). It may be fair to say that the ideologically tinted explanations of return migration tend to be prescriptive, the ad hoc and "positivist" explanations tend to be descriptive. Solutions to problems brought about by returns however tend to be political and tend to reflect, ultimately, the underlying precepts tolerant of human freedom and dignity.

NOTE

(1) It was not until the spring of 1983 that Germany began to institute a cash grant as a return incentive. The results of the program, ill-fated in France, will not be immediately known.

8

PART I

RETURN MIGRATION
AND THE HOME COUNTRIES

National impact of returns

THE ROLE OF RETURN MIGRATION IN ALGERIAN ECONOMIC DEVELOPMENT IN THE 1980's*

Jean-Pierre Garson

Return migration is understood to be the logical termination of the migrant's trajectory. In most instances, it is also understood that migration is an individual choice brought about by various facilitating forces and thus it is also subject to classification into categories. Return migration lends itself as well to classification as to "causes". Cerase (1974) for instance distinguishes return due to failure abroad and return due to a need to demonstrate success. The exploitation of the latter may be seen as a factor in the Algerian drive to attract her emigrants back home.

In view of the fact that prior to the oil crisis migration from Algeria to France had been traditional, some return migration at the present time is all but unavoidable. The volume of the stream of return migrants, enlarged by the specific encouragement of both the French and the Algerian government, is quite considerable but not without its political and economic ramifications. It is the latter which are subject to a brief discussion.

The long history of Algerian dependence on metropolitan France need not be repeated here, as the sources dealing with it are numerous. Suffice it to say that, starting with the early 1970's, there were a great number of Algerians in France but the Franco-Algerian relations were becoming strained. Emerging nationalism and the ideological commitment to genuine independence in Algeria coupled with the economic crisis in France and elsewhere led Algeria actively to harness her labor force for a new thrust into economic development (Benhadji, 1976). Investigations of Algerians in France showed that their willingness to return was considerable. One survey of foreigners in France, including some 450 Algerian respondents identified two thirds as willing to return (Garson, 1977). The Algerian government, as well, was able to create new jobs, some 800,000 of them between 1966 and 1977 (Benachenhoum, 1980: 222). The current Algerian economic plan for 1980-1984 projects 200,000 newly created jobs per annum (RADP, 1980: 85).

----

* Adapted from the French by the editor.

Emigration from Algeria

The Algerian authorities have been preoccupied already by mid-1960's with the impact of emigration toward France, especially the flight of the skilled labor force. The migration was very much related to the conscious efforts on the part of the various French governmental and private agencies to recruit labor for the rapidly expanding French economy. On the other hand, all efforts on the part of Algeria to encourage return migration had only very meager results, not representing more than ten per cent of the return migration which would have taken place anyway. The most crucial set of variables which bear on the willingness to return is that the migrants themselves have experienced a geographical mobility and an occupational mobility which would have to be matched, as it were, in their expectations to return. This applies to the skilled workers in particular who are the mainstay of any industrialization process (Benouamer and Hemman, 1976; Chaker, 1978). Thus, given the fact of migrants' mobility, both geographical and occupational, the country attracting her own nationals is constrained to plan for an infrastructure where the mobility of returnees can be facilitated, mutually dependent as such processes may be. There is a fair amount of capital, not only human but cash and goods which return with the migrants that specific provisions needed to be made in order to make return attractive. Such provisions are outlined below, reflecting the new Algerian return migration policy.

Measures in Algeria to encourage
return migration

There were a number of measures undertaken to encourage return of Algerians in France. In the first place, contact offices were opened in France by the Algerian Ministry of Labor and of Social Affairs to make known jobs available in Algeria. This was done in cooperation with the arm of the economic development, *Caisse centrale de coopération économique*, a governmental agency for economic development. Since the *Caisse* is primarily a financial institution, some of the provisions to return are fiscal in nature. For instance, returning workers are exempt from duty on imported articles from their households, includings one car or one utility vehicle of up to 2.5 ton provided the returned national has lived abroad for at least three years, which is also the maximum age for the vehicles at the time of importation. Furthermore, importation of business or trade with the requisite goods and tools are also exempt from any duties provided the returned migrant is likely to continue in the business or trade. The same three years provision applies.

After five years of stay in Algeria, all the imported goods are freed of all restrictions to sell or barter, but prior to this time limit retroactive import duties would be levied pro rata. Returning residents can exchange their French currency at par for Algerian dinars, which at the time of the regulation, represented an advantage of 12 per cent. On the other hand, those wishing to retain their money in French currency may do so (Article 117, Finance Act 1980, together with the notice No. 4, dated September 14) and their accounts will earn the prevailing interest rates. The accounts are freely accessible (Garson, 1977).

These and other measures make return migration attractive and quite competitive with the occupational and fiscal opportunities abroad. There is no question that nationalistic motives were and are overriding simple economic exigencies. The unilateral suspension of migration from Algeria to France by the edict of September 19, 1973, marked a distinct turnaround in Algeria's emigration policy, and it meant "a new stage in national development and constituted the first effort to make return of Algerians home a reality" (Charte Nationale, 1976: 145). Hand in hand with the financial provisions, private enterprise of returned Algerians is actively promoted. Despite its socialist persuasion, the Algerian government recognizes small enterprises as belonging to the realm of private initiative. This is guaranteed both in the National Charter (May, 1976) and in the Constitution (November, 1976). Nonetheless, the role of private enterprises is likely to remain modest but well within the purvue of individual return migrants and is strictly speaking only supplementary to the main thrust of national development through industrialization.

Two modes of small enterprises are encouraged in Algeria: private business, usually not employing anyone other than members of the family and the willaya or commune which is self-administered and again, supplementary to the major thrust of national development. It is private enterprise and its facilitation to which the new return migration politics are applied. Three such objectives are to be achieved. Service and commerce meeting individual needs for which the national planning system would prove too cumbersome, both in small scale shops (e.g. manufacturing) and in medium enterprises where supplying of parts on subcontract basis would find an outlet for private initiative, as well as other ancillary services where private enterprise is by far more flexibile than large public enterprises. The list of such activities is a long one, ranging from various small manufacturing to maintenance work of any kind, small shops, transport, most of tertiary services, etc.

To the extent that small enterprises get started requires financial help that has been agreed upon between France and Algeria jointly to offer loans of up to 85 per cent of the required capital. The money comes from France but is guaranteeed by the Algerian Treasury. This can be viewed as an indirect French support of Algerians currently employed in France but eligibile to return, thus freeing much needed jobs in France.

In summary, the problem of employment remains crucial for Algeria in terms of being able to sustain a policy of development, which includes development in agriculture where the knowledgeable labor force in the past went to France. Bringing those workers back will go a long way toward achieving the goals of Algerian economic development. From this point of view, the flow of labor between France and Algeria demands close co-operation without which the desired progress can not take place (Tapinos, 1974: 190).

RETURN MIGRATION AND
THE TUNISIAN LABOR MARKET

Georges Abou Sada

The importance of emigration from Tunisia remained limited until the 1960's. At first, only few workers were leaving Tunisia for France in search of a job and better living conditions. Later on, the Tunisian government began to support emigration of its nationals as a provisional placing abroad of surplus labor force. Tunisia concluded bilateral agreements with several labor importing countries to ensure emigration of stable quotas of Tunisian workers. An agreement with France was signed in 1963 (in full force only in 1969), with the Federal Republic of Germany in 1965, with Belgium in 1969, with Austria in 1970 and with the Netherlands and Libya in 1971.

By 1974, after most of the labor importing countries had effectively stopped additional entries of foreign workers, the Tunisian government found itself anew with the old problem of labor surplus, as emigration had virtually stopped and Tunisians had begun to return home. One of the responses the government was able to make was to encourage the establishment of industries producing specifically for export and financed primarily by foreign companies. The number of jobs created by the governmental Act of April, 1972, reached about 20 per cent of all manufacturing jobs in Tunisia (State Economy, 1980). This also meant that priority in this employment was given to returning Tunisians in allocation of resources and privileges, especially if the returnees were able to create their own jobs and contribute substantially to the job creation or if they were entrepreneurs also employing others. From 1976 to 1981, the Agency for the Promotion of Investments (API) approved about 1,000 industrial or semi-industrial projects which led to the creation of 13,400 jobs. To this we may add the creation of 1,000 services and handcraft firms. Of course, the number of "unplanned" returns was much larger, complicating the labor market situation at home. Tunisia has recorded about 5,000 returning workers from France who took advantage of the French *aide au retour* program (Economic Budget, 1981). Furthermore, thousands of Tunisians were flown back by their government from Libya after the political relationship between the two countries deteriorated.

Characteristics of Tunisian migrants

In 1980, Tunisian emigration to all European and Arab countries was estimated at 380,000 of whom 210,000 were living in France, 80,000 in Libya,

25,000 in Algeria, 20,000 in the Federal Republic of Germany and 15,000 in Belgium. Others were in Kuwait and Saudi Arabia (Statistics of O.T.T.E.E.F. P.). There is little statistical information detailing occupational distribution of Tunisians abroad either by the level of skills or by the economic sector in which they work. The statistics of the individual receiving countries are only comparable in an extremely rough fashion. The French INSEE census of 1975 shows Tunisians to be somewhat more skilled, on the average, than Moroccans or Algerians. The census also shows the Tunisians to be much more present in the service sector. A French labor force study of October, 1976 showed the following distribution of Tunisians by sector of activity: construction 37.8 per cent, processing industries 36.4 per cent, trade and services 22.3 per cent, transport 3 per cent and mining 0.5 per cent. Per cent distribution of Tunisian workers in France by skill levels was shown to be as follows: Unskilled 20.3, semi-skilled 38.9, skilled 30.0, salaried employees 8.1, supervisory staff 1.4 and executives 1.0 per cent. Compared to the Algerians, Tunisians seem to have a slight advantage when it comes to holding jobs at higher levels (Ministry of Labor, 1977).

The relatively good standing of Tunisians abroad, particularly in France, can be attributed to the training system which was organized by Office National d'Immigration early in the 1970's and by the French AFTA (adult vocational training) centers. There, 64,000 Tunisians were trained of whom 29,000 left for France and 12,000 for Germany.

The demographic situation in Tunisia

In 1980, the Tunisian population was estimated at 6,402,000 inhabitants. During the preceding twenty-five years, the population in Tunisia had experienced apparent growth rates ranging from 1.8 to 2.1 per cent annually. The actual growth of the population was higher, as emigration affected the growth. Table 1 gives a summary distribution of the Tunisian population by age for the last thirty years.

Table 1: Age distribution of Tunisian population over time (in per cent)

	1950	1965	1980
Less than 20	48	55	54
From 20 to 64	46	41	42
Over 65	6	4	4
Total	100	100	100

Source: CRESGE estimate

Labor force participation rates

In Tunisia, as in other developing countries, the meaning of labor force participation rate (LFPR) is ambiguous insofar as the definition of labor and work is rather vague and the registration of workers is incomplete. The central role farming and tourism play in Tunisian economy makes any statistical assessment of LFPR in these sectors in particular, rather difficult to interpret.

For all males, the overall LFPR is currently about 46 per cent. The highest rate falls in the age group between 25 and 44 years of age (96 per cent), followed by the age group of 45 to 54 (93 per cent) and by the age group between 20 and 24 years of age (91 per cent). For those under 20 years of age, the LFPR is 48 per cent and for those over 65 years of age it is 42 per cent.

For females, the LFPR for 1980 is very low, hardly higher than in other countries of North Africa and the Middle East. By age groups, the female LFPR was 20 per cent for women aged 15 to 19 and 23 per cent for those between 20 and 24 years of age. For women between 25 and 44 the rate was 13 per cent and for those between 45 and 54 years of age, the rate was only 9 per cent.

In 1975, the ILO estimated male Tunisian working age population to be 1,525,000 whereas the Tunisian state estimate was higher, namely 1,622,000. The difference in the estimates can be accounted for by the different assumptions about population growth and about the resulting age and sex structure. The Tunisian figures suggest a growth rate of population in the working age, both male and female, to have been over 3 per cent annually between 1975 and 1980. This growth was undeniably related to the return movement of nationals from abroad.

Return of migrants

The CRESGE has sponsored a study of the impact the return of migrant workers has on the population. An incremental return model proved to have the best fit. The study projected 20,000 returnees annually to increase to 60,000 annually by the year of 1985 and 1986 and then to decrease again to reach a total of 350,000 persons having returned by 1990. It was also assumed that the demographic profile of the returning population was similar to that of the population in Tunisia for the applicable age brackets. Thus, whereas return migration will not considerably affect the age and sex composition of Tunisia, the returnees will, nonetheless, inflate the working age population. Where such a population influx has the most effect, is, of course, on the labor market.

The employment situation in Tunisia has thus far improved in spite of the acceleration of the growth both of the total and the working age population. Since the beginning of the 1970's, 40,000 to 50,000 jobs have been created annually (CRESGE, 1982). These new jobs were in all economic

17

sectors but particularly in those which employ female labor, for instance textile and apparel, reflecting the investments of European firms attracted by the abundant labor pool. The additional job demand should have accommodated 274,000 men and women between 18 and 59 years of age during the 5th Plan (1977-1981) even though only 212,750 new jobs had been created.

Economic performance of Tunisia, although remarkable in certain sectors, often remains below the intention of the state planners. One of the main targets of the 5th Plan, to be extended into the 6th Economic Plan, was to achieve full employment taking into consideration the rapid population increase. The actual job creation and the need for more jobs have thus far not been brought into balance.

The Tunisian government expects, or would like to create 65,000 new jobs annually during its 6th Economic Plan (1982-1986) to accomodate the projected increase in the working age population of 59,000 annually, the expected return migrants and those transferring from hidden unemployment into regular jobs. Needless to say, the achievement of such a plan is very dependent on the overall economic well-being abroad, especially in the "wealthy" countries because a good proportion of Tunisian economy is geared either to export or to tourism.

This type of economic condition, specific to Tunisia among the North African countries, only emphasizes the existing inequalities among the various social strata and between city and country. The return and reintegration of workers from abroad who concentrate in the cities for lack of opportunities elsewhere thus present a real problem for Tunisia. Tunisian workers abroad are not exposed to anything but highly narrow training for well-defined performance. Such a training becomes inapplicable in Tunisia where the industrial and economic development accompanied as it is by diffuse industrialization requires a workforce with more flexible skills. Furthermore, the returning migrants are not likely to replicate the style of life and the income enjoyed abroad which makes for a difficult reintegration.

One of the ways to approach the reintegration of returnees is the exemplary way shown by the ASDEAR (Association for Rural Development). The ASDEAR was created in 1976 as a follow up to voluntary efforts in the area of primarily rural development. The role of ASDEAR is to act as a research and advisory body to the middle class returnees to facilitate their economic reintegration including securing of bank financing for the respective projects they have. The agency acts primarily for returnees from the Netherlands on behalf of the Nederlandse Centrum voor het Buitenland (NCB) foundation. Thus far, in 1980, 22 projects were successfully started, employing 182 persons. Presently, ten more projects are underway and the number of applications currently under review and about to be approved is about 250. About half of the projects are in agriculture, the other half in small industries and in services, all in rural areas. ASDEAR functions as a broker between returnees with complementary skills from different regions so that they, with help of bank support, can realize various economic undertakings which otherwise would not get started. Even though the scope of ASDEAR is limited, the projects and the agency can serve as models for the Tunisian government and its citizens to overcome the difficulties arising from "unscheduled" returns.

THE SPANISH EUROMIGRATION: RETURNEES AND THE DOMESTIC LABOR MARKET

Luciano Berrocal

The estimated volume of emigrants returning each year to Spain increased significantly by 1962 and as early as 1965 began to equal or to exceed the flow of departures. Between 1967 and 1971, the return movement accelerated reaching 74,000 returns in 1976 but then declined to 50,000 returns in 1978 (SOPEMI, 1979).

Usually, the return flows parallel the rate of out-migration which has been responding, in a subordinate way, to the favorable trends in the European economies. One must view the Spanish migration to Europe as part and parcel of the migration which took place within the country (Berrocal, 1981a). The Spanish pattern of internal economic development underlies the out-migration towards Europe. Is this also applicable to return migration?

The few studies available on return migration to Spain tend to confirm that returning migrants usually do not return to their place of origin but rather tend to concentrate in urban areas of Spain which are also centers of industrial production and wealth for the country. Through "Euromigration", the term denoting migration between Spain and industrial Europe, the Spanish countryside suffers not only loss of population but also loss of impetus for development.

The Spanish pattern of development is characterized by a growing overinvestment on the North European model. This model does not contribute to a re-integration of Euromigrants (Moral Santin, 1981; Temprano, 1981). For instance, the average investment needed presently to create one new job tends to be 15 times higher in real terms than it was before the Civil War (Moral Santin, 1981: 131). Needless to say, a returnee is in no way able to contribute significantly from his own means to such an effort of job creation.

The rapid economic growth which Spain experienced in the decade from 1960-1970 led not only to a radical labor mobility of the labor force but also to a fragmentation which the greater flexibility of the market engendered (Berrocal, 1981b; Serrano and Malo de Molina, 1979). At first, this situation facilitated a reintegration of returnees but, while the return movement gained momentum of its own, the Spanish economy suffered a slowdown with a consequent surplus of labor. Currently, unemployment in Spain is high, 14 per cent of the labor force in 1981 (Papeles de Economia, 1980). Given all the apparent difficulties in securing employment at home, what explains the strong return flows of Spanish Euromigrants?

21

The return movement is one essential dimension of the migratory flow towards Europe. Its complex nature is related to the previous fragmentation of the Spanish labor markets and their growing interconnectedness with the rest of Europe in anticipation of the eventual integration into the European Community. There are major differences in the return flow to Spain, from country to country. For instance, return movement from France reached its peak in 1966 and decreased in and after 1973 (Ewenczyk, Garson and Moulier, 1978:116). Spanish official statistics seem to have underestimated the return at first and tend to overestimate it in the later, more recent years. On the other hand, return movements from other countries, especially Germany and Switzerland, increased after 1973. Does this mean that the reabsorption capacity for the domestic markets is an explanatory variable in the return movement? Data suggest that the past experience in the case of Spain shows the pull factors to be more important than the push factors to encourage return (Ewenczyk, Garson and Moulier, 1978:117). The structure of the Spanish labor market has been a major factor in encouraging return of Euromigrants amplifying the dynamics inherent to any established migration stream.

Characteristics of return migrants

What follows is a summary of recent studies on return migrants, specifically their characteristics relevant to their integration into the Spanish labor force. A survey conducted with 133 former emigrants from Sierra Nevada and the Valley of Cadiz Baza (Rhoades, 1977) shows the return trajectory to be a function of the time and age at first emigration, the length of stay abroad, and the level of savings accumulated, marital status and the social status in the community before emigration. Single emigrants under 30 years of age at return are very unlikely to resume any work related to agriculture; they use their savings to buy durable goods and tend to go to cities. Young marrieds use their savings to buy or build a house but they also tend not to return to their community of origin. On the other hand, those who left after they were 30 years of age from rural communities tend to reestablish themselves in the rural area and the rural sector by acquiring land, starting a small trade and also by building a house.

A survey in Barcelona shows returnees tending towards self-employment (Cardelus and Pascual, 1979). Their return seems to be a function of having stayed abroad between 5 to 10 years, enough to save up for the desired goal of savings. It seems that quite a bit of Spanish Euromigration is motivated by a project which can be realized, by working abroad and saving one's earnings.

The most representative large sample among the recent studies was drawn from a study in 1979, with 1567 respondents (Castillo and Castillo, 1980). Over 70 per cent of the returnees were between 30 and 50 years old, that means in their prime as far as reentry into the Spanish labor market.

Those returning after 1974 were younger. Of those returning prior to 1969, 21 per cent were under 39 years of age; for those returning after 1975, this proportion rises to 58 per cent. About two thirds of all returnees interviewed were males, over 73 per cent of them were married, one half of them had left as married. Family reasons were cited as having determined the return. On the whole, return migrants had somewhat more schooling than the corresponding population at home. Tables 1, 2 and 3 summarize succinctly the occupational reintegration process and need not be discussed in detail, particularly since the tables are from a previously published study (Castillo and Castillo, 1980). Suffice it to say that returnees do find a job even though they see it to be a problem. Return into the labor force is particularly difficult for women, many of whom revert to their pre-emigration situation of staying at home. For men, curiously enough, it is harder to find a job if they are younger. Two variables seem to be involved here: older men are more experienced and more accomodating and their willingness to return to smaller places gives them an advantage. Furthermore, older returnees are also likely to become self-employed, diminisching the pressure of a search for a suitable employment.

Perhaps the common characteristics of returnees is their horizontal cross-sectoral labor mobility tending in the direction of the service sector. On the other hand, the presumed occupational mobility allowing upgrading while abroad does not, in general, take place, at least not among the returnees.

Assessment

The Spanish labor market does not seem to be very affected by Euro-migration save in the respect that Euromigration may amplify the mobility and fragmentation of the labor force and polarize the population movements towards the cities and away from the countryside. Return migrants do not seem to be importing new industrial skills and the attempts of returnee women to stay in the labor force complicate and inflate the potential labor force and the concurrent unemployment. It is also noteworthy, however, that during the 1964-1977 period, Spanish Euromigrants were craftsmen or industrial workers to a much greater extent than they were farm workers or fishermen or other workers from the primary sector (Instituto Español de Emigración, 1980).

One has to keep in mind that the official statistics on returnees are of uncertain accuracy. Independent studies seem to indicate, however, that most returnees treat their stay abroad as a part of their life cycle which allows them to speed up the process leading towards accumulation of a little capital and propels them towards an occupational independence, that is, self-employment. Thus, very few returnees return because of a failure abroad. From this perspective, it is understandable that returnees do not present specific problems to the Spanish economy nor the social services and that explains the relative absence of regulations and concern on the part of the Spanish government affecting migration.

Table 1: Per cent distribution of returned emigrants, by time spent looking for job and by the year of return to Spain *

Time spent to find a job	Year of return			
	Before 1969	1969-1974	1975-1978	Total
Did not look Did not need to	17	19	19	19
Had job before returning	20	13	15	15
A few days	15	9	5	9
A few weeks	14.	13	9	12
A few months	20	27	22	24
About a year	4	7	6	6
More than a year	5	4	2	4
Have not found one yet	2	4	18	8
Forgotten	1	2	1	1
No answer	2	1	2	2
Total	100	99	99	98
N	(414)	(626)	(527)	(1,567)

* 75 per cent of those who did not need to find a job are women; not surprisingly, these are housewives.

Source: Castillo and Castillo, 1980: 73.

Table 2: Per cent distribution of returned emigrants, by employment
situation at the time of returning and at the present time

Employment situation	Total population		Working population	
	At the time of returning	At present	At the time of returning	At present
Temporary job	26	8	36	13
Permanent job	46	56	64	87
Unemployed	8	15	--	--
Pensioner	4*	3	--	--
Housewife	15	15	--	--
No answer	2	3	--	--
N	(1,567)	(1,567)	(1,004)	(1,020)

* Estimated figure

Source: Castillo and Castillò, 1980:77

Table 3: Evolution of the employment situation of returned migrants throughout the migratory cycle, by sex (in per cent)

Type of occupation	Before emigrating			First occupation abroad			Last occupation abroad			Present occupation		
	M	F	T	M	F	T	M	F	T	M	F	T
Working for an employer	93	89	92	98	98	99	98	96	97	76	63	74
Self-Employed	7	9	8	1	2	1	1	2	1	26	24	26
Salary earner	31	10	25	33	15	27	45	19	37	42	8	36
Wage earner	45	15	35	56	54	52	43	41	42	23	18	22
Housewife	--	33	10	--	1	--	--	1	--	--	53	15
Domestic service	--	11	3	1	26	9	1	25	8	--	10	2
Property owner	5	2	4	--	--	--	--	--	--	20	28	21
Primary sector	20	9	19	10	3	8	8	2	6	4	--	4
Secondary sector	56	35	53	63	35	55	62	37	55	41	15	41
Tertiary sector	24	55	26	24	59	35	25	59	36	45	83	52

M = male, F = female, T = total

Source: Castillo and Castillo, 1980:85

PORTUGAL'S ACCESSION TO THE EEC AND MIGRATION BALANCE

Eduardo de Sousa Ferreira
José J.R. Leite Pereira

Studies carried out in France and in the Federal Republic of Germany (Poinard, 1979; Amtliche Nachrichten, 1979) suggest that a far greater proportion of Portuguese abroad would return were it not for the presently unfavorable economic situation in Portugal. In Portugal, both the economic reintegration of returnees and the making of simple provisions for return are being hampered by a lack of understanding of the issue of emigration and return. This is despite the fact that there are already a number of projects underway involving governmental co-operation among countries exchanging migrant labor. For instance, an agreement in force between Germany and Turkey since 1972 provides returnee operated industrial companies with financial and institutional support from both parties. Or, the project REMPLOD, which originated in the Netherlands, through which the reintegration of returnees to mostly rural areas in Turkey, Morocco and Tunisia has been facilitated since 1974. A small project of this nature is also underway in Portugal. France has, for a few years, facilitated the return of foreigners by offering cash incentives which the Portuguese in particular took advantage of (de Wenden, 1981). An indirect approach to solving the problem of a massive return of nationals is also being handled by deflecting returnees to other countries, for instance Libya or other Persian Gulf States or South America. There are a fair number of Portuguese involved in these migration flows.

Whatever the problems of migration and return, Portugal, as one of the countries with a large contingent of emigrants, is very much affected by the "migratory chain" of her nationals. The ambiguity of official Portuguese position as regards migration is to be understood in the present-day context of unregulated migration. Portugal has found herself in a position of labor exporter which was meant to solve the unemployment problem, the problem of the influx of settlers from Angola (in 1975 and 1976, about 250,000 Portuguese settlers returned), and the problem of inadequate provisions for the occupational training, of Portugal's workforce.

The remittances, on the other hand became an obvious benefit. Should there be a sudden influx of returnees, the benefits of remittances will end and the current infrastructure will be even less able to absorb the returning workforce. Thus, for instance, during 1975 to 1977, Portugal was unable to reabsorb a rather small proportion of her returnees, with the sizeable remittances

27

still flowing into the country. Between 1978 and 1980, unemployment figures for Portugal were respectively 8.4, 8.1 and 7.9 per cent of the labor force (Banco do Portugal, 1980) and labor demand remained inelastic.

The forthcoming membership
in the European communities

The impact of any present large scale return would be catastrophic for Portugal. The hoped for accession of Portugal to the European Economic Community will, however, affect Portugal's balance of migration. The economic development which Portugal presently faces is a pre-condition for the expected membership in the EEC. It has to be remembered that at the end of 1980, 26.7 per cent of the Portuguese labor force was still employed in agriculture while the proportion of the GNP in agricultural production represented only 12 per cent, a situation very much at variance with the prevailing standards in the EEC and a hurdle to be overcome. Specifically, were Portugal to join the EEC immediately but retain her inefficiency in agricultural production, food prices in the country would rise by some 20 to 30 per cent.

Partial blame for the inefficiency of the Portuguese economy can be laid at the door of the great regional disparities with the interior remaining economically undeveloped. Portugal's product per capita as a whole is thus far only some 55 per cent of that of Spain, the other aspirant for EEC membership, and 60 per cent of that of Ireland (IED, 1981). In view of the fact that a great proportion of the returning settlers from Angola went to rural areas, the rural population and the possible inefficiency have increased. The settlers represented altogether some six percent of the Portuguese population. A similar return to France of her nationals from Algeria was proportionately much smaller (Ayer and Chadhry, 1981).

Return migration of any size would effectively downsize the flow of remittances which, in US dollars have close to tripled between 1977 and 1980. The lion's share of the remittances came from the OECD European countries, about ten billion in 1977 and 22 billion in 1980 (Banco do Portugal, 1980). Not only would the flow of remittances diminish with any increase of return but demand for foodstuff would rise at the time when Portugal is already not self-sufficient in food production. Her deficits in importing foodstuff have doubled between 1977 and 1980.

There are three phases through which Portugal will have to pass before enjoying full status within the European Communities:
— The first phase, expected to end in January, 1984, but subject to a postponement is not likely to have any effect on migration in and out of Portugal. Mean emigration is expected to average some 20,000 person annually and return migration is not expected to increase substantially.
— The second, transitional phase is likely to last about seven years, subject to

an acceptable improvement of Portugal's economy. Prospects by both the World Bank and the OECD indicate an upgrading of the economic performance: in any case, the EEC will probably impose a transition period of 7 years, before granting Portugal the right to free movement of labor, as was the requirement for Greece before attaining her full status in the EEC. The EEC's primary concern is that the large Portuguese birth cohorts between 1955 and 1965 together with the increasingly prevailing practices of bringing one's dependents would represent a potentially threatening influx of freely moving Portuguese looking for employment in Europe, destabilizing the internal labor markets. Some countervailing forces to out-migration can be started by direct investments in Portugal. Already between 1977 and 1980, such investments have doubled allowing for migration substitution (Banco do Portugal, 1979; 1980).

— The third phase will be reached with full member status in the EEC which is not to occur at least until 1991. The free movement of labor at that time will be considered less disrupting as the demographic balance will have become re-established and the economic situation is expected to have improved both in Portugal and in Europe in general.

**Return migration as mechanism
of economic development**

The current problem for Portugal lies in the fact that the imbalance in economic development between her and the member states of the EEC is sufficiently pronounced, implying a migration imbalance as well. Portugal's economic imbalance is unlikely to be adjusted before her formal accession to the EEC. Return migration, which is, of course, uncontrolled, represents an economic burden to Portugal. Even though data are difficult to come by, some estimates are available. For instance, between 1968 and 1975, some 32,000 Portuguese left France annually, presumably for Portugal.

What return movement there was, however, was primarily the result of individual decisions mostly because the goal of migration had been achieved or because the retirement age made return welcome. No doubt, unemployment abroad affects first those with a shorter stay or those without substantial occupational skills. A reintegration into the worklife in Portugal when it occurs is unplanned. In view of the fact that there are no statewide provisions to facilitate returnees into the economy of the country, the modes of economic integration returnees face can be classified as follows: (a) Establishment of small firms, primarily in construction. These enterprises even though small, utilize modern technologies learned abroad. These firms are most likely to be established in the places of origin of the returnees (Poinard, 1979). (b) Resumption of agricultural work when the returnee is in position to acquire some land and thus upgrade his farming status and (c) Entrance into the service sector, particularly in the food branch, or into small salaried positions already held before emigration.

The major impact of migration especially for those originally from agriculture is to change the returnees' occupational preference toward a small enterprise, a shop etc. Here, the returnees with families tend to return to the rural areas, those who are single tend to return to towns and cities.

Necessary changes

In view of her impending accession to the EEC, Portugal will have to redirect her efforts more towards attracting her nationals from abroad inasmuch as she will need to upgrade and enlarge her industrial workforce to meet certain conditions of economic development. In particular, Portugal will have to undertake an inventory of her human resources in order to see which sectors of economic activities will have priority in the intra-European division of labor. Secondly, the Portuguese government will have to come forth with incentives for creation of new enterprises. There exist a number of agencies now the role of which is to rechannel investment capital, specifically, the SIII (Coordinated Program to Encourage Investments), and the SIFAP (Program to Finance Agriculture and Fisheries). Other incentives, which are encountered among other countries concerned with return migration as well, are provisions for duty exemption for goods imported to establish industrial enterprises, unemployment payments to returnees until their reintegration in the labor market and social aid institutions, on a regional basis, to deal with the social aspects of returning.

The provisions listed represent the key measures which will tend also to dissuade the returnees from concentrating on individual consumption, housing etc. Particularly, the government of Portugal is interested in parlaying the substantial savings of individual returnees into investment capital using the following strategies; the regions from where the returnees have come would, spurred by individual municipalities, co-fund at least at parity various enterprises of returnees and create real estate and construction firms helping returnees to find housing and to receive a good return on their invested capital.

Such and similar measures are based on the understanding that return migration of Portuguese has been taking place only with a view to retirement or when the economics of staying abroad become unprofitable. In view of the impending accession of Portugal to the EEC, the re-integration of returnees who are at the peak of their occupational career and skills would go a long way to meet the demands of the membership in an economic system where efficiency of labor is at premium. From this will also follow that some exportation of primarily unskilled labor would continue to be beneficial to Portugal.

RETURN MIGRATION AND SENDING AREAS: FROM THE MYTH OF DEVELOPMENT TO THE REALITY OF STAGNATION

Emilio Reyneri
Clara Mughini

"Temporary" or "target" emigration from Italy to mature economies of Europe implies that the workers will be returning home with years of gainful employment left. Their return would provide a number of stimuli to the domestic economy as it is being heralded in the literature on the subject. The benefits the returning workers will have on the home economies are those of importation of advanced industrial skills, management skills necessary for economic development and as well as an entrepreneurial esprit and some working capital to fuel the development.

Such expectations on the part of the sending countries or sending areas, especially by the government which fostered out-migration in the first place, seem now to have been unrealistic. Here we explore the various "myths" on the example of return migration situation in Southern Italy.

Temporary migration as a factor in vocational and manufacturing training

The myth of occupational mobility through migration presupposes a radical change in one's occupational and social position as a result of migration. People moving from rural and economically backward areas enter a new milieu and they profit by it. Actually, such migrants are usually those who are entering the job market for the first time, either because of their youth if they are males or because of their sex if they are females, the latter having been contrained traditionally not to work outside of home (ISFOL, 1976; ISVI-FOR-MEZ, 1976). If migration involves the entrance into the labor market primarily for women, for men migration means occupational mobility from the primary to the secondary economic sector. In Italy, the presence of only few male rural workers in the international migration streams is explained by previous intersectoral mobility while still in their own country, where they worked in construction, small trade or handicrafts (CSER, 1975; Corsini-Sonnino, 1972; Cella, 1974). Migrants who leave as housewives or students searching for a job or tradesmen or artisans usually become industrial workers mostly in large enterprises, or they become construction workers. Some enter service indusstries but always at a very low skill level.

Therefore, while sectoral mobility is fairly high, occupational mobility per se is low and what there is, is actually downward. Several studies of migrant workers in Germany show that a large proportion of workers with previous occupational training do not practice their trade either because of their insufficient language skills or because the unskilled or semi-skilled jobs they obtain allow them to earn well (Külewind, 1974; Böhning, 1972; Paine, 1974; Abadan-Unat, 1973; Krane, 1975b; CENSIS, 1973; Corsini-Sonnino, 1972; CSER, 1975; Doxa, 1973). Furthermore, foreign workers frequently change their job but tend to remain at the same skill level. This frequent job mobility makes it difficult to accumulate work experience, training or work ethic (Kayser, 1971; CSER, 1975; CEE, 1974).

Migrant workers' low occupational upgrading is further explained by the insufficient information they have about the country of their stay and, even more so, by family obligations which assume primacy in their lives and, ultimately, by their intentions to return home as soon as possible. The migrant, at least the Italian migrant, does not aspire to industrial work but to an independent activity in which he invests the money he earns during migration (Livi-Bacci, 1972a; Castles and Kosack, 1973; Tapinos, 1974).

The "backward" mobility of return migrants

The return to the area of origin means also a return to the occupational situation prior to migration. First of all, for many, return involves leaving the labor market. The aggregate labor force participation rate of migrants falls to the level preceding migration and is due mostly to the fact that women leave gainful employment (ISTAT, 1970; ISVI-FORMEZ, 1976; Tapinos, 1974).

There are some difficulties in reintegration for men as well. Returnees' employment rate is actually lower than that of the population which did not migrate (Leguina, Monreal and Rapado, 1976; Paine, 1974; CENSIS, 1973). For the returnees, the occupational situation is deeply influenced by the condition of economic backwardness in the area to which they returned and thus those returnees still in their working prime have only two alternatives: either to return to the same occupation they left originally, which means agriculture or a precarious secondary sector of the construction or cottage industry, or to enter into the service industries. Agriculture re-attracts only very few returnees (Reyneri, 1979; Livi-Bacci, 1972b).

To maintain employment at a skilled job level or at least to return to industrial employment at home is easier for those few migrants who have acquired such skills abroad (Kayser, 1971). The backward social system in the domestic enterprises discourages returnees who, in any case, aspire to self-employment in some service industry, shops or transportation (taxi service) and who thus lose the little industrial expertise they may have acquired abroad. Primarily, however, those migrants who acquire a good occupational qualification do not tend to return (Böhning, 1972; Paine, 1974; SOPEMI, 1977). This is not surprising in view of the fact that migration also generates expectations of upward mobility which the employment environment back home would frustrate. Those who return displace their aspiration towards acquisition of land and houses in particular as that is the best way of demonstrating one's success.

The myth of socialization
towards industrial occupations

Work abroad, especially in industry, is supposed to produce a "secondary" socialization which, transplanted back home, will prove very successful (Monson, 1975). Actually, it is very difficult to transfer the patterns imposed on the migrant workers while he was abroad to the situation back home where parallel industrial enterprise does not exist. In addition, the population from rural areas like some of those in the South of Italy does not enjoy the "Taylorized" approach to industrial work and the workers acquire a dislike for such work. Becoming socialized for industrial employment would require having some control over one's environment which is certainly not the case of the migrant abroad.

"Return of innovation"

A "circular" migration over relatively short distances as distances have now become in Europe makes an explanation of return migration much more difficult. Out-migration includes both those who emigrate for their first time and those who re-emigrate, while return migration includes both the final returnees and those who may leave again. Thus, among the different classes of returnees (Tapinos, 1974: 186) only two types are more or less unequivocal: the return due to failure which takes place only in a short period after emigration and the return for retirement. As far as the other classifications are concerned, they are more difficult to circumscribe and this includes migration of innovative return. It seems that until at least the mid-1970's very few return migrants who were still in their working prime did not consider re-emigrating (Paine, 1974; Kayser, 1971, 1972; ISVI-FORMEZ, 1976). An analysis of the reasons for return gives very few valid clues as to whether or not the returning migrant considers his move final. Field research shows that migrants attribute their return, either temporary or definitive, more to family and personal reasons than to economic or occupational ones. Therefore, those who return while still occupationally active maintain a short-term perspective which means they are unwilling to commit their resources to any long term project. It is, therefore, paradoxical to attribute to the return migrant the role of agents of innovative social change. They have left originally to reduce their dissatisfaction and to avoid conflicts, the resolution of which would have led to social change.

The traditional hypothesis of innovative return has the following components: (a) the lack of a "take-off" in the sending area is rooted in the apathy of the peasant society which is permeated by fatalism, (b) migrant workers who have had contact with a more advanced industrial society have become re-socialized to new values, therefore (c) having a new mentality they are able, though their actions and leadership, to bring about change in the localities to which they have returned in sufficient numbers. This classical notion of innovative return (Cerase, 1971) is based on return of overseas migrants under different conditions and involving different personality types and different experiences. On the other hand, we have already indicated how difficult it is to become "socialized" into an industrial mode in the large industrial plants where the workers go for avowedly short periods of time and where their contact with the local population is minimal, not to speak of a lack of involvement in the social and political actions in their host country (Talamo, 1967). For most migrant workers, then, the sudden contact with quite a different culture produced either new needs or a crisis of the traditional system of values but it hardly led to a "secondary" socialization making them active agents of innovation back home. By the way, those who succeeded abroad tend not to return. In any case, migration seems to foster individualism deflecting towards satisfaction of personal needs and away from collectivism. The conflict between the receiving and the sending areas in terms of their cultural make-up contributes to the anomie of the migrants (Signorelli, Tirittico and Rossi, 1977).

Remittances and productive
growth in the sending areas

Analyses of the financial contributions which the sending areas benefit from through migrants' remittances have been traditionally carried out on a macro-economic level, focusing on the relationship between remittances and the balance of payments. The individual aspects of remittances have been almost completely neglected. The use of migrants' savings is an important factor which affects the potentialities for development in the sending area. A research project carried out in Sicily (ISVI-FORMEZ, 1976; Reyneri, 1980) concentrated on the use of remittances in the respective families receiving them. Over a period of time some 600 families were studied as to the use to which they had put the remittances received from abroad. For migrants from the area studied the rate of savings was quite high but it was a function of family status of migrants. When migration involved also the spouse, the savings was highest when the length of stay abroad was between 6 and 14 years. Other research shows as well that savings are used first for the current expenses of the families left behind, secondly for the acquisition of durable goods and finally for the acquisition of property. Productive investments play, understandably, a very minor role and to assume otherwise is unrealistic.

Remittances have traditionally been considered a particular form of capital importation to be added to the internal accumulation of capital. The sending areas thus are able to increase their reserves of "strong" currencies considered necessary for any economic development. But the "productive" effect of remittances on such receiving areas is really very uncertain (Böhning, 1976; ILO, 1976). Optimistically, one can call such a process a "virtuous" circle when, thanks to remittances, it is possible to increase imports without increasing the deficit in the balance of payments. Realistically, however, the "vicious" circle prevails inasmuch as remittances increase family incomes *and* consumption of consumer goods produced elsewhere, in more industrialized areas or abroad, leaving the domestic local economy in the status quo ante.

It would be actually surprising were return migrants to behave in any other manner by risking, for instance, all their savings on enterprises likely to fail. Thus return migrants are actually "rational" and not the economists and politicians who wish them to become entrepreneurs. The only activities return migrants can start individually are small businesses which do not figure as variables in the "take-off". In the writings on the role of remittances the Keynesian approach in which consumption, increases the propensity to invest by englarging the market, is an approach which is rarely taken. This could happen only under conditions of very protectionist markets which are presently difficult to envisage given the constraints of the EEC stipulations for member countries.

The sending areas as economically subsidized systems

The difficulty in using the existing surplus in order to start an endogenous process of development is the fundamental problem of all backward economic systems (Baran, 1957; Marshall, 1973). When, as a result of migration, the surplus of available resources increases, the only outcome will be a larger amount of financial resources to be assigned to consumption. It is necessary to overcome the different commercial and financial relations between the national and regional economies which are, at the present time, at different levels of development. This is, of course, a political issue which the relevant literature treats under the headings of a development elite and of a dependent elite (Schneider and Schneider, 1976).

A dominant class which bases its economic power on a backward economic productive system and is dependent on other more developed systems, is interested in maintaining the status quo. Migration reinforces the status quo by removing the threat of unemployment, by increasing family income through remittances and by removing the threateningly active and enterprising persons from a potential collective action. Return migrants, on the other hand, come back often demoralized and disenchanted with the industrial world and tend to deflect their frustrations and aspirations into personal and private consumption.

The old bourgeoisie is tied to declining agricultural production and is being replaced by a new bourgeoisie which is also dependent on outside economic resources the distribution of which it controls. This group is also tied to the governmental machinery which controls the distribution of transfer payments. Such payments, representing pensions and various welfare benefits on one hand and various business incentives on the other are still distributed in the fashion which is particularistic and which allows the office holders a fair amount of personal leeway in the distribution of patronage.

For the return migrants, there are few alternatives for a private financial investment apart from the bank or post office savings accounts, thus they tend to plough their money into land which, in turn, skyrockets bringing sizeable return to the original controlling owners.

All in all, we can say that in sending areas there is a process of modernization without development. The remittance inflow has no positive impact on the productive development; furthermore, when it declines, state policy is necessary to distribute monetary subsidies to support family incomes. In the "Mezzogiorno" the main effects of emigration are a waste of capital and a reproduction of dependent elites: both of which are obstacles to economic growth and social progress.

RETURN MIGRATION TO GREECE AND ITS STRUCTURAL AND SOCIO-POLITICAL EFFECTS

Ross Fakiolas

Overall data on migration

Official statistics for the years 1968 to 1977 show 238,000 Greeks returning home, of whom 161,000 were from Northwestern Europe, primarily from Germany. For the whole post-war period (1946-1981) it is estimated that return migration amounted to about one million persons, including the long term settlers from Turkey and Egypt, and about 30,000 persons returning from the socialist countries in Eastern Europe where they had emigrated as refugees during the Greek Civil War in 1947-1949.

During the period between 1946 to 1973, net emigration was nearly one million persons out of a population of 7.5 million in 1949 and 9.7 million in 1981. Since 1974, net repatriation, including the returning political refugees and the Greeks returning with foreign passports, has amounted to about 25,000 persons annually. However these are only rough estimates as the Greek data on migration are of limited accuracy and coverage. For instance, returnees from Egypt and Turkey, migrants absent for less than one year and migrants to and from the socialist countries are usually not intercepted in the Greek migration statistics.

The causes of migration

The causes of Greek emigration cover a broad range, from political persecution at home to economic migration abroad and emigration to settle permanently in overseas countries. Out-migration to Northwestern Europe was meant primarily as a short term migration with a clearly defined economic objective: to work as much as possible for as much money as possible and to return with some savings.

The causes of return migration are just as many. The majority of those who return from the Middle East and African countries, except Egypt, do so after the expiry of their work contract. Returnees from Turkey and Egypt were compelled to leave those countries for nationalistic reasons, while returnees from the socialist countries repatriate as soon as the Greek government gives them permission to do so. There are some 20,000 persons in the socialist countries still awaiting that permission; the new socialist government, elected

October 18, 1981, had promised return to all political refugees and since December 1982 all refugees have been free to return.

Table 1: Structure of Greek migration by destination 1968 to 1977[*]

	N (000's)	In per cent	Males per cent
Emigrants			
Germany[**]	254	57	57
Other European countries	28	6	62
Australia and North America	146	33	51
Other areas	21	4	66
Total	449	100	
Returnees			
Germany[**]	138	59	55
Other European countries	27	11	57
Australia and North America	48	20	50
Other areas	24	10	50
Total	238	100	

[*]   January 1968 to September 1977
[**]   Includes a small number of migrants to and from the German Democratic Republic.

Source: N.S.S.G. "Statistical Yearbooks of Greece" (1969-1978).

Greeks from Northwestern Europe return for reasons of nostalgia, or because they have attained their economic goals abroad. They also return because of concern for the education and upbringing of their children as Greeks (Unger, 1981; Collarou and Moussourou, 1980). The underlying reasons, however, for most of the returnees are the unsatisfactory social and economic integration abroad and the rapid social and economic development in Greece.

Return from Northwestern Europe had already begun before 1973, the year when the restrictions on a further in-migration began to be imposed by the major receiving countries. The improvement of labor market conditions in Greece with nearly full employment and rising real wages acted both as a restraining factor to emigration and as a strong pull factor for return. The "drying up" of regions of high emigration, mainly in Northern Greece has also caused a reduction in emigration. The social conflicts between immigrants and the indigenous population in the receiving countries helped to create a push factor for return. After 1973, the rising unemployment in the receiving countries and the generous policies to encourage return represented additional push factors. Without the improvement in the labor market conditions in Greece, however, all these factors would have had insignificant effects, as was the case with neighboring Turkey.

The prospects of return migration

The present economic stagnation in Northwestern European countries, their prospects for an average of two to four per cent annual rate of economic growth in the 1980's, the full membership of Greece in the European Community, the established legal protection of immigrants and the continuing economic and social integration of many Greeks in the receiving countries makes it fairly improbable that a massive return migration flow to Greece will take place, despite the high rate of unemployment in receiving countries which is expected to be maintained for a long time.

Effects of return migration in Greece

Return migrants affect economic activity in Greece in several ways. On the negative side, they draw on social funds for pensions, use medical care, take advantage of the educational system and represent an additional drain on the unemployment funds. Proportionally, however, they absorb only a small amount of the total of such funds, under three per cent per annum, but even this marginal load is important for the heavy and rapidly rising financial burden of the welfare system.

On the positive side, returnees contribute to the economy through their savings, their labor and their entrepreneurship. Between 1975 and 1980, official remittances sent by emigrants averaged some $900 million annually, and an estimated additional 10 to 20 per cent of that sum came to Greece in kind or in small undeclared sums brought by return migrants or migrants coming for a visit home. In comparison, during the same period, exports have earned annually about 5.5 million dollars.

Most of emigrant remittances are for current living expenses and immediate investment, while a part is deposited in credit institutions either in foreign currencies or converted into drachmas. Relevant statistics are not available but there are indications that at least half the remittances are used directly or indirectly for capital accumulation. Furthermore, a significant proportion of direct investment is in low productivity business ventures like ownership of coffee houses and small shops, about 80 per cent of which seem to be a one man operation. Other spending goes for prestige consumer goods like big houses and cars, expensive stereo equipment and color television sets (Unger, 1981; Manganara, 1977). An increasing part of emigrant remittances is used to purchase modern equipment for agriculture and machinery and to establish producer co-operatives in which all capital and labor are contributed by return migrants. Between 1975 and 1980, five such companies (co-operatives) were estalished with a total, fully paid-up capital of two million dollars contributed by 311 shareholders. Another two companies were about to get underway and seven more were in the planning stage. These companies enjoy the active support of the Ministry of Coordination; they are in technical fields, in agriculture or in transportation and most are away from large urban centers. One example of an agricultural co-operative is a snail farm.

The early hopes that the process of emigration and return will contribute substantially to raising the skill level of the Greek labor force are not entirely justified. In-migrants to Northwestern Europe were wanted mainly for unskilled, arduous jobs. The migrants were willing to take up any well paid job, irrespective of its prospects for promotion or for occupational training. Furthermore, the low level of schooling of most of the migrants did not allow them to avail themselves of the numerous educational and occupational training opportunities in the host country. Moreover, the migrants were willing to work long overtime hours and were left with little time and energy to improve themselves. Some skills acquired by migrants in highly specialized industrial processes are in low demand in Greece due to the relatively low level of technology prevailing. Many returnees do not like to work in the Greek manufacturing industry where wages are about one half of what they were earning abroad. For instance, a research on returnees to Macedonia in 1976 showed that only 6 per cent of return migrants found employment in manufacturing (Collarou and Moussourou, 1980).

Returnees appear only marginally better off in terms of their industrial skill levels than those who never left Greece and have benefitted both from the formal and on-the-job training at home. Returnees with skills often prefer self-employment anyway and do so in occupations and pursuits where their acquired skills have little usefulness. Also, it must be observed, that returnees tend to revert quickly to the somewhat relaxed approach to work characterizing the domestic labor force.

It must be emphasized, however, that a significant number of leading experts in all walks of life have lived many years abroad where they engaged in studies and in research and that some of the technicians and foremen employed in the most advanced industries in Greece are returnees.

The effects of return migration on unemployment and urbanization are related to the previous large scale emigration. Rapid economic growth and expansion of the educational and social welfare system in Greece have been the main reasons for the substantial decline in unemployment so that return migrants, together with the domestic labor force, have faced so far no major difficulties in finding jobs. The unemployment rate among migrants from agricultural backgrounds who return from Northwestern Europe tends to be relatively high, however (Collarou and Moussourou, 1980). Their situation is due partly to the accumulated unemployment insurance benefits they can draw on in Greece and partly to the adjustment period in Greece and finally their unemployment is also due to their high job expectations in terms of pay and working conditions.

With respect to their occupational qualifications, the majority of returnees enjoy some advantages over their compatriots. For instance, they can speak a foreign language which can be very helpful in finding employment in the rapidly expanding tourist industry or in jobs connected with foreign firms establishing enterprises in Greece. Returnees from Turkey and Egypt are the most proficient in foreign languages. The young returnees from the socialist countries possess a good formal occupational training. Yet, demand for employees speaking a foreign language cannot be always met by returnees because their command of the Greek language is inadequate.

Geographical distribution of returnees

Return migrants tend to settle in cities. Returnees from Turkey and Egypt have had hardly any ties with rural Greece and the same applies to the younger returnees from the socialist countries. The majority of the older returnees from the socialist countries who had been farmers and peasants are now mostly of retirement age. They have lost their property which was confiscated at the end of the Civil War and distributed to others. Nonetheless, some did return to their native village to live as pensioners.

About 80 per cent of returnees from Northwestern Europe and Australia are of rural origin. The returnees from Germany have been away on the average about 11 years; few of them, however, return to their villages for permanent settlement and even a smaller proportion of them engage in agriculture. Although return migration has contributed to urbanization, the latter was being caused mainly by large internal migration fuelled by economic growth in which emigrant remittances played an important role. The rural population of Greece now represents about 24 per cent of the total, whereas thirty years ago it was still over 50 per cent of the total.

41

The social and political
implications of return migration

The longer the migrant has been away, the greater the changes he en-
counters upon return. The rapid pace of social and economic development in
Greece during the entire postwar period translates into serious problems of
reintegration for the returnees. The great majority of returnees have come from
poor peasant families, have low educational attainments and, while abroad,
have worked mainly in low level jobs. They have retained rather traditional
social attitudes. Yet, the long residence abroad, especially in Northwestern
Europe, gives them an air of modernity which they want to act out while in
social situations. Their children who have been to school abroad, quickly
adopt the attitudes of the Greek urbanites.

Even among other returnees a rapid adoption of new middle-class morality takes place, accompanied by conservative political affiliations. A large
number of these returnees are now relatively well off and many have managed
to give their children a good education. The situation is quite different for
returnees from Turkey and Egypt who, as a rule, were born in those countries,
they belong to the middle class and most of them have had more than nine
years of schooling.

Almost all returnees from the socialist countries have a peasant or
working class background and hardly any savings or other property brought
back. The young among them have had many years of formal education and
a fair number hold university degrees in science, medicine or engineering.
Those over 65 years of age receive a small annual grant (not a pension) from
the socialist countries of their previous residence. They have lived in socialist
countries since the Greek Civil War and they have been exposed to situations
of state control, anti-capitalist ideology, limitation of private property and
restrictive political institutions. After return, many of them manage to benefit
quickly from the existence of private enterprise by establishing small private
firms, clinics, consultantships, etc.

Even though traditional values in general are retained or even strengthened among the return migrants, one aspect of the traditional arrangment for
marriage has pretty much disappeared, namely that of the dowry. A survey
of social attitudes of returnees in 1976 showed that the mentality of dowry
diminishes with the length of stay abroad (Collarou and Moussourou, 1980).
Related changes in the perception of sex roles have also taken place, concerning primarily the arrangement for both husband and wife to share responsibility
for housework and the upbringing of the children. Sixty-seven per cent of
returnee respondents accepted the fact that husbands should help with housework, 44 per cent and 60 per cent respectively held that married women with
children and married women without children may or should have a job. No
doubt, this change has come from the circumstances abroad, where it was

customary for immigrants' wives to work for wages in order to meet the goal of rapid capital accumulation.

Politically, return migrants are more aware than they were before migration. Eighteen and thirty per cent respectively of the respondents in the 1976 study indicated they were more interested in politics and trade union activities and spent more time on them. This also is a result of the aging of migrants as interest in politics generally increases with maturity (Collarou and Moussourou, 1980). The increase in interest in the working of the social system is paralleled by the decrease in the interest in religion. Reliance on the parish priest among returnees (male respondents) has all but disappeared.

In conclusion, migratory flows have helped to propel Greece toward modernity. There have been advantages and disadvantages in that change but the overall effects have been positive.

Local impact of returns

MIGRATION, COOPERATION AND DEVELOPMENT: AN EXAMINATION OF A PILOT PROJECT IN PORTUGAL*

Patricia Goldey

Recent Portuguese writings on migration tend to see migration as an inevitable part of increasing modernization or industrialization of the Portuguese economy (Souza Ferreira, 1976). However some writers, including Sousa Ferreira, would admit that after a certain period the influence of migration can have a negative effect on the country of origin producing a serious lack of manpower, especially of specialized and skilled workers while the more heavily industrialised countries continue to pull in a heavy concentration of labour.

Migration from rural Portugal is an endemic social phenomenon. It is not confined to any particular area of the country, or to any particular social group, although the rural sector has been the major contributor to the migratory flow until the late 1960's, due to the predominantly rural nature of Portuguese society, up to 1960 at least.

It is unclear from Portuguese statistics how many migrants have actually returned to Portugal in recent years. Certainly the empirical studies that have been conducted with migrant groups suggest that most labour migrants see migration as a temporary phenomenon (Hoffman-Nowotny, 1978). An "illusion of return" affects statements made by Portuguese migrants and is itself a part of the whole cultural complex surrounding migration in Portugal. Some migrants do return. No one who has visited northern Portugal can doubt the visible material impact on the Portuguese countryside of the *"Brasileiros"* and more recently the *"Franceses"*, those who have come back with something to show for their years of "sacrifices".

In the 1970's the economic recession in northern Europe combined with the end of the colonial regime in the Portuguese territories brought back to Portugal two very different Portuguese migrant types — the labour migrant (*emigrantes*) and the ex-settler migrant (*retornados*). The *retornados*, more

----

* The author wishes to thank the members and executive of the Cooperative of Alvoco das Várzeas, and the technical personnel of the Ministry of Agriculture in the Concelho of Oliveira do Hospital, for their generous assistance and hospitality. Financial assistance for the field trip, in September 1981, was kindly provided by the Nucleo de Estudos de Emigraçao, under the direction of the Secretary of State for Migration and the Portuguese communities, Lisbon. This paper represents an initial evaluation of just one cooperative, as part of an on-going research project to be completed in 1983.

than the *emigrantes*, show surprisingly trouble free incorporation into Portuguese urban and provincial life. Several initiatives in Portuguese agricultural development got underway as a response to the sudden influx of manpower into rural areas after 1977, an unexpected reversal of the historic trend. The "new" manpower stimulated governmental response which, at least partially, is seen in the Pilot Project, to be described.

Agricultural production can be carried out very efficiently on small-scale enterprises. It is not uncommon that output per hectare is higher on small holdings than on large farms; this is perhaps obvious when one takes into account rural underemployment and the total involvement of family labour on the small peasant farm. For people who are still operating at near subsistence level, very small additions to income are major additions to security and confidence. The long-term social benefits can themselves provide economic justification for programmes aimed especially at poor or marginal farmers.

In theory at least, a cooperative gives the farmer the chance to reduce the problem caused by fragmentation, while at the same time keeping the marketing of his produce under his control and influence. Traditional forms of cooperation on *minifundia* make cooperatively organised agriculture a most interesting and viable possibility in the north and parts of central Portugal. Since 1974 collectives and cooperatives have predominated in the south; since 1976 a few "true" cooperatives have started in the northern and central interior in a rather different ideological and social background to that of Alentejo (Goldey, 1980).

There are indications that while full-time agriculture becomes a minority occupation, part-time agriculture continues to be important — socially and economically. Even in towns like Porto and Lisbon, agriculture as a complementary activity to paid employment, to supply subsistence needs, is not uncommon. In Portugal, in 1968, 77.7 per cent of farms were of less than 4 hectares in land area. It has been suggested that 39 per cent of small farms could be regarded as part-time — giving either important supplementary income, or only complementary to off-farm earnings (Cavaco, 1980).

The agricultural project: Alvoco das Varzeas; background information

The district of Coimbra with 391,710 inhabitants in 1970 shows a sharply different socio-economic structure as one goes from the coastal zone to the interior as do many Portuguese districts. Compared to neighbouring districts it is less populous than Aveiro (with 535,815 inhabitants) and Viseu (440,330) but has more inhabitants than Castelo Branco (247,855) or Guarda (205,235). In terms of population density, with 99 inhabitants per km², it occupies an intermediate position between the more densely populated coastal districts of Aveiro and Leiria (197 per km²; 105 per km²) and the depopulating distrticts of Guarda and Castelo Branco (37.3 per km^2; 36.9 per km^2). In the district of Coimbra all municipalities (*concelhos*) show a settlement density pattern of below 100 inhabitants per km^2, but population distribution varies from the coastal strip to the interior east following the standard Portuguese contrast — as dramatic from west to east, as from north to south.

Compared to the districts of Leiria and Aveiro with 33.3 per cent and 48 per cent respectively of the active population in industry, Coimbra had in 1970 only 24 per cent of its active population involved in the industrial sector despite having held for some time the position of third largest Portuguese city. In terms of economic indicators, not merely geographical locality, Coimbra occupies the transitional area between Beira Litoral and Beira Alta.

While rice, maize and olives grow abundantly in the coastal area, production levels fall significantly as one moves east. The rich agriculture of the coastal municipalities, and the industrial off-farm employment alternatives there, along with the excellent north-south communications system linking them with Porto or Lisbon, provide a sharp contrast to the poor agriculture, lack of alternative employment and relative isolation of the more eastern municipalities. While small farmers on the coastal strip of Coimbra district can expect to get a crop of 14-22 cwt. per hectare of maize, those in the interior can hope only for 4-8 cwt. per hectare. In the eastern *concelhos* rye largely substitutes maize as the major cereal crop. Until 1974 the interior municipalities of Coimbra district showed the same population loss due to the migratory flow of labour overseas and to northern Europe as did most of the Portuguese hinterland.

Oliveira do Hospital, one of the *concelhos* of Coimbra, is rather the exception to the rule. In 1970 with a population density of 97.8 inhabitants per square kilometre it was, due to its prospering textile industry, one of the few interior municipalities to retain population, and was even more exceptional in offering, in an essentially agricultural farming area, alternative off-farm employment for men and women. An old settlement — its name originating from its links with the 12th century Order of Hospitalers of St. John of Jerusalem (now the Knights of Malta) — it owes its commercial significance to the old woollen industry as the precursor to the present day textile industry, as do some *concelhos* in the Guarda and Castelo Branco districts. It is also an important centre for the commercialisation of *queijo da serra*, a cheese made from sheep's milk. Less well-known perhaps, but of local economic importance, is the fact that three thousand pigs are slaughtered weekly in the *concelho* of Oliveira do Hospital, as attested by the official veterinary officer, and their carcases circulated by *porqueiras* at fairs in the region, sold from small stalls selling suckling pig and such regional delicacies.

The country town of Oliveira do Hospital — the seat of the *concelho* — in 1981 is undergoing considerable growth, with new buildings springing up everywhere, a new hotel, and daily transport links west to Coimbra and east to Spain. The town itself embraces about one-third of the *concelho's* total population, 9,500 inhabitants out of a total of 29,000. The urban area now includes two nearby civil parishes (*frequesias*) of 3,000 souls. Despite the apparent visible new prosperity the problems typical of many rural municipalities of interior Portugal continue to concern the inhabitants: people from the *concelho* still refer to it as a "backward" area (*atrasado*), they complain of the lack of an agricultural labour force, of the social consequences of emigration, of their distance from good markets and their isolation from the main centres of communications.

The increasing industrialisation of the area, with the growth of textile factories, and more jobs in civil construction, has meant that young men leave agriculture, even if they stay in the *concelho*. Whereas the census returns of 1970 showed over 60 per cent of the active population in the agricultural sector, people estimate now that only 20-25 per cent are actively employed in agriculture-related jobs. The visible modernity of the town of Oliveira do Hospital is recent, some villages only acquired access roads after 1974; the present state of modern building activity is largely the result of the presence in the *concelho* of returned migrants or returned settlers from the newly independent African territories. Along with growth and 'progress' have come some problems: the cost of renting a house now in the town of Oliveira do Hospital is around 8,000 escudos, about 80 pounds monthly, while the national minimum salary stands presently at 10,000 escudos. However, this is an area where women generally work too, either in factories, or on the land if their men are employed elsewhere — so there are frequently two incomes for the household.

Oliveira do Hospital today is a small but growing industrial centre heavily dependent on the textile and civil construction industries, the seat of a *concelho* where two thirds of the municipality are village dwellers dependent upon farming and often supplementary income from off-farm activities. By no means all of its 20 parishes enjoy the same level of modernisation or development.

· The problems of the *concelho* therefore are: 1) how to develop the decaying agricultural sector and control labour availability so that the urbanisation of the seat of the municipality does not overwhelm the still agriculturally based and rural-oriented parishes that make up the *concelho*, and 2) how to keep people on the land to avoid the pains of migration, to prevent a rural exodus, and at the same time to improve the quality of life in the villages of the *concelho* through improved agricultural practices.

The agricultural sector

There are 4,870 farms in the *concelho* of Oliveira do Hospital that are under 20 hectares in size, covering a total land area of 10,423 hectares. There are 32 farms over 20 hectares in size covering 1,830 hectares. This means that the average size farm for most farmers is about 2.1 hectares; while the few big farmers — less than 1 per cent of total farmers — enjoy an average of 57 hectares. The land area of the *concelho* is 23,293 hectares, of which 12,253 appears to be registered as farmed land.

The main agricultural or related products of the area are rye, olives, sheep and pig products. There are only 200 cows in the *concelho*, but 6,560 sheep. Tractors are now commonly used for ploughing — a result of remittances from abroad.

The pilot project

The financial backing for the project comes from a Dutch government agency, which in 1977 offered an aid grant of 12,000,000 escudos over a period of years to the Portuguese government to be administered through the Ministry of Emigration and the Ministry of Agriculture in the area of Coimbra and Castelo Branco. There are three such projects currently underway in central Portugal including two that involve the introduction of tobacco growing in the district of Castelo Branco among returned settlers from Africa (*retornados*). The common social objective of the projects is to try to keep down the flow of migrants to northern Europe by improving agricultural income within the project area. The Dutch represent their interest by sending visiting specialists from Holland once or twice a year. The Portuguese authorities supply the technical expertise within the outline guidelines of the programme laid down by the funding agency. Both the Dutch and the Portuguese agencies involved wish very much for the cooperative to have a continuing self-propelling or at least self-sustaining existence when the Pilot Project period comes to an end.

Objectives of the project

The Dutch agency donors and the Portuguese Ministry of Emigration share the same social objectives — to reduce the migratory flow from the area and to help reintegrate returned migrants and settlers into the rural economy by offering a more profitable approach to agriculture by small farmers. Establishing co-operatives is part of the objectives. The cooperative is an attempt to bring together many small part-time farmers to help solve their marketing and buying problems.

The Ministry of Agriculture (*Ministerio de Agricultura e Pescas, MAP*) is especially interested in the technical problems posed by sheep raising on these hilly, depopulating villages of *minifundia*. In the traditional pastoral economy the sheep grazed year-round on mountain pastures, looked after usually by paid shepherds. With increased out-migration in the 1960's it got harder to find the necessary manpower for shepherding. Going to the hill pastures as a shepherd was a lonely, hard way to earn a livelihood. The MAP then is concentrating on a settled, permanent pasture solution to this problem. To improve pastures with new fodder crops and new irrigation technology and to introduce an increased herd run by the new cooperative in a system of permanent pastures in a traditional semi-pastoral rural economy was a technical challenge to the MAP technicians and one to which they have responded with enthusiasm. If the project were successful it could be repeated in other hilly areas ideal for sheep-raising and with a traditional pastoral economy.

The Cooperative of Alvoco das Varzeas

Alvoco is a village of 640 inhabitants, of whom 455 are over 18 years of age. The cooperative had in 1981, 115 members (*socios*) having grown from an original membership of 74 in 1977. All the cooperative members have more than 1 hectare of land, most have 2 to 4 hectares, and some have over 80 hectares. Members say that they see for themselves only a part-time future in agriculture, even those, the majority, who have between 2 to 4 hectares of land.

There are some women cooperative members, all widows whose husbands were members. No woman has joined in her own right as yet (younger women tend not to have access to ownership of land in their own right and married women's land claims are represented by their husbands). Women members, however, do take an active part in meetings and assemblies; they are often the first to arrive at meetings and speak up without shyness or embarrassment. There is some awareness among members that the cooperative has helped its women members psychologically and materially by giving them an increased security.

For the small farmers of the region, whether or not they are members of a cooperative, the primary emphasis is on self-sufficiency. The problem is to try to make the most of what they all have, and to rationalise the farming effort and introduce new technologies or technical know-how in such a way as to increase farm income on the average or small-sized farms. There are some parcels of land in the village left abandoned due to emigration, and some of these have been bought or are rented by the cooperative which currently works 20 hectares of land for permanent pasture for the sheep herd. Alvoco then is a village where it is claimed that all villagers to a greater or lesser degree own some land. "Here everyone has enough to get by on" ("*Aqui todos tem para sobreviver*") is the generally expressed view of local farmers.

When the cooperative was set up in 1977, members (*socios*) came into the association with land and with pine woods (*pinhal*). The forestry side of the farming enterprise is distinguished precisely from the farmed area — this has obvious implications for assessments of distribution of farm size, i.e. land holding structure and economic viability of farm units. The cooperative functions as a general marketing cooperative, buying and selling from and to its members. There are three major aspects to the agricultural and animal husbandry work of the cooperative: 1) the creation and maintenance of an improved herd of sheep; 2) the production and marketing of sheep products, especially cheese made in the traditional artisanal ways; and 3) the marketing of resin from the pine plantations.

At present (1981) the cooperative herd stands at 130 head plus 60 young of which 30 belong to individual members and 100 to the cooperative enterprise. From February-September 1st, 1981 production of milk was 3,270 litres of which 1,800 litres has been sold as milk through the cooperative, and the rest has been made into cheese (*queijo da serra*) of which 302 kilos have been produced. The year's production has fallen short of the best production rate attainable: the usual 5 litres of milk to 1 kilo of cheese was increased to 6 litres per kilo because of the poor pastures due to the continuing dry spells of 1980 and 1981. There are two women employed by the cooperative making cheese in the traditional way in provisional installations. The importance of the sheep's milk cheese lies in its easy marketability in Coimbra, Lisbon and Porto. The price is high, but there is a guaranteed market demand.

The original 74 cooperative members with forest land all joined in 1977. This year (1980-81) the resin has reached an especially good price of 40 escudos for each tree. Altogether 46,385 kilos of resin were collected representing around 20,000 trees. The payment to members is based on the number of trees a members has, not the quantity or resin. In the four years of the cooperative's existence the resin production has provided the major income of the cooperative.

Many of those village farmers who stayed out of the cooperative do not have pinewoods on their farm and are limited to subsistence farming. Increasingly, these farmers are coming to the cooperative to hire machinery or arrange credit facilities. The only income to be distributed between members thus far has been the profit from resin production.

Members feel that those who benefit most from the cooperative are the pinewood plantation owners. All members of the cooperative own land of some sort in varying degrees. They can join the cooperative with land (i.e. ploughed land) or pinewoods or cash. The striking fact about the Alvoco Cooperative is that all the members presently own pinewood, even if they do not own any arable land. Returns on resin have gone up from 12.50 escudos to 43.50 escudos, so clearly members feel that this is where the present — if not the future — lies.

All present members participate in the buying and selling side of the cooperative's activities, in the resin marketing, and in machinery use, hiring the use of machines from the cooperative. Secondary cash crops like potatoes and maize are also sold through the retail section of the cooperative.

An elected three-man committee administers the Alvoco Cooperative. All three directors (1981) are part-time farmers: one is a road worker, another a businessman and the third, a cattle dealer. All three have houses in the village, and two of the three live there full time. Only the businessman, a returned settler from Africa, has worked abroad. During the week he works in Porto where he has his own store. The General Assembly, however, has more power here than in many other cooperatives.

The book-keeping and tax accountancy side of the cooperative's work is aided by a technician from the regional MAP office in Coimbra who visits the cooperative whenever necessary. This is part of the technical assistance provided officially by the Ministry.

Altogether eleven men are employed by the cooperative from February to December, and two women in the cheese-making in season. Of the eleven male cooperative employees, all are members of the cooperative; six of them are employed full-time in forestry.

Cooperative members give occasional labour, including tractor driving, when needed. Outside tractor drivers now get paid 800 escudos an hour, a high pay in view of the fact that the national minimum salary is 10,000 escudos per month.

There are two technicians, employed by the Ministry to offer technical assistance to the cooperative, an agricultural officer, and a veterinary officer, who have to combine their work on the cooperative with their other work in the *concelho*. They are committed workers but their general work load in the *concelho* is heavy (2 technicians to 4000 farmers).

The extension side of the technical programme in the *concelhos* generally is barely adequate, as the MAP staff are well aware. On the whole, the cooperative is better served than many of the nearby independent small farmers as the technical support is focussed within clear project policy directives, laid down in collaboration between the Dutch funding agency, the Portuguese Ministry of Agriculture, and the Portuguese Secretary of State for Emigration.

Assessment

Given that with the farmers there are four interested parties involved in this project, relations between the parties have been remarkably harmonious, as far as a short visit can reveal. The technical support from the MAP is guaranteed to continue so long as the cooperative stays within the guidelines of the present project, concentrating on improving pastures, and on improved animal production and cheese processing and marketing. There is, however, a possibility that were the cooperarative to decide unilaterally to shift direction and diversify into, for example, vegetable growing, then the MAP might feel obliged to withdraw its back-up services, partly because of a lack of technical expertise and partly because technical interest in the project lies specifically on the side of animal production and the potential for duplicating the project in similar geographic areas.

In so far as problems can be identified at this early stage, two problem areas seem to emerge: 1) whether in fact the primary objective of increasing income of the small farmer to the point where emigration becomes less attractive will be achieved; 2) whether the cohesion within the cooperative under the present cooperative project strategy can be maintained. It is early to assess the success of the primary objective; certainly those farmers who are members of the cooperative are enthusiastic and do see the added income as a distinct improvement to their previous situation.

The second problem area arises in part from the very enthusiasm generated within the village by the cooperative's existence. Some members wish to expand, to diversify. Cooperative members, even those on the Executive Committee, are divided in their objectives, and this may indeed present a problem in the furure to the functioning of the cooperative. Although members of the cooperative tend to be younger than the average farmers in the area which is around 60 years, there is still a generational division between older and younger cooperative members. Some younger members would like to diversify and break away from what they see as restrictions imposed by the Portuguese-Dutch aid agreement. It is possible that when the cooperative does eventually become self-sufficient it is going to be extremely difficult for the technicians, or the directors to hold the cooperative to the original project aims.

One division between members is reflected in two conflicting attitudes regularly expressed by them: *"estamos a viver dos subsidios"* — "we are living off subsidies"; and *"do que precisamos e so o dinheiro"* — "the only thing we need is money".

After four years in existence the cooperative has attained its short-term objective of creating the pre-conditions for successful production and marketing of sheep's cheese and has greatly improved the marketing of resin. It has generated local enthusiasm, and even the differences now expressed by members as to which direction the cooperative should move in are indications of increased self-confidence and revitalisation of the local rural economy. There seems no division along migrant and non-migrant lines among the cooperative membership. However whether the cooperative can maintain its momentum, and generate increased income for members to such an extent that it can compensate for income expected upon migration remains to be seen.

RETURN OF PORTUGUESE: ECONOMIC GOALS OR RETENTION OF ONE'S IDENTITY

Ema Serra-Santana

The town of Braganca is among the smallest county seats in Portugal. In 1960, the population in the district of Braganca was estimated at around 30,000 inhabitants. In 1970, there were fewer than 10,000 inhabitants, 5,000 of whom actually lived within the town (Census of Portugal, 1972). The town is situated in an isolated region in the foothills of the Trasos-Montes, in the northeastern part of Portugal bordering on Spain. Porto is one of the nearest large cities and is eight hours away by train. Economy is agricultural rural, most of it consists in trading within the region. The outside cash, apart from a few public salaries, comes from remittances emigrants send to their families.

A small research project consisting of interviews with 34 families of returnees, between 1978 and August, 1981 provided some data. What all the returnees had in common was their migration pattern: men left first, leaving behind their family, either parents or wives and children. Sometimes wives and also children followed, only to return before the husbands did. The purpose of migration was the "project" that is to save up enough money to be able to return "successfully". Success would not have been possible without the close cooperation of kin. The extended family, mainly parents and in-laws, supervised the local investments (patches of land, what small businesses there were), and took care of the children when their mother followed her husband abroad. Primarily, they supervised the family honor, that is the children but primarily the wife. The wife's support in the project of migration was indeed heroic. Either she stayed at home and managed what there was of the family property or she followed her husband abroad and worked at menial jobs in addition to doing all the housework and taking care of children who were with them.

On the average, the wife followed about two years after the departure of the husband and she went wherever he was. She never changed her habitual mode of work, namely domestic chores and jobs which are essentially an extension of household tasks. The Portuguese woman was able to retain her mode of life, her value system, her convictions, both social and religious, and thus was able to reintegrate without any difficulty when she returned (Petonnet, 1979). Upon return, the women were able to resume all their previous behavior patterns including traditional black dress despite the fact they may have lived for more than five years in very large European cities. The decision to return was made for the sake of the children and for the sake of themselves, "before it is too late".

Impact of returnees on their home town

It is not surprising, given the system of social control operating even during the migratory period and given the very solid ties to their home town while abroad, that returnees do not seem to affect the social structure of Braganca to any great degree. Returnees who had been "peasants" or sons of small landowners became part of the "bourgeoisie" upon return. They may have become craftsmen abroad, and they returned as small businessmen, even administration officials or industrial workers. None of them returned to farming, despite all the traditional ideology they had retained. The returnees adapted to the social structure in their town easily. They bought or built a house for themselves, deposited money in the bank, acquired agricultural land they do not till; they became, in short, "eldermen", the local elite without actually holding the political power which goes with it. That power stays with the traditional elite, the old time businessmen, the large landowners, the few professionals, the public servants. Owning property, however, especially a house, is very important to the returnees and this factor encourages them to support the status quo, which allows the town to retain its traditional ways.

On the whole, the returnees have improved their economic lot, their minds are at ease, they support the community with which they now feel at one, they think warmly of the whole region, of the whole country, they are solid citizens. Their social mobility was individualistic with a firm goal before them. Abroad, they shied away from political involvements. They are not really social climbers as they worked hard for what they achieved. Their wives become their display of success. The wives dress traditionally, stay in the house, do not work the land, they crochet and embroider, following traditional conceptions of what seems proper.

For the Portuguese woman, emigration has given her social promotion, a social reclassification upwards, a payoff for the hard work abroad. All conversations held by returnees during our interviews had a recurrent theme, that of the utmost importance of the family. Thus it is the welfare and an improvement of the individual family which can be seen as the mainspring behind emigration, and behind return as well. To maintain one's identity embedded in the small town, outside of which they did not seem to count, they needed to help preserve such a feeling of identity for their children. Thus decisions to return were often couched in terms of the schooling for the children which would be Portuguese, not French, "before it is too late".

RETURN OF INTERNAL MIGRANTS FROM CATALONIA

Carlota Solé

Catalonia is a part of Spain with a rich historical tradition and with a tradition of internal in-migration dating back to the 19th century to the onset· of industrialization. This tradition has been continued especially after World War I. The last influx of in-migrants took place in the 1960's.

It is the last period of in-migration which is of a particular interest as it represents an in-migration of persons representing a cross-section of Spanish society. That is, people in all walks of life migrate to Catalonia. Barcelona, which is the central place of attraction in Catalonia, is a bustling metropolis of close to three million people as of 1970.

In 1978, a large scale survey of households in the metropolitan area of Barcelona was undertaken by a team of sociologists from the University of Barcelona underwritten by Fundacion Juan March. The sample was a random stratified sample of 1,299 respondents carefully selected so that the sample be statistically representative. From each household, one person over 18 years of age was the respondent. The breakdown of the sample was some 46 per cent in-migrants, the rest was born in the region of Catalonia. The sample reflects the actual distribution of population as found in the census. The main interest of the survey was to determine the variables most responsible for willingness to return or to stay for the in-migrant half of the sample. The native born half of the sample was used primarily to check on the variables of social integration insofar as they would differ from those of the in-migrants.

The project (Solé, 1981) has been reported on at length elsewhere. What is reported on here, are the main variables determining the willingness or the intention to stay or to return of in-migrants to be juxtaposed to situations normally encountered in studies of return migration or of migrants' adaptation where migrants come from culturally *and* politically different areas. What we consider especially significant in this paper is the cultural integration variables which seem to override simple political variables of adaptation or non-adaptation of immigrants.

Normally, studies of return migration concern themselves only with return across political boundaries. In the case of Catalonia, this does not seem to be the case de jure but, from the point of view of the historically embedded cultural differences in various parts of Spain, in-migration of Spaniards to Catalonia can be viewed as de facto immigration and it is treated as such in this paper.

There are several reasons for treating Catalonia as a culturally independent entity within Spain. The language is now an official language in Spain next to Castillian Spanish. It is fiercely maintained in the region so that one can be easily identified as belonging or not belonging to the region linguistically. Secondly, political expression of nationalism (seen as regionalism by the central government) can be seen in the local political allegiances including the participation in the labor union movement which is regionalized. Thirdly, the local social class structure is the most telling of nationalism so that integration into Catalan society cannot take place until one is firmly identified within its social class structure. One also must take into account the Catalan specific symbols, institutions, cultural artifacts etc. This has been traced in our survey be asking the respondents to self-identify themselves within the local class structure.

In order to gauge properly the parameters of social integration of in-migrants, 46 in-depth interviews were conducted previous to the survey so that the complex field instrument for the survey proper be solidly grounded in the cultural base. The field instrument which emerged had 262 items of which 8 were specifically addressed to the question of return. It is the few items on return which will be summarized here.

The most telling indication of whether or not the in-migrants to Catalonia wish to stay was their answer to our question: "Under the same work conditions and opportunities for you and your children would you prefer to live in Catalonia or back home"? 67 per cent preferred Catalonia as compared to 24 per cent preferring living in their place of origin. When the responses were broken down by self-reported social class those of the highest SES were slightly more in favor of staying in Catalonia than the others but differences were slight. On the other hand, when the question was broken down into components indicating that one wished never to return nor to return even though feeling homesick, the lower income groups were slightly less certain that they wished to stay in Catalonia than were the high income groups. In no case, however, was the proportion of those planning or wishing to return any greater than one third of our respondents.

Interestingly enough, the length of stay in Catalonia did not seem to differentiate substantially between those who indicated willingness to return and those who did not, disregarding, again, the social economic status. This is quite an important finding inasmuch as the standard literature on migrant's adaptation (Richmond, 1979) indicates a positive relationship between the length of stay and adaptation, that is a lower propensity to consider return. Among our respondents, of those less than five years in Catalonia, about one third would return either because of family or political reasons. The difference between those staying less than one year and those staying between one to five years, is, naturally, very much skewed in favor of those wishing to return who had the least investment in time in their new "country" of residence. After the magic number of five years, the return due to family ties but not due to employment diminishes quite dramatically. Namely, were the in-migrants to Catalonia able to secure similar and comparable working conditions and jobs in their places of origin, it does not seem to matter how long they had been in Catalonia. Approximately still about one third of them would return or, at least, would consider return. Here, of course, we have to be fairly cautious in our interpretation of the data as the individual cells are becoming quite small despite the large number of the total sample so that sampling variance forces us to discount some of our conclusions. Nonetheless, the logic of the data in our tables (Solé, 1981) allows us to state that among all the in-migrants, the notion of the homeland does not disappear with time. As a matter of fact, and no doubt related to the life-cycle experiences and expectations of the in-migrants to Catalonia, those who have been here for more than twenty years show a proportion of about 25 per cent still expecting to return, in this case, no doubt, to retire. What is also interesting is the fact that some long term migrants, close to three quarters of them, do not foresee a return to home even in case of retirement.

In other words, there seems to be a threshold number of about ten years of residence which differentiated between the potential returnees and the potential stayers, at least for our data. These results are fairly similar to other studies of international migration confirming our notion that migration across a cultural border is as significant as migration across a political border even though the two are not always overlapping.

In the aggregate, there seems to be no difference among the respondents expressing a desire or intention to return by sex. Some of this is the artifact of our sampling method which selected randomly one person per household so that males or females were probably articulating the values of the household. Thus the only perceptible difference by sex was in response to the item that "I would return only under similar conditions of work and housing as I have here", where male respondents (37 per cent) and female respondents (31 per cent) were distributed as expected. Similarly, the proportion of respondents indicating homesickness as temptation to return was duly skewed in favor of female respondents. This means perhaps nothing more than that, culturally, women are more likely willing to name emotional reasons than men are. We think it is not as much culture specific as sex role specific.

Finally, we would like to point out that some three quarters of our sample have experienced the first time migration to Catalonia, the proportion of repeat migrants being slightly higher for men than for women, in keeping with the expected patterns of migration. The fact that women were more likely the first time migrants, even though by a small margin, would reinforce the preceding finding showing them to be more responsive to homesickness.

All in all, the data from our survey which is only sketchily reported here as regards return migration seem to confirm the general findings in the literature that return migration is a function of the length of stay. This, in turn is contributory to putting down roots in the new homeland. The latter finding is corroborated by the process of adapting to the language spoken in Catalonia. Normally, when migration takes place across political borders of nation states migrants encounter a new language to master in order to become successful at all in their new country. The Spanish coming to Catalonia, on the other hand, speak a language reasonably similar to Catalonian so that they are normally quite well understood, non-Catalan Spanish being actually the official language of the country. Migrants indicate their willingness and their success in integration into the Catalan society by adopting the language of Catalan. Our data show that those who have done so show the least willingness to return to their place of origin or to migrate somethere else. Thus, we found the language as a very telling even though not crucial indicator of success in the Catalan society and one feature which occurs at the end of the adaptation process. Salaried employees and skilled workers show proficiency in Catalan when they do not expect to return as compared to those in the same occupational groups who would return. The per cent differences are fairly small, 37 per cent of those not speaking Catalan not wishing to return to 41 per cent of those not speaking Catalan willing to return. The distribution is, however, in the right direction. For the small proportion classified as self-employed, speaking Catalan is obviously important so that it does not discriminate in terms of willingness or unwillingness to return. As we pointed out earlier, Catalan is not indispensable for success in the Catalan society thus its predictive value is confirmatory of a trend.

In the near future, a follow-up study of the potential return migrants will be able to confirm or disconfirm the few tentative findings presented here.

RETURN MIGRANTS TO SARDINIA:
RURAL AND URBAN DIFFERENCES*

Maria Luisa Gentileschi

This paper reports on a survey of ret urn migrants to Sardinia who were registered in various communes as returnees between 1972 and 1977. Migrants returning to rural as well as urban communities were interviewed in order to establish which differences, if any, there were among them which might influence their choice of their return community. Some 150 returnees were interviewed, representing about 9 per cent of all returnees listed on the immigration records of selected communes. While the sample is small, it is statistically representative of local situations.

Urban demography in Sardinia

Cagliari, which is the capital of the island and correspondingly, has the largest concentration of population and the most political and economic power in Sardinia, has recently grown considerably in importance. Twenty per cent of the population of Sardinia lives in Cagliari and the satellite communities. Of the other cities, only Sassari offers some alternatives to the capital city, as it also has a university, daily newspapers and a lively publishing business.

Interregional migration and emigration of population from Sardinian towns varied over the years but was never substantial. Two mining towns, Carbonia and Iglesias, are the only exceptions; their very nature, since they are one industry towns, made them subject to heavier population fluctuations as a result of economic swings. This was especially true of Carbonia, a coal-mining town. It attracted migrants not only from Sardinia but also from the Italian mainland. With the decline in coal mining, the city suffered an exodus of its population (Rudas, 1974; Gentileschi, 1980).

In the 1950's, considerable urbanization started in and around Cagliari, partially as a result of post-war reconstruction but principally as a result of its new position as capital of an autonomous region which Sardinia had become. Given the small number of inhabitants in the rural area of Sardinia, urbani-

_____

* Preliminary report from a research project sponsored by the Working Group on Migration in Italy of the Association of Italian Geographers (Agei).

zation of the island was able to absorb most of the migratory movements so that Sardinians did not resort to emigration to any significant degree (Badas *et al.*, 1977).

In the 1960's, however, the rural to urban migration in Sardinia was supplanted by emigration and migration to the Italian mainland. The province of Nuoro, for instance, was particularly affected. Whereas urbanization in the capital town of Nuoro increased, migration towards Cagliari and Sassari declined. There, the population growth which took place was due mostly to natural increase.

In the 1970's which are known for the overall economic slowdown, industry suffered in Sardinia as well, occasioning a decline of migration related to jobs. Thus the pace of urbanization declined, aided by contributing factors of housing shortages in low income housing which, in turn, was brought about by building regulations to contain an uncontrolled expansion. The return migrants arriving in Sardinia were thus returning to a situation which discouraged a rapid urbanization and thus their choice of places to return to must be seen in this context. Normally, it can be assumed that towns attract more and better qualified return migrants than do villages. Upon their return, intended to be definitive, to their home regions, the younger migrants, those who are better educated, with some savings and perhaps imbued with an enterpreneurial spirit, would be tempted to settle in towns where they could set up a business, for instance. The greater educational opportunities for their children should also make towns more attractive to return migrants. On the other hand, there are strong family ties including those of family property in which some of the savings have been invested while still abroad, which would favor return to the native village. Thus, return to the native village will take place unless specific reasons militate against it. The personal isolation experienced abroad reinforces the nostalgic view of prospects back home which favors a conservative decision as to the place to return to.

Village-town distribution of returnees

Since most return migrants have come originally from Nuoro, Carbonia and Iglesias, one would expect the same communities to experience substantial return flows, reinforced by return migrants who have come originally from small isolated places on the island. An analysis of the distribution of return migrants to Sardinia reveals a clear tendency of returnees to concentrate in only a few communities. During the period under study, 1972 through 1977, 48 per cent of returnees settled in just 38 of the 356 existing communes. Limiting our analysis to four provincial capitals, we find return migration lower than the island-wide mean value. With 27 per cent of Sardinian population, these four communes have received only ten per cent of the returnees. The average rate of return for Sardinia was, during that period, 1.63 per 1000 inhabitants. The capital cities register only 0.62 per 1000 while some communes receive up to 12 returnees per 1000 inhabitants.

Taking into consideration all the communes with at least 20,000 inhabitants, the inflow index increases to 1.36 which is still below the regional average. This is due to the fact both Carbonia and Iglesias fall into the "large" city category and, having sent off many emigrants, they are receiving a proportion of them back. Two categories of communes where emigration has been pronounced are those with fewer than 2,000 inhabitants and those with a population of between 2,000 and 5,000; they are receiving returnees above the island mean return index of 1.62.

What is the impact of return migration on the population growth and the age and sex structure of the various communes in Sardinia? Traditionally, the main source of population growth was natural increase which was substantial both in towns and the rural communes. Averaged over the years studied, the natural increase in the four provincial capitals was 4,850 annually compared to a positive migratory balance of 494. Gains from international migration were higher than from internal migration. Annually, there were 104 emigrants and 224 registered return migrants compared to internal 100 outmigrants and 104 in-migrants. On the average, 253 return migrants were registered annually.

Socio-demographic profile of returnees

An age pyramid constructed for Nuoro and one for two rural communes show that in Nuoro, which is the capital of Barbagia province, the age distribution does not seem much affected with return migrants included. Smaller communities, however, will show a marked distortion of the population pyramid where children under 15 and adults from 30 to 45 "extrude" from the pyramid. No doubt, young migrants who left in the 1960's have returned with their families ten years later and set themselves apart demographically from the otherwise aging population distribution in the rural areas.

We have interviewed at length 45 returnees in two urban communes, Nuoro and Quartu S. Elena to look for determinants of community size choice upon return. The profiles are summarized in Tables 1, 2 and 3. The tables are quite self-explanatory. While urban communes do not attract proportionately as many returnees as do the rural communes, returnees to urban communes have a more varied background as regards their pre-emigration residence and work histories. Thus, it is natural for migrants with higher occupational characteristics to tend towards cities. On the other hand, although returnees to rural communes, had usually been farmers, mostly agricultural day laborers prior to emigration, they do not resume agricultural work but for 20 per cent of them.

In short, the qualifications of emigrants returning to towns contribute indirectly to further impoverishment of talent in small rural communes by drawing away that particular demographic reserve consisting of emigrant workers and their families, together with their savings. Perhaps the most interesting development which is the result of return migration to rural communes in Sardinia is the settling there but commuting to work in adjacent urban areas. The savings and the property and housing in the rural area allow the workers who have gained some industrial experience abroad, to utilize this experience for employment which may not be very stable but allows them to combine rural residence with urban employment. Thus, for a time, a decline in the nominally rural population has been slowed down in Sardinia.

Table 1: Distribution of returnees by commune of birth, of departure and return

	Urban communes		Rural communes	
	perc.	nos.	perc.	nos.
Same commune for birth, departure and return	57.8	26	89.0	57
Commune of return different from that of birth and that of departure	11.1	5	3.1	2
Commune of birth different from that of return	31.1	14	6.3	4
Other	--	--	1.6	1
Total	100.0	45	100.0	64

Table 2: Educational level of returnees to urban and rural communes

		Primary school unfinis.	Primary school	Lower second. school	Training school	Upper second. school	Univer- sity	Total
Urban communes								
	perc.	13.3	66.7	13.3	2.2	4.5	--	100.0
	nos.	6	30	6	1	2	--	45
Rural communes								
	perc.	40.6	51.6	6.3	1.5	--	--	100.0
	nos.	26	33	4	1	--	--	64

Table 3: Return migrants by work experience before and after
emigration and by return to urban and rural communes

		Urban communes		Rural communes	
		perc.	nos	perc.	nos.
	agriculture	2.8	1	70.7	41
Before departure	industry	77.8	28	24.1	14
	services	19.4	7	5.2	3
	Total	100.0	36	100.0	58
Non active			9		6
	agriculture	--	--	26.0	13
On return	industry	59.5	22	66.0	33
	services	40.5	15	8.0	4
	Total	100.0	37	100.0	50
Non active			.8		14

RETURN MIGRATION IN
FRIULI-VENEZIA GIULIA

Elena Saraceno

The purpose of this paper is to report some of the findings on the patterns of settlement of returning migrants to the Friuli-Venezia Giulia Region (CRES, 1981). Work and family history of some 1500 returnees were sought in interviews conducted between September 1980 and March, 1981. A random sample was drawn from a list of 10,929 heads of families receiving travel refunds from the region between 1970 and 1979.

In that region returning migrants are part of the tradition established after World War II and lasting well to the end of the 1960 decade, main movements being between the region and Northwest Europe (CRES, 1977; Saraceno, 1978; CRES, 1979). Among returning migrants in the 1970's, the different generations that had left over time were represented. Much of the reason for return was seen in the job opportunities created by recent industrial development in the region. Since 1968, consequently, return migration rates were higher than out-migration rates, predating thus the European energy crisis of 1973 which only amplified the return stream.

Migration in Friuli-Venezia Giulia had been one of the most intense waves since the second half of the last century. The presence of small agricultural holdings, a relatively weak urban bourgeoisie and a growing rural-artisan class provided a different social background for migration than that of southern out-migration areas, for instance (Saraceno, 1980).

Soon after the Second World War, an attempt at industrialization with largely extraregional investments (shipbuilding, textile industry) but highly concentrated in the urban eastern part of the region, failed to provide the right conditions for an industrial take-off. In the second half of the 1960's, a second attempt at industrialization took place but with a completely different approach. Small and medium size firms developed quite spontaneously, in a geographically dispersed pattern in rural areas. Such firms maintained a continuity with the previous local artisan crafts in the production of steel cutlery, metalworking in general, machine tools and wooden chairs and furniture. The goods were mostly for export and expansion was fast. Not only was the economic expansion able to absorb most of the return migrants but it could take those laid off from the big older industrial concerns as well and there is evidence of additional immigration into the region (Saraceno, 1981).

The transformation of local demand for labor should be considered as the most important factor for changes in return migration flows. Specifically, two aspects were important: 1) the occupational opportunities in the region and 2) the undiminished significance of owning real estate property back home, the latter particularly dominating the preparation for return while abroad.

Job opportunities in the region

During the 1970's, returning migrants found a job in an unusually short time: 67 per cent of our respondents found a job within a month after return and another 24 per cent had a job within six months. Table 1 shows the history of the occupational careers of returnees. Their present occupation is much more similar to the one they held abroad before returning than to the one they had held before leaving home. This represents a classical scheme of labor force evolution in the face of modernization (Paci, 1973), from agriculture to construction and industry and finally into the service sector.

Table 1: Occupational development of returning active males at
different points of their migration cycle

Professional sectors	Before migration		Last abroad		First after reentry		Present (1980)	
Agriculture	19.3		0.4		2.9		2.8	
Construction	36.8		45.3		41.5		37.5	
Mining		0.5		0.8		0.2		0.3
Mechanics		17.3		25.1		21.8		23.2
Woodwork		10.1		11.4		13.2		13.1
Other industrial		4.9		4.9		4.5		5.2
All industrial	32.8		42.2		39.7		41.8	
Commercial		3.6		4.4		6.9		6.0
Transport		2.0		2.8		4.0		4.5
Services		3.0		1.5		2.7		4.4
Technicians/employees		1.8		3.4		2.3		3.0
All tertiary	10.4		12.1		15.9		17.9	
Total	100.0		100.0		100.0		100.0	
Apprentices	16.3		--		--		--	
Unskilled	35.4		14.0		23.8		25.0	
Skilled	33.4		50.1		48.5		46.8	
Specialized	13.1		32.5		25.4		25.2	
Employees	1.8		3.4		2.3		3.0	
Total	100.0		100.0		100.0		100.0	

The change in the type of employment was accompanied by a change in occupational skill levels, only that the last jobs held abroad represented a higher level than those held after return. This setback characterized specifically the specialized workers who were unable to find a similar industrial placement back home. Specialization of jobs held is often a function of the size of the enterprise which, in the region, tended to be smaller than those the workers left in their country of immigration. Abroad, 47 per cent of the returnees had worked in medium and large size firms (with more than 100 workers), while back in the region only 24 per cent of our respondents held jobs in larger enterprises. More than half of the returnees (53.3 per cent) found jobs in firms with fewer than 20 employees. The difference in the size of firm is most apparent in the building industry, where an informal organization and diffuse job descriptions are rather common and result in a decreased level of specialization. The relatively recent industrial expansion has not produced as yet a clear differentiation of skill levels.

Job mobility has been high among our returnees. Only 16 per cent have had one job in one employment sector; others had on the average four or five different employments. The oldest returnees had a higher job mobility than the younger returnees which is related not so much to age as to the level of schooling. The older migrant started quite often in agriculture and moved around into other industrial employment. The younger migrants, with a better training, went directly into industrial employment, for instance.

From the point of view of job careers, the return did not represent a clear break with their previous work history. Occupational stability between the job at departure and the last job abroad characterized some 30 per cent of our respondents and 52 per cent held the same kind of job abroad and upon return. If we define the employment sectors in a broader fashion, the occupational stability increases to 55 and 64 per cent respectively, that is, remaining within the industrial sector, etc. The "building" sector seems to offer more occupational mobility abroad, the typical sequence being from labourer to mason to tile layer, to electrician or plumber or master mason. Occupational stability abroad was more likely among those who worked in factories, where skills were more clearly defined and where the foreign workers are usually recruited for prespecified jobs. After return, building and construction employment falls into disfavor despite the extraordinary rise in demand for construction workers. Apart from the lower pay in the region than abroad for such work, returning migrants are looking for "easier jobs" in the industrial or in the tertiary service sector.

The manufacturing industry, especially in machining and woodworking, allows for occupational mobility of the returnees. The increase in the local demand for labor both in manufacturing and construction provides the opportunity for the returnees to settle in the area of their departure and in the same type of job. Many returnees become seld-employed. While abroad only

11 per cent of our respondents were self-employed, mainly in the building sector; after return the proportion of self-employed increases to about 30 per cent overall, but in small business the proportion increases to 67 per cent, in building to 40 per cent and in machine and mechanical sectors to about 16 per cent. The figures refer to the proportion of returnees working in the same sector who are self-employed as opposed to working for an employer.

One should indicate, however, that self-employment is related to the notion of pre-retirement. Returning family heads, in their fifties, even with a high level of industrial skills, tend to open a shop or a bar or restaurant using the savings accumulated abroad, or in turn, look for jobs as watchmen, caretakers or sales assistants. In other words, they treat their new jobs as compensation for the hard work abroad.

The property and the family

In our study, 82 per cent of respondents returned to the same community they had left originally. Seventy-three per cent of them returned with the expected savings, 84 per cent owned a house which was either recently built or renovated. These figures are extremely high and indicate the central value of property in the minds of the "temporary" migrants (OECD, 1978; Reyneri, 1979). Almost three quarters of our respondents had come from small communities (under 10,000 residents), scattered rural towns, had been farmers and owners of small and agriculturally insignificant plots of land. Even though many ceased to farm, they retain their residence in the rural areas. On the other hand, those who have never left or had left the families continued farming even if on a part-time basis only.

Throughout the post Second World War period, it was the rural environment that reproduced migration with the establishment of an interdependence between migrants' remittances and subsistence farming, allowing a substantial rural population to remain in areas where there was an insufficient demand for labor (Corsini and Sonnino, 1972). This surplus population could then migrate "temporarily" to return again. The system of "temporary" migration produces a dissociation between work integration in the receiving country and the social value frame of reference which remains home-oriented. This dichotomy is reinforced by job mobility and by frequent returns home for vacation (72 per cent of our respondents came home at least once a year), by marriage ties (72 per cent of respondents had wives from their own place of origin) and by the continuous sending of remittances.

Temporary migration contributes very little then to a social transformation of the sending areas since the value system of the migrant remains fixed and may even become exacerbated towards traditionalism during his stay abroad. The returnees often complain about the change taking place at home and think the development is "ruining" people back home.

The single most important issue in the determination of the timing of return is the increasingly difficult situation in which the migrant finds himself abroad: the process of familiarization that takes place comes into conflict with the maintenance of the home place social and value orientations typical of the temporary migrant. Family and property prove to be more significant in the end than jobs or careers. A great majority of our respondents who have left home as single men (87 per cent) return married (85.4 per cent). The average size of the returning family is three or four persons, returning together in 47 per cent of cases, returning individually otherwise. Most of the wives are themselves migrants from the same area but most of the children were born abroad. Those who return have successfully resolved their value orientation conflict in favor of tradition. This limits somehow their contribution to the process of modernization and industrialization that has been taking place at the regional level. (1)

NOTE

(1)   The data presented here refer to the returned, occupationally active males, single for heads of families. Employed sons living with their families are excluded.

EMIGRATION AND AGRICULTURE IN A SICILIAN VILLAGE*

Robert L. Vivolo

The research for the present study has been carried out in Mirabella Imbaccari, a Sicilian agrotown on the border of the provinces of Catania and Enna. Although the town has an official population of nearly 9,000, the actual resident population is much closer to 4,500. The resident population is predominantly composed of the old and of the school-aged young. The last published census lists the number of emigrants from Mirabella as 412. A better gauge of the magnitude of emigration is the fact that, since at least 1977, more than 50 per cent of the children born to citizens of Mirabella are born in the Federal Republic of Germany.

Mirabella is experiencing what Rhoades has described as "physical growth and population decline" (1979: 61). During the past twenty years as the resident population has diminished the town has expanded. Entire new quarters have arisen on formerly cultivated land. Houses "alla tedesca" have been constructed complete with lawns and gardens. Physically, the town has the air of a prosperous suburb. In reality, it is a ghost town which comes to life for two months each summer when the "Germans" return.

In order to view the effects of this migration on agricultural structure and production, informal interviews have been conducted and census data from 1961 (the period prior to heaviest migration) have been compared with census data from 1970 (the period of peak migration). However, before examining the present situation of Sicilian agriculture a brief historical description of agriculture in Sicily is warranted.

For centuries, the problems of agriculture in the interior of Sicily have been small, fragmented holdings, an over-reliance on the production of wheat and absentee landlords. After the Second World War various attempts at land reform were tried. Generally speaking, land reform was a failure. Land was either appropriated in parcels too small to be effectively utilized or it was of such poor quality as to make it agriculturally useless. Much land, distributed via the clientelistic system of local level politics, never found its way into the hands of those entitled to it. Nonetheless, the area used for the cultivation of wheat actually declined and there was some movement towards crops which could be cultivated more intensively and which required more labor. But as if

* The research for this study was funded in part by Fulbright-Hays and Nazional Science Foundation grants.

73

in proof of the failure of the Land Reform Act of 1950, the next two decades saw a massive emigration of peasants and farm workers. This emigration, predominantly towards Latin America during the 1950's, became increasingly directed towards Northern Europe when such countries as Germany, France and Switzerland found themselves short of industrial workers in the 1960's.

Despite the earlier, limited gains made after the passage of the land reform acts, the decade between 1961 and 1971 has witnessed a 31 per cent increase in the amount of land under wheat cultivation and a 52 per cent decrease in the amount of land used for viticulture. These figures, when compared with the figures on the number of work days per hectare for various crops, prove very interesting. The cultivation of wheat requires 12 work days per hectare each year. In contrast, the cultivation of wine grapes requires 70 work days per hectare each year. Not surprisingly, it is precisely those crops which require intensive cultivation and more manpower which suffer the most during a period of heavy culturation. 14,000 hectares of formerly cultivated land have been taken out of production between 1961 and 1970. This loss of potentially productive land stems from two sources, both of which are directly related to emigration. First, there exists a process of suburbanization whereby formerly cultivated lands are used by migrants for the construction of new homes.

A more serious problem is the abandonment of agriculture by those with a migratory history. Their land is generally left uncultivated or it is left to the care of their aged parents. The remittances sent back by the migrant and the savings which they bring back to Sicily permit the family to leave their land uncultivated or to the limit cultivation of those crops which are used for home consumption. The abandonment of agriculture, according to studies done in the interior of Sicily by ISCI (1976, 1979) tends to be permanent, especially for those who, prior to emigration, had some experience in non-agricultural work.

The consolidation of smaller holdings, often predicted as a result of emigration, has failed to occur in the area under study. In fact, since emigration, there has been an increase not a diminution of fragmented holdings. The percentage of total holdings in one piece has declined from 51 per cent to 46 per cent while the percentage of holdings fragmented in five or more pieces has increased from 7 per cent to 11 per cent. With respect to size of holdings, Table 1 demonstrates that there has been very little change in the size of intermediate size farms. Although there is a slight reduction in the percentage of holdings of under one hectare, one must keep in mind that it is precisely these small holdings, formerly listed in the census as cultivated land, which have been used for the building of houses. The change in percentage of very small holdings results not so much from consolidation but from the more recent withdrawal of these small holdings from culturation.

The land situation in Mirabella is similar to that described by Reyneri (1979) in his study of the Sicilian interior. Land which is held by migrants is rarely sold. Even if he leaves it uncultivated during or after his emigration, the migrant tends to retain possession of his land. Remittances and savings protect the migrant from the necessity of selling his land. These same remittances and savings also permit the migrant to buy up other small pieces of land, often from middle and large owners, thereby further contributing to the fragmentation of holdings. In Table 1 one can see that the percentage of land surface of farms between ten and one hundred hectares has actually diminished. The combination of a reduction in the percentage of land surface of larger farms and an increased percentage in the land surface of holdings fragmented in five or more pieces clearly points out that the migrant, rather than consolidating, is aiding the process of further fragmentation.

The increasingly high rate of inflation of land prices has made land a considerable investment opportunity and by not cultivating the land the migrant is not disposed towards consolidation (Reyneri, 1979). The present study confirms the results of exodus already described for other countries (Rhoades, 1978, 1979; Rubenstein, 1979; Swanson, 1979; Wiest, 1979).

The aging of the agricultural work force is a process which is common throughout Italy, not merely in the zones of emigration. Census figures for the entire country in 1971 show that 77 per cent of those working in agriculture were over 35 years of age. However, since emigration usually occurs between the ages of 17 and 35, the period in which the individual is best suited for agricultural work, the areas affected by heavy emigration show an even greater degree of aging than the national average. Table 2 shows that in the zone in question 94 per cent of the work force in agriculture is over the age of 35.

The process of aging in the zones of exodus appears to be irreversible. An entire generation of *de jure* residents of Mirabella is being born and raised in the industrialized cities of West Germany. Even assuming a mass return of these migrants (an unlikely event), there would still remain the problem of not only the lack of interest of the young in agriculture, but also their total lack of experience.

The same situation holds true for those children left behind in Mirabella by migrating parents. The remittances sent by migrant family members allow those left behind to continue their schooling. It is extremely difficult, if not impossible, to convince someone with a high school diploma or a college degree to assume a career in a non-profitable agricultural system. "Only with a new agricultural policy capable of creating farms of a certain dimension and efficiency and with various types of association and forms of cooperation is it possible to attract the young" (Zampaglione, 1977: 632).

The only change from 1961 onward which appears to be beneficial is that of mechanization. The number of tractors and motorized tillers has increased dramatically. But, the motorization of agricultural work has created a situation whereby it is becoming increasingly difficult for workers to find manual jobs in the fields (Rhoades, 1978, 1979). The shift away from labor intensive crops coupled with greater mechanization has left many with no op-

75

Table 1: Size of holdings, hill zones of the provinces of Catania and Enna

Hectares	Year	Number of holdings	Perc. of total holdings	Area	Perc. of total land surface
Less than 1	1961	39,860	41.6	19,527	5.0
	1970	31,600	38.2	16,386	4.3
1.01-2	1961	19,982	20.8	29,168	7.5
	1970	16,755	20.3	24,700	6.6
2.01-3	1961	9,646	10.0	23,800	6.1
	1970	8,553	10.3	21,487	5.7
3.01-5	1961	11,234	11.7	43,839	11.3
	1970	10,725	12.9	42,167	11.3
5.01-10	1961	8,533	8.9	59,651	15.1
	1970	8,651	10.4	60,027	16.1
10.01-20	1961	3,822	3.9	52,504	13.5
	1970	3,640	4.4	50,037	13.4
20.01-30	1961	1,122	1.8	27,664	7.1
	1970	1,050	1.2	25,760	6.9
30.01-50	1961	797	0.83	30,466	7.8
	1970	758	0.91	27,345	7.3
50.01-100	1961	582	0.60	41,089	10.6
	1970	• 528	0.63	37,125	9.9
100 plus	1961	282	0.29	59,728	15.4
	1970	270	0.32	67,672	18.1

Source: ISTAT

Table 2: Age groups of those actively employed in agriculture,
hill zones of the provinces of Catania and Enna

Age	Number of workers	Percent of total
14-34	5,042	6.0
35-40	7,395	8.9
41-45	8,595	10.3
46-50	10,811	13.0
51-55	8,860	10.6
56-60	12,307	14.8
61-65	9,989	12.5
65 plus	19,876	24.0
Total	82,875	100.0

Source: ISTAT

tion but to migrate. In this way, the investments of returned migrants in farm machinery, instead of creating additional jobs in the areas of exodus, have contributed to greater migration.

Infrastructural changes, which are sorely needed in this area, did not take place. In the ten year period in question, there has been no major road construction in the countryside. Electricity is still lacking. Despite the financial resources available to the migrant, the amount of land under irrigation in the hill zone of the province of Enna, where most of the land of Mirabella residents is held, has increased by only 4.3 per cent.

Perhaps the greatest threat to Sicilian agriculture caused by emigration is that which has been the greatest handicap in the past, that of absentee landlords. Those who work the lands of migrants have little incentive to improve the yields of the fields. And the return migrant, with his savings and various government pensions and subsidies no longer has an interest in agricultural work.

RETURN MIGRATION AND THE DEVELOPMENT OF THE ITALIAN MEZZOGIORNO

Russell King
Jill Mortimer
Alan Strachan

This is a progress report on a two-year programme of research[*] on the economic impact of return migration in the Italian Mezzogiorno. Within the Mezzogiorno we have selected the three southernmost regions of Puglia, Basilicata (sometimes known as Lucania) and Calabria as our regional frame of reference. This spatial limit is partly dictated by the simple logistical desire not to spread fieldwork and interviewing over too wide an area, but it can be justified on other grounds too. Other south Italian regions, like Abruzzo and Campania, have characteristics which make them transitional to the Italian Centre-North or, as islands (Sicily and Sardinia), possess rather more unique migration traditions. Above all, we believe that our three chosen regions contain an excellent cross-section of the Mezzogiorno's physical, social and economic geography. There are extensive areas of upland and mountain country, especially in Calabria and Basilicata, as well as lowlands and plateaux, chiefly in Puglia. Settlement sizes range from major cities like Bari and Reggio Calabria to tiny communes of a few hundred inhabitants. Agriculture ranges from the intensive vineyards and orchards of the Bari littoral and the Metapontino to the wild pastures and forests of the Calabrian Sila. Industrially the Bari-Brindisi-Taranto triangle of growth poles has witnessed one of the most significant industrialization efforts of the Mezzogiorno in the post-war period. Administratively the three regions contain ten provinces (Bari, Brindisi, Taranto, Foggia, Lecce, Matera, Potenza, Cosenza, Catanzaro and Reggio Calabria) and 788 communes. As our project was being set up, the south Italian earthquake of November 1980 struck, affecting many settlements in the province of Potenza. Whilst we acknowledge that the effect of natural disasters on migratory patterns may be a useful topic for research, we decided at an early stage that it would be unwise to try to carry out interviews in this difficult and tragic environment, and so we omitted Potenza province from our research plan.

----

[*] Financed by the British Social Science Research Council under Grant HR 6977.

Statistics

Italian demographic and migration statistics are plentiful and extremely detailed. The decennial censuses are presented with a wealth of data at the commune level. Annual publications by the Central Institute of Statistics (ISTAT), such as *Popolazione e Movimento Anagrafico dei Comuni* and *Annuario di Statistiche Demografiche* enable shorter term migration trends to be charted at the provincial and communal levels. Such detail lends a false impression of accuracy, however. Our experience in communal offices leads us to believe that official Italian statistics are a miasma of arbitrary approximations and often deliberate falsifications. If such data have value, it is as an indicator of long term trends and of broad geographical patterns. Our account will, therefore, be cast in terms of generalizations and round figures.

During the period 1946-76 Italy experienced an emigration, according to official figures, of approximately 7.5 million people, of whom 5 million went to European countries. The pace of the outmovement has fluctuated quite markedly, but the highest peaks were recorded during the early 1960's, since when there has been a fairly steady decline. The total recorded return migration for the same thirty-year period has been 4.5 million, including 3.5 million from Europe. The annual quantity of returns matches rather closely the pattern of emigration, but with a lag of one or two years, and with a slower rate of decline since the peaks in the early and mid 1960's. During the 1970's returns have tended to balance or slightly exceed new emigration, 1973 being the turning point since when the migratory balance has been positive.

The importance of migratory movements in our three study regions of Puglia, Basilicata and Calabria can be gauged from the fact that they account for 11.5 per cent of the Italian population (6.4 million out of 55.5 million) but 23 per cent of both the emigration and return migration of Italians over the 1946-76 period. Table 1, which is compiled from various ISTAT sources, splits the post-war migration into two periods. It is possible to identify, in a crude sense, the increasing importance of returns in the later period, and to observe some simple regional contrasts: Calabria was initially the region of heaviest outmigration, being replaced after 1961 by Basilicata; rates of return, relative to outmigration, are slightly higher in Puglia. The effect of migration on regional population totals is also illuminating. In spite of high rates of natural increase, Basilicata and Calabria lost population between 1961 and 1976. Puglia, with lower rates of outmigration and a slightly higher ratio of returnees to emigrants, gained over 330,000 inhabitants.

Figure 1 presents a provincial level picture of the character of emigration and return migration from our study area. Quantities of emigrants and returning emigrants are standardized as proportions of the resident population (per thousand) to account for varying population size in the ten provinces. Considerable variations in rates of migration are revealed, especially in the Puglian provinces. Economically prosperous provinces like Taranto have low emigration, and, therefore, low return rates. Lecce province has very high rates of external movement, but these are largely related to the importance of seasonal and short-term movements which are traditional to this province and which mean that it is the same migrants who are recorded over and over again in the various annual totals. It is also somewhat surprising to find that these two provinces, with the lowest and highest rates of movement out of the whole set of ten, are actually geographically adjacent. Figure 1 also reveals differing temporal patterns of migration between the provinces: in particular the tendency of the Calabrian provinces to have a second peak of emigration and return in the late 1960's.

Table 1: Emigration and return migration for Italy, Puglia,
Basilicata and Calabria, 1946-61 and 1962-76

1946-61:

Region	Population 1961	Emigrants	perc.	Returnees	perc.
Puglia	3,439,806	385,721	11.2	185,363	5.3
Basilicata	642,362	110,322	17.1	48,119	7.4
Calabria	2,045,965	420,525	20.5	93,818	4.5
Italy	50,624,000	4,452,200	8.8	1,913,760	3.8

1962-76:

Region	Population 1976	Emigrants	perc.	Returnees	perc.
Puglia	3,771,329	470,782	12.4	338,513	8.9
Basilicata	614,596	132,134	21.4	107,835	17.5
Calabria	2,034,425	331,847	16.3	207,239	10.1
Italy	55,510,000	2,995,130	5.4	2,426,162	4.4

Source: ISTAT

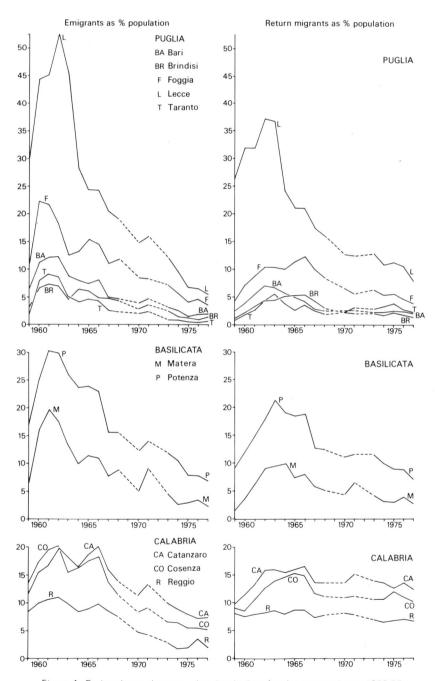

Figure 1: Emigration and return migration indices for the ten provinces, 1959-77

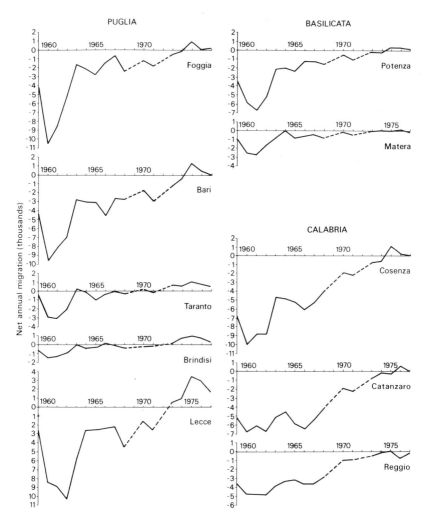

Figure 2: Net emigration balance for the ten provinces, 1959-77

When the absolute net external movements are plotted for each province (Figure 2), most provinces reveal a switch to a positive balance around 1973, part of the national trend. Taranto, however, experienced an excess of returnees as early as 1963, which can be hypothesized as reflecting the strong build-up of new industries there at this time (steelworks, port and other industrial concerns). Calabria, on the other hand, achieved a positive migration balance later (1975 or 1976) and, by 1977 (1976 in the case of Reggio Calabria), had reverted to a net loss of migrants.

Economic impact of return migration

The prime focus of our research concerns the economic impact of returnees. Specific information is sought on employment patterns before and after return and on the use of savings and remittances. The relevant migration literature presents a conflicting picture, thus far. Economically derived theories point to return migration as a dynamic force for development. Returnees, it is suggested, bring capital in the form of remittances and savings as well as experience of different types of work and new ideas from their period abroad (Miracle and Berry, 1970), all of which can, theoretically, be harnessed for development of the region of origin. Much of the empirical research, on the other hand, demonstrates that this stimulus to development simply does not happen. Returnees are found to be economically conservative: they depress agriculture, inflate land prices, reinforce traditional social structures and so on. Their only desire seems to be to buy a plot of land in their native village and to build a new home (Reyneri, 1979; Merico, 1978). Similar conclusions have been reached by Rhoades (1978, 1979) for Southern Spain, by Baucić (1972) for Yugoslavia and by studies of return migrant behaviour in Malta and Gozo (King 1980, King and Strachan 1980). Longer review papers of this evidence have been prepared by Gmelch (1979) and by King (1979a).

Most of the studies which contain a conservative model of returnee behaviour are based on rural areas, looking at migrants who return to their native villages. Two critical points can be made here. Firstly, these are areas where developmental preconditions are often lacking in the first place. This leads to a dangerously tautological argument: return migration does not lead to development largely because developmental stimuli are lacking-hence, the high outmigration of these areas in the first place. Most rural areas in Southern Italy, and in southern Europe generally, especially remoter upland regions, have not experienced any really positive changes over recent decades. Hence migrants return to an economic environment which has scarcely changed during their period of absence.

Secondly, not all returnees go back to their native villages. Studies which look at return migration from the origin village perspective are, in one sense, examining a biased sample. For just as the original outmigration is not representative of the total population, and just as the return flow is not a representative cross-section of the migrant stock in the destination society, so too the returnees who go back to their native villages are not a representative sample of the return flow as a whole. The village flow will be disproportionately made up of rural-oriented, conservative, older returnees. The younger, more modernistic, industrially-oriented returnees will go to cities, even though they may have originally come from villages. It is, therefore, important to investigate returnees in urban as well as rural contexts.

Returnees coming back to urban areas have a range of employment choices open to them: they can try for work in various types of industry, in construction, in the service sector, or, if they live in peri-urban communities, even in intensive agriculture geared to supplying the local urban market. Migrants returning to their native villages have no such breadth of choice. Agriculture often remains backward and depressed and holds little attraction anyway, industry is non-existent, construction activity is feeble apart from the new houses of the returnees themselves, and the limited amount of service sector employment is controlled by traditional village elites with whom migrants, almost by definition, have had little contact or influence. The new house and the small independent business, so often condemned as anti-economic, are the only alternative. Such an economic destination may not, therefore, be the result of a returnee mentality (the new house, small shop kind of bourgeois ideology) but rather an event conditioned by the absolute lack of alternative outlets *in loco*. Studies on returnee occupations at the village level rarely ask returnees what they would have *liked* to have done or what their attitudes towards different types of employment were at the time of return or are now.

One of the objectives of our study then, is to clarify returnee economic behaviour into *types*, for instance: a) migrants who return home to their native villages and set up in employment as best they can, perhaps in self-employed businesses such as the familiar shops, bars, taxis etc.; b) migrants who return but fail to find satisfactory work and who maintain themselves in temporary retirement, perhaps in anticipation of a second emigration; and c) migrants who return not to their native settlements but to a town where industrial and service sector jobs are more plentiful.

Economic activity after the return may reflect the original occupational and educational background of the migrant before he left for his period abroad. Or it may be the fulfillment of the original expectations and aspirations which lay behind the emigration viewed as a means to an end. The length of time spent abroad, and the type of work and cultural experiences attained, may also influence post-return economic behaviour and achievement. By structuring interviews to migrants so as to elicit information on the pre-migration state and the experience abroad as well as the situation since return, it will be possible to build up life histories or longitudinal profiles of migrants returning to the Mezzogiorno. Some earlier work along these lines in Malta and Gozo

(King 1979b, King and Strachan 1980) suggests that modal profiles do exist (although there will, of course, be different modal types for Southern Italian migrants), but this also raises certain more fundamental questions of definition of such phenomena as circulatory and repeat migration (cf. Bovenkerk 1974).

Questions and hypotheses to be examined

The questionnaire used for the field investigation contains 30 pages and some 230 questions. The questionnaire was piloted in April 1981. On an average, each interview lasts about one hour. The following questions give an idea of our main analyses.

Are migrants' employment patterns since return influenced by their work experience abroad? Do returnees, for instance, tend to opt for non-rural or factory jobs similar to the ones they did abroad, or are their aspirations in completely different fields, such as non-manual or service sector employment? How far are their job aspirations matched by local employment opportunities? How widespread is the desire, observed in other studies to which attention has already been drawn, for economic independence through the 'small business ideology', or do these activities spring up in rural areas because of the lack of acceptable alternative job opportunities? How strong, for instance, are the traditionally inculcated values of prestige attached to land ownership in village areas? Does the migrant who emigrates with his or her family follow a different migration and return pattern than the migrant who goes abroad alone?

Do returnees tend overwhelmingly to return to their native communities or are there net inter-regional, rural-urban or interior-coast movements produced via the emigration-return process? Official statistics give few clues to the importance of these internal movements that are the result of external movement. Are migrants spatially mobile after return? Identification of these geographical mobility paths associated with return migration is important in the context of return migration planning policies.

STRATEGIES OF RETURN OF YUGOSLAVS IN FRANCE AND THE FEDERAL REPUBLIC OF GERMANY

Mirjana Morokvasić

Economic emigration from post-war Yugoslavia is now two decades old. Emigration was barred after World War II but resumed gradually in the 1950's. From 1965 onward, Yugoslavia signed bilateral agreements with countries of immigration in Northwest Europe as a short term solution to increasing unemployment at home and the negative balance of payment.

From the very beginning, return migration of out-migrants was fully expected both by the Yugoslav policy makers and the migrants themselves, fitting well with the schemes of worker rotation of the host countries (Friganović, 1972). Soon enough, however, studies of migrants began to point out the disadvantages of out-migration for the sending countries (Baucić, 1982; Abadan-Unat, 1982; Trebous, 1970; Böhning, 1982). In the Yugoslav case, the authorities were able to control the movements of workers but little. Actually, until 1981, there were no specific measures to make the policy of "temporary" emigration effective, related as it was to the continuing high unemployment in Yugoslavia. The effective halt to labor in-migration by the European countries in 1974 forced Yugoslavia to face the issue of return realistically, that is, to make a better use of the remittances and of the skilled work force abroad so that domestic economic development could take place.

To attract foreign currency together with the returning workers, the Yugoslav government issued legislation which paid competitive interest rates as well as offering business credit in dinars to returnees. The purpose of this was to establish enterprises utilizing both the foreign reserves and the skills of the returnees. The first such "hard currency factories" began to be established from 1971 onward, but remained limited in scope and effectiveness due to administrative difficulties and bad co-ordination (Beroš, 1975; Vedris, 1975, 1978).

Motivation to return

A very strong component of return migration is the readiness of migrants themselves to do so, whereas various incentives for return provided by the respective administrations in the countries concerned remain ancillary. What follows is a brief summary of a survey of 58 Yugoslav couples residing in France and in Germany who were interviewed at length about their motivation and actual plans to return. Inferences are also drawn from various earlier studies (Morokvasić, 1972, 1973, 1980, 1981b); detailed information on the study is found elsewhere (Morokvasić, 1982)*.

Yugoslavs were leaving with a vague idea of length of their stay abroad and with a firm intention to return. They organized their lives so as to anticipate return. As their stay began to lengthen, they also became aware of how little it was in their power to achieve what they set out to do. Despite all this, return, sooner or later, has remained their goal.

Family reunion

The arrival of wife and children normally means an increase in expenditures which, in the long run, diminishes savings, encourages settlement abroad and diminishes chances of return (Böhning, 1972). The return-oriented Yugoslavs are well aware of such dangers but they keep separate in their minds the members of the family who join them to work and those who remain their dependents. The former contribute to the goal of savings, the latter detract from it. Our study of Yugoslav couples shows that the arrival of the working wife increases the value of remittances sent home and doubles the saving capacity of the migrants (Morokvasić, 1981a, 1982). In Germany, where the majority of Yugoslav women came as workers, whether married or single, the couple was not always living together but rather in separate workers' hostels or in different parts of the country so as to remain in the work force (Morokvasić, 1980). Those Yugoslavs who already had children at the time of emigration left them at home while children abroad would in time be sent home to school.

In 1976, 51 per cent of Yugoslavs had one or all of their children in Yugoslavia (Böhning, 1980: 39), while 24 per cent of families had no children at all and the rest had one or two children with them. Bock and Tiedt (1978) found that the majority of the Yugoslav parents do not have their children with them in Germany. The likelihood of children remaining with their parents diminishes after the child's sixth birthday when the child goes to school at home. A study of Yugoslav women in France, Germany and Sweden (Morokvasić, 1980) showed that about one half of the women interviewed had left their children at home. This became most likely when the distance from home was short, like in the south of Germany. The present study of couples shows that all, or at least some of the children of these couples are in Yugoslavia. "Had the children been here, we would have waited, the conditions would

----

* The research was carried out thanks to a grant from the "Rockfeller and Ford Program for Population and Development Policy Research".

never be ripe for return. Had they gone to school here, we would never have returned. This way, we force ourselves to return (interview transcript)". Thus, children of the return-oriented Yugoslavs are used to assure the temporariness of the stay abroad, even though the temporariness lasts much longer then originally anticipated.

Table 1: Yugoslav couples by number of children, by country

		Number of children present				
Country	0	1	2	3	4+	N
France	0	8	17	4	1	30
Germany	5	7	12	3	1	28
N	5	15	29	7	2	58

Source: Morokvasić, 1982

Savings and remittances

Studies of the economic behavior of Yugoslavs in France (Morokvasić, 1981: 293) show that more married than single Yugoslavs remit more money home and they do so more often when the spouse is present. It has also to be borne in mind that the per capita income of Yugoslavs exceeds that of other non-EEC nationals in France and the savings rate is about 50 per cent of the income per couple when both are working. Baucić and Maravić (1972) show that Yugoslav workers transfer 20 per cent of their wages to Yugoslavia. Later studies suggest that up to one third of wages are remitted but this also includes cash brought home when on vacation in Yugoslavia.

The majority of Yugoslavs keep their savings in Yugoslav banks and the amount kept in foreign banks is limited to the equivalent of one month's salary. The reason for this is the various advantages Yugoslav banks offer their depositors, advantages which are not matched by banks in France or Germany, for instance. Hard currency savings are still mostly used for durable goods and, in particular, for housing (Baucić and Maravić, 1972; Morokvasić, 1981). The couples' study shows that the intended use of savings is primarily for housing. All but 10 Yugoslav couples have either built a house or bought an apartment in the place they intend to return to. Others are still building or already have a building lot and, perhaps, some land.

Productive investments on the other hand, are rare. Only in two cases was agricultural machinery purchased and, one worker was planning to buy equipment for a workshop to be opened together with his brother in Yugoslavia. In terms of material achievement Yugoslavs are not far from having their original objectives met: they all have a good car, most of them have built a house. These seem to be important preconditions for return, since housing problems in particular were mentioned as the reason for migration in the first place, next to a lack of good employment. To have a job back home is thus a necessary precondition for return. In order to find a job, the emigrants must be well-informed about conditions back home.

The role of information

A return-oriented migrant is interested in two types of information: what are the incentives to return offered by the host country and what are the incentives back home. Information media are primarily Yugoslav newspapers, radio broadcasts in his own language, as well as Yugoslav commercial banks, consulates and national clubs and associations.

In the couples' study, the most often mentioned incentive was the French *aide au retour* (discontinued as of November, 1982). All our respondents felt that the amount offered was quite low and thus good only for those returning in any case. The disturbing part of the aid was the need to relinquish one's documents, that is, the residence and work permits, thus foregoing the possibility of re-emigrating.

Our respondents seemed to be well-informed about the various Yugoslav customs regulation; their complaint was the rapidity with which such regulations were changing, not allowing them to plan well ahead. In comparison with a 1975 survey in France (Morokvasić, 1981), the information level of respondents in the couples' study was much higher. This again indicates a serious concern with return, fueled, no doubt, by the dismal economic prospects in the host country.

One issue which aroused lively interest on the part of the expatriate Yugoslavs were the various investment schemes in Yugoslavia. In a nutshell, the returning worker lends his hard currency savings to a Yugoslav enterprise, his loan is supplemented as needs be by the Yugoslav government in dinars and the worker is assured a job with the enterprise. Attitudes towards such schemes were rather mixed among the interviewed Yugoslav couples, only about one half were positive. Those from the more industrially developed regions in Yugoslavia (Vojvodina, for instance) felt the schemes were suitable for the less developed areas or for enterprises in financial difficulties. Furthermore, they felt that unskilled workers who had, however, savings, would find it a good vehicle for regaining a job in Yugoslavia. Nevertheless, the prevailing attitude seemed to be a general distrust of the Yugoslav state machinery guarantees, which were regarded as not entirely reliable.

The actual idea of job creation through the use of personal savings was felt to be good. The way in which it was being carried out was found to be unsatisfactory, however. For the expatriate Yugoslavs who had some industrial skills the attraction of the private sector in the Yugoslav economy was much more tempting, primarily in view of the fact that small enterprises, e.g. taxi services, were being established. But here the bureaucratic complexity and taxation were considered a deterrent to private initiative. "Sometimes one has to have some forty different certificates", was one description of the matter.

Agriculture remains a sector that offers numerous possibilities and yet, the migrants feel that the Yugoslav policy makers have neglected to make it more attractive. Only very few of the expatriates contemplate returning to agricultural pursuits and even then there is the question of who is actually going to work the land. Men think their wives should do it but the wives, who have worked in industry, find the idea unattractive without the reward of a cash income.

Search for jobs back home

More than one third of the couples interviewed have gone beyond simple collection of information. Aware of the fact that without skills they could not expect much back home, they have enrolled in various skill improvement courses offered by Yugoslav agencies abroad. Both men and women are completing their primary schooling and some secondary training as well, in adult education programs. Women tend to take courses in textile related occupations or in tourism services, men in truck driving and related courses. Quite often they pay considerable fees for such courses.

The attempts to find jobs directly were often frustrating, again due to the bureaucratic maze on one hand and the actual scarcity of jobs on the other. The present economic situation in Yugoslavia has made people suspicious of everything and everybody. They only trust themselves and their own resources and do not really expect help from anywhere. Nevertheless, the return of one third of the respondent couples was imminent. A few had opted for a radical solution. They had returned their French permits, and were waiting for the *aide au retour* and a supplement from their employer, the Michelin plant in Tours. As one respondent indicated: "I will get 10,000 F, my wife will get 10,000 from the French government. I will get 20,000 F from my firm plus 1,000 F for each year of service. Altogether I will have 50,000 F, more than I could possibly save in two years".

Despite preference for private initiative, half of the couples who were respondents in this said they would opt for employment in the socialist sector because it offered security. Among those returning, most found jobs in socialist state enterprises at wages much below than their wages abroad. They expect supplements from the land they own and, perhaps, farm, the pension entitlements earned abroad and the interest they get on their savings.

Yugoslavs' intentions to return were demonstrated by a series of concrete steps to make return possible, the strategy being as follows: savings and remittances, schooling of children back in Yugoslavia and keeping informed about the conditions at home and, finally, searching for jobs directly. This also means that during their stay abroad they remain "temporary", isolated, apolitical, stretching their stay, waiting for the right time to return.

OCCUPATIONAL PROFILE OF
RETURNEES IN THREE GREEK CITIES

Klaus Unger

The study reported here deals with a sample of returnees from West-Germany to three Greek cities: Athens, Salonica and Serres. Interviews with 574 respondents were conducted in 1980, with per city distribution as follows: Athens 226, Salonica 217 and Serres 131.

The mean age of our respondents, all males, was 42 years, the mean age at emigration was 28 years. Every fifth respondent was a repeat migrant in that he had returned to Germany at least once. The mean stay abroad was 11.4 years with three years on the average back in Greece at the time of the interview. About 80 per cent of our respondents returned between 1976 through 1979, evenly divided for each year.

Some 70 per cent of our respondents had finished primary school (until 1976, compulsory school attendance in Greece was limited to 6 years), about 10 per cent had finished their secondary school, leaving the remainder without a primary school leaving certificate. On the average, our respondents had completed 6.7 school years.

The current proportion of unemployed among the respondents was 11.9 per cent counting those who had returned recently and were still looking for a job. On the other hand, among those who had found jobs after return, the proportion unemployed was only 1.8 per cent. The length of time returnees had to spend looking for a job was 9.5 months on the average with a median value of 6.1 months. This figure also includes, however, those still looking for a job and those who consider themselves retired. Excluding these respondents, the two respective values are 7.8 and 5.9 months.

Of those currently employed, 58.4 per cent are wage and salary earners, 35.9 per cent are self-employed and 5.6 are employers. The high proportion of self-employed is at least partially due to a lack of job alternatives. As a matter of fact, the majority of our respondents would have preferred to work in a factory setting like the one they had experienced in Germany. The smaller the city to which our respondents returned, the fewer employment alternatives there were so that self-employment became a necessity. Thus, Serres, the smallest return community in our sample with some 50,000 inhabitants shows the highest proportion of returnees being self-employed. Among our 207 self-employed returnees, three out of four were in the service sector; specifically, 9.7 per cent were in construction and 14.0 per cent in trades but the main occupations were taxi-driving (17.9 per cent), running a small grocery shop

Table 1: Profile of returnees by occupational categories in per cent (Ns)

Profile items	Wage and salary earner	Own account worker	Employer	All
			per cent	
Place of residence now				
Athens	66.8	29.1	4.1	100.0	39.4
Salonica	58.6	35.9	5.5	100.0	36.3
Serres	44.6	47.1	8.3	100.0	24.3
				100.0
	(291)	(179)	(28)	(498)
Now living in the same community as before emigration	45.7	59.8	75.0	52.4
	(291)	(179)	(28)	(498)
Age at return				
under 35 years	48.8	40.9	10.2	100.0	25.5
35 to 40 years	58.2	35.2	6.7	100.0	33.1
more than 40 years	64.6	33.5	1.9	100.0	41.4
				100.0
				(498)
Return period				
last 2 years	62.1	35.5	2.4	100.0	24.9
2 to 4 years ago	60.4	36.1	3.5	100.0	45.6
more than 4 years ago	52.4	36.1	11.6	100.0	29.5
				100.0
				(498)
Would perfer to work in a factory similar to those in Germany	90.1	72.4	48.1	81.4
	(284)	(174)	(27)	(485)
Return to Greece was not worthwhile	43.4	37.9	21.4	40.1
	(286)	(177)	(28)	(491)
Migration plans realized				
not at all/little	26.0	19.1	18.5	23.1
partly	54.3	46.2	33.3	50.3
fully	19.7	34.7	48.1	26.6
	100.0	100.0	100.0	100.0
	(289)	(173)	(27)	(489)

Table 1: cont'd

Profile items	Wage and salary earner	Own account worker	Employer	All
Improvement of income after migration: not at all/little	68.5	55.2	38.5	62.0
	(260)	(154)	(26)	(440)
Improvement of occup. situation: not at all/little after migration	61.1	49.0	40.7	55.6
	(262)	(155)	(27)	(444)
Advice to Greek emigr. to return to Greece				
should return	9.4	9.8	13.6	9.7
should return under the pre-condition of economic security	27.5	36.8	36.4	31.3
should not return	63.0	53.4	50.0	58.9
	100.0	100.0	100.0	100.0
	(265)	(163)	(22)	(450)
Would prefer to re-emigrate	58.6	51.2	37.5	54.8
	(269)	(168)	(24)	(465)
Good chances for themselves to find an appropriate job in Greece	20.1	37.1	57.1	28.5
	(269)	(170)	(28)	(467)
Good chances for non-migrant Greek to find an appropriate job in Greece	36.8	26.6	37.5	33.3
	(242)	(143)	(24)	(409)
Would prefer to change the present occupation	80.1	54.8	35.7	68.5
	(287)	(177)	(28)	(492)

(12.6 per cent) and managing a cafe or a restaurant (20.8 per cent). Fewer than one per cent of our respondents were in a position to employ five or more employees.

Changes in the distribution of returnees by occupation as a result of migration show a fair occupational stability for the semi-skilled and skilled workers, some up-grading of unskilled and white collar workers and an increase in those who became self-employed. Specifically, while the modal form of employment in Germany was in semi-skilled jobs, such jobs were difficult to find upon return. Thus, whereas about 95 per cent of our respondents had worked in Germany in industrial jobs as primarily semi-skilled or unskilled workers, upon return only about 45 per cent of them stay in such jobs. There was some improvement in their overall occupational status by moving into white collar jobs and self-employment.

Table 2: Per cent distributions of returnees by occupational classification and migration

Classification	Before emigration	Last job in Germany	Present job
Unskilled worker	31.7	28.2	13.5
Semi-skilled worker	31.3	50.9	26.9
Skilled worker	3.7	16.0	3.8
White-collar worker (clerical worker/civil servant)	9.6	4.0	14.2
Own account worker	22.4	0.9	35.9
Employer	1.4	-	5.6
Total	100.0	100.0	99.9
N	514	574	498

Looking at the displacement into different occupations after return, we see that from the number of returnees who were unskilled upon leaving less than one half took up unskilled jobs again. There were 145 respondents in our sample who were semi-skilled workers at emigration but only 117 resumed that type of work upon return. Whereas among our respondents 93 were self-employed before emigrating, 155 were self-employed after return.

Change in occupation upon return

The shift in occupation upon return is understandable. While in Germany, most respondents worked in large scale industries, like metal working, automobile and similar, inasmuch as the recruiting for workers in Greece was done by large industrial corporations. The Greek expatriates did not experience much of job mobility while in Germany, their first and last job there being a comparable type of work.

The major switch in the work orientation of the Greek migrants was away from agriculture. Before migration, one fourth of our sample had an agricultural background which was all but lost at migration and remained lost after return. Some of this is due, naturally, to the fact that we have interviewed returnees in cities. Another interesting observation that can be made on the occupational changes our respondents experienced is that the pre-migration work experience in construction was not utilized while in Germany but was partially resorted to again upon return. The tendency to turn to service occupations upon return is connected to the switch to self-employment.

Surprisingly, there was no significant impact of the length of stay abroad on occupation pursued after return, nor was there any significant difference between those who received vocational training in Germany and those who did not. Only some 16 per cent of the total sample had received any vocational training abroad of whom only 40 per cent were able to make any use upon return. After all, the kind of migration experienced by our respondents was deemed temporary and it was a period during which the migrant saved up money, for whatever purpose, faster than would have been possible at home. He did not intend to acquire occupational skills during his period of migration.

Some 55 per cent of those who set out to save up for a small enterprise at home did actually succeed and are now self-employed. These were also the respondents who expressed a greater satisfaction with the migration experience than the rest of our sample. Those respondents returning to jobs not much different from those they had held in Germany were not as sanguine about the success of their return. Only one in five felt that return to Greece was worthwhile. Close to six out of ten would have re-emigrated to Germany, had it not been for the current immigration restrictions, or so they said. Although Greece is now the tenth member of the European Community, the free movement of labor for Greeks will not come into effect until 1988.

The self-resported satisfaction or dissatisfacion with return is related to a number of variables: Education influences positively occupational success abroad and upon return. Age, on the other hand, influences occupational success adversely, that is, older returnees do not fare as well as younger ones. Education and age are, of course, inversely related and thus confound each other. By dichotomizing our sample into two groups, those with low and high occupational status (unskilled and semi-skilled and others), we notice that the larger the city the more it attracts low status returnees who are older with less schooling; the interviewees were reluctant to return to places from whence they had come and returned to other places, they had an agricultural or construction work background and their occupational classification did not change after return.

Table 3: Comparison of occupational composition of the returnee sample and the total population (1971) (in per cent)

Occupation	Athens		Salonica		Serres	
	Sample	Census	Sample	Census	Sample	Census
Wage and Salary earners	66.8	71.3	58.6	65.3	44.6	51.1
Own account Workers	29.1	20.6	35.9	24.7	47.1	42.1
Employers	4.1	8.1	5.5	10.0	8.3	6.8
Total	100.0	100.0	100.0	100.0	100.0	100.0
N	196	648,980	181	138,400	121	10,020

Census data refer to the male population only (as well as the sample).

Source: National Statistical Service of Greece, Results of the Population and Housing Census, 1971, Vol. II, Athens 1973.

Conclusions

The research reported here (Unger, 1983) shows results which are not at variance with similar studies on return migration in the Mediterranean basin. We have focused here specifically on the occupational changes return migration may produce. Such changes were few. In the first place, the number of returnees is not sufficiently large to affect the receiving communities. Actually, the smaller the community to which our respondents have returned, the more similar their occupational distribution was to the community-wide occupational distribution. This fact should not escape those interested in promoting returnee satisfaction. On the other hand, those returning to a large community like Athens, found themselves at a disadvantage both occupationally and as regards their social integration. Their chances for employment were perceived as less than those of non-movers and their willingness to return to Germany, were it possible, was much greater than that of the other returnees. Returnees are more likely to re-emigrate when their household income is low, when the unemployment after return has been extended, when chances for employment in Greece appear grim and the chances of a job in Germany appear better. To dissentangle all the minutiae of the relationship between the variables is a considerable task and cannot be undertaken here. Suffice it to say that return migration of workers is not a last link in the migration process unless the migrants are near retirement.

RETURNING AND REMAINING: RETURN AMONG TURKISH MIGRANTS IN GERMANY

Czarina Wilpert

Return migration of Turkish workers from Germany has recently re-gained attention in the political debate. Up until now, the stabilization and growth of the Turkish population in Germany since the 1973 recruitment stop and the recession has lent support to the general assumption in research as well as in policy-making that guestworkers have become immigrants.

Yet, in spite of this, some workers have been returning. Little is known about the motives and experiences of these returned workers, and even less is known about the situation of their children.

Characteristics of returnees and stayers

The one study of Turkish migrant workers in Germany which provides some answers to the question of return compared two samples of Turks in Berlin (Kallweit and Kudat, 1976). A sample of 1,632 Turkish workers who returned from Berlin between 1975 and 1976 were compared to a cross-sectional sample of Turkish workers in Berlin in 1974 (Kudat, 1974). The returnees in 1975 had, on the average, a shorter length of stay abroad, tended to be separated from their families and more often came from and chose to return to rural areas in Turkey than did the average Turkish worker in Berlin in 1974.

Distinction was made between "voluntary" and "forced" return migra-tion. "Voluntary" referred to those who claimed to have planned their return, "forced" to those who gave unemployment as their reason for return. If the amount of savings was used to indicate achievement of migration goals, the comparison of absolute monthly savings of the 1975 sample returnees with the 1974 sample of stayers does not indicate success. Both voluntary, as well as the unemployed returnees had lower total monthly savings than the stayers. Moreover, the single most important factor distinguishing the 1974 stayers from 1975 returnees was the extent of family fragmentation. The spouses of more than half of the returnees (54 per cent) but less than one-fifth (17.6 per cent) of the 1974 Berlin Turks were still in Turkey.

The returnees were among the least secure economically. They were more likely to be employed in the least stable sectors of employment, e.g., in construction (Dohse, 1981). The longer unemployment and the shorter length of stay tended to interfere with the renewal of their work and resident permits. Most importantly, the separation from their family did not give them the possibility of income supplement through work of another family member, while they drew unemployment insurance and looked for another job.

Most returnees came from rural areas so that it remained easier for them to keep their families at home. In fact, their families served as a pull factor, making the return more attractive.

Attitudes about return

Studies of migrant workers in Germany generally conclude that migrant workers tend to prolong their initial plans to stay while abroad, that their desire to stay permanently increases with length of stay and that the 1973 halt to in-migration resulted in a stabilization of the Turkish population and in the growth in the number of family dependents. In 1972, only 9 per cent of Turkish workers expressed interest in staying permanently in the Federal Republic (Bundesanstalt für Arbeit, 1973). In 1974, the percentage was 29.1 per cent (Jurecka and Werth, 1981), but still lower overall among the Turks than among other nationalities. The authors explain this by the shorter history of Turkish migration to Germany as well as by the religious differences between Turks and Germans.

A survey conducted in Berlin in 1979 found that only 7 per cent of the Turkish population desired to stay permanently in the Federal Republic. While 22 per cent were as yet undecided, approximately one half had not set a date for return (Social Data, 1980). It is this inability to set a specific date which affects conclusions about the permanency of the Turkish population in Germany. Unfortunately, each survey contained different questions as to plans to return or to stay, limiting the comparability of the studies. The latest survey of foreigners in the Federal Republic (Mehrländer et al., 1981) compared plans to return across nationalities and age groups. It remains unclear, however, whether the category "return not planned" is an indication of a decision to stay or, more likely, reflects uncertainty about the date of return. The survey shows that 40.1 per cent of the Turks have no plans for return. Another nationwide survey of foreign youth in Germany in 1979, between the ages of 15 and 25, found that 24 per cent of the Turkish youths wanted to remain in Germany (Hecker, 1979). This was only slightly less than the 30 per cent of youths of other nationalities who made this choice. The differences between the lesser desire to stay permanently found among all nationalities in Berlin, and the result of surveys in the rest of the Federal Republic may be attributed to the fact that foreigners in Berlin are more acutely aware of their being marginal. Many foreign workers, especially Turks, see their future in Germany pessimistically and in comparison to Germans they feel especially underprivileged in all aspects of life (Forschungsverband, 1979).

One study of Turkish and Yugoslav school children dealt with the question of their return as well (Wilpert, 1980). In 1975, very few 12 to 14 year-old Turkish and Yugoslav youths expressed preferences to work and live in Germany rather than in their country of origin. In fact, an astonishingly high percentage of Turkish youths preferred to finish school in the home country. Children of both nationalities were aware of discrimination, but what was surprising was the likelihood that the youths with the highest occupational and educational aspirations were also more positively disposed toward return. Nonetheless, an increased length of stay in Germany does lower the homeward orientation even without a change in the perception of opportunities in Germany. The perception of personal opportunities in Turkey seems to diminish with increased length of stay in schools in Germany.

Taking into consideration the legal and political rights of foreign workers in the Federal Republic of Germany, it is questionable whether or not the necessary conditions for a decision to settle exist for Turkish or other migrant groups. A series of special directives regulating where foreigners may live or may attend school affected directly the foreign workers and sharpened their perception of barriers and discrimination. The regulations have been established primarily for the protection of the German population, thus limiting the expanding of civil rights of migrant workers (Dohse, 1981a, 1981b; Weihdacher, 1981).

The original motivation of the migrant worker was to improve his family's social and economic status at home. Although this attempt has rarely been successful, the migrant retained this goal especially for his children. The decision to work abroad continues to be perceived instrumentally. Is this true for children as well as for parents? Can we differentiate between the desire to return as a normal goal and the "illusion of return" as an anomie-reducing factor?

Case studies

The following analysis of Turkish case studies addresses the future perspectives of migrant families and youth (1). The case studies draw on the personal accounts of the migration experience and motivation of 30 families who had been abroad for over ten years.

The families were selected from a 1975 sample of school youth (Wilpert, 1980). Parents and children were interviewed separately in 1980. Only parental perspectives are reported here and specifically, those factors contributing to the perception of advantages and disadvantages of staying in Germany.

Finances

Financial factors include the need to pay off debts incurred for large investments in apartments, shops, or property.

Case A is of rural origin and a member of the Alevi Muslim minority. He is 41 years of age and father of three children. He began working in Turkey when he was 14 years old, and had worked in mining before he came to work in Germany 10 years ago.

> The work here has ruined me — that's why I want to return. And since I plan to return some day, I'm building a four-storey house in Istanbul — that's also why I still have debts and that's why I sold my car. In fact, every three or four months I go over to Istanbul and look and see how the construction is going. I have quite a few debts with this house. There are six apartments and two shops but I want it to be built of the best material. I'll only be able to pay up the debts in another five or six years, and by then it should be clear what the children will be doing.

Occupational training

In instances where there is at least some hope for vocational training, the father often plans to set up a shop, or place of work after the son has acquired the necessary skills.

Case B, a Kurd, is currently a construction worker, and comes from the town of Erzuran. He has 6 children and is 52 years or age. His wife is not employed. The children weren't able to learn German here.

> Our daughter went to school, but I have never even heard her speak one word of German. In fact, in school she only had one or two hours of German lessons. At home she speaks her mother tongue. And I didn't see that the boys learnt anything at school either. In fact I saw that they learned nothing in school. I begged them at least to attend a course to learn an occupation and to improve their German, but no one listened to me.
> If they would just go to a course then I would give them the money: I would do anything they want for them. I want them to get themselves settled. They should at least learn an occupation, because we don't want to stay here forever.

Schooling

Emphasis on academic or professional education has been interpreted as an orientation toward a greater economic security and social mobility at home. This certainly was the original ambition of parents. Educational assimilation of children into the German educational system, however, means that the children, though Turkish speaking, no longer think of themselves as academically competent in their native language. Such families, expecting higher income, job security, and good education for their children as a result of the educational achievement, have decided to stay while remaining oriented toward their home country.

> *Case A* (continued) I'm not thinking about returning right now, and if the children do study then I won't return. My wife feels the same way as I do. The only thing I want is for the children to study. If they go to university then I'll stay, even if I have to stay another fifteen years here. And I would continue to work so that they could do well.

Case H is a family of rural origin which has been in Germany for 10 years. Both parents are factory workers. They have three children. The eldest daughter was married and sent back to Turkey. The 14 year-old son attends the *Realschule* and has hopes of going to the *Gymnasium* (2). They have made numerous investments in Turkey.

> Actually we could return any time, but it just doesn't work out. Now we are waiting for our son to finish school. He's very good in school. How can you interrupt the education of a child and return?

Case D is an urban family. They have three children and have been in Germany for 10 years. Both parents work. The mother was the first to migrate. The father, aged 55, works as a carpenter. The two eldest daughters, 10 and 13 at the time of their arrival in Germany, were later able to qualify for the *Gymnasium*. The pressure and competition, however, turned out to be too much. The parents have invested much in their children's education. Now, the family is waiting for the youngest son to enter university.

> Now our youngest son is in the *Gymnasium* — just what he wanted — and I really want him to study. Of course, he had a lot of help from his sisters, and now we are not thinking about returning — of course, who wants to stay forever? We'll wait until my husband gets his pension and then we'll return.

I have confidence in our children that they'll get an education; I
know that. Since we have been here the children have been our
only aim — we work for them.

Kin and village networks

Those who have been the most successful in establishing kin and village
social networks in Berlin find it easy to alter migration goals and to deal with
their minority status in Germany.

Case G is a Kurdish family from a village. The 40 year old father is employed
by the municipality as a garbage collector. He has been in Berlin for 13 years.
The mother stays at home. The two eldest children, 17 and 15, live at home
and attend a *Gymnasium*. The father has brought 42 people here from his village. They also bought property in the village and houses have been built in
Istanbul and Erzurum. The father explains how he feels about returning:

> We have many friends from our village — that's why we always
> have a lot of visitors. If we didn't have so many friends here, we
> probably couldn't stay. We're Turks. We don't go out like Germans
> to bars and places like that. I don't go to any pub; the only thing
> we can do is to visit our friends and talk to them and if we don't go
> to friends we stay home. And I can't let the children go out on
> their own. Anyway, if we went out a lot we would never manage to
> save 5 pfennings — there are eleven people in the house — and I'm
> the only one working.

Life cycle and aging

An earlier "maturing" common among Turkish peasants and workers
with respect to age at marriage, entry into the workforce and starting a family
leads to the both subjective and the normative feeling of being "old" as early as
at 40 or 50 years of age. Parent's primary interest is to help their children in
their education, training, or business and then return themselves to their
home country.

> *Case D*: (continued) The children may do what they like. It's most
> likely that they'll stay here. And then the two of us will return to
> Turkey. Of course, we are also thinking about what my husband
> will do when he returns to Turkey. It's hard to make a new begin-
> ning. First, we will have to have a house and then we'll be able to

live with the money from his pension. He'll be eligible for retirement in about 6 or 7 years. Only then can we return.
There is no use thinking about my retirement since I have never worked in Turkey. I'd have to work a long time here to earn it. For my husband to earn a little bit more, he'd have to stay here 25 years but the 600 DM per month that he can get now will be enough for us — we can't wait 25 years. But in the meantime, our son will finish school.

Case F is a rural worker. Father of four children, he has been in Berlin 14 years, and now works for the municipality.

I still have to pay some money into my retirement fund — I'll have to stay until that's completed. But otherwise I'm fed up here. I have 10,000 to 12,000 DM still to pay, but then I'm going to go. Up until now the situation in Turkey hasn't been good — that's another reason that we haven't been able to return. But when we return, then we'll be able to become self-employed. We have to return — we can't stand it here any longer.
Soon I'll be able to apply for my pension in Turkey and then I'll see what I can do. When I'm retired I'll continue to work too. When I return to Turkey, I'll get my pension — maybe I'll open up a shop or a coffee house. And then, we'll get some rent from our apartments and then we'll be able to manage on that.

The original ability of deferred gratification for future security at home makes sense as long as goals appear within reach. However, the time span must be clear. To work in order to save for the future becomes less attractive. "At last, I want something out of life" summarizes the feelings of many. In some cases, even the return to retire appears to be hard, and too far off. Strategies are developed for cashing in retirement funds and investing in Turkey.

Case G is a 40 year old worker from a rural background. Currently he works as a carpenter in a construction enterprise. He has four children and has been in Berlin for 16 years, since 1964.

I have to get back as quichly as possible and secure my situation there. If the boys want to return, then I can set up a shop for them. If I compare myself with the Turks here, I live a normal life. There are some people here that only buy bread and onions in order to save money. They take the handle off the door so that they do not have any visitors and they don't have to spend any money. A man like that may earn a lot of money, but then he lies in the hospital two years because his health is ruined. The work isn't easy — it kills you.

107

I haven't invested very much in Turkey. I bought some property in Istanbul. My brother and I bought some property and a house, and for about half a million Turkish lira I took over a shop. My brother works there now.

I want to return at last to Turkey. I've had enough of Germany. I've wanted to return since 1978 but it hasn't been possible so far; something always got in the way. We've reached the point where we can't save 5 pfennings. So, by the end of 1982, I want to return to Turkey once and for all.

Naturally when I return I will go to Istanbul. There I will work with my brother in his shop and we will share the profits. I really don't want to work very much anymore. I'm sick and tired of getting up at four o'clock in the morning.

Others who plan to return to retire express similar feelings with respect to their working hard in Germany.

Case E: Our economic situation is okay. If we had stayed in Turkey it certainly would have been bad times for us. I only need to look at the situation of my friends who are still there. On the other hand, actually, I'm fed up here. I get up in the morning, you don't even see the sun, you don't see anything but work! Of course, it's better in Turkey and we want to return, but we just haven't managed so far.

Through the permanent extension of the "temporary" stay, the aging worker begins to think about the quality of life for a Turkish worker in Germany. Only the temporariness and the hope of return make the combination of alienating work and frugal living conditions bearable.

Case G: (continued) Germans are not like us. The Germans work the whole day but in the evening they go out where they can forget their problems. They're not very happy with their life either. After all, Germans are forced to work here; that's not the case with me. If I want, if I don't like it here anymore, then I can go back to my country. Of course, Germans are not forced to save money. Whatever they earn they spend, whereas some of us Turks feel forced to save. But then, we don't live humanly.

Case H: (continued) Well .... the life of a Turk here is not to be envied. Both in Turkey and here working people are looked down upon. But the conditions of work are tough here, too. I used to envy those who drove a Ford. But in those days I didn't know how one earned such a Ford. Fords and houses are built, but no one appreciates the work which goes into it. Ten people live in one room eating potatoes and onions — that's how it's done!

Minority status

Migrant workers are not only aware of their inferior legal status and rights, but also of discrimination in social life.

Case J: The 48 year old father of five children, of rural background, has been in Germany for 13 years. The family has a large social network in Berlin. Although only German families live in their apartment building, the family has no contact with them. There are Turks in the immediate neighborhood, though.

It's hard to find an apartment. Germans don't want to rent to us. And at my age, I don't want to get into difficult situations. A new apartment, and then maybe they don't like us and they won't want us. At my age it's hard to take being mistreated. That's why I avoid new situations.

I live here and speak to the people who are like me, who come from my country. That will continue the same way. When you go to a new area, you meet a lot of dirty words and criticism — I understand some German, so I don't like it. Well, I've gotten used to this area. Nobody says anything, and you are not forced to comply with   the ways of others. Even if I had enough money to move into a better apartment, it's better the way it is.

Case H: (continued) We have a couple of friends from our home country whom we meet occasionally. We also have a couple of Pakistani friends my wife met through her work. I don't like Germans, that's why I don't meet them. In fact, I only know one single German. He's of course a very good sort of man. We are the only Turkish family in this house. A lot of families here we don't know at all. And they don't want anything to do with us.

Well — I personally look for our faults. It's our fault that the Germans don't like us. But the German government should also behave like a man. If they don't want the foreign workers any longer, they should say so openly. And, since our government does nothing for us — we're in an especially bad situation.

Feeling of discimination and social marginality tends to develop into prejudice toward Germans. The Turks fear the disrupting effects German lifestyle and German peers may have on their own children.

Case H: As a whole the school situation of our children is bad, too. Sometimes they follow German children and do bad things... but a German is never guilty! If a Turkish child does the least thing there's an uproar. Even though they're just children, and may be imitating a friend. If Germans do anything, it's hush-hush, but the goings-on of Turks end up in the newspapers.

Case I is an upwardly mobile family. The parents have been in Berlin for 12 years and they have 10 children. The three daughters qualified for the *Gymnasium*. They live among Germans in an outlying Berlin district.

Our children plan their life here according to the life of their German friends. Germans don't want to go to school very long; they want to learn an occupation in the shortest way possible. Our children are beginning to think in the same way. I wanted them to become doctors, but they say they cannot wait until they're 30 years old to become a doctor. They too, just like the Germans, want to learn an occupation in the shortest way possible. Germans don't think about the future, and now our children begin to think that way too. Some of the behavior of our children is similar to that of Germans. They say whatever comes to their mind, and we don't like that.

We do feel that we live between two worlds, and that is hard. It's the same for the children; they are neither like the Germans nor like the Turks. All Turks have the same problem. Germans don't have any family life. The German working class have no morals and they are corrupt. They cannot be brought together with us. I don't want my children to become like the Germans. Neither of us, nor our children, have much to do with them. It's not possible for us to come to a common understanding with them.

"One foot in Germany"

In cases where parents no longer are willing to bear the hardships of later life under the foreign working and living conditions, they make plans to leave one or more sons, at times even daughters, at least, if married or cared for, to secure the family income when they return (3).

Case L, a fifty year old member of a Kurdish rural minority in Turkey, 11 years in Berlin, is a construction worker. He is the father of four children. The eldest daughter is married in Turkey. The family socializes exclusively with the 60 families from their village.

110

It was good for me that we came here, but now I think it's enough. I am building a house with six apartments and two shops in Istanbul. It was begun in 1978. I go to Turkey about two or three times a year to check what's being done.

I'm tired. I would return this very day, but I cannot swing it yet. One never feels at home in a foreign place. At the latest I will return in 1984, when the youngest son has gotten a job, then everything will be all right. I'll arrange my daughter's marriage, too. The children will stay and I will return with their mother. My wife doesn't want to return, but she can stay with the children if she wants. I can't stand it here any longer. We've waited long enough now for the children. By the time we return, we will have paid the debts on our house. I think that I will live in one of the apartments, and work in one of the shops. Then I'll manage to live on the rent. The children may stay here as long as they want.

Case G: (continued) I think I'll leave my boys here, but the girls I'll take with me in any case. The girls may not stay here with their brothers, either. The oldest son is getting married this summer and when the youngest son is engaged then my obligation to him is taken care of as well. The girls, I will take with me. I don't want to take the boys very much, because well you know — this anarchy in Turkey. They can stay here for a while.

Concluding note

In the above-mentioned cases, the first generation Turkish migrants show strongly their desire to return. Decisions about return are not questions of individual taste or independent choices. For the first generation migrant the nuclear family and their reference groups play a decisive role. These interpretations are made in the context of the perception of economic and political developments in Turkey and in Germany. Workers whose children foresee prospects of higher education are more willing to express a possibility of staying in Germany themselves. These, and families with numerous village and kin networks in Berlin are the only workers with some positive words about life abroad. Yet they, too, remain basically return-oriented.

Additional factors support the retention of the original temporary goals of work abroad. Reference groups have evidently not been replaced. Recognition and satisfaction for what has been achieved, whether it be education for the children in Germany or the numerous investments for the family in the home country, are found only with respect to former status among peers and kin. This lends support to the above findings among the educationally successful and those with close kin and village networks abroad, who may find some positive status in Germany. Yet prestige needs alone are not reason enough for continued return orientation.

Furthermore, deferral of gratification assumes a long-range goal which can be achieved. To some, this may appear near achievement. Investments have been made. Return is possible. But, even if original investments no longer appear so lucrative as at the outset or goals are no longer feasible, retirement is near. Goals may be transferred to children. Aging, poor health, and hard work take their toll. Rest and unmet social and emotional needs may be satisfied by return. Hard work and frugal living for return goals lower the quality of life abroad. "If you live like a German" ...... "like a human being" ...... "you can't save 5 pfennings" ...... "the work here kills you" ...... To raise the quality of life means to stop saving, to consume, and give up betterment at home. Return may be seen as an improvement in the quality of life.

Ultimately, the "return of retirement" is the goal of the majority of first generation Turkish workers. This is clear from a number of surveys and little change in this orientation toward a decision to stay in Germany has become apparent since 1972. Intensive interviews with families of different backgrounds and experiences in Germany demonstrate the rationale and the primacy of instrumentality in the choices that may appear to others as "planless". In fact, our studies lead us to see the migrant as goal-oriented attempting to plan for self and children under conditions where he is unable to predict the future for his class at home or abroad. Yet, plans for a retirement at home may also be altered at any time due to dramatic economic or political events in Turkey. But even when return plans are definitive, the strategy of "one foot in Germany" for sons and daughters, is common.

NOTES

(1) The in-depth interviews for these case studies were carried out by Ali S. Gitmez and Zerrin Iren, in connection with a larger project on future perspectives of migrant families and youth financed by the Volkswagen Foundation (Wilpert, 1983).

(2) These are occupational and academic secondary schools, respectively. The *Realschule* educates for middle level white collar occupations, and the *Gymnasium* qualifies for university education.

(3) This strategy would also explain the greater willingness of Turkish workers in Berlin who would accept that sons and daughters stay, if they themselves return. 41 per cent of Turkish fathers would accept that sons stay as compared to 3 and 2 per cent of Yugoslav and Greek fathers, respectively. Also a similar greater willingness to allow children to marry German citizens was found among the Turkish first generation than among the other two nationalities (Sozial Data, 1980).

GEOGRAPHICAL AND OCCUPATIONAL REINTEGRATION OF RETURNING TURKISH WORKERS

Ali S. Gitmez

Migration and return in brief

About 816,000 Turkish workers were officially sent to Western Europe during the fifteen-year period between 1961 and 1975. In addition, a large number of workers, estimated to be around 150,000, emigrated illegally as "tourists", whose presence is not reported in official figures. The flow has largely been reversed since 1975, with a net repatriation of about 20,000 to 30,000 persons annually.

The stock of Turkish population in Western Europe at the end of 1980 was around two million, only 40 per cent of which were actually workers; the rest were their spouses and children. As the size of present stock indicates although many workers have returned home since the recession of 1973, Turkish population in Europe shows an increasing trend. This is due mainly to family reunion and new births. The increase from 1979 to 1980 was, for instance, 13.5 per cent.

The Federal Republic of Germany has always taken some 80 per cent of Turkish immigrants to Western Europe. At the end of September 1980, 1,462,442 Turks, of which 520,374 children under the age of 16, were living in the Federal Republic of Germany. Thus Turkish nationals accounted for 32.8 per cent of the total foreign resident population and Turkish children under 16 for 46.4 per cent. The Turkish population in the FRG increased by 42.3 per cent between 1974 and 1980, 15.3 per cent increase being during the year period from 1979 to 1980 (SOPEMI, 1981).

Turkish governmental agencies do not provide official information on the extent of return migration. There are estimates by researchers however, which indicate that about one-half of the out-migrants to Northwest Europe usually return (Gökdere, 1978; Gitmez, 1980). For instance, between 1967 and 1974, there were some 30,000 returnees annually, during 1975 and 1976 this number ranged between 55,000 and 60,000, after that date up until 1980 it is estimated that the annual number of returnees were about 15,000 to 20,000 persons (Gökdere, 1978). The return movement has however gained new momentum since 1980, exceeding 70,000 persons annually.

The number of Turkish workers in the Federal Republic of Germany dropped from 605,000 in 1973 to 521,000 in 1976, and the number of Turkish workers leaving the FRG increased to a large extent (Entzinger, 1978):

whereas the annual number of returnees was 40,508 in 1973, it increased to 51,281 in 1974 and to 64,933 in 1975, and dropped back again to 44,505 in 1976 and to 30,000 in 1977 (Werth and Yalçintas, 1978: 63). The figures include not only workers but also dependents and relatives. While OECD had estimated a total of 80,000 returned Turkish workers in the period of 1974 to 1976 (SOPEMI, 1977), another reliable estimate presents the number at 35,000 for the year 1974 (van Gendt, 1977). All evidence and observations show that return migration came to a stable low level after a few years of temporary increase following the recession.

Despite the considerable number of returnees annually, governmental interest in the issue is lacking. There was an earlier government-sponsored study on migration underwritten by the Turkish State Planning Organization in 1963 (Abadan, 1964) and another study on return migration in 1965 (Tuna, 1967). Other studies, such as there were, were undertaken by individual social scientists (Abadan-Unat et al., 1976; Yasa, 1978; Gitmez, 1977). The most recent such study is reported here.

Reintegration of returning migrants

A purposive sample of 1365 returnees was interviewed in 1978 (Gitmez, 1980) covering three distinct regions in Turkey: an industrialized region of Bursa, a semi-developed region of Afyon and the region of Kirsehir still primarily agricultural and governed by a traditional economy. The sample included all returnees who were resident in one of the three regions in the year 1978. The study yielded 515 interviews from Bursa, 488 from Afyon and 362 from Kirsehir. In addition, 30 returnees were interviewed in depth to tap their experience of migration and return in the greatest possible detail.

Results of the study presented here have to be accepted with a caveat inasmuch as the sample was purposive, the returnees to these particular regions were self-selected and no controls were available on other migrants and other returnees. The findings may well be idiosyncratic even though the literature on return migration contains similar findings elsewhere. Two interrelated general findings are of interest: 1) the geographical distribution of returnees by regions and by the size of community as compared to the respondents' pre-migration geographical distribution and 2) the occupational distribution of respondents by area, size of community of settlement and the pre-migration occupational classification. Both findings have a bearing on the central question surrounding the study of return migration, namely, *to what extent does migration and return migration contribute to socio-economic change and industrial development in the sending country.*

It has to be borne in mind that our sample was a demographically biased population. The mean age of respondents was 39.1 years, most returnees were under 50 years of age, 93 per cent of the returnee respondents were males.

Two thirds of our respondents have returned after the 1973 oil crisis; between 1974 and 1975 some 38 per cent of our sample came back. Of the respondents, 61 per cent migrated to Northwest Europe, primarily to Germany, after having been recruited for work officially, a further 18 per cent went to work "unofficially", that is as tourists at first. There are however noticeable differences between the emigrants of different regions, concerning the channel of emigration: while 31 per cent of the returnees in underdeveloped Kirsehir and 22 per cent in semi-developed Afyon had gone abroad as "tourists", only 4 per cent of those in developed Bursa had done so.

An average length of stay abroad was 5.5 years but only 22 per cent of our sample had their families with them. There are again, large differences between the subsamples concerning "family migration": 32.5 per cent of Bursa as against 18 per cent of Afyon and only 9 per cent of Kirsehir respondents had taken their families with them.

About one half of our respondents live now in villages, about the same proportion as before migration. Only 13 per cent are new to the area where they live now; 78 per cent had been living in the same region before migrating. They seem to be simple men in terms of schooling, with 12 per cent having gone past the primary school, whereas about 6 per cent remained illiterate. Some two-thirds felt that their migration experience was worthwhile, only 7 per cent became dissatisfied and 20 per cent saw not much difference in their lot before, during or after migration.

Geographical distribution
of return migrants

It is instructive to look into the geographical distribution of return migrants. Given their socio-demographic profile, it is not surprising that a fair proportion of the returnees have come back at least into the region they came from originally. Furthermore, their pre-migration background in terms of the size of the community seems to have predetermined the place to which they returned. Whereas other migration studies in other countries indicate that return migrants are not likely to return to their rural areas of origins, our respondents did so in fair numbers. Compared with the general population trend in Turkey, the rate of urbanization among returnees appears to be considerably smaller than that of the population in general.

Looking at the size of community of origin and the size of community upon return (Table 1), we notice a stability of some 80 per cent for larger cities and for villages, while towns re-attracted slightly over 60 per cent of return migrants who had left them to emigrate. There was an understandable upward bias for the size of community to settle in upon return. Of the approximately 80 per cent of our sample resident in cities, three quarters had lived in

Table 1: Geographical distribution of returnees by size of community, by three regions and by pre-migration residence. Per cent in ( )

Present residence Region	City		Pre-migration Residence Town		Village		Total	
City								
Bursa	259		38		38		335	
Afyon	67		5		9		81	
Kirsehir	34		3		26		63	
Total	360	(75.0)	46	(10.0)	73	(15.0)	479	(100)
	(80.5)		(20.7)		(10.4)		(35.1)	
Town								
Bursa	11		47		3		61	
Afyon	14		63		29		106	
Kirsehir	5		31		8		44	
Total	30	(14.0)	141	(67.0)	40	(19.0)	211	(100)
	(6.7)		(63.5)		(5.7)		(15.5)	
Village								
Bursa	18		7		94		119	
Afyon	26		8		267		301	
Kirsehir	13		20		222		255	
Total	57	(8.0)	35	(5.0)	583	(86.0)	675	(100)
	(12.7)		(15.7)		(83.8)		(49.5)	
All								
Bursa	288		92		135		515	
Afyon	107		76		305		488	
Kirsehir	52		54		256		362	
Total	447	(32.7)	222	(16.3)	696	(51.0)	1365	(100)
	(100)		(100)		(100)		(100)	

cities prior to migration. Only 7 per cent of our respondents were residing in towns at the time of interview of which about two thirds had resided in towns prior to emigration, about 14 per cent in cities and about 19 per cent in villages; 86 per cent had lived in a village before migrating, while about 8 per cent had lived in cities and 5 per cent in towns.

The three subsamples representing regions at a different stage of socio-economic development also offer some clues to the redistribution of returnees by size of community of origin. The region of Bursa is the most industrially advanced, with the greatest proportion of its population living in cities. On the other hand, the opposite is true about the region of Kirsehir. Of the three quarters of all returnees living now in cities in the region of Bursa, 77 per cent had lived in a city in that region before migrating. About 16 per cent of all respondents living in villages lived in the region of Bursa of whom four fifths had lived there before but 15 per cent had come from a city. The region shows a fair exchange between the city and the village and one could presume that at least some of the exchange is a function of the life cycle of individual migrants. Those who emigrated from cities for abroad but returned to a village may have come originally from the village and the pre-emigration community represented a link in their migratory chain, a situation quite common for migrants.

The region of Kirsehir contains only slightly over 9 per cent of all our respondents living in cities. Of these, 54 per cent had lived in a city before emigrating but 41 per cent had lived in villages. On the other hand, 38 per cent of all returnees presently living in villages live in villages in Kirsehir of whom 87 per cent had lived there before emigration while only 5 per cent had lived in a city. Thus, the drift toward urban residence is more pronounced in the rural than in the urban region which, again, indicates perhaps more the developmental stage of migration than any pattern which could be defined as culture and country specific. Here, Afyon represents a unique example to show the drift toward small towns after return.

Occupational distribution
of return migrants

One cannot really understand the geographical dispersion of return migrants adequately unless one considers their occupational characteristics as well. The interplay between the size of community and the job opportunities is only too well known to be disregarded. Inasmuch as most of the out-migrants to Northwest Europe were working there in large industrial plants, their occupational experience and classification was fairly uniform. It is their original occupational background and their post-migration jobs which represent the measure of the impact of migration on socio-economic development in the direction of a desired social change.

Out of all respondents whose pre-emigration employment was in agriculture, about 59 per cent were working in agriculture after return. Interestingly, the highest proportion of those returning to agriculture was found in the region of Afyon, which is at a halfway point in socio-economic development between the regions of Bursa and Kirsehir; these two regions show the return to agricultural employment for our respondents to be about 48 and 45 per cent respectively. The "loss" to commercial and service employment (retirement) explains most of the move away from agriculture by returnees. Actually, Table 2 shows rather clearly the shift into service related occupations some of which are, not surprisingly, the result of becoming self-employed.

Table 2: Respondents by type of work, by region, before and after migration. Per cent ( )

Before Migration	Regions	After migration					
		Agriculture	Industry & construction	Own business (Machine shops etc.)	Services	Not working	Total
Agriculture	Bursa	36	5	8	15	10	
	Afyon	152	3	13	25	28	
	Kirsehir	49	-	19	18	23	
	Total	237 (58.6) (61.2)	8 (2.0) (5.5)	40 (9.9) (14.4)	58 (14.3) (20.8)	61 (15.1) (22.2)	404 (29.6) (100)
Industry & construction	Bursa	9	48	48	28	47	
	Afyon	9	21	24	14	15	
	Kirsehir	4	3	9	4	5	
	Total	22 (7.6) (5.7)	72 (25.0) (49.3)	81 (28.1) (29.2)	46 (15.9) (16.5)	67 (23.3) (24.4)	288 (21.1) (100)
Own business (Machine shops,etc.)	Bursa	2	4	21	7	5	
	Afyon	6	3	13	4	11	
	Kirsehir	-	-	9	2	2	
	Total	8 (9.0) (2.0)	7 (7.9) (4.8)	43 (48.3) (15.5)	13 (14.6) (4.7)	18 (20.2) (6.5)	89 (6.5) (100)
Services	Bursa	4	14	17	27	15	
	Afyon	9	6	16	42	13	
	Kirsehir	2	-	5	15	9	
	Total	15 (7.7) (3.9)	20 (10.3) (13.7)	38 (19.6) (13.7)	84 (43.3) (30.1)	37 (19.0) (13.4)	194 (14.2) (100)
Not working	Bursa	24	30	23	18	50	
	Afyon	16	3	12	23	7	
	Kirsehir	65	6	40	37	35	
	Total	105 (26.9) (27.1)	39 (10.0) (26.7)	75 (19.3) (27.1)	78 (20.0) (27.9)	92 (23.6) (33.5)	389 (28.5) (100)
TOTAL		387 (28.4) (100)	146 (10.7) (100)	277 (20.3) (100)	279 (20.4) (100)	275 (20.2) (100)	1364 (100)

Unemployment or not working among returnees has a broader definition than the standard concept of unemployment used, for instance, in Northwestern Europe. Our "unemployed" respondents included also those who are not actively looking for a job, are living off their savings or supervise their investments in the family establishment without actually holding down a job. Among those whose pre-migration jobs were in agriculture, some 15 per cent are presently not working, somewhat more so in the agricultural region of Kirsehir. Interestingly enough, among those who had been unemployed prior to migration, some 24 per cent are unemployed again, and disproportionately so in the region of Bursa. For all of our respondents, the current proportion falling in the "unemployed" or, more likely, currently not working category was about 20 per cent at the time of interview, a figure not actually high provided the circumstances for not working are made clear. Given the chances of receiving unemployment insurance payments earned abroad and paid in hard currency and given the capital accumulation brought back, a proportion of unemployed are simply not working.

Concerning differences between regions, returnees to Bursa appear to have been distributed rather evenly among various sectors of employment, whereas those to Afyon and Kirsehir are concentrated in limited job sectors.

For most of the returnees, the period following return seems to be one of extended inactivity and dislocation, a period in which they feel they can afford to remain unemployed, and live on their savings. They seem to care about the social prestige of work they are to do and this requires a period of search for job/investment. Mainly because of this, and not because they originally desire to do so, some finally take jobs as wage earners in the service or industrial sector, but considerable time may elapse before they settle on permanent employment.

Investment practices of returnees

There is no doubt that the most important, or probably the only asset of many returnees is their savings, since repatriation seems to have little impact on the skill level of labor force. Thus, about four-fifths of the respondents report some form of investment. About 37 per cent of all investments were made in housing and building lots, 34 per cent of investments were in agricultural land or in machine shops and the like. Service sector investments represented only about 23 per cent of all investments made by our respondents.

With the exception of housing and investment in land, either for building or for agriculture, investments were related to job creation. Nonetheless, the enterprises created are quite small and are more likely than not to be established in villages or in small towns. The enterprises are often nothing more than a truck or similar commercial vehicle, a small shop or repair shop. Some

25 per cent of investors in commercial enterprises, 24 per cent of investors in non-agricultural production and one half of investors in commercial vehicles live in villages where some 40 per cent of the housing investments has also been made. The dominant economic activity in each region and each type of settlement seems to be reflected in the type, number and distribution of self-employment jobs.

The distribution of housing, occupations and investments is not unusual with returnees who were able to save up money while working abroad. It is the same distribution which is often at variance with grander designs for socio-economic development expected as a result of migration exchanges to and from industrialized countries.

Many seem to have developed social status expectations which makes them very selective in investment and employment choices. In most cases migration confers local social status which is compatible with the previous holders of such status and has to be maintained by investing in traditional symbols of prestige. Most of them use their savings in a way that reinforces their would-be social status. This usually means a self-employed, one-man business venture. In this case, they seem to have become economically and indeed socially integrated in the home country because they are their own "bosses" and not "dependent" workers.

Conclusions

The central question surrounding the evaluation of return migration is twofold; one aspect is the extent to which it contributes to socio-economic development in the home country, and the other is the extent to which the individual returnees take advantage of their experience abroad in some way as they readapt to the socio-economic structure of the country. When evaluating the contribution of migration to the individual and to the home economy, it is clear that these two conflict with each other. Whatever the impact of personal ventures, such as small-scale investments, these do not imply socio-economic development, as they have nothing to do with development in the productive process and therefore, do not represent any real response to the needs of the country. Nor are they effective in terms of variability, size, and distribution within each specific region. Furthermore, as returnees raise considerably the amount of capital available for such small ventures, this usually causes, and indeed forces, already existing enterprises of a similar nature, owned by non-migrants, to go out of business.

In terms of their contribution to the skilled labor force, return migrants do not seem to be a significant source of industrial skills, even if they have acquired some useful industrial skills, as they are reluctant to enter the wage-earning labor market in industry.

Their social reintegration is connected to how satisfied they feel with their decision to return. Their deep dissatisfaction with the social administration of the country and the criticism they express, certainly hinders their smooth reintegration. This feeling seems to be temporary, however, and tends to become attenuated with the passage of time.

Policies of integration of returnees

RETURN MIGRATION TO ITALY
AND THE
REINTEGRATION OF RETURNEES

Claudio Calvaruso

The problem of the re-entry of emigrants from abroad has deeply concerned Italy since the first few years after the Second World War. The periods of greatest mobility of the Italian labor force out of the country meant for Italy an equally strong return movement. For example, in 1961 there were 329,000 emigrants and 210,000 returnees and in 1966, 219,000 people left the country and 208,000 returned. In the 1970's, however, the flow slowed down (Table 1) with positive migration values for the returnees. This process created considerable flexibility in the Italian labor market. It is true both for the agricultural labor force and for the industrial and service sectors of the Italian economy.

It was not until the constitution of individual Italian regions into autonomous local authorities that the problem, despite its gravity, began to receive some serious attention. Actually, only in the 1970's a debate began on the problems caused by the return of emigrants, at the time when the economic crisis provided a rapid drop in workers' mobility and, paradoxically, a decrease in the number of returnees. From 1970 to 1980 both the number of people leaving the country and of those returning fell progressively from 115,000 emigrants and 142,000 returnees to 83,000 and 86,000 respectively in 1980, the last year for which data were available (Table 1). The newly constituted regions thus faced a positive migration balance and with it, new problems.

The impact of returning emigrants on the local labor market to which they return is still insufficiently researched. We wish to report briefly on a study carried out in the Molise region for the FORMEZ by the CENSIS (1981). The study shows that the returning migrants possessed occupational skills and technical knowledge which were considerable in comparison with the levels prevalent in the area. In addition, the return migrants had accumulated savings which, even though individually not sufficient for any large or even medium scale investment, were significant in their aggregate value as a potential for investment in economic development of the region.

Our study showed specifically too, that with regard to occupational skills, and the diffusion of skills among the skilled workers, even those with a training period of less than 3 months, and among the semiskilled workers, the area benefitted by the importation of skills and knowledge of working in large scale organizations. The latter included, significantly, the awareness of a new social and work ethic acquired abroad and the workers were inculcated with this.

123

The study has also shown that a turnaround time of about three years abroad brings to the area significant positive cultural and occupational elements irrespective of the net inflow or outflow of migrants. For example, net organizational gains were noted in the area studied, not merely in social life but also in productive structures, political, institutional, trade union and social action and in forms of interpersonal and family behavior.

Table 1: Migratory movements Italy-abroad 1964-1980

Years	Emigrants	Returnees	Balance	Returnees emigrants x 100
1964	258,482	190,168	− 68,314	73.6
1967	229,264	169,328	− 59,936	73.9
1970	151,854	142,503	− 9,351	93.8
1973	123,302	125,168	+ 1,366	101.1
1974	112,020	116,708	+ 4,688	104.2
1975	92,666	122,774	+ 30,108	132.5
1976	97,247	115,997	+ 18,750	119.3
1977	87,655	101,985	+ 14,330	116.3
1978	85,550	89,897	+ 4,847	104.2
1979	88,950	91,693	+ 2,743	103.1
1980	83,007	86,061	+ 3,054	103.7

Source: Compilation by the CENSIS of data from ISTAT (Italian Central Statistical Bureau).

These great advantages, however, were thus far underutilized by the political and other institutions representing the local bodies, the political and union organizations which do not seem to have the suitable channels through which they can exploit the skills imported by the returnees. For instance, the local organizations responsible for economic and social planning do not tend to co-ordinate the isolated and individual efforts of the returnees in their economic activities. Thus the returnees start up commercial enterprises which do not earn enough to support a family, they set up tourist facilities in areas of few tourists and they move into sectors of occupations different from those in which they acquired some skills while abroad, thus experiencing a "backward" mobility and a downgrading of their effectiveness. The failure on the part of the responsible agencies to exploit the occupational skills of women returning from abroad causes the women to revert to subsistence agriculture or to artisanal or agricultural activities, which have no market and thus are wasted. As far as social and political institutions in the region are concerned, it is difficult to confront adequately the problem of reinsertion of re-entrants into the productive life if the political institutions are not set up to exploit such human resources. Primarily, it would require proper monitoring of returning migrants as to their numbers, skills, resources and availability on the one hand, and as to the wherewithal to involve them with the local population in employment in local social and economic projects which are feasible and which promise fair economic returns, on the other.

Regarding the expectations of the returnees, the objective to pursue here is the development of forms of collective solidarity and will to utilize their own accumulated experiences. The end product is thus a collective and not individual resource available to the local community. Our study has, in fact, produced evidence that such involvement is very much age dependent. The willingness to integrate into projects of a collective scope decreases very dramatically past the 35th year of age of the returnees.

All in all, familiarity with the situation of return migrants and the results of the study on Molise briefly reported here encourage us to make the following recommendations regarding the integration and utilization of return migration, that is, of return migrants: 1) take the greatest advantage from the occupational skills learned abroad, in whatever economic sectors these skills may have been acquired, 2) utilize the imported knowledge of methods of production and styles of work, including the new appreciation of work efficiency, and 3) take advantage of the skills returnees have in political and trade union activities. On the economic investment side, 4) pooling of remittances and savings away from individual consumption to collective investment related to development in the local area should be encouraged together with the exploitation of 5) the EEC Regional and Social Funds which provide financial assistance to the less developed regions in any of the member states of the European Communities.

Table 2: Re-entry by geographical district from 1975-1980

District	1975		1976		1977		1978		1979		1980	
	V.A.	%	V.A.	%	V.A.	%	V.A.	%	V.A.	%	V.A.	%
North-West	13,407	10.9	13,027	11.2	11,962	11.7	11,946	13.3	14,050	15.3	12,515	14.5
North-East	23,008	18.7	21,989	19.0	20,500	20.1	19,206	21.4	19,431	21.2	18,668	21.7
Central	11,105	9.0	10,858	9.4	10,079	9.9	9,572	10.6	10,038	10.9	9,533	11.1
South	56,403	46.0	51,950	44.8	44,572	43.7	36,177	40.2	36,094	39.4	32,928	38.3
Islands	18,851	15.4	18,173	15.6	14,872	14.6	12,996	14.5	12,080	13.2	12,417	14.4
ITALY	122,774	100.0	115,997	100.0	101,985	100.0	89,897	100.0	91,693	100.0	86,061	100.0

Source: Compilation by the CENSIS of data from ISTAT (Italian Central Statistical Bureau).

Table 3: Migratory balance by region of origin

Region	1975	1976	1977	1978	1979	1980
North-West	− 78	− 2,828	− 1,935	− 3,173	− 1,854	− 1,619
North-East	+ 5,068	+ 3,848	− 3,622	+ 2,314	+ 2,536	+ 2,882
Central	+ 4,362	+ 3,822	+ 3,635	+ 2,164	+ 2,520	+ 2,315
South	+ 14,243	+ 10,071	+ 5,650	+ 1,308	− 269	− 274
Islands	+ 6,513	+ 3,837	+ 3,158	+ 1,012	− 190	− 240
ITALY	+ 30,108	+ 18,750	+ 14,330	+ 3,045	+ 2,743	+ 3,054

Source: Compilation by the CENSIS of data from ISTAT (Italian Central Statistical Bureau).

Table 4: Re-entry of Italian emigrants from abroad by country. Per cent in ( )

Country of stay abroad	1973	1975	1976	1977	1978	1979	1980
Europe	101,771 (81.3)	101,948 (83.0)	96,150 (82.9)	81,042 (79.5)	68,086 (75.7)	61,537 (73.7)	62,240 (72.3)
EEC	52,435 (41.9)	50,089 (40.8)	47,593 (41.0)	43,616 (42.8)	38,613 (43.0)	39,116 (42.7)	37,183 (43.2)
United Kingdom	2,998 (2.4)	2,622 (2.1)	2,550 (2.2)	2,581 (2.5)	2,441 (2.7)	2,398 (2.6)	2,542 (3.0)
France	7,733 (6.2)	6,685 (5.4)	6,533 (5.6)	6,255 (6.2)	5,350 (6.0)	6,006 (6.6)	5,194 (6.0)
W. Germany	37,751 (30.2)	36,789 (30.0)	34,527 (29.8)	30,624 (30.0)	26,895 (29.9)	26,732 (29.2)	25,535 (29.7)
Other countries	3,953 (3.1)	3,993 (3.3)	3,983 (3.4)	4,156 (4.1)	3,927 (4.4)	3,980 (4.3)	3,911 (4.5)
Other European countries	49,336 (39.4)	51,859 (42.2)	48,557 (41.9)	37,426 (36.7)	29,413 (32.7)	28,421 (31.0)	25,058 (29.1)
Switzerland	47,094 (37.6)	49,985 (40.7)	46,602 (40.2)	35,590 (34.9)	27,472 (30.6)	26,603 (29.0)	23,106 (26.8)
Other countries	2,242 (1.8)	1,874 (1.5)	1,955 (1.7)	1,836 (1.8)	1,941 (2.1)	1,818 (2.0)	1,952 (2.3)
Non-European countries	23,397 (18.7)	20,836 (17.0)	19,847 (17.1)	20,943 (20.5)	21,811 (24.3)	24,156 (26.3)	23,821 (27.7)
USA	5,924 (4.7)	5,699 (4.6)	5,541 (4.8)	5,363 (5.3)	4,997 (5.6)	5,264 (5.7)	4,822 (5.6)
Canada	3,775 (3.0)	2,770 (2.3)	2,622 (2.3)	2,764 (2.7)	2,664 (3.0)	2,784 (3.0)	2,732 (3.2)
Australia	4,274 (3.4)	2,528 (2.1)	2,245 (1.9)	1,829 (1.8)	1,349 (1.5)	1,663 (1.8)	1,499 (1.7)
Other countries	9,424 (7.6)	9,829 (8.0)	9,439 (8.1)	10,987 (10.7)	12,801 (14.2)	14,445 (15.8)	14,768 (17.2)
TOTAL	125,168 (100.0)	122,774 (100.0)	115,997 (100.0)	101,985 (100.0)	89,897 (100.0)	91,693 (100.0)	86,061 (100.0)

SCHOOLING OF CHILDREN RETURNING TO ITALY: PROBLEMS IN THE SYSTEM

Luigi Favero
Graziano Tassello

In answer to the new immigration policies pursued by receiving countries, labour exporting nations have planned special policies for returnees. The increased awareness of the interdependence of the European nations' economic labour markets makes the coordination of such policies more urgent than ever. The specific field of education pertains to this category. The EEC Directive of July 25, 1977 on the education of migrant workers' children is an indication of such a trend. The premise of the Directive clearly states its two aims: (a) to make possible the integration of the children of migrant workers into the school systems or professional training courses of the host country, (b) to help their possible re-integration in the country of origin.

Only in 1977, the year in which the EEC Directive was promulgated did the Italian educational institutions feel the need to take into consideration the problems that returning children face in the Italian school system. Instructions given by the central administration (Directive of the Interministerial Committee for Emigration (CIEM) of 1977, Circular n. 163 28th June, 1978 of the Ministry of Education) underline the importance of starting surveys to find out specifics of school re-integration (Augenti et al., 1982).

In the meantime, Italian universities and regional bodies had started their own surveys on specific aspects of re-integration. Regions (with the D.P.R. 616; 1977, in compliance with the law no. 328) have now a larger jurisdiction and a greater power in the field of welfare, education and professional qualification courses. Within the framework of their economic development plans, regions may now organise specific projects utilizing the aid of the European Social Fund for the return of migrant workers: professional qualification courses, culture and language classes, training of teachers etc.

Specific activities in this field have been undertaken by some regions like Friuli-Venezia Giulia, Umbria (1), Latium (2). At the provincial level, ACLI-ENAIP undertook in 1979 a survey on the phenomenon of repatriated children of school age in the province of Foggia. EISS-FORMEZ planned a project of intervention in the field of teachers and local administrators' ongoing education in Calabria (Comunità Montana Silana). In the same geographical area Centro Studi Emigrazione in Rome (CSER) has begun an experimental project for the linguistic of migrants' children (CSER, Progetto PELFLE,

Progetto Educazione linguistica per i figli dei lavoratori emigrati, 1979). The project envisages the continuation of the teaching of the language of the country from which the children have returned as well as the teaching of the mother tongue.

The only nationwide survey aimed at finding out the statistical distribution of returnee children in Italian schools was held by the Ministry of Education, between September and December of 1979. In this manner students enrolled in primary, and junior and senior high school grades for the school year of 1979-1980 were enumerated. Unfortunately, the enumeration did not seem to be complete due, primarily, to non-responses of some school districts, particularly those with a presumedly high proportion of returnee children, e.g. Calabria (3).

Preliminary results

Almost one third of the Italian municipalities have schools with pupils who have returned from abroad. The amount of the phenomenon is underestimated because in the provinces where all schools were canvassed the proportion of municipalities interested in returnees' integration ranges from 41.5 per cent of schools with returnee pupils (Cagliari) to 100 per cent (Brindisi, Ragusa). In Puglia 80 per cent of the municipalities fall into this category; in Friuli-Venezia Giulia 65 per cent, in Sicily 55 per cent.

The total number of surveyed children who were enrolled in the school year 1979-1980 and fell into the category under investigation (i.e. returned from abroad not before 1979 and having lived abroad for at least one full year) were 22,674. Of these almost one fifth were enrolled in the schools of the Puglia region. The leading regions in exporting manpower are also those with the highest percentage of children who have returned (Puglia and Sicily alone account for more than one third of the total number).

Territorial and school distribution
of the returnees

The phenomenon of re-entries in school age, even if more concentrated in some areas, presents a multifaceted territorial and scholastic distribution. We notice few units for each classroom or section (except in a few cases) and great variations from school to school, often within the same municipality.

As for the distribution of returnee pupils according to the school system, we find three fifths of them in primary school, 30.5 per cent in junior and 9.5 per cent in senior high school. On the other hand if we take into consideration the total of pupils in the Italian state schools during the year 1979-1980, we find the following distribution: 46 per cent in primary school, 30,5 per cent in junior high, 23.5 per cent in senior high school.

The enormous gap existing between the percentage of students enrolled in senior high school who are returnees and those who never left is due to the age distribution of the two categories of enrolled students; (a) the age distribution of migrants is distorted due to their irregular return and their stay abroad on one hand and, on the other, (b) the selection process into school grades both abroad and in Italy slows down the migrants' progress through the grades (Rosoli, 1980; Falcinelli, 1980; Marcuccini, 1980; Faina, 1980; Cavallaro, 1980). To confound the matter, there is still a dire lack of accurate data available which makes interpretation of the existing data hazardous. What has to be particularly stressed is the circumstance where Italian students abroad do not fare well for whatever reasons in the host country schools which retards their progress through the grades abroad.

Distribution according to area of departure, age and re-entry regions

Forty-five per cent of the returnee pupils come from German-speaking areas, 22 per cent from French-speaking areas, 18 per cent from English-speaking areas, and 5.5 per cent from Spanish-speaking areas. In the province of Reggio Calabria and the Latium region 41 per cent and 38 per cent respectively come from English-speaking areas.

If we take into consideration the age at the moment of re-entry in Italy, we have the following distribution: 40 per cent have returned between the ages 0-7 years, 30 per cent between 8-10 years, 21 per cent between 11-13 years. More than 3/4 of the pupils have returned during their compulsory schooling age. Since in many nations (especially German-speaking) compulsory schooling begins at 7, we notice that a vast majority of children return before that date. Thus it is incorrect to speak of school re-integration. The fact that at least one-fourth of the returns from German-speaking areas and one-third from French and English-speaking areas have taken place while the child was between six and seven years old suggests that education for one's children is a driving factor in the motivation for return.

Only 3 per cent of the returnee pupils had been enrolled abroad in classes higher than the 8th grade. 13 per cent were enrolled in classes equivalent to our junior high school classes. ISTAT figures on returns show that the percentage of family members, aged 0-14, who had returned from European country in 1975 made up 52 per cent of the entire return migration flow. The percentage drops to 51 per cent in 1976 and to about 49 per cent in 1977.

Table 1: Relationship between classes of enrollment at re-entry and last class attended abroad

At re-entry	pre-sch.	kinderg.	Abroad 1	2	3	4	5	6	7	8	9	10	11	12	13
Kindergarten	81.8	18.1	0.1	-	-	-	-	-	-	-	-	-	-	-	-
Primary School:															
I (1)	66.5	16.4	13.3	2.4	0.8	0.3	0.2	-	-	-	-	-	-	-	-
II (2)	2.1	1.2	62.0	26.7	5.7	1.4	0.5	-	-	-	-	-	-	-	-
III (3)	0.2	-	2.4	62.9	26.9	5.6	1.5	0.5	0.1	-	-	-	-	-	-
IV (4)	0.1	-	0.3	1.7	67.3	26.2	3.5	0.7	-	-	-	-	-	-	-
V (5)	-	-	0.1	0.3	1.9	69.3	23.8	3.8	0.6	0.2	-	-	-	-	-
Junior H.S.:															
I (6)	-	-	0.2	0.1	0.1	2.2	66.4	27.2	3.2	0.6	0.2	-	-	-	-
II (7)	-	-	0.7	0.2	0.1	0.2	1.6	76.5	17.4	1.9	1.3	-	-	-	-
III (8)	-	-	0.2	0.9	0.2	0.2	1.4	4.6	70.9	15.2	4.6	1.4	0.3	0.2	-
Senior H.S.:															
I (9)	-	-	0.1	-	-	0.1	0.1	0.6	2.1	63.4	23.6	7.2	2.5	0.1	0.1
II (10)	-	-	-	-	-	0.7	0.7	0.7	-	9.2	61.2	16.4	10.5	-	0.1
III (11)	-	-	-	-	-	1.1	-	-	-	2.2	3.3	66.7	16.7	8.9	1.1
IV (12)	-	-	-	-	-	-	-	-	-	-	-	14.8	48.1	29.6	7.4
V (13)	-	-	-	-	f	-	-	-	-	-	-	-	33.3	53.3	13.3

Data collected in the survey show instead that 51 per cent of the returnees fall into the age bracket 0 to 8 years. Ninety-five per cent of family re-entries involve children aged through their 14th birthday. A comparison between the two distributions in Table 1 underlines the seriousness of premature leaving of school to enter the labour market. This is, no doubt, a result of labour migration orientation encouraged by the administrative obstacles to schooling.

Age-grade school classification
of returnee children

Re-integration into Italian grades takes place mainly during primary school age. Forty per cent of returnee children are enrolled in the first grade. On the whole, 74 per cent of returnee pupils were enrolled in primary school, 17 per cent in the junior high and only 5.5 per cent in the eighth grade or higher. Also, about 3.5 per cent were enrolled in kindergarten classes. In primary school, except in grade one, approximately 25 per cent of the pupils enroll in the same grade they were in abroad. In fact, they have become repeaters. It is a common practice to "park" the returnee pupil in the grade corresponding to the one he has been in while abroad in order to be able to assess his scholastic abilities. In the high school, this applies to between 15 and 29 per cent of the returnees. The effective down-grading by at least one year affects 3 per cent of all students in the primary grades, 6 per cent in the junior high grades and 7 to 10 per cent in the senior high school grades.

At the time of their re-entry, starting with the first grade, about one half of pupils are initially enrolled with a delay of one year, in the fifth grade only one third of the returnee pupils are in line with the expected age grading. The sixth grade shows a further decrease to two fifths and then to one fourth for the remaining junior high grades. The delays are even more considerable for the senior high school. During the school year 1979-80, at the time of the survey, more than one half of all enrolled students corresponded to their age grading; the proportion reached two fifths in the seventh grade, dropped off to one third in the 8th grade and to one fifth in the higher grades.

An analysis of Table 2 confirms the "parking" explanation of returnees. Eventually, the returnee students are switched to the classes corresponding to their age. It would be interesting to find out the actual practices which determine transfers from grade to grade, to establish how scholastic recovery takes place and what instruments of evaluations are used by the teachers responsible. Even though, ultimately, the system returns a good percentage of returnee children to their proper grade in the primary school, this does not happen at the higher levels of high school, the years of schooling particularly significant for any successful re-integration into the modernizing Italian society.

Table 2: Age and class of enrollment after re-entry (Tot. pupils)

Age	Kinderg.	Prim. School					Junior H.S.			Senior H.S.				
		1	2	3	4	5	1	2	3	1	2	3	4	5
5 years	39.6	60.4												
6 years	2.1	93.9	4.0											
7 years	0.4	50.2	43.4	6.0										
8 years		11.2	38.9	43.8	6.0									
9 years		4.9	12.3	37.8	38.6	6.5								
10 years		1.6	3.7	15.6	37.1	35.4	6.6							
11 years		0.6	1.3	5.3	15.7	33.3	40.0	3.7						
12 years		0.7	0.2	1.6	5.2	15.8	45.3	27.8	3.3					
13 years		0.2	0.4	0.6	1.8	4.9	24.9	37.2	24.9	5.0				
14 years			0.1	0.5	0.1	1.7	6.1	18.3	35.0	36.6	1.6			
15 years					0.2	0.4	2.6	6.6	16.0	56.6	14.8	2.8		
16 years		0.3	0.7	0.3			1.4	1.0	3.1	58.5	20.7	11.9	2.0	
17 years							0.8	0.8	1.5	40.0	16.9	26.9	8.5	4.6
18 years		1.7					1.7		6.7	33.3	11.7	20.0	15.0	10.0
19 years		2.6		2.6	2.6				2.6	34.2	2.6	21.1	13.2	18.4

Age and class attended in 1979-80 (Tot. pupils)

Age	Kinderg.	Prim. School					Junior H.S.			Senior H.S.				
		1	2	3	4	5	1	2	3	1	2	3	4	5
6 years	88.9	11.1												
7 years	16.1	75.2	8.7											
8 years	2.2	21.9	67.8	8.1										
9 years	1.4	4.0	28.0	58.5	8.1									
10 years	0.5	1.2	6.5	30.7	53.9	7.1								
11 years	0.2	0.9	1.7	10.0	37.7	43.2	6.3							
12 years	0.3	0.1	1.0	3.4	13.5	35.6	40.7	5.3						
13 years			0.6	0.8	4.0		17.7	41.6	32.3	3.1				
14 years		0.1	0.1	0.1	0.8		6.2	22.4	47.9	19.9	2.2			
15 years				0.1	0.2		2.5	10.1	32.9	32.9	19.5	1.8		
16 years							0.5	2.0	13.1	30.0	35.2	17.4	1.8	
17 years							1.1	1.1	2.8	16.9	24.9	31.4	18.4	3.4
18 years									2.0	5.1	13.8	36.2	24.5	18.4
19 years		0.5							0.5	8.2	7.2	10.3	30.8	42.1

In fact, the loss of one year increases progressively from 16 to 48 per cent between the first and the 9th grade. Similarly, the delays of two years increase from 2 to 22 per cent for the same grades and delays of 3 years from 1.4 to 6 per cent. The most serious problem seems to be in the high school. At the age of 14, 30 per cent of pupils are two or more years behind, a serious situation indeed for the returnees.

The major difficulties with re-integration and the highest number of repeats and delays are to be found in the Southern regions. At the age of 14, 24.5 per cent of the returnee pupils were re-enrolled in the North, 21 per cent in Central Italy and only 17.5 per cent in Southern Italy were re-enrolled in their proper age grade.

Conclusions

Returnees of school age find themselves in a double bind. While abroad, their progression through school grades was often slowed due to various factors, cultural and language ones in particular. When they return, at least those who are returning during their mid-schooling, they are penalized by being "parked" in the same grade they have already attended abroad. Some of this is no doubt the fault of the Italian school system the gatekeepers of which are unduly cautious about admitting returnee students to their proper grades. Primarily one may seek the differential school success of emigrants and of the stay-at-home population in a selectivity which is work force-oriented for the emigrants and, perhaps, does not encourage the children into schooling given the occupational characteristics of migrants.

Much more information is needed on this particular problem of school attendance by returnees. The existing school system must be utilized where present educational programs (DPR 416/74 and Law 515/77) foresees some improvements in the situation which, thus far, has taken time to be implemented.

NOTES

(1) The project undertaken by the Umbria Region, the first of its kind in Italy on the school re-integration of migrant children returned from abroad, was presented at a Seminar held in Trevi, February 27 and 28, 1979.

(2) The Latium Region reported on a similar project in Terracina, September 22, 1979.

(3) The results of the survey, promoted by the Italian Ministery of Education in collaboration with the CSER, are published by the Ministero della Pubblica Istruzione and Istituto della Enciclopedia Italiana, *La Scuola italiana e gli alunni migranti*, edited by Augenti, *et al.* Rome, 1982.

AN ACTION PROGRAM TO ATTRACT SLOVENE WORKERS TO RETURN HOME

Silva Meznaric — Peter Klinar
Niko Tos — Franc Zizek

Return migration is particularly salient for Yugoslavia as out-migrants usually represent an outflow of skilled workers difficult to replace. Return migration is normally understood as containing within it a potential for socio-economic development in the area where it takes place. In order to identify the "migration component" in development, a region in Slovenia was identified for a "field experiment". The region of Pomurje and, specifically, Murska Sobota commune were selected as the target area for "action research".

The "action research" is variant of a field experiment but differs from the latter in that no new components are experimentally introduced as would be the case in the application of the migration disturbance model suggested by the OECD. This model requires that a state agency either increases or decreases the migration component in one area, controlling the "natural" migration in a comparable area to see how the differing migration flows affect socio-economic development. The "action research" variant was chosen to avoid the field difficulties in matching of areas. Two sub-populations were identified to serve as targets for our action research: the political influentials in the region of potential return and the potential returnees currently working in the Federal Republic of Germany and in Austria. An operational definition of action research is to (a) identity the role of change agents, (b) make the role clear and desirable to the change agents and (c) let the change agents and the target population interact with the goal of facilitating return migration where such was desired.

The Pomurje region

The region of Pomurje is part of Slovenia, one of the Yugoslav republics. In 1982, the region had a population of close to 130,000, Slovenia had about 1.9 million. In the region, the employed population increased from 19.2 per cent of the total in 1970 to 26 per cent in 1978, while in the whole Republic of Slovenia the 1978 proportion was 42 per cent. Of all the labor force, farming occupied 51 per cent still in 1978 (Vesnik, 1979: 9). The estimated latent unemployment in 1981 was some 18,400 persons (Department for Regional Economics, 1981: 48), even though the increase in social product and per capita income was considerable during the past decade. The rise in the social product, however, was not any faster than was the national increase (Vesnik, 1979: 9). The share of per capita income in the region was 3.9 per cent in 1977 while the share of the region's population in the whole of Slovenia was 7.1 per cent. An index of national income in the region was 55 per cent as compared to the republic wide income levels. Thus, in the region there was plenty of room for improvement which was to be at least partially brought about by an influx of returnees from abroad with industrial skills.

The return of workers from abroad as well as the intrinsic growth of the labor force in the region are now projected to represent an increase in employment at a rate of 4.5 per cent annually which will require innovative measures to create employment.

The potential returnees

Whereas the influentials in the region of return are charged with developing job creation programs, those to benefit from such programs are, or were, still abroad, primarily in Germany and Austria. Their demographic profile is as follows: men represented 76 per cent of the potential returnees, their modal age ranging from 26 to 48 years (89 per cent). Their domicile is the region of Pomurje. They have been abroad on the average for 11 years. Their occupational distribution included 43 per cent of unskilled and 26 per cent of skilled industrial workers; the rest were working in various service occupations. Our respondents were administered a questionnaire abroad. Those already returned to the region were also interviewed. The interviews yielded a list of 49 items (variables) characterizing our population. The items were descriptive of the demographic and social profile of the respondents and of their economic behavior including investments. The items were subjected to a standard factor analytic program to identify clusters of variables which would be associated with return and those associated with staying abroad. Out of 12 factors, only three factors, unnamed but designated F 1, F 2 and F 9, were identified as describing return migrants with some degree of predictability. The components of the three factors, in no specific order, were as follows: the wife of the worker is in Yugoslavia; remittances are sent home with a fair regularity; the respondent lives abroad in a boarding house as a lodger without own furniture; his children are in Yugoslavia at school. Also, his wife may be in Germany with him but both send remittances home, or, the potential returnee is still single but owns property in Yugoslavia. Other contributing factors to the willingness to return is owning a house in Slovenia, including a mortgage or loan back home and, frequent travel home. The respondent has few social contacts with the host population.

One factor (F 10) clearly clustered around traits predicting the desire to stay abroad namely: enjoyment of good health with no work related accidents, all savings in a German bank, and own independent housing. Other factors were not clearly articulated to predict return migration. It has to be remembered that factor analytic approach is a difficult analytic tool unless the N is extremely large, which in our case it was not. Nonetheless, the analysis essentially confirmed the findings in the literature on return migration which links a lack of success abroad with a willingness to return.

The role of governmental policies in attracting returnees

The major problem facing any region of out-migration is to modify the situation encouraging out-migration so that the regions become friendly to in-migrants or, in our case, to return migrants. The problem in Yugoslavia in particular is that of attracting back those workers from abroad whose industrial skills would benefit the development at home while all the research indicates that those most willing to return are those who retain strong ties to their community of origin and cannot be described as successful migrants. In other words, those most likely to become returnees are those whose stay abroad was not very satisfactory and whose stay abroad may not have advanced sufficiently their industrial skills and orientation towards a western-type productivity ethos so essential for any economic "take-off".

It is at this point that the role of the influentials in the community of return comes into play. Given the fact that Yugoslavia is a socialist country, a fair amount of economic stimulation lies in the hands of the governmental apparatus. Whereas there are some clear disadvantages to such a system in that it is bureaucratically cumbersome, the advantages could lie in the breadth of measures which can be put into effect not only to provide financial stimulus for new industrial plants but also to provide various individual incentives for returning workers as regards tax advantages, liberation from import duties and the like.

There is a great number of desiderata as regards stimulation of economic growth in Yugoslavia and such desiderata are echoed by the planners in the region of Pomurje. Planned measures include but do not exhaust the following list: dissemination of information about job opportunities in the region; encouragment of small private enterprises be it in farming or in the service sector or in industrial production including a favorable tax treatment; promotion of improved housing.

As a concrete example, a current program in the Murska Sobota commune deserves a brief mention. The program includes the building of an electric tool factory, funded by the Iskra Organization of Associated Labor which is a nationwide and very successful manufacturer of electric handtools. The specific plant in the commune would produce components for the tools and the labor force would be recruited primarily from among returnees who have had similar factory experience and training abroad.

In summary, regional development is enhanced by flexible policies towards returning migrants such that a form of affirmative action, to borrow the phrase from the American policy vocabulary, comes into existence. It should be recalled that action research meant exactly that, namely identification of variables characterizing the population needing intervention and identification of the influentials who can deliver policies favorable to the population of returnees.

POLICIES ON THE RETURN
AND WORK REINTEGRATION OF

Mladen Vedris

The Yugoslav migrant population is young both in absolute and relative terms when compared to the population of the receiving countries and other foreign nationals working there; for instance, two thirds of Yugoslav nationals were in the age group of 21-45 years in 1977 in the Federal Republic of Germany. Also, Yugoslav migrant workers have much higher educational and occupational qualifications on the average than the Yugoslav population as a whole. Furthermore, there are regional differences in migration from Yugoslavia. The rate of out-migration ranges from 1.5 per cent in Montenegro to 3.7 per cent in Bosnia and Herzegovina and to a high rate of 5.1 per cent in Croatia. The average rate is 3.3 per cent.

More than 70 per cent of about 700,000 Yugoslav migrant workers in European countries at the end of 1977 had been abroad for a period longer than 6 years. Almost all migrant workers had believed that their stay would be a temporary one and that they would return to their homeland having worked in the foreign country for two or three years, or five at the most, but their stay is being prolonged considerably, affecting adversely their decision to return.

Effects of out-migration on Yugoslavia

In the period of the most intensive outflow of Yugoslav workers abroad, from 1968 to 1972, 740,000 workers found jobs abroad, or an average of about 150,000 a year. For the sake of comparison, in the same period, an average of 100,000 workers a year found employment in Yugoslavia. Working abroad had the function of a "safety valve" in the domestic labor market. Workers employed abroad have remitted to Yugoslavia in the past decade over 21 billion U.S. dollars, that is about one fourth of Yugoslavia's overall foreign exchange earnings. Migrants' foreign exchange remittances in 1980 amounted to about 4.8 billion in U.S. dollars, that is 26.7 per cent of Yugoslavia's overall foreign exchange earnings in that year; the remittances covered as much as 95 per cent of the foreign exchange deficit in Yugoslavia's foreign trade in 1980.

In the past, remittances have played a significant role in consolidating domestic economic flows, making it possible for the national economy to be supplied with the necessary primary materials, manufacturing components and industrial equipment; for instance, the entire importation of the "means of production" was covered in 1976, and 86.1 per cent of it in 1977.

Of the overall savings of the population of Yugoslavia at the end of 1980 (393 billion dinar), as much as 58.5 per cent was deposited in foreign currency savings accounts in Yugoslav banks, i.e. 230 billion dinar or 7.85 billion U.S. dollars. In addition, Yugoslavs temporarily employed abroad keep considerable amounts in foreign banks.

With the resources in savings accounts, new, well-furnished, modern houses have been built, often entire settlements. Migrant workers participated in a number of local self-imposed taxation projects for the construction of transport routes, schools or communal facilities of common interest for the local community, commune or region. These investments influenced the dynamics of overall economic activity, increasing the rate of capacity utilization in certain industrial branches, especially in construction.

Other positive effects of migration are manifested in learning foreign languages and in acquiring new knowledge, work experience, training and skills.

The negative effects of migration tend to become increasingly evident with the length of stay and work abroad. The large scale but unorganized, employment abroad until 1973 can be seen as unfavourable from Yugoslavia's standpoint. About every second worker left his workplace in Yugoslavia for temporary work abroad. Among them were often skilled and highly educated people, the leading figures in the production process in their circles and of optimal working age and potential. The vacancies left by them were filled with new workers, frequently without the appropriate training. Subsequently, this replacement had a negative effect on productivity or, in broader terms, on the growth rate and pace of economic development. Resources invested in the education and training of workers temporarily employed abroad represented a direct loss. Other expenses were incurred by the areas of migrants' origin. The construction and maintenance of infrastructural facilities are primarily financed from taxes while the costs of schooling migrants' children left behind, and the costs of other social infrastructural facilities are largely financed from taxes and contributions levied on the income of those employed in Yugoslavia.

Social effects of out-migration were also felt. Prolonged or long-term separation of family members brought about an increasing number of migrant family divorces. Out-migration accelerated the aging of households especially in rural areas. Migrants' prolonged stay and work abroad aggravated the problem for their children, the second generation who are torn between the host country, to which they have insuffiently or not at all adpated themselves, and the country of their parents' origin, which they have often not even seen.

On the whole, international migration of Yugoslavs: (a) provided a solution to an imbalance in the economic development at home but; (b) the initial advantages have in time become disadvantages, leading to the question of ensuring conditions for return and successful reintegration.

Implementing return

In 1973 a law was passed in Yugoslavia relating to the basic conditions for temporary employment and protection of Yugoslav citizens working abroad (The Gazette of the S.F.R. of Yugoslavia, No. 33, 1973). It led to the adoption of The Social Compact on the employment of Yugoslav citizens returning from work abroad. The Social Compact regulates: i) the bases for the organised employment of Yugoslav citizens abroad and the return of Yugoslav citizens from work abroad; ii) the conditions for employment and priorities when granting it; iii) the employment scheme; and iv) the program of measures for the return of Yugoslav citizens from work abroad (cf. The Gazette of the S.F.R. of Yugoslavia No. 39, 1974 of August 2, 1974; pp. 1339-1342).

Upon returning home, some migrants have ceased to be economically active due to retirement, living from an annuity, savings, and the like, but most have continued to be economically active at home, using one of the numerous possibilities, e.g.: (a) investing money into a modernized, capital-intensive agricultural production. (b) investing money in private workshops (crafts) or services, or (c) keeping foreign exchange savings in bank time deposits or buying bonds issued by co-operatives. This form of migrant workers' investment has also opened a possibility for the parallel and further employment of non-migrant labour.

A special "act relating to the conditions under which work organizations may issue bonds paid in foreign currency", in 1972, allows work organizations to ensure foreign currency for themselves by issuing bonds which are paid in foreign currency and which can be subscribed to only by citizens of Yugoslavia. Work organizations may also undertake to grant the subscribers to bonds some other special benefits, in addition to interest.

The Constitution of the Socialist Federal Republic of Yugoslavia proclaimed on 21st February, 1974 ratified this matter as follows (Art. 28): "In order to expand the economic foundations of labour, organizations of associated labour co-operatives may collect financial resources from citizens and ensure them in addition to the repayment of these resources, compensation for investment in the form of interest or other benefits determined by statute". This constitutional provision was elaborated on in the Associated Labour Act, enacted on 25th November, 1976 (Art. 91):

"Organizations of associated labour may collect financial resources from citizens with a view to expanding the material base of labour. Citizens shall have the right to the restitution of the resources referred to in section 1 of this Article and the right to compensation for such resources in the form of interest or other benefits determined on the authority of law".

"When the resources referred to in section 1 of this Article are used for providing new workplaces, the basic organization concerned may, in conformity with the Social Compact and law, undertake to establish a labour relationship with the citizen who has given resources to the basic organization, provided that possibilities are thereby created for his employment or for expanding employment opportunities in general".

The results achieved to date show that through this kind of investment of foreign exchange savings of migrants about fifteen work organizations have opened altogether about 2,000 new jobs. On the other hand, migrant workers have not shown any major interest in investing their savings in farming because of some still unsolved system-related problems, primarily in the sphere of health and pension insurance, and because of insufficient security regarding the marketing and prices of agricultural products. This turning away from agriculture is interesting especially if one bears in mind the fact that over 50 per cent of workers temporarily employed abroad had been farmers before leaving the country.

Investment in service enterprises has been rather modest. Empirical research shows that only 5.5 per cent of returnees and 1.3 per cent of migrant workers invested or intended to invest money in this sector of economic activity. This can be accounted for: (a) by a longer period of absence from home and, consequently by insufficient information on possibilities; (b) by a lack of knowledge of legal formalities required for starting such undertakings; and (c) by a lack of knowledge of possibilities offered by new organizational forms (e.g. contractual organization of associated labour).

Because of this, a faster and more successful realization of migration policy is sought in links with big organizations of associated labour in developed industrial centres. This also entails a more intensive use of funds for fostering development in economically underdeveloped regions, and also broader forms of international cooperation with the labour-receiving countries.

The Organization for Economic Cooperation and Development (OECD) launched in 1977 a multilateral project known as the "Experimental Schemes for Increasing Employment in High Emigration Regions". The project is of a research-operational character, its aim being to accelerate work on the provision of appropriate space and possibilities for the opening of new jobs in the countries and regions of returning migrants' origin, by making use of the resources, potentials and participation of the "three subjects": migrant workers, the countries of their origin and the host countries. The following receiving countries have taken part in the implementation of this project: Belgium, France, the Netherlands, the Federal Republic of Germany, Sweden and Switzerland, as well as the following countries of migrants' origin: Greece, Italy, Portugal, Spain, Turkey and Yugoslavia. The project has been implemented in three Yugoslav republics; Bosnia and Herzegovina, Croatia and Slovenia. Other regions have expressed their interest in being included, as well.

The use of foreign financial resources has also been given an institutional framework with the establishment of a fund for financing an increase in employment in underdeveloped and high emigration areas of Yugoslavia (The S.F. R.Y. Gazette No 22/1978). "The Fund's duties are to collect resources which other countries have given to the S.F.T. Yugoslavia in the form of grants-in-aid or loans on the basis of cooperation in the employment sector, and to channel resources thus collected into increasing employment in economically underdeveloped and high emigration regions of the S.F.R. of Yugoslavia, in line with interstate agreements and provisions of this law" (Art. 2, section 1).

"Credits from the Fund's resources are also granted to investors who operate in regions which are neither economically underdeveloped nor high emigration areas, if they invest resources from such credits together with their own funds in the development programmes of the economically underdeveloped and high emigration areas of the S.F.R. of Yugoslavia, or in other words, if they contribute to the development of their economy" (Art. 7, section 2).

The first resources provided on the basis of cooperation with the host countries were used in 1977 to co-finance two investment projects in the areas of the commune of Rozaj (Montenegro) and Struga (Macedonia).

Conclusions

The period of the past five years represents the period of the social community's intensive efforts to control and guide all the three stages of migration flows: departure abroad, stay and work in migrant-receiving countries, and creation of possibilities for returning home. At a certain period of economic development external migration from Yugoslavia was one of the solutions for a less painful transition from the country's extensive to an intensive form of business. With changes in the economic structure and the economic growth recorded in recent years, there is less reason for going abroad and opportunities are being created to attract the return of migrant workers.

A migration policy consistently defined and implemented at all levels of socio-political communities should enable Yugoslav society to affect migration flows in the best manner possible: for migrant workers to become a force upon their return that will speed up the community's progress through their work, experience and resources, instead of their being a "problem" the solving of which slows down the economic and social development of the country.

TEN-YEAR EXPERIENCE IN PLANNING AND IMPLEMENTING THE RETURN OF MIGRANTS IN YUGOSLAVIA

Ivo Baucić

At the end the 1960's and in the early 1970's, it became obvious that despite certain favorable, short-term effects, migration did have adverse economic and social effects in Yugoslavia: (a) due to the departure of workers who were needed by the Yugoslav economy; (b) the unfavorable age structure of the returning migrants, and (c) the continuing increase of the number of Yugoslavs abroad. At the end of 1973 there were about 860,000 Yugoslav migrants in European countries, and more than 200,000 post-war economic migrants in overseas countries. The most important political platform for Yugoslavia's current migration policy was provided by the Conclusions of the Presidency of the League of Communists of Yugoslavia and the Presidency of the Socialist Federal Republic of Yugoslavia on the "Problems of the Employment of Yugoslav Citizens Abroad". The conclusions were adopted at a joint meeting on 5 February, 1973. The necessity of gradually reducing the number of workers going abroad and the need to open the way for their return, especially the return of skilled workers and experts was affirmed clearly.

Article 5 of the Law on the Basic Conditions for the Temporary Employment and the Protection of Yugoslav citizens Employed Abroad (Yugoslav Official Gazette No. 33, 14 June, 1975), adopted in 1973, stipulated that "at the end of every year, the Federal Employment Bureau and employment organizations in the republics and autonomous provinces, agree on a programme of measures for the return of Yugoslav citizens from employment abroad".

In summer 1974, the executive councils for all the republics and autonomous provinces of Yugoslavia adopted a "Social Compact (1) on the Temporary Employment of Yugoslav Citizens Abroad and the Return of Yugoslav Citizens from Employment Abroad" (Yugoslav Official Gazette No. 39, 2 August, 1974). This was the first and so far the only legislation adopted by a labor-supplying country in which the very title emphasizes the return of workers from employment abroad. Chapter IV of the same Social Compact is entitled "Programme of Measures for the Return of Yugoslav Citizens from Employment Abroad". Due to its exceptional importance, I am quoting extensively from Article 24: "In order to put into effect the principle of the temporariness of the employment and stay of Yugoslav citizens abroad, and their gradual return to Yugoslavia, socio-political communities, organizations of associated labor and their associations and self-management communities of interest — on the basis of the measures of the country's development policy — opened the way for a gradual return of Yugoslav citizens from employment abroad and their inclusion into active economic and social life in Yugoslavia, by developing earning on the basis of personal work, by a more productive engagement of labor in agriculture, by investing part of workers' savings to open new jobs, by facilitating the purchase of equipment for economic operations, by suitable tax policies etc."

Article 25 of the Compact states that "the Federal Employment Bureau lays down especially the following particulars: 1) the measures which must be undertaken by employment organizations in order to obtain an exact picture of the requirements and possibilities for the employment at home of Yugoslav workers employed abroad; 2) the measures which must be undertaken by the Federal Employment Bureau and by employment organizations to ensure the realization of the programs of socio-political communities; 3) the role and tasks of the Federal Employment Bureau and employment organizations, regarding the information of workers about the prospects and conditions of employment in Yugoslavia, and regarding their mediation in providing employment within the country; 4) the measures, which are to be undertaken regarding the technical training of workers employed abroad, in keeping with the existing possibilities and requirements for the return of workers and their active engagement in Yugoslavia".

A program of measures and actions for a gradual return of Yugoslav workers from employment abroad and their work-engagment in Yugoslavia was adopted first. By the end of 1978, the program had been established in all of the republics and autonomous provinces in Yugoslavia. To date, no less than one fifth of the communes in Yugoslavia have adopted such a program. Nevertheless, there is still only a very small number of enterprises offering provisions that migrant workers require upon their return from employment abroad, mostly due to a lack of sufficient number of returnees.

The policy of return has become an integral part of the Yugoslav legislation to influence the return and the productive employment of migrants directly and indirectly. Specific provisions relate to custom duties and tariffs, foreign exchange and the development of small and medium-scale enterprises both in industry and agriculture.

Although according to the obligations arising from the Social Compact, concrete programs for creating the necessary conditions for the return of migrants should primarily be adopted by communes, the greatest activity in this respect so far has developed in certain federal institutions.

The federal Fund for Financing Increased Employment in the Economically Underdeveloped and High Emigration Regions of the Socialist Federal Republic of Yugoslavia was established in 1978 (Yugoslav Official Gazette No. 22, April 28, 1978). The primary task of the Fund is to gather resources obtained from foreign countries in the form of soft credits or grants and to utilize them for increased employment in the underdeveloped and high emigration regions in Yugoslavia.

The most recent law on the protection of the citizens of Yugoslavia temporarily employed abroad (Yugoslav Offical Gazette No. 15, March 26, 1980) includes the obligations of organized social forces concerning the implementation of the policy of migrants' return. This is to be accomplished by a dissemination of information on possibilities for and conditions of employment in Yugoslavia, by mediation on behalf of returnees to obtain employment and, by vocational education and training during employment abroad.

Citizens temporarily employed abroad are to contribute to the creation of conditions for their return and employment, and by occupational training in Yugoslav enterprises. The existing legal regulations which deal with the return migrant workers will have to continue being changed, adjusted and supplemented, especially in the sphere of excise and banking and investment policies. It is obvious that the concepts and practical solutions for a better economic inclusion of returning workers and their savings in a speedier development of individual regions and the country as a whole must be worked out primarily by enterprises and their associates.

The acceptance by Yugoslavia of employment abroad as a temporary necessity in a certain stage of the country's socio-economic development was soon followed by the development of services which help in the comparatively simple task of securing employment abroad and in the legal and social protection of Yugoslav workers during their employment in foreign countries. This social practice preceded legislation. At present, the situation is the other way around: there are fully defined political positions and a legal basis for social activity for providing the necessary conditions and for working out programs for the return and the economic reintegration of migrants, while the realization of this policy and of legal regulations is slow and ineffective.

The realization of an active policy for the return of migrants is certainly a much more complex and difficult task than the organization of employment agencies and foreign employers. Therefore, the policy for the return and reintegration of migrants cannot be expected to be successfully realized without suitable social services. It is not necessary to set up any new and separate services, but it is necessary above all to ensure a greater and more organized utilization of the existing services. A successful realization of the objectives of the return of migrants requires a more intensive activity on the part of Yugoslav services in the labor-receiving countries and a better cooperation between services in Yugoslavia and the corresponding foreign services. This requires amendments to the existing bilateral agreements.

Yugoslavia has had several models to stimulate migrant return by offering returnees possibilities for productive employment. Results have been achieved. The evidence of an increasingly longer average stay of Yugoslav citizens abroad however, and a gradual increase in the total number of Yugoslav

149

citizens in West European countries in recent years, suggest that the effects of the return policy have been thus far insufficient.

NOTE

(1) Social compacts are self-management enactments concluded on an equal basis by organizations of associated labor, chambers of economy, government agencies and socio-political organizations under which the parties thereto ensure the regulation of socio-economic and other realizations of a broad interest.

PART II

RETURN MIGRATION

AND THE HOST COUNTRIES

RETURN MIGRATION FROM FRANCE: POLICIES AND DATA

André Lebon

In the case of economic migration the notion of return represents the "normal" conclusion of the "migratory chain" (OECD, 1978: 5). As an example, in France, during the last intercensus period (February 1968 - February 1975) the number of incoming foreigners is estimated at more than 1.6 million of whom about 1.1 million were coming to work. The number of those leaving France during the same period, is estimated at 750,000 (Lebon, 1978). Recently, however, a new situation has arisen as a result of the interplay of two countervailing forces. On one hand, immigration to France began to be restricted as of 1974 to maintain the number of foreigners already in the country and, furthermore measures began to be undertaken to actually reverse the flow, thus encouraging return migration. On the other hand, resident foreigners have increasingly become part and parcel of the French economy, their movements have ceased to be cyclical and their long residence in France and their children schooled there, made them unwilling to return.

In this paper we can outline only the general situation surrounding return, with respect to the policies of the government of the day, of the body politic and, primarily, with respect to the foreigners themselves.

The policies of return

Three periods can be identified in the development and implementation of the French policy regarding return migration; each period reflects fairly well the incumbency in the office of the Minister (Secretaire d'Etat) in charge of migration. As early as October 9, 1974, the newly established Ministry issued 25 directives concerning immigration, with the overall intent "to allow either a complete integration into the national community of those foreign workers who so desire.... or to encourage the preservation of socio-cultural links with their country in view of the prospective return home" (Ministère du Travail, 1976). The three cabinet meetings which defined the overall immigration policy, namely those held on October 9, 1974, May 21 and December 9, 1975, dealt with the return problem with a view toward organizing vocational training which would help the return migrant to re-integrate in his home country and offering him money to facilitate his resettlement. Free transportation home for needy foreigners had already been provided since 1974, but only to about 200 claimants a year. The general philosophy at the basis of the mea-

153

sures was stated as follows: "Our intention is to create a regular return flow, but we wish at the same time to respect the free choice of the migrant and to remain in close contact and consultation with the countries of return" (Dijoud, 1977: 124).

A few months after the appointment of the new Secretaire d'Etat in charge of migration affairs, Mr. Storelu, France stepped up her efforts to encourage voluntary return by two means, namely unilateral financial assistance to returning workers and an expressed desire for close co-operation with countries concerned. On May 30, 1977, *aide au retour* was officially announced. It aimed at inducing foreigners receiving unemployment benefits to return to their home country in exchange for a sum of 10,000 francs plus whatever other emoluments they were entitled to. On October 1, 1977, this arrangment was extended to all unemployed foreigners, whether they received unemployment assistance or not and to all employed foreign workers who had worked in France for at least five years.

Aide au retour proved politically embarrassing, however and was repealed by an order of the Conseil d'Etat on November 24, 1978. Nonetheless, the program continued to be implemented but it was modified in that the number of nationalities eligible for *aide au retour* was to be reduced, in stages, from 23 to 18. At the end of 1979, nationals of three Black African states were to become ineligible for the aid; then, as of December 31, 1980, the ineligibility was to be extended to the Spanish and the Portuguese as well. It should be noted here that the latter two groups represent roughly 55 per cent of all foreigners who benefitted from aid to return and almost 70 per cent of those who have actually returned.

As a result of the Franco-Algerian agreement, signed on September 18, 1980, Algerian nationals also ceased to be entitled to aid to return but remained eligible for an "allowance" (*allocation-retour*). On the other hand, the program of vocational training, concurrent with *aide au retour* was extended both as to the number of countries covered and to the types of training. An example of the program is best seen in the Franco-Senegalese agreement of December 1, 1980 in which the *formation-retour* was assured to all Senegalese wishing to go home.

The present situation

In the spring of 1981, the new government through its Secretaire d'Etat in charge of immigration proposed that "we must at the same time change the spirit of the so-called policy to return.... by better respecting the free choice of migrants", by questioning the strictly financial measures of the previous policy and by stressing the vocational training as devised in co-operation with the developing countries affected by the return of their nationals (Autain, 1981).

The reaction of society to return migration is, of course, the backdrop against which one can follow the development of the French immigration policy. That means that public opinion plays some role and the political parties, the labor unions and the employers all represent pressure groups to effect policies most advantageous to themselves.

The public

An opinion poll carried out by SOFRES between January 9 and 15, 1981 summarizes the state of the public opinion as follows: Seventy-one per cent of the 1,000 respondents thought that the in-migrated workers should not be sent back but that entry of new foreign workers intending to join the labor force must be blocked. Only 17 per cent were in favor of a compulsory return, 8 per cent would still allow new immigration and 4 per cent had no opinions (*Le Journal du Dimanche*, January 18, 1981).

The parties

The power vested in the government of the day to act on unemployment in France through the return or sending back of foreign workers reflects a clear division between the political parties. On one hand there are those who were in power until May, 1981 and then there are those who came into power after that date. The first group, primarily the Parti Républicain and the Rassemblement pour la République, both fairly conservative politically, took a stand in favor of return over time in the expectation that French manpower would slowly replace the foreigners who left the country. Their stand was based on an ideological re-evaluation of manual labor which should be afforded more esteem (Falala, 1979; Barre, 1978).

The political parties presently in power, mainly the Parti Socialiste and the Parti Communiste have, on the other hand refused to consider the migrants' return as a remedy against the economic crisis in France. They do, however, favor return as part of a global reintegration program supported by vocational training in France and by economic aid for development to the affected countries. The true right to return is only there when the right to stay is clearly stated (Le Garrec and Perraudeau, 1980). One should be mindful, though, of the fact that some local factions of the Communists were very much in favor of the return policy while they were still in the opposition.

The unions

The three main labor unions, Confédération générale du travail (CGT), Confédération française démocratique du travail (CFDT) and Force Ouvrière (FO) have, generally speaking, taken quite similar positions. For the unions, the implementation of a policy of return implies that the three following conditions be met: freedom of choice for migrants, vocational training in France in preparation for return and co-operation between the countries concerned. The unions have reacted strongly against the institution of aid to return calling it deceptive (CGT, 1977) and branding it as a mechanism of "deportation in disguise" (CFDT, 1977) while the FO remained critical of the very notion of a possibility of replacement of foreigners by Frenchmen (FO, 1978).

The employers

In January, the deputy-chairman of the Confédération nationale du patronat français (C.N.P.F.) declared himself in favor of reducing by half the number of foreign workers in France over an eight year period, thus bringing down the number employed in France to one million by the end of 1985 through a "cautious but continuous action" (*Le Monde*, January 20, 1978).

The foreigners

Two large-scale surveys of foreigners in France included a question regarding the migrants' willingness or plans to return or their intentions to stay in France. Although these studies date to 1970 and 1976 respectively and thus reflect the different political and economic conditions prevailing at that time, they are very representative due to the large size of their samples and they are, thus far, the best available. The first survey of 2,046 foreigners with families resident in France in 1969 and 1970, showed that 38 per cent of the respondents wished to return while 38 per cent wanted to stay in France. The remainder was, as yet, undecided. On the other hand, of the 1,990 workers without their families in France in 1975 and 1976, 57 per cent expressed a wish to return while only 23 per cent wanted to stay in France permanently. One can surmise that both the changed economic situation and the different family status explain the greater willingness to return among the respondents of the second study. As regards ethnicity, Italians in the first study and Spanish and Portuguese in the second were overrepresented among those wishing to stay while North Africans were underrepresented in the same category. The studies were not primarily directed to the issue of migration, thus the conclusions must remain tentative. The first study dealt with housing and the second with the sending of remittances.

A number of small studies of non-random samples dealt with the question of return migration for second generation migrants. A study of Algerians and Portuguese (N of 121) in Northern France showed 28 per cent wishing to return (Abou Sada and Jacob, 1976), a study of the same nationalities (N of 191) in the Rhone region showed 35 per cent thinking about return and a study of Maghrebinians in Paris (N of 100) showed 36 per cent willing to return (Chazalette, 1977; Camilleri, 1979). Disregarding the variables of sex, age, ethnicity and education and disregarding the different wording of the questions as well as different methodological approaches which make such studies incomparable, what strikes one most in the literature on return migration is the need for integration of the respondents who then either wish to return or wish to stay depending where they presume they will be more successful fitting in.

A follow-up study of returnees is usually quite difficult. Nevertheless, three recent small surveys with numbers ranging between 80 and 150, of mainly Portuguese and Algerians, offer some information on the adaptation of returnees at home. All the respondents were relatively young, mostly under forty years of age, so that the issue of retirement did not figure in the decision to return (Chazalette, 1979; Cordeiro and Guffond, 1979; Poinard, 1979). Both pull and push reasons for return were identified. A positive attitude to the home country stemming either from an assurance of a job back home was coupled with maintenance of strong links with home while abroad. A negative attitude toward the host country usually resulted from perceived xenophobia and homesickness. The latter was expressed primarily by women respondents; other reasons were a bad state of health due to work injuries and, finally, unemployment.

Result of the return migration policies

In order to understand the French immigration policy better a few statistical indicators of the foreign presence in France will be helpful. At the time of the last census in 1975 (a new census took place in 1982 but results are not yet available), there were 3,411,415 foreign nationals residing in France. The Ministry of the Interior in its annual statements reports a higher figure, slightly over 4 million since 1974. For the last three years, 1979, 1980 and 1981, the number of reported foreigners was: 4,170,353, 4,124,317 and 4,147,978 respectively. The Ministry derives its figures from the national register of aliens, but the figures are believed to be inflated. Table 1 shows foreign population by nationality as of January 1, 1979, a distribution which is believed to be fairly accurate and not undergoing substantial change at the present time.

France does not register the departure of the foreign nationals or of her own citizens. In order to arrive at some estimate of return migration, we have to resort to the population accounting formula whereby the number of foreigners enumerated in two different censuses is corrected on the basis of

157

arrivals (births and immigration) and on the basis of deaths and naturalizations; this results in a figure which reflects the return flow. The last intercensus period available (1968-1975) shows an annual average of some 90,000 to 100,000 returns (Lebon, 1979). Without the benefit of census data, only a very approximate estimate of return migration can be made. In view of the fact that any considerable immigration to France of new workers has been all but stopped, the normal return flow of those who leave within the first half a year or so because they are discouraged, dwindles sharply, diminishing the overall return flow. The immigration of family members and of refugees also slows down return migration. These two arrival streams represent approximately 45,000 persons annually coming to join somebody working in France, of which refugees represent an inflow of about 5,000 persons annually. Given the stronger flow of immigration of persons not likely to return soon, our estimate based on calculations not shown here is about 70,000 to 75,000 persons leaving France annually. Some of the departures are brought about directly by the various programs of return and we shall look at these programs and try to assess their success.

Table 1: Estimate of the foreign population residing in France, January 1, 1979
(In thousands)

Nationals	In the Labor Force	Not in the Labor Force	Total
Italy	175.3	290.1	465.9
Other E.E.C.	66.2	86.8	153.0
Spain	184.5	322.8	507.3
Portugal	385.0	438.0	823.0
Yugoslavia	43.1	30.9	74.0
Turkey	36.3	21.6	57.9
Poland	19.3	77.9	97.2
Morocco	181.4	118.5	299.9
Algeria	361.0	431.0	792.0
Tunisia	73.7	73.4	147.1
Other Africa	50.7	41.9	92.6
Others	65.8	124.3	190.1
Total	1,642.8	2,057.2	3,700.0

Source: Mayer and Lebon, 1979, "Rapport d'un groupe interministériel sur la mesure de la présence étrangère en France", Ministère du Travail.

Vocational training for return

Programs designed to offer occupational training to potential return migrants have been in existence in France since 1975. The implementation of such programs implies close collaboration between France and the countries of origin and, in most cases, such programs are a part of bilateral agreements. The country of origin stipulates what kind of trained manpower it would like to have and has a use for. Then, in France, potential candidates are selected from among the specific nationals who are willing to return. The French government organizes and funds the training program using the facilities of the National Education Administration or the Association for Adult Vocational Training (A.F.P.A.). An interministerial group oversees the programs. This group in turn, answers to the Secretary of State in charge of immigrant workers and includes representatives from the Ministry of Foreign Affairs and the Ministry of Cooperation and from the Vocational Training Authority. Finally, the Caisse Centrale de Co-opération Economique is entrusted with the actual implementation and the management of the programs as approved by the interministerial group.

Table 2: Trainees benefitting from the vocational training
for return, by nationality (1975-1980)

Nationality	1975	1976	1977	1978	1979	1980	Total 75-80
Algerians	28	27	201	312	375	496	1,439
Tunisians	-	36	1	-	-	15	52
Moroccans	-	-	-	4	-	-	4
Malians	-	15	15	14	14	15	73
Mauritians	-	-	-	-	-	36	36
Senegalese	-	18	2	-	23	1	44
Portuguese	-	-	-	-	-	12	12
Others	-	-	-	3	1	5	9
All	28	96	219	333	413	580	1,669
Program cost in francs (in millions)	0.65	3.65	10.15	13.1	17.0	28.0	72.55

Source: Caisse Centrale, 1981.

The country of return, on the other hand, takes care, either partially or fully, of the expenses associated with return travel; the country also provides a guaranteee of employment at home or, in the case of some countries in Black Africa provides the returnees with arable land, either as a land grant or as a land-lease.

Thus far, more than 1,600 foreign workers have benefitted from such vocational training (*formation-retour*), the great majority of them being Algerians. The total cost of the program for five years was over 72 million francs amouting to about 43,000 francs per trainee. The training courses fall into two categories: (a) industrial training, which interests mainly North African countries like Algeria and Tunisia, and (b) agricultural training which interests mainly the countries of Black Africa, mostly Mali and Senegal. Among the skills specifically needed are those of instructors for vocational training, technicians and foremen for building trades, or agriculturists to develop the region of the Senegal river.

Starting in 1977, the vocational training has been extended to young Algerians aged 18 to 25 so that eventually the entire family may return and become occupationally integrated. Young Algerians receive a Certificat d'aptitude professionelle (C.A.P.) which is recognized in Algeria.

Aid to return

In addition to occupational training, France provides the much discussed *aide au retour*. Between June 1, 1977 and December 31, 1980 over 45,000 applications to receive aid to return were approved. The approved applications cover some 85,000 foreign nationals, including the family members of the applicants. Table 3 offers a breakdown of applications over time.

Tables 3 and 4 help explain why the program met a fair amount of criticism. In the first place, interest in the program seems to have dropped considerably by the end of 1979 (Lebon, 1979). Even though the aid was meant to help France to rid herself of unemployed workers, only slightly more than one fourth of the approved applicants for aid were unemployed. The eligibility of employed workers went into effect four months after the inauguration of the program, provided they had worked in France for at least five years. Portuguese and Spaniards in particular made a good use of the aid to employed workers, whereas workers from French Black Africa were evenly divided between those who were and who were not employed at the time their application for assistance was approved. The eligibility of the Portuguese and the Spanish was suspended in December, 1980. It is worth recalling that both Spain and Portugal were countries which traditionally supplied France with manpower and their nationals are considered the most assimilable. Their return often represented the return of whole families while the return to Africa was a return of individuals. To encourage the return of Algerians, a specific Franco-

Algerian agreement was made to serve as a stimulant to return, on the request of the home country. That the return program was not successful becomes clear from Table 4. Algerians and Portuguese are about equally represented in France with some 350,000 persons each. As regards return, however, Algerians did not seem to take advantage of the program to return for the period for which we have data.

Table 3: Aid to return applications approved from
June 1, 1977 till December 31, 1980 (1)

Period	Unemployed (a)	Employed (b)	Total (a+b)	Number of individuals (2)
6.1.1977/12.31.1977	3,667	3,359	7,026	13,313
1.1.1978/12.31.1978	3,390	12,884	16,274	31,735
1.1.1979/12.31.1979	3,167	12,449	15,616	30,957
1.1.1980/12.31.1980	1,666	4,882	6,548	12,537
Total	11,890	33,574	45,464	88,542

(1) There is only one application per family even when several members of the same family meet the conditions for the granting of the allowance.

(2) Including *all* the members of the families (wife or husband, children under majority age) of the unemployed workers and the employed ones having applied for the aid to return.

Source: Office National d'Immigration.

Table 4: Breakdown of applications granted and of
individuals concerned, by nationality

Nationality	Applications granted (unemployed + employed)		Individuals concerned		Number of persons per application (b) / (a)
	Number (a)	%	Number (b)	%	
Spaniards	8,456	18.6	23,428	26.5	2.77
Portuguese	16,885	37.2	35,631	40.3	2.11
Algerians	2,674	5.9	3,257	3.7	1.22
Moroccans	3,720	8.2	5,263	5.9	1.41
Tunisians	4,789	10.5	6,865	7.8	1.43
Turks	2,292	5.0	3,125	3.5	1.36
Yugoslavs	2,687	5.9	5,713	6.4	2.13
Black Africans (+ Mauritius)	3,936	8.7	5,219	5.9	1.33
All Together (1)	45,464	100.0	88,542	100.0	1.95

(1) Including 25 applications pertaining to migrants of "Other nationalities" and concerning a total of 41 persons.

Source: Office National d'Immigration.

Characteristics of the departing migrants

Only a few studies dealing with the characteristics of return migrants from France have been conducted so far. Studies on the impact of return on the French population and or the labor market in particular are lacking. There are, however, two studies by Office National d'Immigration (ONI) on the socio-demographic and socio-economic characteristics of migrants leaving France and on the effect of their departure on the employment situation in France.

An analysis of the files of 26,574 migrants who returned between June 1977 and December 1978 and who received aid to return, shows that they were mostly quite young, and had worked in France in the secondary sector and in construction and public works (road maintenance, refuse collection and related) (Lebon, 1979). Fifty-five per cent of these workers were 40 years old or younger and 57 per cent of the unemployed at the time. By nationality, the proportion of returnees under the age of 40 years was as follows: Yugoslavs 79, Black Africans 77, Turks 72, Tunisians 63, Moroccans 59.5, Algerians 55.5, Spaniards 55 and Portuguese 45 per cent. By drawing the line at 45 years of age, the proportion of returnees falling under this age limit is raised to 70 per cent, thus indicating rather clearly that the returns were not very likely for the purpose of retirement.

The distribution of the returnees by occupation and the sector of employment in France and by the employment status can be summarized as follows:

Employment sector	Recipients of aid to return		in per cent.
	Unemployed	Employed	Total
Primary (agriculture, etc.)	2.3	4.2	3.7
Secondary (industry, construction, etc.)	81.0	67.3	70.7
Tertiary (services)	16.7	28.5	25.6
Total	100.0	99.0	99.0
N	6,968	19,606	26,574

While construction and related occupations employed some 27 per cent of the registered non-EEC foreign workers, 37 per cent of the recipients of financial aid to return were in that category, reflecting the instability in the construction employment at that time. A question then arises: what happened to the jobs left by the returning migrants?

A study of employers carried out between October 1979 and the beginning of 1981 by contacting enterprises in 17 different "départments" of France was designed to trace down the fate of the 4,645 jobs left vacant by foreigners who had accepted aid to return. In view of the fact that the time period of the survey was extended, that those responsible for employment were not always contacted immediately after the foreign worker had left and that the survey was by phone, the results can be considered only indicative and not strictly speaking, statistically valid. The results are summarized in Table 5.

Table 5: Jobs left vacant by departing foreigners

| Sector of activities | Total jobs freed | Jobs replaced by | | | Jobs eliminated | Jobs still vacant | Undeter-mined (1) |
		French nationals (a)	Foreigners (b)	Together (a) + (b)			
Primary sector	151	40	51	91	56	1	3
Secondary sector, of which:	3,841	975	1,094	2,069	1,325	88	359
industry	(2,290)	(749)	(559)	(1,308)	(744)	(44)	(194)
construction and public works	(1,551)	(226)	(535)	(761)	(581)	(44)	(165)
Tertiary sector	653	248	185	433	153	2	65
Total	4,645	1,263	1,330	2,593	1,534	91	427

(1) At the time of enquiry the employer no longer knows what happened to the job left vacant following the departure of the foreign worker.

Source: Office National d'Immigration.

It appears that one third of the jobs left vacant were eliminated for one reason or another. This proportion reaches 37.5 per cent in construction jobs which were affected more severely by the economic slowdown. Actually, foreign workers have replaced the departing foreigners in a greater number of cases than have Frenchmen, the figures being 1,330 and 1,263 respectively. The 2,593 vacancies created and not abolished after the departure of returning foreigners, were filled by new workers as summarized in Table 6. Figures in Table 6 are self-explanatory, namely, the better the job, the more likely it would be filled by a French national but there are enough jobs which at the moment would be unattractive to Frenchmen and which go, by default, to foreigners, despite the overall high unemployment.

In order to put the information summarized in the two preceding tables into another perspective, a note on the development of foreign manpower during the corresponding time period is in order. The Ministry of Labor carries out surveys of foreign manpower every three years. Only firms employing ten or more workers and belonging to the industrial and commercial private sector are surveyed. State services are reserved for French nationals. Foreigners are of course, active also in other enterprises not surveyed. Nonetheless, the Ministry of Labor survey covers approximately two thirds of all foreign workers in France. Table 7, reflecting data from recent surveys, shows that the number of employed foreigners decreased between 1973 and 1976 by some 135,000, that is by about 11 per cent, while the decline slowed down considerably thereafter, that is during the following three years the decline was about 30,000 workers or 2.7 per cent of the foreign labor force surveyed (Villey, 1981).

The small decrease registered between 1976 and 1979 is paralleled by the labor market behavior of French nationals whose employment decreased by 0.3 per cent. The decrease conceals structural changes in the employment situation. Whereas many jobs in industry and construction have disappeared, foreigners in particular registered an increase in employment in the service sector of 20.2 per cent. It appears, thus, that the return migrants who have left jobs in industry and construction were replaced *numerically* in other jobs by other foreigners in France who were entering the job market for the first time. The pool of potential workers are the spouses and children of foreigners as well as the incoming refugees who are more likely than not to find jobs in the service sector, e.g. hostelries and related, as well as industrial cleaning services.

The development of unemployment among foreigners in France

Aide au retour was set up with the official purpose of inducing, first the unemployed, and then all foreigners from non-EEC countries to return. The effectiveness of the program should be considered in the light of the overall unemployment statistics for the period in question, that is as of June, 1977. Table 8 offers a fairly clear overview of the unemployment situation in France between 1977 and 1981. It should be noted again that only non-EEC nationals were eligible to receive *aide au retour,* subject to various restrictions.

Two things stand out in Table 8. In the first place, the employment situation of non-EEC nationals deteriorated continuously all through the period in question. Specifically, the deterioration took place from the middle of 1977 to the middle of 1980 paralleling the similarly unattractive employment situation for all workers. During 1981, however, unemployment among non-EEC foreigners increased more rapidly than the unemployment among French nationals, by 38.9 per cent and 24.1 per cent respectively. It is difficult to link the more rapid increase of the non-EEC unemployment to the decline in aid to return. It bears repeating though that in spite of its modest results aid to return has helped to avoid an even greater disparity between the increase in the unemployment of foreigners and that of French nationals. The lack of interest in aid to return must be sought in other variables, like the relatively small

Table 6: Per cent distribution by nationality of the workers recruited for jobs vacated by returnees

Sector of activity	Replacement by			By occupational qualification	Replacement by		
	French nationals	Foreigners	Total		French nationals	Foreigners	Total
Primary sector	44	56	100	Unskilled workers	36	64	100
Secondary sector, of which:	47	53	100	Skilled workers	52	48	100
industry	57	43	100				
building & public works	30	70	100	Tradesmen	49	51	100
Tertiary sector	57	43	100	All together	49	51	100
All activities together	49	51	100				

Source: Office National d'Immigration.

sum offered which has remained unadjusted to inflation over the years, the progressive restrictions imposed as to eligibility and, particularly, the requirement that work and residence permits be surrendered to French authorities, with little hope of regaining them in the near future. Parenthetically, it should be noted that possibly due to the exclusion of Portuguese from the eligibility for aid to return, their unemployment has increased by 44.9 per cent compared to an unemployment increase of 38.9 per cent for the rest of the non-EEC foreigners during 1980 and 1981.

Table 7: Change in the number of employed foreigners by sector of activity, between 1973 and 1979* (in thousands and per cent)

Date	Industry	Building	Services	Together
October 1973	602.9	407.5	216.2	1,226.6
October 1976	540.1	333.3	217.8	1,091.2
October 1979	489.6	310.0	261.7	1,061.3
1973/1976	− 10.4	− 18.2	+ 0.7	− 11.0
1976/1979	− 9.4	− 7.0	+ 20.2	− 2.7
1973/1979	− 18.8	− 23.9	+ 21.0	− 13.5

* survey on foreign manpower

Source: Ministère du Travail.

Table 8: Unemployment by nationality (End-of-quarter
trend in job applications)

| Date | Non EEC foreigners | | EEC foreigners | French nationals |
	Number of unemployed	ratio 1	ratio 2	ratio 3
6.30.1977	93,456			
		+ 10.7	+ 8.5	+ 7.0
6.30.1978	103,464			
		+ 15.2	+ 11.6	+ 19.1
6.30.1979	119,206			
		+ 0.1	- 5.4	+ 5.8
6.30.1980	119,337			
		+ 38.9	+ 19.1	+ 24.1
6.30.1981	165,783			
change 6.30.1977/ 6.30.1981		+ 77.4	+ 36.6	+ 67.4

Ratios: Increase of the number from one year to the next of:
 — non EEC unemployed foreigners (ratio 1)
 — EEC unemployed nationals (ratio 2)
 — unemployed French nationals (ratio 3)

Source: Ministère du Travail.

Conclusions

The problem of specifically allocating a proper interpretation of population figures as related to population policies remains a very difficult one. For
instance, were one to project the population composition in France without
the contribution of the foreign nationals to its demographic structure, one
would find that France is much older demographically than is the case now.
But, then, the presence of foreign nationals is not likely to disappear in view
of the fact that the French population policy was favorable to immigration
for a long time. The temporary adjustments stemming from the market forces
which seem to demand that some unemployed nationals leave do not seem to
work nor do they fit into the overall demographic plan for the country. As

things stand, foreigners contribute to the reproduction of the country's population and they are also, in their majority, likely to stay. What is important to note, however, is the lesson we can perhaps draw from our juxtaposition of the recent governmental policies on return migration and from the actual situation of migration flows as they have developed. The extent to which the policies of return had any effect, can only be gauged from the data. The results are modest but nonetheless, slightly positive. The situation is perhaps, related to the situation in another important demographic process, namely that of fertility. Over the years and across different countries, variations in fertility were also variations in the age of implementing one's need to have children. So here too, those who were inclined to return may have accepted the additional financial and other incentives to do so earlier than anticipated, thus slightly modulating the stream and counterstream of migration for the time being. In the long run, one has to assume that a great majority of migrants will stay even though there were periods in French history as well as elsewhere where the flows and counterflows were fairly in balance.

Today, practically all European countries of immigration and others as well, are struggling with the notion of closing their borders. Such measures are more likely to discourage return flows than were there a possibility to return. Migratory traditions in the Mediterranean basin are old and stable and they nourish migration but also return migration. To what extent would one wish to tamper with such tradition remains to be seen.

RETURN MIGRATION IN FRANCE AND THE FRANCO-ALGERIAN AGREEMENT OF 1980

Catherine Wihtol de Wenden-Didier

The Franco-Algerian Agreement was signed in September, 1980. This Agreement, followed a few months later by the Franco-Senegalese Agreement went a long way to weaken the French "aid-to-return" legislation of May 30, 1977 (de Wenden, 1981). Finally, in June, 1981, after the national presidential elections and under a new Secretary of State for migration affairs, the policy encouraging return has been all but abandoned.

What these changes represent is, perhaps, nothing more than a modification of current policies and a political expediency, as a dramatic departure from a long standing immigration policy would be difficult to bring about. Here, we shall indicate some of the changes which are taking place in the French migration policy. The following are, perhaps, the most important. They reflect the philosophy that the French government does not see the return of foreigners as its main objective, despite the efforts in that direction in 1977 when return legislation was promulgated. In the first place, the anticipated replacement in jobs left vacant by French nationals does not seem to have occurred. Secondly, it became clear that any unilateral arrangement is unworkable in today's political climate so that bilateral agreements are essential. Thirdly, the highly controversial financial subsidy to those wishing to return was found discriminatory and addressing the "wrong" population. Finally, simple administrative provisions seem to be ineffective when considerations of primarily sociological variables of job training and reintegration in the home country have been omitted. Despite all this, return migration remains a viable and valuable option for foreigners in France but the decision to return must remain strictly voluntary (Briot and Verbunt, 1981: 84-85). It is in this context that a short overview of one bilateral agreement, the one between France and Algeria, should throw light on one aspect of return migration.

The presentation of the Agreement to the public

The results of the return migration policies of 1977 were indeed meager, in spite of the financial incentives provided. The desired quota of some 35,000 returnees per year had not been achieved as of May, 1981 (Cordeiro, 1981: 120-121). Between June 1, 1977 and January 1, 1981, only 2,604 Algerian

171

migrant workers had asked for aid to return, representing only about three per cent of the 86,000 or so, eligible (OECD-SOPEMI, 1981).

The Agreement was to address the issue of return indirectly, namely by providing mechanisms of return to those who so wished but also providing mechanisms for integration into the French society for the others. The French and the Algerian press carried extensive coverage of the Agreement, a number of excerpts from which follow as an illustration of what the goals of the Agreement were: "Point de départ d'un renouvellement et d'un développement de la coopération entre nos deux pays" (François-Poncet, September, 1980). "L'accord est un moment historique du dialogue Nord-Sud" (Stoléru, September, 1980). "La liberté de choix qui est laissée aux intéressés exclut toute forme de contrainte" (*El Moudjahid*, September 14, 1980). "Cet accord répond au bon sens économique qui permet, dans le cadre du respect humain, de soulager le marché de l'emploi en permettant la substitution de chômeurs français et étrangers aux postes de travail volontairement libérés" (Stoléru, September 18, 1980).

Of course, with presidential elections in full swing by May of 1981, the attractiveness of jobs vacated by returnees made the pre-accord migration policy irresistible to the incumbent party. It is therefore not surprising that financial incentives to return did not entirely disappear from the Agreement. The incentives to return were seen, however, after the presidential elections in June, 1981, only within the theme of cooperation, dialogue and freedom of choice for Algerians in France.

Again, the public utterances in the press echo the prevailing official sentiments by the parties to the Agreement. "La coopération... est une attitude commune des deux parties... Cet aspect particulier de la coopération ne peut être séparé de l'ensemble des domaines dans lesquels se déploie aujourd'hui la coopération bilatérale entre les pays concernés" (CCCE, 1981: 24). "La France entend proposer aux pays d'origine des accords bilatéraux définissant les conditions de travail, de séjour et de retour des travailleurs étrangers en France et des Français à l'étranger" (Mauroy, July 7, 1981). "Le problème de l'immigration ne peut être isolé de la politique de coopération de la France au développement des pays d'origine" (Conseil des Ministres, July 23, 1981). "Changer l'esprit de la politique dite de retour; sortir du faux dilemme: assimilation ou retour..." (Autain, August, 1981). Against the public utterances, however, we must look at the actual situation and the specific provisions the Agreement initiated.

Financial aid, occupational training, reintegration and aid to development

As of June, 1981, the mechanism of financial aid to returnees became sharply contested. A report commissioned by the Caisse Centrale de Coopération Economique defined the aid as "étrenne dérisoire au terme d'un exil souvent douloureux" and found that financial incentives to encourage return proved futile. The rapid fall in the number of departures between 1978 and 1980 from 36,359 to 14,509 can be explained by changes in the payment of the aid. The aid, first offered to nationals of 23 countries became progressively more restrictive to the point of becoming very rare. The primary beneficiaries were those nationals who were not threatened by deportation and whose status was not in doubt. Thus, the Spanish and the Portuguese represented two thirds of all beneficiaries.

The unilateral aspect of the aid involved neither a previous agreement with the sending countries nor a choice between the different possibilities for "organized" return for foreigners in France. Finally, in July, 1981 the *Cour des Comptes* criticized the current migration policy and, in August, Mr. Autain, the current Minister responsible for immigration, declared he was willing to suppress the aid altogether, as it had been formulated then.

On September 18, 1981, in the wake of the Franco-Algerian Agreement, Mrs. Questiaux, the Minister for National Solidarity, announced that financial aid to return would soon be paid in full in France, while prior to that, the payment prior to departure was only partial. This received full support of the Algerian government.

The report of the *Cour des Comptes* was also critical on another issue, that of occupational training (*formation-réinsertion*) of the potential returnees. Special concern was expressed about the delays in starting the program and when started, the difficulties in establishing its actual pay-off. Nevertheless, by June, 1981, close to 2,000 migrant workers in France had benefitted from vocational training to prepare them for re-integration in their home country (CCCE, 1981). At the present time (November, 1981), French government officials use the term training for re-integration (*formation-réinsertion*) in lieu of the earlier used term training for returnees (*formation-retour*). The new term emphasizes the qualitative aspects of the program which aims at real cooperation with developing countries.

In July, 1981, the French government seemed willing to abandon the idea of the pre-set 35,000 annual departures of foreigners and did propose instead, an organization of effective occupational training programs for Algerians in France and a grant of 320 million francs to develop vocational training programs in Algeria. The special needs of Algeria were to be met. A permanent Franco-Algerian Committee was set up as a result of the Agreement, and on September 18, 1980, the committee was charged with the implementation of training for re-integration and also with the placement of the trained returnees. Similarly, Algeria committed herself to provide jobs to all the beneficiaries of the training program. The aspirations of the program have, however, been much scaled down, from some 12,000 annually to the realistic 1,000 trainees annually. The length of training is no longer determined in advance. Still, the number of candidates for retraining remains very low. Of the 1,000 applications for return received from Algerians in France in less than half a year since May, 1981, only 30 have requested re-training.

In spite of the very modest result of the program, the French government has sought to make the program for integration via occupational training one of the main points of its migration return policy. The Ministry of National Solidarity announced an immediate implementation of training for re-integration, to take place in France as of September, 1981. There are signs that the program will ultimately work.

The second main goal of the new French migration policy dealing with return migration takes into account the interest of the country of origin and the personal needs of the returnee. This plan designed to aid small and medium size firms is presently under active consideration by the Algerian government. The project is to assist returnees by creating industrial and handicraft enterprises in Algeria by offering low interest, long term, loans guaranteeed both by the French and the Algerian government.

At the present time there is not enough evidence to judge the future of the project. A preliminary survey of Algerian applicants for aid to return, conducted by the Office National d'Immigration, shows a positive acceptance in general. The fact that only a small proportion of migrants replied to the questionnaire, makes the error of self-selection too large to ascribe any significance to these preliminary results.

All in all, the Franco-Algerian Agreement is an innovative instrument for the persistent issue of in-migration and the return of migrants. Whereas unilateral measures ran counter to the spirit of co-operation, bilateral agreements will go a long way to enable those who wish to return to do so and those who are not certain will stay in their host country for the time being.

RETURN MIGRATION FROM THE FEDERAL REPUBLIC OF GERMANY

Heiko Körner

German migration statistics reflect an intra-European migration dominated primarily by the pull effects of labor market conditions characterizing all the Northwest European countries (Böhning, 1980). The respective political actions of the Federal government up to the year 1973 coupled with a good economic performance in the Federal Republic Germany and the efforts on the part of the German Labor Market Administration to supplement spontaneous labor in-migration by a direct recruitment of workers abroad have produced heavy in-migration. During this "phase of liberal circulation of manpower in Europe" (OECD, 1978: 16), return migration was a primarily statistical phenomenon reflecting return flows as a proportion of the in-migration flow with a time lag.

The Federal Government decided to cut off recruitment of foreign workers as a direct result of the oil crisis in 1973. Subsequent legislation was aimed at limiting the proportion of foreigners in certain designated regions of Germany, mainly in the south, to a stipulated percentage of the current labor force and also at limiting work permits granted to children of foreign immigrants who had not been in the country prior to 1973. As a result of these measures, immigration was reduced sharply during the ensuing years. In the meantime, return migration proceeded as before so that for the first time in 1974 out-migration exceeded in-migration, actually diminishing the stock of foreigners in the country.

Between 1974 and 1977, the negative net immigration persisted but by 1978, the situation was reversed and the net immigration became positive again. There is no doubt that the decrease in return migration is at least partially a consequence of the recruitment stop of 1973. During the phase of liberal circulation of manpower each migrant returning home was free to re-enlist with the German Labor Commissions in his home country and to return to Germany to work. After the recruitment stop when free entry was granted only to European Community nationals and barred, for instance, to Turks, a departure from Germany became irreversible. Thus, a growing number of potential returnees ended up staying on in Germany, despite the fact that the labor market statistics show consistently higher unemployment rates for foreigners than for Germans from 1974 onward.

The resumption of the increase in the number of foreigners immigrating into Germany is attributable to political and humanitarian factors: during the

1970's there was an increasing number of entrants seeking and being granted political asylum and, a liberal interpretation of the principle of family reunification brought more family members to Germany. Partially, the second influx was brought about by the German regulation disallowing payment of children allowances (Kindergeld) to foreign workers whose children were living abroad (Mehrländer, 1978: 127). The effects of the family re-unification program are to be seen also in a widening disparity between the number of foreign residents and the number of foreign workers. The labor force participation rate of foreign residents fell markedly from 71 per cent in 1970 to 53 per cent in 1980. This is only temporary, though. From now on, an increasing number of migrants' children will be taking up employment in Germany. The "second generation" in substituting, at least partially, the manpower losses arising

Table 1: Federal Republic of Germany: migration of foreigners (1967-1980)

	Immigration	Emigration	Balance of migrat.
1967	330,298	527,894	- 197,596
1968	589,562	332,625	+ 256,937
1969	909,566	368,664	+ 540,902
1970	976,232	434,652	+ 541,580
1971	870,731	500,258	+ 370,479
1972	787,162	514,446	+ 272,716
1973	869,109	526,811	+ 342,298
1974	538,574	580,445	- 41,871
1975	366,095	600,105	- 234,010
1976	387,303	515,438	- 128,135
1977	422,845	452,093	- 29,248
1978	456,117	405,753	+ 50,364
1979	545,187	366,008	+ 179,179
1980*	631,400	385,800	+ 245,600

* provisional figures

Source: Statistisches Bundesamt: Statistisches Jahrbuch für die Bundesrepublik Deutschland, various issues, Stuttgart 1967 sq.

Table 1: Foreign residents and persons employed (1) in the Federal Republic of Germany 1967-1980 (2) (1000 pers.)

| Years | All foreigners | | | Selected nationalities | | | | | | | | | | | |
| | Resident Population Total | Population up to 15 years | Persons employed | Greeks | | Italians | | Yugoslavs | | Portuguese | | Spaniards | | Turks | |
				resid. pop.	pers. empl.	resid. pop.	pers. empl.	resid. pop.	pers. empl.	resid. pop.	pers. empl.	resid. pop.	pers. empl.	resid. pop.	pers. empl.
1967	1,806.7	-	991.3	201.0	140.3	412.8	266.8	140.6	95.7	24.0	17.8	177.0	118.0	172.4	131.3
1968	1,924.2	-	1,089.9	211.8	144.7	454.2	304.0	169.1	119.1	26.9	20.0	175.0	115.9	205.4	152.9
1969	2,381.1	-	1,501.4	271.3	191.2	514.6	349.0	331.6	265.0	37.5	29.5	206.9	143.1	322.4	244.3
1970	2,976.5	-	1,949.0	342.9	242.2	573.6	381.8	514.5	423.2	54.4	44.8	245.5	171.7	469.2	353.9
1971	3,438.7	-	2,240.8	394.9	268.7	589.8	408.0	594.3	474.3	75.2	58.4	270.4	186.6	652.8	453.1
1972	3,526.6	-	2,352.4	389.4	270.1	581.7	426.4	608.6	478.9	84.7	66.0	267.2	184.2	712.3	511.1
1973	3,966.2	603.9	2,595.0	407.6	250.0	630.7	450.0	701.6	535.0	112.0	85.0	287.0	190.0	910.5	605.0
1974	4,127.4	715.3	2,286.6	406.4	229.2	629.6	331.5	707.8	466.7	121.5	78.5	272.7	149.7	1,027.8	606.8
1975	4,089.6	809.3	2,038.8	390.5	196.2	601.4	292.4	677.9	415.9	118.5	68.3	247.4	124.5	1,077.1	543.3
1976	3,948.3	838.1	1,920.9	353.7	173.1	568.0	279.1	640.4	387.2	113.7	62.3	219.4	107.5	1,079.3	521.0
1977	3,948.3	868.2	1,869.5	328.5	155.5	570.8	283.3	630.0	373.7	111.0	59.7	201.4	97.2	1,118.0	508.6
1978	3,981.1	887.4	1,864.1	305.5	142.6	572.5	290.5	610.2	366.7	109.9	58.3	188.9	90.9	1,165.1	511.2
1979	4,143.8	937.4	1,947.5	296.8	136.1	594.4	304.3	620.6	363.6	109.8	58.5	182.2	88.9	1,268.3	542.1
1980	4,435.3	1,059.0	2,015.6	297.5	129.7	617.9	308.4	631.8	348.9	112.3	58.0	180.0	84.9	1,462.4	588.0

(1) persons employed liable to social insurance — (2) all data as of Sept. 30.

Source: Statistisches Bundesamt, Fachserie 1, Reihe 1.4: Ausländer, various issues, Stuttgart 1974 sq.
Bundesanstalt für Arbeit, ANBA Sonderhefte: Arbeitsstatistik-Jahreszahlen, Nürnberg 1976 sq.

Table 3: Unemployment of foreign workers in the Federal Republic of Germany 1970-1980

	1970	1971	1972	1973	1974	1975	1976	1977	1978	1979	1980
Unemployed, total (1000 pers.)	148.8	185.1	246.4	273.5	582.5	1,074.2	1,060.3	1,030.0	992.9	876.1	888.9
German workers	143.8	173.3	229.4	253.7	513.4	922.7	954.2	932.3	889.4	782.5	781.5
Foreign workers	5.0	11.8	17.0	19.8	69.1	151.5	106.1	97.7	103.5	93.5	107.4
Unemployment rate, total (per cent.)	0.7	0.8	1.1	1.2	2.6	4.7	4.6	4.5	4.3	3.8	3.8
German workers	0.7	0.8	1.1	1.2	2.5	4.6	4.7	4.2	4.0	3.4	3.4
Foreign workers	0.3	0.6	0.7	0.8	2.9	6.8	5.2	4.9	5.3	4.7	5.0

Sources: Bundesanstalt für Arbeit, ANBA Sonderheft: Arbeitsmarktstatistik 1980 - Jahreszahlen, Nürnberg 1981.

from return migration. The Deutsches Institut für Wirtschaftsforschung (1978) has forecast in 1978 that the stock of potential foreign workers will approach about two million persons in 1985. This number was reached, however, already in the year 1980. The restrictive policy regarding in-migration after 1973 did not seem to diminish the labor market pressures in Germany which are felt today. The ever increasing number of primarily young foreign workers is competing with Germans for the decreasing number of jobs available. The situation of foreign workers is complicated by the fact that they lack occupational training comparable to that of their German counterparts. A recent investigation showed that only 26 per cent of employed foreign workers were holding jobs requiring occupational training in industrial skills. The overwhelming majority had no training to speak of (Mehrländer et al., 1981: 138). The profile of the "second generation" does not differ much from that of their parents. The proportion of young foreigners without any vocational training currently employed in industrial jobs is about 75 per cent. This is not surprising since only 46 per cent of young foreigners succeeded in finishing their compulsory schooling by earning a school completion diploma (Mehrländer et al., 1981: 45). In the near future, the educational achievement of foreigners in Germany is not likely to improve (Körner, 1978). The disparity between the low skill levels of the abundant foreign labor force and the growing need to employ highly skilled personnel in German industrial production to meet the requirements of modern technology may prove disadvantageous to the German economy in the long run (Körner, 1981a).

German policies of return migration

The development of policy approaches vis-à-vis the problem of return migration reflects the changing socio-economic environment in Europe. During the phase of liberal circulation of manpower in Europe the majority of observers agreed that return migration was the logical consequence of a presumably temporary stay of migrant workers in the Northwest European industrialized countries. Under normal conditions, the sending countries were expected to benefit from migrants' savings, skills and experience gained abroad. The resulting economic development in the South of Europe then would enhance the attractiveness of return. Hence, neither the host nor the sending countries felt the need to develop specific policies to encourage return migration.

The oil crisis and its economic consequences brought about a fundamental re-assessment of the costs and benefits of worker migration (Stahl, 1982). In the sending countries there grew disillusionment with the results of return migration. Instead of the expected trickle effects of migration to speed up economic development there arose additional labor market and balance of payments deficit problems. These problems not only acted as a burden to the

Table 4: Foreign residents and labour force (1) in the Federal Republic of Germany 1961, 1970, 1974 - 1980

	1961	1970	1974	1975	1976	1977	1978	1979	1980
Resident population, total	56,175	60,651	62,061	61,886	61,542	61,420	61,321	61,315	61,516
Germans	55,489	58,212	58,039	57,863	57,672	57,551	57,394	57,254	57,186
foreigners	686	2,439	4,022	4,023	3,870	3,869	3,927	4,062	4,330
rate of foreigners (2)	1.2	4.0	6.5	6.5	6.3	6.3	6.4	6.6	7.0
Labour force, total	26,821	26,610	27,234	26,878	26,696	26,855	26,952	27,199	27,640
Germans	26,361	24,883	24,760	24,572	24,529	24,710	24,821	25,061	25,357
foreigners	461	1,727	2,474	2,306	2,167	2,146	2,131	2,138	2,283
rate of foreigners (2)	1.7	6.5	9.1	8.6	8.1	8.0	7.9	7.9	8.3
Labour force-participation, total	47.7	43.9	43.9	43.4	43.4	43.7	44.0	44.4	44.9
Germans	47.5	42.7	42.7	42.5	42.5	42.9	43.2	43.8	44.3
foreigners	67.1	70.8	61.5	57.3	56.0	55.5	54.3	52.6	52.7

(1) 1961: data from population census as of June 6th, 1961
1970: data from population census as of May 27th, 1970
1974-1980: all data from micro-census statistics as of April 30th.

(2) foreigners in per cent of total

Source: Statistisches Bundesamt, Fachserie 1 - Reihe A.6.1: Entwicklung der Erwerbstätigkeit, Stuttgart 1975 and corresponding years; Fachserie 1 — Reihe 4.1.1: Bevölkerung und Erwerbstätigkeit, Stuttgart 1977.

economies of the sending countries, but also the resulting slowdown of development tended to widen the gap of socio-economic opportunities in Europe, diminishing the attractiveness of return from abroad. The resulting stabilization of the foreign labor stock in the industrialized countries combined with the effects of family re-unification programs coincided with increasing unemployment in the host countries. Thus, the previously large benefits of imported labor tended to disappear while the social and economic costs of a large number of foreign residents became more and more apparent. The response of the German authorities to this new situation was a moderate one (Unger, 1980; Weidacher, 1981). Under the label of *Konsolidierungspolitik*, the number of foreigners in the country was to be stabilized by disallowing additional worker immigration and by promoting return migration. The latter was to be encouraged by generating jobs and investment opportunities in the sending countries. On the other hand, those foreign workers and their families opting for a prolonged stay in Germany were to be given all possible assistance allowing them to become integrated in the country, both economically and socially.

In 1980, the German Federal government proposed three main guidelines to implement the new thrust in dealing with the issue of foreigners (Bundesrepulik Deutschland 1980). 1) Opportunities were to be created for young foreigners in the country to have equal treatment in their search for employment, in their access to schools and in their participation in the social life in Germany without forfeiting their national and cultural identify. 2) No new adult foreign workers were to be accepted into the employment market, excepting, of course, nationals of the European Economic Community and others specifically exempted. Finally, 3) potential return migrants were to be strongly supported by assisting their various self-help undertakings.

Underlying these guidelines was the principle of voluntariness. No foreign migrant is obliged to participate in schemes for social integration (with the exception of those underlying the school attendance legislation) and there is no official pressure to return to one's country. Actually, the Federal Republic has no legal means to enforce return migration be it to relieve its own unemployment situation or to assist some countries wishing to entice their own nationals to return.

Early instances of policies favoring return emerged already in the 1960's (Entzinger, 1978; Werth and Yalçintas, 1978). Bilateral agreements were concluded with a few countries where workers were recruited, particularly with Italy, to set up vocational training courses potential returnees could benefit from. These efforts were, however, fairly sporadic. A more systematic effort concerning Turkish in-migrants became the basis of the Ankara Agreement of 1972. This Agreement between the German and the Turkish governments provided for vocational and lower management training courses aimed at the semi-skilled Turkish workers in Germany who intended to return home. It was hoped that the up-grading of abilities would enable the return migrants to meet the needs of the Turkish economy for skilled industrial personnel.

Most of the needed financing for the program was contributed by the German government, the rest by the Turkish government. A special fund was created to be administered by the *Turkiye Halk Bankasi* (Turkish People's Bank) which in turn offered soft loans and advice on a consulting basis to returnees setting up an enterprise in Turkey.

In spite of the widespread publicity the training courses received, only a few of Turkish migrants showed any interest in them and only a small number of participants actually returned home. The reasons for it are to be sought in the prevailing prosperity in Germany which absorbed the trained Turks very quickly. The co-operation between Turkish and German authorities proved not to be very fruitful in this respect. The financial credit and the consultancy arrangements were difficult to translate into reality due to the cumbersome administrative procedures and the remarkable lack of enthusiasm particularly on the part of the Turkish government.

Better results emerged from the German-Korean Program to repatriate Korean workers. This program was based on an agreement between the Office of Labor Affairs of the Republic of Korea and the German *Bundesministerium für Wirtschafliche Zusammenarbeit* (BMZ : Ministry for Economic Co-operation) in 1975. According to this program, Korean migrant workers willing to return home were to be trained as instructors for metal and electrical machinery industries, as factory foremen and as foreign language secretaries. The training courses in Germany are complementary to training programs in Korea where modern centers for vocational training were set up with the help of the Federal Republic. Thus, the courses offered in Germany can be designed with regard to the structure of the Korean labor market and the local needs for industrial development. Moreover, the Korean Administration of Labor Affairs was charged with channeling the qualified returnees into adequate work places in Korean industry or in the training centers themselves. Additional opportunities are open for return migrants wishing to establish small scale industries.

A new impetus for the Turkish-German re-integration program arose from the coming into existence of Turkish workers companies (Günce, 1978; Penninx and van Renselaar, 1978). The first workers' joint stock company, *Turksan*, was created in 1965 by Turkish workers in Germany as a result of private initiative of Turkish intellectuals living in Cologne. Afterwards, the development of other self-help organizations gained momentum. Turkish workers' companies began to mushroom in Northwest Europe after 1970, especially in Germany. Despite the slow growth of most of such companies, the idea of being able to create one's own work places by investing in small scale industries and managing them became popular among Turkish migrant workers. It is estimated that during the mid-1970's at least one in ten Turkish workers in Germany was shareholder in at least one such company. More recent figures show even better results.

The BMZ began to support Turkish workers' companies as part of its policy to link return migration to the economic development in Turkey. In

1974, it undertook two broad programs: first, it encouraged the various workers' companies already in existence to form a federation to strengthen the voice of the Turkish constituency. The Federation's major tasks were legal and economic counselling of the enterprises as well as training workers and managers to be. Second, the Ministry commissioned a private German consulting firm, ISOPLAN in Saarbrücken, to undertake the economic and technical counselling and the overseeing of those companies' investment plans, the financing of which was sufficiently underway to be considered by the Ministry for support. The activities of ISOPLAN covered feasibility studies, business consulting, management promotion and location of experts to operate the enterprises in Turkey. Due to some difficulties in dealing directly with the Federation of Turkish Workers' Companies, the Ministry began to channel its financial support to the Federation through ISOPLAN as of 1978.

Negotiations between the German and the Turkish authorities brought resumption of the financial aid which was then channeled through the *Turkiye Halk Bankasi*. In 1976, a special credit fund had been created with the provision that both the Turkish and the German governments participate half and half in the Bank's capital endowment. The Turkish workers' companies became heavily dependent on governmental and private credits which implied heavy debt servicing commitments. The German Ministry had to extend financial aid to the companies to help them in servicing their debts. The Turkish government offered financial incentives to the workers' companies as well, particularly exemption from taxes, accelerated depreciation allowances and exemption from import duties on imported machinery.

During the years 1977 through 1980, the German government through the BMZ allotted some eight million DM to consulting and management training programs in Germany; another twenty million DM were channeled into a special credit fund jointly created by Turkey and Germany to subsidize the workers' companies. During this time, the number of workers' companies actually in operation rose with increasing momentum.

The example of the German-Turkish co-operation created interest among other foreigners' groups in Germany. The Greeks in particular were eager to have a similar program. In 1978, a federation of Greek workers' associations was created with the backing of the *Diakonisches Werk* of German Protestant churches. By the end of 1980, five Greek workers' companies were started in Greece and several others were in the planning stage. The BMZ designated about 3 million DM to this program. The Greek government concluded an agreement with the German government in 1980, technical and financial provisions of which paralleled the Turkish-German program.

German policies to induce return migration and re-integration at home by supporting foreign workers self-help organizations can best be described as learning by doing. In order to underline the voluntary character of return migration, any consideration of lump sum payments to would-be returnees, as it was instituted in France for instance, has, up to now (1983) never been seriously considered by the Federal government. Moreover, no central agency had been created to deal with return migration. The dealings with the individual workers' associations or national groups were made through social institutions like churches or the *Deutscher Gewerkschaftsbund* (Labor Federation). The aid program concentrated exclusively on individual projects tutored by private agencies. Government to government co-operation was thus reduced to channeling financial assistance to the sending countries and to outlining the ultimate responsibility and supervision of the program. The BMZ has the ultimate responsibility for planning and financing the various aid programs. The Ministry is also responsible for the co-ordination of activities with other Federal ministries, the authorities in the sending countries and the international organizations such as the ICEM (Intergovernmental Committee for European Migration).

The execution of the programs falls to the responsibility of the *Zentralstelle für Arbeitsvermittlung* (ZAV, Central Labor Exchange) of the *Bundesanstalt für Arbeit* (Federal Labor Agency). The ZAV has had a long standing involvement in the problems of return to their home countries of foreign specialists, scholars and other highly skilled personnel. In 1980, the ZAV together with the *Gesellschaft für Technische Zusammenarbeit* (Technical Co-operation Corporation) formed an integrated organization named *Centrum für Internationale Migration und Entwicklung* (Center for international migration and development) which is to act as the central agent for all return migration and re-integration activities of foreigners in programs directly supported by the Federal government. The activities of the Center are (a) to support self-help organizations of migrant workers and foreigner experts with a view toward their return home; (b) to support creation of jobs in developing countries, especially by providing technical and economic advice; (c) to extend vocational training to migrant workers who wish one; (d) to maximize contacts between potential employers in Third World countries and foreign workers willing to relocate from Germany; and finally, (e) to organize the appointment of German experts to assist with the operation of migrant workers' projects in their home countries. The technical and economic consulting and progress evaluation remains in the hands of individual private agencies which act as agents for the center, maintaining thus the decentralization typical of the German approach to the complex issue of return migration.

Evaluation of return policies

The return migration policies of the Federal Republic are anchored in the premise of support to individual self-help organizations of potential return migrants. The main instrument of such policies is counselling and financial aid channeled through a private independent agency. Thus far, the policies came to a test primarily in the Turkish workers' companies case. In 1980, there were 98 such fully operating companies and 109 companies were either in the planning stage or just beginning operation (Werth, 1981; Jurecka and Werth, 1980). The funds invested in these companies since 1972 are about 600 million DM. The companies in operation have created some 9,600 new jobs. Only 10 per cent of the jobs went to returnees, but the employment spin-off is estimated at some 45,000 to 50,000 jobs. This record is actually quite modest when considered against the background of Turkish return migration. Return migration to Turkey from Germany between 1972 through 1979 amounted to some 745,000 persons and their savings transferred back to Turkey have amounted to some 15 billion DM between 1972 and 1978. The unemployed population in Turkey is now about 2.2 million.

The only moderate performance record of the Turkish workers' companies can be explained by two main circumstances (Bahadir, 1978). In the first place, the Turkish workers' associations in Germany were not always reliable partners to negotiations either with the individual Turkish workers or with the German agencies. In the second place, the Turkish government and its agencies proved unable to give full support to the workers' companies. The rank and file bureaucrats in Turkey were un-cooperative and the complexity of administrative procedures to handle foreign trade and finance has created seemingly insurmountable problems. Thus, the developmental effect of the workers' companies must be described as very slight. The trickle down effect of development is not apparent. The one merit of the Turkish workers' companies can be seen in the experience gained by creating small scale companies in a developing economy.

Such a state of affairs should be interpreted as the result of the German policies supporting return migration on an individual or, at most, associational level. Not connected with measures geared for regional or national development, the Turkish-German program did not succeed in closing the gap in social and economic opportunities between the two countries. This gap still plays a major role in Turkish migration to Germany; for instance, most shareholders of the Turkish workers' companies tend to remain in Germany. Their stay is longer than originally intended. A recent survey of foreign workers in Germany shows only 30 per cent of the respondents as having had plans originally to stay longer than five years, but it also shows some 76 per cent of respondents who have been in the country for more than five years (Korte, 1980). A return home is envisaged usually only under pressure of personal reasons.

The question remains whether official return and re-integration programs should rely solely on addressing individual needs or needs of interest groups. Proposals to the OECD as well as to the Federal government have been made repeatedly to undertake complementary programs towards regional development in the main out-migration areas using the technical and financial resources of the Federal Republic (Baucić, n.d.; Körner, 1981b). Although good theoretical reasons underlie such proposals (Hiemenz and Schatz, 1979), the

Federal government as yet has not reacted positively to them mainly so as not to appear admitting any formal obligations to recompense the sending countries for their outflow of manpower.

Inasmuch as the success of the workers' companies depends rather heavily on the overall development of their region, it would seen advisable to supplement the individual level efforts with regional and national level efforts requiring, naturally, greater and more direct intergovernmental co-operation.

DILEMMAS OF SWEDISH IMMIGRATION POLICY: THEY WERE INVITED TO STAY PERMANENTLY. - DO THEY WANT TO RETURN?

Tomas Hammar

Return migration from Sweden

Emigration of foreign citizens is not equivalent to return migration from Sweden since there is a small number of naturalized Swedish citizens born abroad who return to their country of origin and among the foreign citizens who leave the country a number were born in Sweden. When plotted, the emigration curve can be used as a lagged approximation of the return curve, since a major part of return migration takes place a few years after immigration, however, and it has often been concluded that return migration from Sweden has been influenced less by changes in the employment situation in the country than immigration to Sweden. Economic booms and recessions in Sweden have, in other words, not exercised a substantial impact on the rate of return.

The propensity to return varies with sex and age. Women have lower return rates than men, and the highest return rate is found among men 20-35 years old. Most people who immigrate to Sweden are at this age.

In Table 1 both absolute and relative figures are given for return immigration for each year 1968 through 1977. Out of a total of about 32,850 foreign citizens who immigrated in 1968, almost 50 per cent or about 15,750 persons had returned ten years later. The number of returnees was high during the first three years but fell every year afterwards. The same trends are shown by each of the following immigrant cohorts, those of 1969, 1970, etc. The final total for return seems to approach but not to exceed half of the original immigrant group.

Many of those who returned to their country of origin did not stay there, however, but re-immigrated once again to Sweden. We do not know the size of this return for all immigrants, only for some of them. Table 2 shows the re-immigration of Yugoslavs, 1968 through 1978 by year of return to Yugoslavia. For instance, in 1968, 2,264 Yugoslavs immigrated to Sweden and 944 Yugoslavs returned to Yugoslavia. Ten years later 214 of them or 23 per cent returned to Sweden again. During the same decade the Yugoslav return rate was about 25 per cent, far below the average figure for about 50 per cent of all immigrants (Table 3).

Table 1: Return migration from Sweden, by sex and year of immigration,
1968-1977 (1) - Proportion male in ( )

Year of emigration	Year of immigration									
	1968	1969	1970	1971	1972	1973	1974	1975	1976	1977
1968	1,294 (51)									
1969	3,025 (52)	2,142 (62)								
1970	2,199 (55)	6,007 (58)	4,930 (67)							
1971	2,296 (54)	5,539 (59)	10,384 (60)	3,248 (62)						
1972	2,293 (58)	5,097 (60)	6,542 (60)	5,364 (55)	1,822 (55)					
1973	1,982 (59)	4,107 (60)	5,175 (59)	3,627 (58)	3,853 (57)	1,696 (57)				
1974	1,028 (57)	2,324 (58)	2,813 (58)	1,950 (56)	1,944 (59)	3,144 (56)	1,524 (56)			
1975	726 (57)	1,378 (58)	2,002 (57)	1,473 (54)	1,410 (56)	1,953 (57)	4,477 (60)	3,351 (67)		
1976	629 (55)	1,112 (62)	1,323 (59)	1,177 (54)	1,032 (55)	1,351 (56)	2,625 (57)	5,068 (61)	1,770 (58)	
1977	289 (54)	498 (57)	719 (57)	661 (54)	531 (56)	675 (56)	1,514 (56)	2,853 (57)	3,841 (58)	1,809 (54)
Total	15,761 (55)	28,204 (59)	33,888 (60)	17,500 (57)	10,592 (56)	8,819 (56)	10,140 (60)	11,272 (62)	5,611 (58)	1,809 (56)

(1) A small number of Swedish citizens, mostly naturalized, is included.

Source: SOS, 1977: 175.

Table 2: Return immigration of Yugoslav citizens to Sweden

Year of emigr. from Sweden		Year of immigration to Sweden											Total
		1968	1969	1970	1971	1972	1973	1974	1975	1976	1977	1978	
1968	944	56	83	36	20	4	2	5	5	1	2	0	214
1969	712		60	72	21	10	4	1	7	1	1	1	178
1970	800			45	82	16	10	8	5	4	4	2	176
1971	1,345				63	91	40	19	13	8	1	2	237
1972	1,901					93	159	62	44	20	18	5	401
1973	2,166						119	162	70	37	35	6	429
1974	1,237							93	134	52	17	13	309
1975	1,305								52	144	50	21	267
1976	1,023									63	85	31	179
1977	660										41	43	84
1978	943											73	73

Source: The National Central Bureau of Statistics, Stockholm.

Table 3: Re-emigration of Yugoslav citizens from Sweden, 1968-1978

Year of immigr. to Sweden	Year of emigration from Sweden											Total
	1968	1969	1970	1971	1972	1973	1974	1975	1976	1977	1978	
1968 (2,264)	48	70	49	87	86	86	42	51	37	24	22	602
1969 (3,596)		26	124	152	166	182	80	94	64	23	34	945
1970 (8,812)			122	342	404	469	249	257	214	84	141	2,282
1971 (4,836)				155	226	263	179	199	170	81	84	1,357
1972 (1,649)					44	81	61	83	59	29	38	395
1973 (1,237)						21	36	51	42	22	31	203
1974 (1,370)							21	66	67	27	45	226
1975 (1,384)								26	28	28	56	138
1976 (1,278)									13	36	52	101
1977 (1,283)										13	39	52
1978 (935)											18	18

Source: National Central Bureau of Statistics, Stockholm.

Only those who returned are included in the figures in Table 4. In absolute numbers, twice as many went back to Finland in 1974 than in 1977. The main reason for this is that immigration to Sweden from Finland had been much higher in 1970 and 1971 than in 1973 and 1974. The return in 1974 included many more Finns who had stayed long in Sweden before they returned; 42.5 per cent of those who left Sweden in 1974 had been more than 4 years in Sweden. In 1977 the corresponding figure was 30.1 per cent. In 1974, 23.1 per cent left during the first two years. In 1977, the return after a short stay in Sweden had risen quickly, to 54.9 per cent.

After a short stay in Finland, some returnees decide to re-immigrate to Sweden again. The differences shown for the years 1974-1977 (Table 5) may

Table 4: Return migration of Finnish citizens to Finland
in 1974-1977 by duration of stay in Sweden

Duration of stay in Sweden	1974	1975	1976	1977
< 1 year	13.3	21.3	25.3	37.0
> 1 year	9.8	10.1	13.4	17.9
> 2 years	6.2	6.1	5.9	8.2
> 3 years	11.8	5.4	4.4	4.0
> 4 years	16.5	9.9	3.9	2.8
5-10 years	10.4	19.7	23.9	14.8
Return migration < 10 years	67.9	72.6	76.7	84.7
Born in Sweden or immigrated before 1968	32.1	27.4	23.2	15.3
Total	100.0	100.0	100.0	100.0
Numbers	11,205	7,969	6,505	5,345

Source: SOS 1977, 177.

Table 5: Re-immigration and immigration to Sweden of
Finnish citizens by duration of stay in Sweden

Duration of stay in Sweden	1974	1975	1976	1977
< 1 year	14.9	9.0	6.2	5.6
> 1 year	9.0	7.1	4.8	3.1
> 2 years	4.9	5.2	3.9	2.3
> 3 years	2.9	3.6	3.7	2.2
> 4 years	0.8	2.6	2.6	2.4
5-10 years	0.5	1.4	3.4	4.3
Re-immigration				
< 10 years	32.9	92.0	24.6	19.9
> 10 years or born in Sweden	67.1	71.0	75.4	80.1
Total	100.0	100.0	100.0	100.0
Numbers	9,672	12,212	15,800	14,900

Source: SOS 1977, 176.

be explained by the very large immigration that took place in 1969 and 1970. The waves of return and then of re-immigration are seen in the higher percentage of re-immigration in 1974 and 1975. Of all immigrants from Finland to Sweden in 1977 about 20 per cent were repeat migrants. A small number of persons in fact are recorded for three or four immigrations and returns, but we must recall that Swedish statistics include only recorded migrations and that repeated and short term movements often are not officially recorded.

The Finnish return migration in 1977 took place after a much shorter stay than the Greek and Yugoslav return migration (Table 6). Among all returnees to Greece and Yugoslavia that year less than 25 per cent had only four years residence in Sweden. This indicates that there exist inherent differences between Nordic and non-Nordic migration, even if it is also true that a part of the explanation may be found in the fact that immigration from Greece and Yugoslavia was strong during a period from 1965 to 1967, but never again reached the same volume.

Table 6: Return migration in 1977 by duration of stay and citizenship

Duration of stay in Sweden	Finland	Greece	Yugoslavia
< 1 year	37.0	4.1	4.6
> 1 year	17.9	3.4	4.1
> 2 years	8.2	5.2	4.2
> 3 years	4.0	5.3	3.9
> 4 years	2.8	4.3	4.1
> 5 years	2.2	8.1	6.5
6-7 years	9.0	18.6	22.6
8-9 years	3.6	4.7	5.5
Return			
< 10 years	84.7	53.8	55.5
Born in Sweden or immigrated before 1968	15.3	46.2	44.5
Total	100.0	100.0	100.0
Numbers	5,345	677	660

Source: SOS 1977, 177 ff.

Swedish immigration policy and return

Sweden has become well known as a country of immigration with enlightened policies. For instance, Swedish language courses have been free since 1965 and, since 1972, such classes take place during paid working hours. Immigrant foreigners have voting rights and are eligible to stand for office in local elections if they have resided legally in the country for three consecutive years. National associations of immigrants are supported financially by the state, and local communities provide immigrant associations with meeting places. Unemployed immigrants are entitled to the same public labor market service as are Swedish citizens, their social benefits are the same as for Swedes, etc. Immigrants are organized in trade unions to the same very high extent as are their Swedish workmates: more than 90 per cent of blue-collar and more than 75 per cent of white-collar workers are unionized.

Generous immigrant policy has one absolute prerequisite, which is that immigration be strictly controlled. The number of persons admitted to Sweden from countries outside the Nordic labor market is decided on the basis of what is good for Sweden and for all its inhabitants, including those who are not yet Swedish citizens. Labor immigration from non-Nordic countries has been reduced to a small number of experts who are needed in Sweden. Family reunification is permitted, however, and political refugees are granted asylum or admitted to Sweden from the world's refugee camps on the basis of a quota of about 1,250 persons a year. The composition of present immigration to Sweden can be seen from Table 7 including figures from 1979.

Table 7: Immigration to Sweden 1979, by categories of admission

	N	per cent
Non-Nordic Immigration		
Adopted children	1,300	4
Refugees	3,650	11
Family reunion	9,000	28
Labor immigration	1,450	5
Guest students	800	2
Total outside Nordic area	16,200	50
Immigration from Nordic countries	16,200	50
TOTAL	32,400	100

Source: SCB 1981, 15.

194

To understand return migration from Sweden it is important to know a little about the regulation of immigration into the country. The Nordic labor market agreement of 1954 was renewed and somewhat modified in 1982. According to this agreement, Finnish citizens may take up employment and residence in Sweden without any permits. Through special agreements, the public employment service offices of both countries have been instructed to cooperate in order to prevent unnecessary migration; Swedish enterprises have undertaken to use employment offices instead of directly recruiting in Finland. There are no obstacles, however, for individual Finns to go directly to Sweden and to seek a job there, and in most cases this is the way it is done. The number of Finns in Sweden is so high that the unofficial, personal paths to a job in Sweden are innumerable.

A non-Nordic migrant's scenario

A Yugoslav, a Turk, or a Greek worker who would like to join a friend or distant relative working in Sweden must apply for a work permit before arrival in Sweden. Such a permit is not given to anyone who applies after arrival in the country, and since 1981 the same is true also for residence permits. Let us now say that this job-seeker is successful and gets his permits. He is then one of the extremely few persons who obtain a new permit. But with a work permit for one year in his hand, he can be rather certain that his permits will be renewed the next year and also extended in such a way that they will be valid for any job in Sweden and not only for one kind of industry. He may obtain a permanent permit after the first year, both for residence and for work in Sweden. Let us now say that this immigrant wants to return to his country of origin, but perhaps not for good; he may not yet be quite sure, but wants to see what job opportunities he has back home. He might then depart without giving notice to the Swedish population register that he is leaving definitely, i.e. for more than a year.

Though this imagined person in fact returns to his country of origin, he may in this case not return according to Swedish official records or statistics. If he is skilled in managing his personal bookkeeping with the Swedish population officers he can stay in this same position for a long time. He may work in his country of origin or somewhere else, but according to the Swedish registers he resides in Sweden. And if one day he finds, as is often the case, that he would like to immigrate again to Sweden, he will have no problem doing so because he will have all the necessary permits and he will not, of course, be counted as an immigrant. It is even conceivable that he apply for Swedish citizenship on the basis of the length of his legal stay in Sweden, the required five years.

Since it is very hard to obtain a permit of immigration, a strong incentive exists for unregistered return migration. Swedish regulation covers only non-Nordic immigration. This means that Finns, Norwegians, and Danes do not have the same incentive not to report their movements in and out of Sweden. They may forget or they may not care to register their movements for other reasons. Such differences should be kept in mind when dealing with statistics on Swedish return migration.

Immigration policy and return migration

Swedish immigration policy combines strict regulation of immigration with generous provisions aiming at equal socio-economic conditions for immigrants and Swedes. When this policy was initiated in the 1960's, official terminology was changed. The word "utlanning" (foreigner) which had come to have a negative connotation, was replaced with the word "invandrare" (immigrant). For example, the National Board for Immigration Control was called "Staten "Statens utlanningskommission" up until 1969; its successor was named "Statens Invandrarverk". But after a while even the word "immigrant" lost part of the inviting ring. Moreover, the word has a very broad meaning. It includes all foreign citizens and all Swedish citizens born abroad and sometimes it is even used to refer to their children born in Sweden. One consequence of this usage is that people who have no intention of remaining in Sweden often find themselves cast in an "immigrant" role. Another consequence is that Swedes are made to believe that every resident foreign citizen plans to stay for good, which of course is not the case.

The terminology was adjusted to policy, but words can influence thinking and policy making. We shall give examples from some sectors of immigrant policy, starting with education for children of immigrants.

Thanks to a reform in education in 1977 all children "from homes in which another language than Swedish is in active use" are entitled to instruction in their language. About 500 million SwCr ($100 million US) were used in 1981-82 to implement this principle and about 50,000 children are taking part in "mother-tongue" instruction in schools all over Sweden. However, most children receive very few hours per week, though there is a growing interest in using available resources for mother-tongue classes. In such classes all instruction is given in the mother-tongue and Swedish is taught as the first foreign language. This has created a demand that all-Finnish schools be es-established in places where there are numerous Finnish speaking children.

The general policy aim is a multicultural society in which ethnic groups can develop their language and culture, and socialize their children into this culture and teach them the language. Schools are asked to assist with this process, but they must at the same time prepare immigrant children for the Swedish labor market, teach them Swedish, and give them a good vocational training. "Active bilingualism" is the term often used to denote the goal of this school policy.

It may be too early to evaluate the outcome. In 1981 the reform started in its 4th school year and, far from being implemented in the same manner everywhere, local schools show very different interest in immigrant education and use widely varying models of education. This much can be said, however: all agree that most immigrant children only get two hours per week of instruction in their mother-tongue and this is absolutely insufficient. Children who already know a great deal cannot develop their language further, while those who know only a little can hardly learn more. Good progress both in mother-tongue and in Swedish is found only in mother-tongue classes. The number of such classes is increasing rapidly.

Schooling in mother-tongue has a number of consequences for return migration: First, language training has up to now been insufficient for children who transfer to schools in the country of origin. They are not able to follow classes without preparatory instruction, either organized in Sweden by their parents (e.g. Greeks) or — which is rare — organized after arrival in the new school. The new mother-tongue classes (at present about 10 per cent of all immigrant education) will give much better preparation for a possible return. It is still too early, however, to evaluate their results. Even if an active bilingualism is achieved, this will not necessarily imply increased return migration. Immigrant children will learn Swedish and they will get Swedish vocational training, which might make them stay in Sweden, although their language skills will open up for them the option of return.

The improved schooling may reduce the rate of return since parents may be less inclined to go back in order to insure their children's education. Up to now many parents have returned before the start of school, or in some cases before the start of the 4th or 5th school year, which is considered especially crucial in Turkey, for example. Many Greek parents have sent their children to grandparents or relatives in Greece, while continuing to work in Sweden. This may also change if classes in Greek are available to the children and, if so, return migration might diminish.

The propensity to return may also be influenced by the Swedish policy of encouraging immigrants to organize themselves as national associations and in the long run to form immigrant minorities of Sweden-Finns, Sweden-Greeks, Sweden-Turks, etc. Two principles are inherent in this policy, the freedom to choose one's cultural identity as well as the idea of partnership. Minorities need a number of basic resources in order to cope with problems of cultural activities in a group numbering only a few thousand persons. They must organize themselves and elect their own representatives, for only then the leaders of the majority listen to their demands.

All major immigrant groups have accepted these principles and have organized themselves as local associations and national federations. They have even started two confederations, each consisting of six associations, in order to increase their negotiating power. They get financial support for their organizations as well as for their periodicals. They are called upon to give advice in several councils, and they have access to the Swedish legislative procedures in the same way as have other "interest groups".

Now, what might be of importance for return migration is first of all the extent to which immigrants take an active part in these organizations. If they do, then this may help preserve their cultural ties to the old country and also bring the second generation into the minority group. But it is not certain that this would also lead to more return migration; it might have the opposite effect if the ethnic associations can offer at least part of the things that many of their members feel are lacking.

In the same way, lower return migration can be expected the more the socio-economic position of immigrants is improved. The strong labor unions in Sweden have never accepted anything less than equality in wages and working conditions for all employees. This has not meant that immigrant workers have had the same jobs as the average Swedish worker, but instead that they have had the same job as a Swede employed for the same period of time. Newcomers more often have routine jobs, more monotonous and heavier and riskier, and all of this is true for immigrants during their first years. But they also improve their work positions, though this mobility comes slower for them than for Swedes.

Relatively good working conditions reduce the incentive to return. This has sometimes been a policy dilemma for some emigration countries, which maintain that their workers are temporarily abroad. If the working conditions, housing standards, etc. offered to their workers are too good, there is an increased risk that they will eventually stay.

Sweden has both facilitated naturalization and has granted foreign citizens voting rights. These two measures are in a way the most explicit expressions of the idea that immigrants living in Sweden will not return. After five years in Sweden they are entitled to full citizenship and after only three years they automatically receive full political rights on the local and regional level.

These provisions have resulted in increased interest in the Swedish society and polity by immigrants who are learning more about the functioning of the system and political issues at stake. They become members of political parties, are elected representatives, etc. Of course, this is an integration into the political system which first of all involves those who were already integrated before, i.e. who had lived long in Sweden, were married to Swedes, knew the language well, etc. But the effects spread to those among their compatriots who were not so well integrated, and there is little doubt that especially the political rights granted to immigrants may bring them closer to Sweden and further away from their countries of origin. This is thus one more instance where Swedish immigration policy may impede return migration.

Measures to facilitate return

Actually very little has been done to assist immigrants who want to return. Some steps have been taken, however. Agreements have been concluded between Sweden and several sending countries concerning old age pensions, unemployment benefits, child allowances, and so on for persons and families who return. There has been up to now no vocational training in Sweden especially aimed at those who want to return. Such courses are to be started on a experimental basis. Workers facing lay-offs or termination have recently been given the chance to get full wages while looking around for other jobs. The National Labor Board has decided, for example, that Finns affected by unemployment in Sweden will be allowed to look for jobs in Finland on the same terms. Remittances to dependents in the country of origin may be partially deducted from the taxable income in Sweden.

Table 8: Immigration to and emigration from Sweden 1968-1977
by country of citizenship

Country by citizenship	Immigration	Emigration	Emigration in per cent of immigrants
Finland	185,497	105,782	57.0
Yugoslavia	27,694	11,709	42.3
Greece	15,261	8,501	55.7
Turkey	10,823	1,883	17.4
Italy	3,032	5,160	170.2
Poland	9,443	1,029	10.9

Source: SOS 1977.

Conclusions

This paper dealt with two problems. One is the relation of immigrant policy to return migration. The argument is that it is very likely that many Southern Europeans would have returned, had they not been offered reasonable socio-economic conditions. It has been shown that very few measures have been taken to give direct assistance to those who want to return.

The other problem refers to the question whether Nordic return rates are higher than non-Nordic, as a consequence of the free circulation in the Nordic area. The common labor market might mean that Nordic citizens in Sweden enjoy even more of a generous policy than other immigrants to Sweden, and therefore would be more likely to stay. The geographical distance is short in the Nordic area, and the strict regulations of non-Nordic immigration makes return less tempting for non-Nordic immigrants.

For Turkey and Poland return migration has been only a small proportion of immigration to Sweden. For Yugoslavia and Greece this proportion amounts to about 50 per cent. It is a little higher for Finland but not as much as could have been expected according to our assumptions. Return migration was 170 per cent of immigrants from Italy during this ten-year period. The reason for this is that immigration from Italy started much earlier than immigration from other countries. The proportion for Turks is low exactly for the reason that large scale immigration came about only in 1976 and 1977. The low return migration of Poles is understandable. The statistics that are available give some weak support to the idea that limiting immigration also limits return migration.

The rate of return migration is by far more significant than might have been expected in the case of Sweden. Immigrants to Sweden are almost guaranteed a permanent stay in the country, once they have received their first labor and residence permits. Furthermore, they are given access to work and living conditions equal to those of the indigenous population. But they tend anyhow to return about as often as do their compatriots in other European immigration countries.

Is there a gap between policy and reality in Sweden that can help us explain this, or does policy not play the role that is expected here? A tentative answer is that immigration policy does not have a strong impact on the rate of return, so that other factors must be invoked to explain the outcome. Most immigrants initially want to return, for many this becomes an illusion, and for some it becomes a reality. The determining factors are, perhaps, not found in the country of immigration but in the country of emigration.

ECONOMIC CHANGE AND
MIGRATION: THE FINNISH CASE

Tom Sandlund

The Nordic countries are often seen as fairly similar, even though the differences in economic development are rather great (Allardt, 1975; Alapuro, 1980; Valkonen, 1980). While economic and social development in Sweden was slow and stepwise, the development in Finland and Norway was in leaps and bounds.

As a starting point, we shall compare the distribution of the gainfully employed population in various economic sectors in Finland with that of Sweden in the same years and juxtapose the data on emigration supplied by Finnish and Swedish official statistics and the Mobility Project (MOB) of the Finnish Academy of Science (Sandlund, 1980). Additional findings concerning willingness to return to Finland from Sweden and the problems connected with such returns will be added.

There was a net outflow of population from Finland to Sweden after the Second World War up to 1970. The reversal in migration flows in the beginning of the 1970's can be partially explained by an economic boom in Finland. More likely than not, however, a new type of migration pattern has developed between Finland and Sweden which brought along new problems as well.

This new pattern in migration is due to the change in the socio-economic structure of Finland producing new structural relationships between the two countries.

In comparison with the early 1970's the economic situation in Finland is not good today (1981). Another contrast is even greater, namely the economic situation in Sweden is worsening and immigrants are being adversely affected. It is therefore tempting to point at the economic recession in Sweden and the relatively good situation in Finland, even if unemployment remains high, as the most important factor determining lower out-migration figures and increasing return migration. There are, however, other factors pointing toward a qualitatively new situation. These factors are historical, structural and social.

Migration between Sweden and Finland is no new phenomenon (Swanberg, 1980). After the Second World War Sweden was the main receiving country for Finns. In the middle of the 1950's, passports were abolished between the Nordic countries (Denmark, Finland, Iceland, Norway and Sweden) and these countries (plus Iceland later) also introduced a free labour market, which in practice means that a citizen of one country has free access to the labour market in another.

201

Table 1: Migration between Finland and Sweden 1968-1981

Year	To Sweden	To Finland	Net
1968	17,239	6,360	- 10,879
1969	38,556	5,974	- 32,582
1970	41,538	11,033	- 30,505
1971	16,584	18,841	+ 2,257
1972	10,284	17,618	+ 7,334
1973	8,999	15,917	+ 6,918
1974	9,601	10,729	+ 1,128
1975	12,137	7,699	- 4,438
1976	15,734	6,358	- 9,376
1977	14,825	5,253	- 9,572
1978	11,951	5,320	- 6,631
1979	12,485	6,812	- 5,673
1980	12,003	9,926	- 2,077
1981	6,919	11,617	+ 4,698

Source: Befolkninsrörelsen 1980. Part. 3. Table 6.17. Sveriges officiella statistik. Stockholm 1981. For 1981 monthly preliminary data summarized.

It is hard to estimate the importance of historical connections but it is a fact that the Finnish immigrants have deeper roots in Sweden than many other immigrants. This is true not only of Swedish Finns from Finland but also of the Finns themselves. The historical factor may contribute to the increasing tendency to see migration to Sweden as a form of internal migration, often of short duration.

Migration

Since the Second World War, Finland has taken a social and economic leap that has reduced the gainfully employed population in farming from 63 per cent in 1940 to 12 per cent in 1980; this figure is expected to decline further. At the same time, the service sector has risen from 17 per cent to 52 per cent. In short, Finland has in one great leap gone from a farming society to a post-industrial one. The most visible result of this process is a population concentration in the south coupled with high emigration.

Both internal migration and emigration have been heavy in Finland after the war. Between 1945 and 1980 well over 400,000 Finns migrated between Finland and Sweden. The reasons for emigration were several but the main reasons were to be found in the structural change of economy in Finland, the higher living standard in Sweden and the complementary economic structures and labour markets of the two countries up till the 1970's.

Geographical mobility coincided with social mobility. The movements from rural to urban areas have been large and in most instances brought with them social mobility either of an intra- or inter-generational kind. Emigration and return from abroad involved interesting forms of joint geographical and social mobility.

Table 2 shows the concentration of Finns towards Uusimaa that has taken place attracting migrants from all parts of Finland. The population of Finland is no longer so equally distributed, as it was in 1950. The concentration in Uusimaa (and here especially in the Helsinki region) stands out clearly. The changes in the distribution of the Swedish speaking population, on the other hand, are clearly smaller. These was a small increase in the Uusimaa share of the population but the Swedish population shows a decrease also in this district, in sharp contrast to a heavy surplus for the Finnish population in 1975. The distribution of the 1931-1950 cohort in 1970 by county of birth is the same as the distribution by county of residence in 1950. Emigration has been high, therefore it seems reasonable to conclude that emigration has not affected this age group differentially in different parts of the country.

Among Swedish Finns, internal migration has been small (Sandlund, 1981). This has been negatively "compensated for" by a higher emigration. The differences in the actual amount of geographical movements between the language groups seem to be small (Finnas, 1981), but the differences mean that the Swedish-speaking population has suffered more definite losses during periods of high emigration.

The Finnish population shows a total loss of only 9 per cent while the Swedish loss amounts to 29 per cent. The Finnish concentration in Uusimaa has been more than equalled by a migration of nearly one fourth of the Swedish age group to Sweden. But regardless of this heavy loss which includes deaths the total migration among the Finns seems higher due to the high internal migration. Losses in the Swedish group also include a certain loss due to negative net language shift, estimated at the most to be only 3 per cent (Finnas, 1981).

After 1970, the migration gap between Sweden and Finland began to close. The higher figures for 1977 and 1978 should be seen partly as a result of earlier emigration, i.e. they include many who over-optimistically returned in 1972 and 1973 and left again after the economic boom in Finland had changed into a depression (Table 1).

Table 2: Per cent distribution of residence in Finland 1970 by county of birth and sex for age group born 1931-50, for Finnish and Swedish population and by regional distribution of age group 1950 and 1970

county of birth	Men county of birth	Uusi- maa	other coun- ties	tot.	Women county of birth	Uusi- maa	other coun- ties	tot.	Distribution 1950	1970
Finnish Population										
SOUTH										
Uusimaa	84	(84)	16	100	79	(79)	21	100	11	23
Turku & Pori	77	11	12	100	73	12	15	100	15	15
Häme	71	18	11	100	63	21	16	100	14	15
Kymi	71	16	23	100	66	16	18	100	8	7
EAST										
Mikkeli	57	16	27	100	43	22	35	100	7	4
Pohjois Karjale	53	27	20	100	48	26	26	100	14	4
Kuopio	59	20	21	100	53	20	27	100		5
MIDDLE										
Keski-Suomi	65	16	19	100	60	16	24	100	15	6
Vaasa	65	11	24	100	64	13	23	100		7
NORTH										
Oulu	74	10	16	100	64	14	22	100	11	9
Lappi	78	7	15	100	66	11	23	100	5	5
Swedish population										
Uusimaa	93	(93)	7	100	90	(90)	10	100	45	50
Turku & Pori	67	27	6	100	64	29	7	100	10	9
Aland	93	2	5	100	96	4	-	100	7	6
Vaasa	90	6	4	100	89	8	3	100	37	33

Source: Sandlund, Tom. 1982. Social structure and social mobility: a study of the Swedish population in Finland 1950-1975. Ethnicity and Mobility Research Report no. 10.

Reasons for Return

Studies show that return migration takes place mostly within five years of emigration. Between 1946 and 1975, 40 to 50 per cent of the Finns who had emigrated to Sweden returned. The figures increased towards the end of the period; two thirds of return migration can be explained by the amount of emigration two years earlier. About 85 per cent of the returnees have been in Sweden less than five years (Borgegard, 1976) (1). The largest emigration to Sweden took place between 1960 and 1970 however, and return migration took place in the early 1970's suggesting that the emigrants from Finland to Sweden during the 1950's and 1960's who have not returned thus far will likely remain in Sweden, at least for the rest of their working lives. In this population there are also those who returned at the beginning of the 1970's but became disappointed and moved back to Sweden.

There have been only a few studies dealing with return migration from a sociological point of view. The economic determinants of migratory flows have been studies, whereas sociological studies mostly dealt with the situation of Finns in Sweden. Research results from the 1970's show that about half of the immigrants say that they will return "sometime later". About 30 per cent answer that they will return within a year and the rest that they will not return at all. The ideal returnee at that time was a person under 35, unmarried, with a fairly high level of education and poor or no knowledge of Swedish (Lind, 1977). A study of Finnish Swedish-speaking immigrants in Sweden in 1979 showed that slightly under 40 per cent said they would not return while only 14 per cent said they would and the rest contemplated a return, but had either not yet decided or considered return not possible at the moment (Kommitteebetankande, 1980). Among the returnees to Finland the education of children in their native language is quoted as the foremost reason for return, despite the increasing number of Finnish schools in Sweden. On the other hand, what makes return migration easier is that in many areas to which the return migration is directed, an effective school system in Swedish exists. To many potential return migrants a "soft landing" in these areas can be contemplated with the intention to move on to unilingual Finnish districts after the children have settled in and picked up enough Finnish to change the language of instruction.

Swedish schools also exist in some localities which are officially unilingual by Finnish and these attract children of return migrants (Rosenlew-Cremieux, 1980). Many of the children have difficulties, including language difficulties, in school after return. In many districts, the possibility exists of placing the children directly after return in Swedish or Finnish schools and deciding on the proper school later.

The high percentage of return migrants that give the children's education as a reason for return may be due to the fact that more returnees in the 1982 study were married than they were in the earlier studies, but it may also

Table 3: Distribution of population gain and loss between 1950 and 1975 for the age cohort born 1931-1950. Finnish and Swedish population are separated

County	Finnish population gain (loss)		Swedish population gain (loss)	
	N	per cent	N	per cent.
Uusimaa	+ 160,651	+ 103.2	- 9,710	- 20.0
Turku & Pori	- 26,517	- 12.4	- 3,919	- 35.3
Häme	- 7,196	- 3.7		
Kymi	+ 3,358	+ 2.9		
Mikkeli	- 40,690	- 42.8		
Pohjois Karjala & Kuopio	- 87,645	- 44.4		
Vaasa & Keski Suomi	- 54,088	- 26.4	- 14,366	- 37.7
Oulu	- 54,109	- 33.0		
Lappi	- 23,850	- 31.0		
Aland			- 1,414	- 37.0
Total gain	+ 164,009			
Total loss	- 294,095		- 29,409	
Net loss	- 130,086	- 9.2	- 29,409	- 27.2
Whole age group 1950	1,414,615		108,043	

Sources: Official Statistics of Finland VI C:102. 1950 Population census volume I and VIII. Helsinki 1956 and 1958.
Official Statistics of Finland VI A:138. Vital Statistics. Helsinki 1978 and unpublished tables, Central Statistical Office. Helsinki.

| | Returnees | |
	1968-69, -71	1981
Worse economic situation in Sweden	4	8
Comparatively better in Finland before	19	10
Childrens' education	4	19
Language difficulties	7	3
Homesickness	21	16
Family reasons	16	9
Personal reasons	4	6
Studies or military service	14	13
Aims of migration fulfilled	3	9
Other, no answer	8	7
Total	100	100
	(N=1998)	(N=485)

Source: Heikkinen, 1974:45; Korkiasaari, part results 1982.

reflect the debate about language of instruction and language development that was taking place both in Sweden and in Finland.

Economic reasons are not very prominent among the returnees' answers, neither among the earlier nor the later returnees. Social and cultural alienation in Sweden is one of the main reasons for returning to Finland. Potential returnees are quite willing to accept a lower living standard in Finland in return for a greater psychological well-being (Korkiasaari, 1982; Heikkinen, 1974), even though the situation is not always so good after returning to Finland. The experience of unemployment has obviously been quite high among the returnees but, nearly four fifths of them feel secure in their present jobs (Korkiasaari, 1982).

The study by Korkiasaari suggests that Finnish return migrants can be divided into two groups, one that has experienced a great deal of unemployment and one that has not. The feeling of job security was not the very best among the returnees. Among the 14 per cent unemployed returnees, many said they were not at present looking for work but intended to go back to work later. Seventeen per cent of the returnees were at present furthering their education and about 15 per cent said they contemplated a move abroad again.

Two other reasons for return should be mentioned: old age and land-ownership. Many studies show that when parents become old some Finns move back in order to be near them. As long as Finland was an agricultural country a movement back implied taking over the farm. This is hardly so any longer. The ownership of land, however, representing mostly small holdings has provided the foundation for farmers and return emigrants to establish, especially in Ostrobothnis, a fur industry which is the leading fur industry in the world as far as mink and fox furs are concerned. The ownership of land is distributed differently in different parts of the country. Where ownership has been rather widely distributed, access to land in order to build a one-family house is easy — a very different situation from multi-storey flats in Sweden. A fairly easy access to building land induces return migration.

After the great emigration to the USA, Finland experienced a return migration of pensioners in the 1930's. Such a return migration can be expected now again. The attitudes in Finland to such migration are ambiguous and these attitudes in themselves contribute to establishing the threshold level for return emigration.

In dealing with the extent of movement between the two countries, it should be pointed out that in absolute numbers the return migration is to a great extent a function of the extent of out-migration. When the emigration figures were very high, as was the case in 1969 and 1970, return migration figures are also apt to be high a few years later. The high return migration in 1971-74 might therefore not only be an effect of the economic boom in Finland during that time, but perhaps largely an effect of the common return stream based on out-migration in preceding years. Mostly single people were returning at that time but, frustrated with the economic situation in Finland, many re-emigrated.

"The second generation" migrants have seldom been asked where they want to live. It was taken for granted that they are going to "stay" in the host country. This may be less true in the case of migrants in Sweden and Finland than in many other cases in Europe. In a situation where the parents return and grown-up children remain abroad, they establish a link to the home country which may encourage their "return" in the future.

Complement and competition

Up till the 1970's Sweden and Finland complemented each other, where-by Finland supplied labour to Swedish industry. The surplus population in Finland did not become the problem it would otherwise have been. Today, the two countries have both a high standard of living and high unemployment. This gives rise to new problems. While earlier the task for Swedish in-migration policy was that of trying to make the situation in Sweden attractive for the Finns, a stricter Swedish immigration policy will probably ensue now. The existing Nordic agreements will make it difficult to effect changes quickly, however.

The Finnish authorities on their part begin to worry about a brain drain effect and about the tendency of the Swedish authorities to look to Finland to take care of the welfare and education of the Finnish community in Sweden. With high unemployment and difficulties in expansion in the public sector, citizens of the two countries may well be divided into "wanted" and "less wanted". Wanted may well be young people with particular skills and specialists in certain fields. Unwanted will be the sick, the old, the unemployed, the unskilled, and costly minorities. Such a policy by both countries, even if not even hinted at officially, will diminish migration between the countries but may for the time being keep the returns from Sweden to Finland high.

Conclusions

Finland in 1950 was about 20 to 30 years behind Sweden in most social and economic respects. The rapid industrialization of Finland uprooted the population with two very visible consequences. First, the population that in 1950 was geographically quite evenly distributed became very heavily concentrated in the south, around Helsinki. Secondly, the surplus population was so great that 400,000 Finns have migrated for a period of time to Sweden, mostly for economic reasons. Between 1960 and 1980, Finland has made social and economic leaps in development characteristic of "interface regions" (Alapuro, 1980). For many years Finland has been an "odd" country in two respects among the countries of out-migration: (a) Finland belongs to the world's richest nations in terms of income per capita and (b) income distribution is, in comparison to other countries of out-migration, comparatively even. Differences with Sweden remain on both counts but are negligible.

The reasons for moving to Sweden today are no longer economic even if differences, for instance in housing remain. Quality of life factors became prominent as reasons for migration. Excluding the specialists in professions who remain in Sweden, quality of life factors tend to raise the return migration figures from Sweden to Finland. It is therefore to be expected that the amount of net movement between the two countries will remain low although the short time migration may stay high. This will be due partly to the unemployed either trying to find permanent jobs or holding relatively short time jobs in both countries. As a consequence of the highest out-migration figures at the end of the 1960's, Finland now has both a migration of previous economic migrants returning for quality of life reasons and a short term migration for quality of life reasons to Sweden and back.

(1) Borgegard and other researchers' estimates contain however, methodological difficulties. Studies of emigration cohorts almost only concern the 1970's. The beginning of that decade was exceptional due to peak emigration in 1969-1970 and the economic boom in Finland in the beginning of the 1970's. If one just looks at the difference between out and re-migration the problem of the size of those who have moved twice (or more) arises. Logically, if all have moved twice to Sweden and then stayed the net return over the period would be nil.

PART III

PERSPECTIVES ON RETURN

MIGRATION

Historical antecedents

RETURN MIGRATION FROM THE USA TO POLAND

Adam Walaszek

Poles have always emigrated to other countries with the intention of returning to their native land. This has been so, irrespective of whether the dominant motive of emigration was economic or political (Kubiak, 1979; Golab, 1977). The fact that later on the majority of emigrants did not return to the old country, however, must be explained not by individual motivations preceding the emigration but by a set of objective events that occurred both in the country of settlement and in Poland.

The intention of Polish emigrants to return followed a regular pattern: to save money earned abroad in order to invest it in the old country to buy land, to build a new house or to have a small workshop. One significant consequence of their savings habits meant a delay in their socio-economic advancement and their relatively slow integration and acculturation in the country of settlement.

The history of the Polish migration to the United States may be dated to the beginning of the 17th century. Political emigration between 1776-1870 reflected the Napoleonic wars and national insurrections in the years 1794, 1830-31, 1848-49, 1863-65. Individual cases of return were also linked with political events in Europe (Stasik, 1973).

From 1870 to 1914 there was a mass economic emigration of peasants from Central and Eastern Europe to North America. Poles formed a significant portion of this mass migration, with 2.7 to 2.8 million people. At the beginning of the 20th century, they occupied second position next to the Italians among new immigrants arriving in the United States.

After World War I, the U.S. restrictive immigration bills significantly limited mass immigration from Poland. Between 1919-1922 the volume is estimated to have been around 180,000 persons, including 140,000 Jews. The annual immigration quota initially granted Poland the right to send 25,827 immigrants, and after the Polish postwar borders had been finally settled, the quota was 31,146 persons. After the Johnson-Reeds bill of 1924 the quota was 5,982 and since 1930, 6,524 persons per annum.

The last phase in the history of Polish emigration to the United States began during World War II. After the war, there was a political emigration, a response to the new political situation in Poland. The majority of emigrants were intellectuals. The Displaced Persons Act of 1948, amended in 1950 made it possible for 165,000 Polish immigrants to come to the USA. Until the beginning of the 1970's, over 300,000 Polish immigrants arrived in the USA including those who qualified under the immigration quota system.

The new postwar emigration had a very different social composition from the preceding one. Due to the higher level of education and greater political experience, the newcomers were able to secure better employment in the United States. The new emigrants also wished to become political and ideological leaders of Old Polonia. This gave rise to conflicts between the two, the old and the new leadership among the immigrants. The new immigration was composed mainly of soldiers of the Polish Army in the West, and of the intelligentsia connected with the political machinery of the Second Polish Republic. These people treated the United States as the place of their temporary settlement and also as a means in their political struggle for a non-socialist Poland (Kubiak, 1969). They intended to return but only if the political regime in Poland changed, with the result that they have ended up remaining in the USA.

Return migration before World War II

Return migration from America to the Polish territories prior to World War I was estimated at approximately 30 per cent of the original emigration (Caro, 1907, 1914; Brozek, 1977; Pilch, 1976). From 1908-1918, 221,176 Poles (so classed according to "race and nationality") left the United States. Since 1920 both criteria have been applied. Between 1908 and 1914, returns averaged about 30,000 annually. Among those who left, 54 per cent went to Austria, 0.5 per cent to Hungary, 0.7 per cent to Germany, 42.4 per cent to Russia. Before World War I, 1.1 million people left the Austrian part of the divided Poland for the United States, almost 1.1 million people left the Russian part and 450,000 to 600,000 the Prussian part. During the same period some 660,000 persons returned to all the Polish territories (Schlag, 1961; Ferenczi, 1929). Return movement after World War I was different from the preceding one. Between 1919 and 1923 return migration was described as a "fever" by the press. From 1919 to 1923, slightly fewer than 100,000 Poles returned. Three fourths were males, 73.6 per cent in the age category between 16 and 44 and 23.6 per cent were over 45 years of age. Most often they returned after a stay of 5 to 10 years (72.2 per cent), and some 8 per cent returned after 10 to 15 years abroad. In addition, 985 Poles already naturalized in the U.S. returned to Poland to stay.

According to American statistics, 53.7 per cent of the returnees were unskilled workers, 6.2 per cent skilled, 10.6 per cent were self-defined as farmers, 2.3 per cent as farm workers, and 25 per cent fell into "other jobs". Polish statistics offer a different picture. There, 52.9 per cent were workers, 33 per cent, farmers, 1.7 per cent, merchants and industrialists and 10.4 per cent, representatives of "other jobs" (Commissioner, various years; Archives; Polish Embassy; Polish Consulate, various years and numbers). For specific years these percentages vary.

Table 1: Return migration from the United States to Poland, 1919-1939

Years	Polish Data	American Data (a) "race, nation"	"country of birth"
1919	15,000 (b)	153	
1920	26,328	18,190	18,392
1921	50,205	42,207	42,572
1922	8,939	31,004	33,581
1923	2,096	5,278	5,439
1924	5,048	2,590	2,594
1925	2,639	3,693	3,721
1926	2,552	2,823	2,881
1927	2,295	2,725	2,650
1928	1,565	3,046	3,071
1929	942	2,316	2,273
1930	1,096	1,924	1,979
1931	1,024	2,101	2,119
1932	632	2,375	2,408
1933	227	1,627	1,675
1934	308	733	785
1935	229	457	458
1936	419	443	442
1937	179	413	422
1938	160	409	400
1939		322	315

(a) fiscal year ends on June 30.
(b) estimates.

Source: Annual Report. Commissioner General of the Bureau of Immigration, Washington, D.C. 1919-1939; Rocznik Statystyki RP, Warszawa 1924-1939; Wiadomości Statystyczne GUS, Warszawa 1930-1939. Archives of New Files, Warszawa, Ministry of Foreign Affairs set, 9886, p. 142.

The role of the Polish ethnic organizations
in the USA in the return movement

The Polish ethnic group in the United Stated emerged slowly as a result of mass immigration. The peasant who had come to America from the Russian or Austrian part of Poland acquired a consciousness of the fatherland and the national culture only after he had emigrated. The activities organized by the Polish organization, societies, parishes, schools and the press and the direct links with the local community of the region of origin, became supplemented by a pan-Polish consciousness. The beginning of the change can be seen in the religious and mutual aid organizations. National organizations such as the Polish National Alliance appealed to peasant emigrants. A push for the restoration of an independent Poland assumed importance only when emigrants stated that their identity was Polish in the period directly preceding and during World War I (Kubiak, 1979).

Before and during World War I, there was a Polish national minority in the States. In 1918-1919 it reached the peak of its development: it had its own treasury, its own army considered to be an independent force involved in the world conflict, its own political representations. It was a "state", although with no territorial state organization. It had its own legislature, *Sejm Wychodźstwa* (the Emigration Diet), making decisions about taxes and even exacting them. "The external manifestation of progressive changes of consciousness were, among others, public demonstrations, congresses, organizations and institutions, and finally the three first "Emigration Diets" (Kubiak, 1979: 59).

In the consciousness of the Polish masses a specific image of future Poland was coming into being - free, democratic, just, crystallized. It was also assumed that the country destroyed by the war and deprived of industry awaited the emigrants' initiative. The return to the country was viewed as the pioneer crusade of progress. The patriotic watchwords called for reconstruction of Poland and promised simultaneously a good future to the returnees (Pamietniki, 1977).

People were also disposed to returning due to the recession in the USA in 1920 and 1921. It soon appeared, however, that the Poland they imagined and the true Poland were not one and the same. Return often meant economic ruin and psychological setback.

In the United States, the wave of patriotic enthusiasm began to decline. New problems also appeared. One, for instance, was created by "legal and international consequences of the existence of the independent Polish state: ... To serve the Polish cause meant then to serve the Polish state" (Kubiak, 1979: 59). This fact created a complex dilemma over citizenship, and as emigration became more permanent, the drama of double identification arose.

Other causes cooling the attitudes of the Polish communities towards return were the tragic situation in Poland of the returning Haller's soldiers who, as Polonia's volunteers fought during the war for the independence of Poland, the crash of the Polish currency, and the bankruptcies of corporations investing emigrants' savings in Poland; and the conflicts and tensions between the Polish community and the Polish diplomatic agencies.

A new identity of Polish immigrants emerged in the United States. The emigrant community wished to decide its own fate and to fight for its own interests in the USA as an American ethnic group. From the loyalty to the independent country demonstrated during the war and in 1918-1919, from the watchwords "Let us save Poland first of all", opposite viewpoints gradually developed. The Emigration Diet in Cleveland in 1923 expressed its stand with the slogan "The emigrants for themselves". This program finally won at the Polish Congress in Detroit in 1925 (Kongres, 1925), where the necessity of so-called Americanization was stressed. The return movement began to deline in 1923 and ceased almost altogether afterwards. Contrary to expectations, the mass return movement did not occur even in the period of the Great Economic Depression. Those few people who left for Poland were retirees.

During World War II, the Kongres Polonii Amerykanskiej (The Polish American Congress), was founded in Buffalo in 1944 to "defend the interests of the free postwar tate, independent of foreign influences" (Pienkos and Pienkos, 1981). Today, KPA still pursues a change in the present political system in Poland. Equally, the KPA shows a growing interest in Polish issues in the United States. Since 1968, among other things, the Congress has fought against commentaries insulting Poland, which appear in the American mass media. The KPA works to heighten the prestige of the Polish ethnic group.

The return of the Polish and other ethnic groups from the USA

What was observed with reference to the return migration of the Polish ethnic group from the USA, can be extended to other groups of new immigrants from Southern and Eastern Europe. The demographic and occupational structure of the return migration to Poland, Greece, Czechoslovakia, Roumania, Slovakia, Hungary and to the territories of later Yugoslavia, reveals significant similarities both before and after World War I. In general, the people who returned were relatively young, less than 45 years of age. Seventy per cent of them were employed in the USA in industry as unskilled workers, they lived and worked in cities of central and Eastern states. The majority left for America in order to save as much money as possible, to be able to return and spend it in Europe. In general, they spent not more than 10 years abroad.

The break of communications caused by World War I, and the patriotism of emigrants strengthened the desire to return. Patriotism was created by the consciousness developed during the emigration, that one belonged to a European nation. The political unrest and conflicts experienced by the young states which emerged in Europe after World War I led the ethnic organizations in the United States to advise a delay in the return. The ethnic organizations started to treat the return movement with concern. Their concern was mainly to work for the benefit of the group in the United States, clarifying the issues of naturalization and Americanization.

Table 2: Permanent departures from the United States
to Poland, 1939-1957 and 1959-1975 (a)

Year (b)	Number	Year	Number	Year	Number
1939	315	1951	72	1964	2,056
1940	81	1952	68	1965	2,123
1941	4	1953	71	1966	747
1942	-	1954	219	1967	1,827
1943	1	1955	182	1968	319
1944	1	1956	67	1969	288
1945	-	1957	91	1970	448
1946	24	1959	564	1971	1,588
1947	55	1960	281	1972	3,791
1948	127	1961	445	1973	9,242
1949	133	1962	467	1974	20,588
1950	106	1963	1,490	1975	30,122

(a) according to the place of landing; including the tourist movement.

(b) fiscal year ends on June 30.

Source: United States; Department of Justice. Immigration and Naturalization Service, duplicated material.
Statistical Abstract of the United States. 1939-1957, US Department of Commerce, Washington D.C., Government Printing Office.

Finally, one should mention the changes in the American immigration legislation. The introduction of the quota system, limiting the access to the USA, forced potential returnees to analyse the decision about return more carefully.

All these circumstances caused return migration to slow down. In 1919 the American press published articles full of anxiety if not panic about the impending exodus of hundreds of thousands of people. The Immigration Commissioner F. C. Howe expected the departure of 1.5 to 2 million people. Certain financiers, fearing the decline in manpower, suggested bringing in 5 million Chinese to replace the departing Europeans (Saloutos, 1974). The anxieties proved to be premature. The return movement declined in the following years. In the years 1925 to 1939, 562,357 persons left for Europe, compared to 895,832 persons who left in the years 1919 to 1924 (US Department of Labor, individual years). Nor did return migration intensify in the period of the great economic depression (Saloutos, 1974). The immigrants set their roots in the American soil irreversibly.

RETURN MIGRATION OF THE
FINNS FROM OVERSEAS COUNRIES

Keijo Virtanen

European research into the history of overseas migration has paid very little attention to return migration, mainly due to a lack of comprehensive statistics corresponding to those available for emigration. The large-scale statistical study of migration by the United States National Bureau of Economic Research (1929) did pay attention to return migration, but was limited — because of the unreliable statistics on returning emigrants — to five European countries: Spain, Britain, Italy, Sweden, and Finland (International Migrations I, 1929). Similar difficulties are evident in studies of recent return migration, e.g. from Canada (Richmond, 1967) or intra-European migration (e.g. Seferagic, 1977).

In general, the most thorough research before 1980 — outside the Finnish research — on the history of overseas return was carried out with Swedish and Italian data (Lindberg, 1930; Tedebrand, 1976; Foerster, 1924; Cerase, 1970; Caroli, 1973). Also the works on Greeks (Saloutos, 1956) and Irish (Schrier, 1958) should be mentioned. By 1980 there were only three monographs on the history of overseas return migration (Saloutos, 1956; Caroli, 1973; Virtanen, 1979).

The Finns are one of the few well-documented migrant groups. The data sources are varied: passport lists, passenger lists, church records, and the district court registrars' records.

Both the background factors and the actual conditions of migration had changed radically by the end of the 19th century, when Finnish migration began to reach its peak. The host country, mainly the United States, had changed into a rapidly expanding industrial society, while at the beginning of the century, when large scale migration started from Western Europe, it was still a country where the majority of immigrants went into agriculture.

The attraction of the United States was based on the higher rates of pay compared to Finland, for example. For the individual emigrant the most essential feature was precisely higher wages, about which information spread through letters and returning migrants. While a farmhand or a lumberjack earned two or three marks a day in Finland during the late 19th and early 20th centuries, the wages of an immigrant working on railroad construction in the United States were two dollars a day around 1910; one dollar was more than five Finnish marks in the early 1900's (Toivonen, 1963). From the point of view of an individual emigrant this difference was the main "pull" factor in

America. In broader terms, the rapid growth of American economy attracted labour from Europe, where the development was slower.

The conditions for the Finnish return migration were completely different from what they had been in the overseas migration of the early 19th century. Firstly, the supply of free farmland, which had been readily available in North America earlier ran out towards the end of the century (Lindberg, 1930; Hvidt, 1971). Consequently, immigrants tended to engage in those occupations which they could leave fairly easily to transfer to the other kinds of work, to move on somewhere else, or to return.

A second vital precondition for return migration, a form of intercontinental commuting to work, was the development of transportation. The voyage on a sailing ship used to last as long as three months in some cases; now, steamships were able to transport emigrants over the Atlantic in two weeks. By the 1870's, steam had replaced sail in the transport of emigrants (Engelberg, 1944; Jones, 1960; Kero, 1974; Hell, 1976). The level of comfort for the passengers was still far from satisfactory, however, despite the faster passage.

In 1891 the Finnish Steamship Company started sailings between Hanko in Finland and Hull in England specifically with emigrants in mind, which also meant better opportunities for return migration. From 1894 on, the Finnish Steamship Company established itself as the main carrier of Finnish emigrants as far as England. By the time of the First World War, improvements in the cleanliness of the ships and in cabin space had made the passage more comfortable due to competition between the shipping lines for overseas traffic in the 1920's (Engelberg, 1944; Kero, 1974).

While it cannot be shown that emigration increased due to the improved transportation, it did make return easier (Engelberg, 1944; Hell, 1976). There was a mutual interaction between emigration and the development of sea transport; emigrants enjoyed the benefits of improved transport, while the shipping lines profitted by carrying large numbers of emigrants overseas and back again. This was true not only for the Italian shipping industry (Caroli, 1973) or Greece (Saloutos, 1956), carrying the large migration waves, but also for the "small" migration countries like Finland. In both cases, the emigrants of this period were regarded only as temporary labour in the host countries. And that is exactly how they considered themselves at the moment of emigration. The great majority of Finnish migrants, for instance, left for economic reasons, wishing to earn as much as possible and then return home. The comment of one emigrant from 1922, now resident in Florida, to the question as to the intention to return at the moment of emigration, was "I should think everyone intends to". Another stated that he had intended to remain abroad until he had a "pocketful" of money. Very few intended to leave their home country for ever, even though they were "pushed" overseas (Virtanen, 1979).

The original cause for this mass movement of people was the "push" rooted in a radical change in the traditional basis of Finnish society. The increase in population became so rapid that the economy could not keep pace with it, leading in Finland as elsewhere in Europe to the emergence of "relative surplus population", which the economy could not adequately support (Jutikkala, 1953).

This "relative surplus population", had become problematic in Finland already in the 1840's. Between 1815 and 1875 the main increase in population occurred in rural areas, leading to population pressures since economic opportunities did not expand accordingly. In the 1860's, 85 per cent of the Finnish population was still engaged in agriculture. The Finnish industrial revolution had its beginning in the following decade, but it was not until the last decade of the century that industrialization really got under way (Haatanen, 1965).

In this transitional period the population pressure in Finland was concentrated in the countryside. An increasing proportion of the rural population became landless, since the number of farms did not increase as fast as the number of potential farmers. The division of farms was blocked both by prevailing law and the prevailing custom, i.e. that the entire property be taken over by one child only. The other children had to seek their living in other ways. The proportion of landless population steadily increased towards the end of the 19th century, while opportunities for employment deteriorated (Lento, 1951; Haatanen, 1965).

The Finnish society in the 19th century was characterized by internal migration which was greater at the beginning of the century than at the end. The increase in emigration abroad seems to explain the reduction in internal migration towards the end of the century. Internal migration did decrease as emigration abroad became more widespread, with Sweden as the major destination in the period 1861-1890 and North America thereafter. In the transitional period, the tradition of emigration to Sweden was for a short time a barrier to emigration to North America, but it did establish the habit of going abroad to find work. Once emigration to a particular destination (e.g. North America) had gained momentum, self-perpetuating factors came into play: factors such as family ties, with different members of the family emigrating at various different times, and the migration tradition in a given area, with emigration gradually becoming a collective form of behaviour, or social norm (Wester, 1977).

Overseas emigration from Finland took on the nature of mass migration at a later date (in the 1870's) than did overseas emigration from many west European and Scandinavian countries; it was at its peak at the turn of the century, when the movement overseas from some of the countries in Southern Europe was only beginning (Saloutos, 1956; Schrier, 1958). The beginnings of the emigration proper from Finland thus fall somewhere into the middle of the European migratory development. The Finnish return migration is similar to the movements from other Scandinavian countries. The Finnish return rate among those emigrating between 1860 and 1930 was about one-fifth (of the 380,000 emigrants about 75,000 returned permanently), which is similar to the return rate for Sweden and Denmark (Hvidt, 1971; Tedebrand, 1976). The situation was quite different for countries such as Italy and Greece, which were typical "new" migration countries, where a very large proportion of migrants returned home, perhaps subsequently to "commute" overseas to work again (Foerster, 1924; Lindberg, 1930; Saloutos, 1956; Caroli, 1973).

The return migration to Britain (an "old" migration country) was also very high (International Migrations I, 1929; Caroli, 1973), so that the division of reference to the return rate or to the temporariness of the migration (only 10 per cent of the Finnish emigrants made two or more trips) cannot be sustained in the Finnish case, which has been defined as belonging to the "new" migration (Virtanen, 1979).

Analysis of the return migration factors in the area of origin may stem from the fact that about 10 per cent of the Finnish emigrants originated from towns (Kero, 1974). The return rate of urban emigrants was only around 5 to 10 per cent. The return rate also in Sweden has been lower to towns than to the country as a whole (Tedebrand, 1976).

Secondly, farmers and crofters returned relatively more frequently than their children, and the latter in turn more frequently than members of the landless peasant families. Farmers and crofters usually returned permanently, whereas their children tended to migrate more than once, due to their lack of a sure source of livelihood in Finland. The return rate to low emigration areas (eastern and northern Finland) was clearly lower than to high emigration areas (western Finland).

Thirdly, the age structure of emigrants from different areas was fairly consistent: over half of all emigrants were under 25 years of age. Among the returnees, the older the emigrant was at the time of emigration, the more likely he or she was to return subsequently to Finland. The only exceptions were those who were over 50 at the time of emigration, whose return rate was low. More likely than not, they were joining their emigrated children abroad.

Fourthly, there were relatively more men among the Finnish emigrants than among the Swedes. Finnish emigration was more rural in origin than Swedish emigration (Kero, 1974) and the proportion of women was higher in towns than it was in the country. Around two thirds of the emigrants from Finland were men (Toivonen, 1963). In terms of the "old" and "new" division of migration, the Finnish emigration was not exceptionally male dominated; men made up a considerably higher proportion of the emigrants from some Southern European countries than from Finland (Saloutos, 1956). The return rate for men was relatively much higher than that for women. Consequently, the return migration was even more male dominated than the emigration. In Finland 75 to 85 per cent of the migrants returning permanently were men.

Fifthly, married male emigrants returned normally after a few years to rejoin their families. Some sent tickets for their families in Finland to start a new life abroad. About three quarters of the emigrants were unmarried, but

224

the rate for permanent returning married emigrants was much higher than that for the unmarried. Consequently, nearly half of those returning permanently to Finland were married. The corresponding figure for Sweden appears to be about 30 per cent (Janson, 1931). The married emigrants from Sweden probably included more couples and families arriving later than did the emigrants from Finland, as family emigration had an effect of binding the people to the adopted country. The return rate of widowed emigrants was lowest, however, similar to those of the oldest age group.

Although Finnish emigration began later than emigration from other Scandinavian countries, the peaks in the return migration occurred in approximately the same period: the period before 1893, 1893 to 1914, and the period from the First World War up to 1930 (this return period continues up to the present day). Return migration only achieved real significance from the second phase onward, and then reached its peak in absolute number in all the Nordic countries. These trends can be explained to a large extent by means of very general factors: the rapid industrial expansion in the United States and the development of transport and communications, which changed the nature of manpower needed in the country of destination as well as increased the ease of migrating.

The main flow of the Finnish overseas emigration was directed to the United States and Canada. It was not until the 1920's that other countries and continents began to attract more attention from emigrants. Of about 380,000 Finnish overseas emigrants before 1930 approximately 315,000 went to the United States, 60,000 to Canada, 2,000 to Australia, 1,000 to South America, and 1,000 to South Africa (Finnish Official Statistics XXVIII-2: 22; XXVIII-18: 23; XXVIII-21: 13; International Migrations I, 1929; 364-365, 452, 552; Kero, 1974: Appendices A and F; Raivio, 1975: 113-114).

Migration to other destinations was rare, but the return rate from Australia was extremely high: approximately 50 per cent returned permanently. The main reason for this was that Australia was a second choice country of destination; also, supportive Finnish communities did not exist there to the same extent as in North America. The Australian immigrants also took up work which was not binding in nature. And for the same reasons, even higher return rates occurred among the Finnish emigrants to South America and South Africa. The countries or continents of "small" immigration were thus unable to attract or retain immigrants to anything like the same extent as did North America. The hypothesis that increasing distance had a diminishing effect on the return migration rate (Akerman, 1976), is not borne out when the Finnish emigration to North America and other overseas countries are compared.

The economic depression periods in North America increased the return migration. Return migration, however, was not as closely connected to economic cycles as emigration, since personal motives had a more important position in the decision to return than to emigrate.

The first job obtained by Finnish men was typically in mining, forestry, or in a factory, while women mainly worked in service occupations. The motivation of the women to return was reduced by this work, which provided more favourable conditions for learning the new customs and language than did the men's occupations. The men's employment was relatively more sensitive to economic fluctuations in the host country. These are contributory factors in the relatively lower return rate for women than for men. The Finnish return migration was not as dependent on economic cycles as that of the countries in Southern Europe; unlike the typical "new" migrants, Finnish immigrants did not usually work in large gangs in the cities as the Italians (Foerster, 1924; Caroli, 1973) or the Greeks (Saloutos, 1956).

Apart from mining and forest labour, the occupation in which Finns most frequently engaged was agriculture, the "right" form of livelihood for the "old" migrants, according to the Dillingham Commission. With the passage of time, many men began to establish farms, though often on very infertile land; the best land had already been taken by other ethnic groups by the end of the 19th century. In any case, farming had the effect of binding the immigrant to his adopted country. The general tendency of Finnish immigrants to settle in the countryside or small towns and their eagerness to set up farms of their own must have been a particularly strong factor reducing the probability of their return.

The Finnish immigrants in the United States spread to the northern states of the country, from the Atlantic seaboard to the Pacific coast, and in Canada went mainly to Ontario and British Columbia. The return rate from the eastern states and provinces appears to have been the highest, and seems to drop as one moved west to the Pacific coast. One reason for this was a form of stage migration. Living further west usually meant the gradual abandonment of the idea of returning. Additional factors were the availability of different kinds of work in various parts of North America. The eastern regions were far more important places for immigrants to settle immediately on arrival than they were a few years later.

The distance factor alone was nevertheless not decisive as can be seen in the relatively high return rate from Australia, South America and South Africa. Internal mobility within North America, on the other hand, did have a significant effect on the ties of the immigrant to his adopted country. Thus the hypothesis, that return migration rate falls with increasing distance (Akerman, 1976), is applicable to North America. It represents a more significant geographical factor in the return than does the distribution of migrants between the United States and Canada. The east-west factor was more important than the north-south factor (USA-Canada) in determining the probability of return from North America.

Finally, we need to analyze the strictly personal factors influencing the decision of migrants to return. The predominant motive for emigration, both in Finland and in many other countries, was the search for better earnings with a subsequent return home in mind. Consequently, if migrants were going to return, they would do so rather soon after arrival overseas. Over half of the Finnish migrants who returned did so within five years of emigration. Similar return strategies are identifiable in the migration patterns of many countries both of the "old" and "new" migration (Foerster, 1924; Semmingsen, 1950; Saloutos, 1956; Richmond, 1967; Caroli, 1973; Tedebrand, 1976).

Having achieved their objectives was, however, not the only motive for return, since adversities might also send them back home. Correspondingly, there were immigrants who were not able to return even if they had wanted to do so. The most frequent cause of return, however, was probably homesickness, arising from a failure to adapt to the host country, and this was at its strongest soon after arrival.

Return did not necessarily mean that the migrants would be happy back in Finland, however. During their years of absence, changes had taken place in their home area, as also in the migrants themselves. About 10 per cent of all the Finnish migrants made two or more journeys overseas in the period up to 1930. Those who made at least two trips were more likely to return permanently to Finland than those who had emigrated only once. An emigrant who revisited Finland and attempted to readjust to Finnish conditions without succeeding and therefore decided to re-emigrate was, nevertheless drawn again to his or her old home area even at a later stage in his life than those who had emigrated only once.

Similarly, those who had already moved at least once within Finland before emigrating overseas were more likely to return than those who had lived all their lives in one place before emigrating. The former group was more used to moving, so that the return was also "easier" for them. The differences in the return rate between these groups are not big, however.

In general, returning migrants had a relatively good chance of readjusting to life back home, primarily due to the fact that in most cases they had been abroad for only a few years. They also tended to be fairly well-off when they returned. Since they often invested their savings either in farming or some other form of real estate, this too was likely to strengthen their ties to the area they had settled in and lead to the abandonment of ideas of re-emigration overseas.

In terms of the return migration in a wider context, the final balance of Finnish overseas migration was definitely negative, for Finland only regained 75,000 of the 380,000 persons who had emigrated overseas prior to 1930. The final balance in a "new" migration country such as Italy was quite different, where the economy visibly prospered from the busy movement back and forth between Italy and the overseas countries and from the capital brought back with those who returned.

The analysis also demonstrates that Finnish migrants cannot be classified under the "new" migration; rather, in its main features Finnish migration showed extensive similarities with migration from the Nordic countries, and differed radically from the overseas migration movement in Southern European countries, which was essentially a temporary phenomenon, a form of intercontinental commuting to work. The application of the terms "old" and "new" migration as such in this context is thus rendered rather questionable, since in many of the component features, the analysis of the "counter-current", i.e. the return migration in relation to the emigration, shows the division to be contradictory.

The alternatives confronting the migrant, to settle in the new country or to return to the old one, depended on extremely complex interactions of factors, which this paper has attempted to illuminate in terms of certain central concerns. Unquestionably, the low number of those returning is a crucial factor in the history of Finnish overseas migration, even if it does not on its own permit conclusions to be drawn on the significance of the migration for the Finnish society from the 1860's to the present day. The similarity between the overseas migration of several decades ago and the recent migratory history between Finland and Sweden should not be overlooked. There are, of course, considerable differences too, but in any case the history of overseas return migration helps us to understand these present phenomena.

THE RETURN OF DUTCH MIGRANTS FROM AUSTRALIA, NEW ZEALAND AND CANADA

Wim Blauw
Joed Elich

Until the early 1970's, the Dutch government deemed the foreign work-ers in the country to be there for a temporary stay but presumed that the Dutch citizens who had emigrated did so for good. Emigration from the Netherlands was quite heavy during the first decade after World War II, when, in 1952, some 50,000 persons emigrated overseas. In 1980, on the other hand, the total for emigrants was only about 5,000 but interest in emigration is on the increase again.

Whatever return migration there was, used to be attributed either to a failure in the emigration policy itself or to the failure of individual emigrants (Hofstede, 1964). Now, however, a lot of international migration is not for keeps. The Dutch Department of Emigration (part of the Ministry for Social Affairs and Employment) monitors not only emigration but also tries to monitor return migration. There are indications that the number of returns particularly from Australia, New Zealand and Canada is increasing and that the returnees are relatively recent emigrants themselves (Elich and Blauw, 1981). The official definition of an emigrant is a person who intends to stay abroad for at least one year or for an indefinite period. Hence the figures for emi-grants are likely to contain a large number of those who did not intend to emigrate in the traditional sense. A return migrant is then a person who has officially emigrated and was noted to have done so in the records and perhaps with the help of the Department of Emigration and then has returned to the Netherlands supposedly to stay.

Return migration to developed countries has not been studied exten-sively thus far (Appleyard, 1962; Richardson, 1968; Richmond, 1968). In the Netherlands, there are two extensive studies on return migration from over-seas (Harvey, 1980; Nozeman, unpublished), both of which use small samples of returnees to probe for reasons for return. Both studies were exploratory and based on purposive sampling. The study reported here is based on semi-struc-tured interviews administered to 113 respondents. Family units were treated as one respondent, so that our 113 cases represent 162 persons. Eligible for sampling were emigrants or emigrant families who left the Netherlands in 1970 and in 1975 and returned before August, 1980. The two years and the three countries have 100 cases each, in our sample, yielding 596 usable cases. More than 30 per cent returned (1). Of those who emigrated in 1970 to Australia and New Zealand, 37 per cent returned and of those who emigrated in 1970 to Canada, 29 per cent returned.

The main purpose of the study was to gather the life histories of our respondents particularly with a view toward unraveling motives for emigration and for return. Coding of responses proved, of course, difficult but the main purpose of our exploration was to flesh out, as it were, the standard findings on the demographic profile of migrants. Since our respondents were not migrating primarily to work abroad, non-economic variables influencing both the emigration and return proved salient.

In addition, to recreating a profile of returnees, some comparisons were drawn between emigrants and the future returnees. Data on emigrants to match our study years (1970 and 1975) were available from a recent study of 410 Dutch emigrants (Kruiter, 1981). The differences between emigrants and returnees are important. Whereas there were no significant differences in the age, sex and marital status of emigrants or of our returnees at the time of emigration, there were substantial differences between the two groups as regards occupation. Service occupations characterized returnees much more than emigrants, 24 per cent and 7 per cent of the two samples respectively. Obversely, high skill occupations were less frequent among returnees than among emigrants, 16 and 25 per cent respectively. Education tended to differentiate mainly between the countries emigrants were going to but did not differentiate between emigrants and returnees. Thus, New Zealand attracted and lost highly educated Dutch migrants, whereas emigrants with only secondary schooling were more likely to go and also to return from Australia. Emigrants to Canada were on the middle educational level.

Comparing the reasons for migration, return migrants had a greater proportion of "adventurer" types, who were also younger than the emigrants who stayed abroad. Altogether, 10 per cent of our return migrants had left originally to escape from personal problems or because social problems around them had bothered them. On the other hand, more sincere emigrants showed an overall displeasure with the state of things in the Netherlands. Returnees were more likely to have come from urban areas in the Netherlands and stayed in urban areas while abroad. Upon return, however, 63 per cent of them settled in communities smaller than 50,000 or in suburbs. No doubt, this may be simply a function of the relative difficulty in finding housing in cities. Finally, for those who return after a relatively short period of time, the modal length of stay abroad is about two years. Emigrants to Canada have a slightly faster turnaround than emigrants to the other two countries but the differences are small. The return curve when plotted, has a sharp rise peaking at the two year point and a fairly steep decline thereafter. Most of our respondents here returned before five years were over.

Motives to return

Two underlying clusters of motives for return were found among our respondents: 1) culture shock and 2) personal problems. Even though the countries of immigration are superficially similar to the Netherlands in the quality of life, material amenities and basic belief systems, there were enough nuances in the conduct of everyday life which our returnees found difficult to adjust to. Some of the difficulties encountered were the perceived discrimination against women on the job, particularly in the still male dominated societies of Australia and New Zealand. The open friendliness displayed was often difficult to translate into genuine friendships. As one respondent put it: "Australians are friendly but they don't like to make friends". Our returnees who had a higher education tended to complain about the "lack of mental freedom", meaning primarily the absence of serious intellectual discussion in the circle of their acquaintances. In this cultural isolation the returnees tended to realize that it is also their lack of willingness to adapt to the new cultural mode. As one of them said, "the first person one meets there is oneself". In the immigration countries, however, there were better opportunities to start a business, there was less social distance between people of different social classes than in the Netherlands and social control by others was informal.

On the other hand, many returnees held the opinion that there was a stricter discipline in schools, that people were less involved in politics and that societal problems like vandalism, drugs, alcohol, criminality and environment pollution were common in cities. Dutch emigrants missed the domesticity and the cozy, safe streets of Dutch towns.

Personal problems, even though related to the culture shock, were of a different nature. Homesickness, which affected one out of five returnees was not only brought about by missing family relations but also by missing the familiar low country and the sea, for instance. Married women and single men suffered more from homesickness than other respondents and keeping in close contacts by letters and tape recordings only drove home what was amiss abroad. Other essentially personal problems encompassed unemployment or an unsatisfactory job (20 per cent) and breakdown in marriage (14 per cent). Those who were trying to escape personal involvements at home by emigrating also tended to return as such problems did not go away.

Experiences after return

Return migrants have to overcome the aura of returning due to a failure abroad. Nonetheless, two out of three maintained that their emigration experience had been positive. Actually, the unemployment rate of our returnees was only four per cent as compared to the nationwide rate of eight per cent. Considering their qualifications and experience, however, this did not mean much.

Interestingly enough, 70 per cent of our returnees continue to maintain contact with their previous country of emigration where they may have friends or some members of the family. Only 8 per cent of our respondents regretted the fact that they had emigrated in the first place. Actually, 18 per cent regretted having returned and some of them expect to re-emigrate. Prior to their return, many harbored romantic images about Holland, her friendly people, cozy social relationships. Upon return, naturally things did not look so rosy and cozy as in their imagination and the big cities in the Netherlands had the same problems of vandalism and social disorganization as those overseas.

To summarize briefly our impressions gained from the interviewed returnnees, the following observations can be made: 1) distance does not seem to influence the decision to return; there were more returnees proportionately in our sample from Australia and New Zealand (37 per cent) than there were from Canada (29 per cent). 2) Return migration peaks at about two years, then it declines rather sharply. After some ten years, it is rare. 3) Whereas most immigrants expected conditions abroad to be similar to those they left behind, the real differences in the style of life left them with a culture shock and those unable to adapt, returned. 4) Economic motives turned out to be quite subordinate to other reasons for emigrating and for returning.

Such conclusions are not likely to fit into the theoretical framework such as there is where economic motivation is understood as the main underlying force behind migration.

NOTE

(1) Price (1976) in his study of return migration from Australia calculated that in the period 1947 to 1980, 29.5 per cent of the people who had arrived in Australia from the Netherlands departed again. In fact, this percentage also includes people who arrived before 1947 but excludes the peak of return of the people who arrived in Australia in 1978 and 1979 (the peak of return is two years after emigration). However, this non-realized return applies to small numbers of emigrants, so that our figure remains a good approximation of return migration.

Theoretical stances in

explaining return migration

THE OECD AND RETURN MIGRATION: NOTE ON THE ROLE AND ACTIVITY OF AN INTERGOVERNMENTAL AGENCY IN THE STUDY OF RETURN MIGRATION

Abridged version of a contribution submitted to the Conference by the Secretariat of the Organisation for Economic Cooperation and Development

The OECD and return migration

In 1967, a report was prepared which directed OECD* activity towards the elimination of discrimination against foreign workers in the host countries and the study of the economic effects of migration on both groups of countries, thus laying the foundation for the development of the concept of the "migratory chain", with its alternative outcomes of integration in the host country and reinsertion in the home country, which has underpinned the Organisation's approach since. This concept draws together in a "chain" of phenomena and reactions the various stages of migrants' physical movements (departure, entry, access to the labour market, settlement or return, possible re-migration) and the repercussions (economic growth, labour-market structure, balance of payments, development) on the immigration and emigration country.

In November 1973 the migration situation in Europe changed dramatically. The Federal German government imposed a ban on the recruitment of foreign workers, except those covered by the European Common Market and certain other agreements or freedom of movement, which has remained in force. The other main immigration countries adopted similar policies. It was feared that massive returns, caused by the refusal to renew work or residence permits on the part of the host countries, would have catastrophic effects on the labour market situation, already taxed by the incipient recession, of the home countries. Fortunately this did not occur, but the OECD decided nevertheless that its effort should be directed towards discouraging unilateral action and accordingly, in 1975 a document "The OECD and International Migration" first announced the idea of "concertation" between partner countries in migration policy, producing a set of "Guiding Principles" which ought

---

* The Organisation for Economic Cooperation and Development, successor to the Organisation for European Economic Cooperation (OEEC): a grouping of the world's main industrialised market-economy countries with headquarters in Paris.

to govern the action of member countries in this field. These "Guiding Principles" were included in the "Recommendation of the Council on a General Employment and Manpower Policy" which was the issue of a meeting of Ministers of Labour held in Paris in March 1976.

The ministerial meeting of 1976 had two other important consequences in the field we are discussing. First, a proposition by the Turkish Minister requested the organisation to constitute a high-level group which would study the inter-relationship between migration, growth and development. This group was in fact constituted and produced in 1978 a report with the same title ("Migration, growth and development"), known generally as the Kindleberger Report after the distinguished professor who acted as chairman. Second, following a proposal by the Greek Minister, the organisation developed in 1977 a set of guidelines for negotiation between countries in the matter of returns, including certain suggestions for the creation of appropriate institutional mechanisms, entitled somewhat colourfully the "moden machinery for the reinsertion of migrant workers returning to the home country".

Parallel to this work leading to and emerging from the ministerial meeting of 1976 were two other strands of relevant activity. First, a further series of projects was undertaken on the economic effects of migration in the home countries, with reference to some of the institutional factors involved. The results of these projects were used in the production of an important published report, "The migratory chain" (1978), which completed the development of the migratory chain concept outlined above, supported by examples of the chain reaction in operation. Second, the area of institutional factors was more deeply explored in an operational activity of the Co-operative Action Programme of the OECD Technical Co-operation Service; this was concerned with the provision of reintegration and other services for returning migrants, culminating in a conference at Helsinki (May 1976) and the publication of a substantial report. Following the conference it was decided to concentrate the activity of the Co-operative Action Programme on the promotion of pilot projects for job creation in regions of high emigration.

Such was the situation at the beginning of 1979. The principle of bilateral concertation between countries in formulating and implementing migration policy, rather than the taking of measures unilaterally without the involvement of the partner country, had been incorporated in a formal recommendation of the organisation. The concept of the migratory chain, linking the various stages of migrant movement with their economic and social effects, had been refined. The high-level report on migration, growth and development had been published. The Co-operative Action Programme was actively encouraging job creation projects in the emigration countries. At this point it was decided by the Council of the OECD to reconstitute the Working Party on Migration, the original purpose of which had been to monitor a former decision of the OEEC on the liberalisation of manpower movements, with new terms of reference which still apply.

The new mandate of the working party was given to it by the Council of the Organisation in April, 1979. The terms of reference establish the working party as a forum for the discussion of migration issues, in the light of the Kindleberger Report, with particular attention to the alternative final "links" of the "migratory chain", namely the integration of the migrant and his family into the society of the host country or his return to, and resettlement in, his country of origin.

In December, 1980 a meeting of government experts was organised on "migration and regional labour markets" at the invitation of the Italian government. The purpose of the meeting, held near Trieste, was to examine concrete examples of the resettlement of migrants in the region of origin and study *in situ* the applicability of the guidelines for reinsertion action. Background documentation had been prepared by experts from the Centre for Economic and Social Research in Udine, and further papers submitted by national participants from Finland, Portugal, Spain, Turkey and Yugoslavia. The region in question — Friuli-Venezia Julia — had been chosen because it had experienced a significant return of migrants.

It emerged from the discussions that the successful outcome of the returns had been due more to initiatives taken by the population itself (for example, effective exploitation of measures taken at national level for the promotion of small enterprises) than to deliberate government policy for returns. This pattern was confirmed by the contributions from other countries. On the other hand, some individual assistance had been necessary (travel grants, priority in public housing, help with the transfer of social security benefits and educational problems) and in this area specific institutional arrangements were useful, as also for the provision of reliable information on which migrants could base their own decisions and for the creation of a framework in which their own initiative, particularly the use of their savings, could operate to advantage. It is in this area — the orientation of migrants' savings — that OECD work on returns has since been concentrated.

RETURN MIGRATION:
AN ANALYTICAL FRAMEWORK

Rita L. Chepulis

A more comprehensive understanding of the particular and general ramifications of labor migration requires both a socio-economic analysis and an historical interpretation. To understand the thinking, behavior and difficulties that migrants encounter, both in the receiving countries and upon return, necessitates placing the whole migration process within a larger framework.

When we speak of migration, we are not only dealing with individual migrants. We are also dealing with their countries of origin, the receiving countries, as well as with larger interlinking economic and political processes. Continuous actions, reactions and subsequent developments that occur on varying levels affect different countries, regions, villages, urban centers, and naturally, the migrant or would-be migrant in particular ways.

Societies have for centuries been part of large scale political and economic processes. The effects of this on the path of development in each respective country are both historically specific and linked to internal and external factors. This directly affects the people, how they use their environment, their subsistence, as well as the structuring of their social relations (Cole, 1977).

An historical analysis of the dependent inter-relationship between the "core" or industrialized societies and the "peripheral" or developing countries, which became the migrant-sending countries, would help to explain, for example, the nature and cause for their labor surplus. A cursory look at the colonialist nature of foreign investment in the periphery reveals the effects of an almost complete underdevelopment and involution of the economic structure of the former colonies (Bagchi, 1982; Szentes, 1976). Generally speaking, the type of investment was such, that it developed only certain sectors of the economy, while systematically hindering the native incipient development of other branches of the economy. This resulted in the distortion of economic diversification of these industrially underdeveloped countries. Those branches of industry that were developed, i.e. extractive industries, were geared completely to the needs of the industrialized countries. This kept them "dependent on the export of a few valuable resources, thus making these economies extremely vulnerable to the effects of changes in the needs of the core (industrialized) economies" (Chirot, 1977: 34) and fluctuations in world market prices. The unbalanced development of only certain sectors of industry, obviously had repercussions throughout the entire society and affected the capacity to absorb the potential labor supply. The effects of such development or rather underdevelopment are still manifest to the present time. One such result is/was the migration of workers from North Africa to France, from India and Pakistan to Britain, from Indonesia to the Netherlands, to name but a few examples.

While migration obviously implies change, such as change of residence on the most basic level, we must be careful to separate the notion of change from development, since one does not imply the other. For example, by the late 1950's, most of the less industrialized countries of the Mediterranean Basin — Greece, Portugal, Spain, Turkey, Yugoslavia — adopted an overall export-led development strategy, which included the *export of labor* (Woodward, forthcoming). However, the changes that occurred as a result of migration and what the effects have been on the sending countries' development are two distinct issues.

In order to understand the roots, causes and shifts in the direction of labor migration, several levels of analyses are proposed: macro, regional and micro level. The levels are not contradictory, but rather supplement each other, and the existing migration theories can be applied to each level.

Macro level

The macro level refers to international economic and political relations of integration and dependency of the developing countries on the highly industrialized ones.

Temporary European labor migration is not just a product of the postwar period. The historical dependency of "core" and "periphery" had very concrete manifestations prior to that. For example, before World War II, Yugoslavia had quasi-colonial relations with Germany. Her mines and other extractive branches of industry were a cheap source of raw material and foodstuffs for industrialized Germany. Not only did Germany have at its disposal eighty-eight percent of Yugoslavia's metal ore production, but it also forbade the development of any locally owned industry in metallurgy and other fields. In conjunction, between 1933 and 1941, more than 40,000 Yugoslavs went to work in Germany's factories, often organized through recruiting agents (Cifrić, 1981).

Postwar developments, therefore, had obviously been affected by previous international relations. An understanding of what has preceded, helps to illuminate changes and continuations in relations and labor migration between the highly industrialized countries and those which were predominantly agricultural, until rather recently.

The effects of the penetration of the international market has caused an increased integration of national economies into the world economy. This has effects throughout the entire society, affecting social relations as well, which tend to become organized around the opportunities and constraints of the world economy (Markoff, 1977). Thus, the expansion of postwar highly industrialized Western European economies and the demand for foreign labor, coincided with the export-led development strategies of the sending countries. According to this strategy, their exports would repay debts (incurred for industrialization programs) and during the early period of development, exports of labor would bridge the gap to be ultimately filled by domestic production (Woodward, forthcoming).

Migration, therefore, remains dependent not only on individual aspiration, but also on larger socio-economic and political factors. Changing conditions in the world economy affect the direction of labor migration in general, and return migration in particular.

This can be understood more clearly within the present world economic situation and the problems of deep-rooted economic recession facing all the countries. The impact, however, tends to be greater on the sending countries, because of the "fragility of their domestic industrial structures" (Woodward, ibid., 11-12). This means they have fewer resources to deal with increased unemployment, rising inflation, and massive foreign debts which results in a significant decline in the standard of living.

Consequently, projects for integrating return migrants into their own economies, also face increasing difficulties in implementation. If the sending country does not have the hard currency necessary to import needed materials and components for production, production capacities become underutilized, leading to further underemployment or unemployment.

The migrant workers, despite the desire to return, are thus constrained by lack of employment prospects in the home country. The dilemma becomes even greater as recession in the receiving countries causes factory shutdowns and rising unemployment. During such crisis periods, the foreign worker often becomes the scapegoat for attack by politicians, trade unions, mass media and national citizens. This may increase the desire to return home, on the part of the migrant workers, but the economic realities may not always permit such a decision.

Regional level

The starting point for this type of consideration is the fact that great internal heterogeneity in some societies is as great as between national aggregates, if not greater. Many developing societies are really a mixture of developed and underdeveloped regions and their problems result from this imbalance (Linz, 1966). The distribution of income can be highly unequal, "both among persons and households and among regions" and poorer regions are less likely to attract initial industry (Woodward, ibid., 10). Thus, the development of one region may be at the expense of another, creating even greater disparities between them.

Local stratification systems, local political processes, and even local culture become responses to a region's place within the world economy (Markoff, 1977). New modes of production can have a direct influence on the labor absorbing capacity of the traditional sectors. The growth of the modern sector can actually create underemployment and reduce the level of income in the traditional sectors. Even handicraft industries can be ruined by competition from cheaper machine-made goods imported from abroad (Szentes, 1976). Thus, the underemployed or unemployed worker may leave the community and seek employment elsewhere, either in the home country or abroad.

Environmental conditions, such as poor soil quality, cannot always explain why a particular community or a region is economically undeveloped. Other factors, such as the concentration of land ownership, utilization of actual surplus, agricultural policies, both national and international (e.g. European Community), the production of cash or subsistence crops can all be very significant factors in influencing local employment, local production, income creation and subsequent migration.

The dispensal and decentralization of industry into less developed, rural regions can have an impact on the success of the reintegration of returning migrants. However, even this is dependent on the entire economic situation in the sending country, especially if foreign technology and foreign components need to be financed and imported.

The generalizations that can be made from regional patterns of organization are clearly of greater comparative relevance than those drawn either from community or national studies alone. According to Smith (1976), by viewing complex societies as nested regional systems, analysis can be focused directly on the organizational determinants of societal integration. A regional analysis can build system variability into its models of explanation, thus allowing reasonable kinds of comparisons between equivalent units. Any regional system once defined, can be broken down to a particular hierarchical level, and systems at a given hierarchical level become standard units of comparison.

In such a way, the type and level of industry, as well as the relations of production in a particular region can be ascertained. An analysis of the existing different categories of agriculturalists, industrial or peasant-workers, for example, can show not only the inter-relationships between these categories, but also help to explain which group would tend to migrate. The different rates of migration of different regions, for example, where one has a higher rate of migration abroad, while another one has a higher rate of internal migration, may be explained by such factors as proximity and ease of access to nearby industrial centers. Return migration will subsequently be affected by the type of socio-economic organization in a particular area, depending on the constraints and opportunities, such as employment and investment possibilities.

242

Micro level

The micro level is the level of the individual migrant, who is operating not only within a given socio-cultural framework, but also within the constraints of larger economic and political factors in both the sending and receiving societies. Political decisions and legislation can severely constrain the alternatives from which the migrant may choose. Also, which foreign workers are more or less favored as a group in the receiving society, has little to do with their capabilities as "good workers". The reasons can range anywhere from whether their sending country is a member of the European Community (Cornelisen, 1980), to social, religious and political reasons.

The role of the migrant worker can be interpreted as being both an active and a passive one. Generally, they have very clear socio-economic reasons for going to work abroad and for return. While the reasons for out-migration tend to be predominantly economic, voluntary return reasons often include those of a purely social nature, such as the desire for their children to be schooled in their own societies. This in turn is linked to larger issues such as integration and assimilation of the foreign population into the receiving society.

Their role is passive, however, in the sense that the foreign workers are part of a larger movement of both labor and capital, which has its own specific rationale and means. These roles are paradoxical, even though they are manifestations of the same process. The returning migrant, for example, may himself experience a general increased personal economic well-being, but may be returning to a region or country that has not developed in the meantime. The disparity between one and the other will concretely affect the returning migrant in terms of employment possibilities and social mobility. The increased personal economic well-being may turn out to be short-lived, for example, as savings dwindle while waiting to become employed.

Employment possibilites for returning migrants can also be affected by such criteria as age and sex. The possibility clearly exists, that if a migrant worker family has returned for the purposes of schooling their children in the home country, the returning women may find it more difficult to find employment than the returning men. If the returning female migrant worker can not find employment, the chances are that she will simply leave the labor market, either definitely or temporarily. Her mobility tends to become less for family reasons, while the husband, if he cannot find employment, may return to work abroad, given the opportunity in a receiving country. The women may also return earlier than the men, for given family reasons, and the lack of employment possibilities may be rationalized as a desire to stay at home with the family, especially in cases where the parents and children have been separated, the children having remained in the sending country.

Whether the vocational training that the migrants may have received abroad will be utilized depends on whether similar employment opportunities exist at home. The opposite, de-skilling, may even occur. The nature of industry in the receiving countries, especially the branches in which the migrants tend to be employed, may demand a very narrowly defined specialization or repetitive short cycle operations. This can actually lead to the loss of skills and qualifications because the worker is not able to use the know-how attained previously. While migrants as a whole have lower levels of formal qualifications than the domestic European working class, a part of the migrant population does jobs for which they can be considered as overqualified (Primorac, 1976; Schierup, 1983). Furthermore, programs may be undertaken in the home country in the meantime, which specifically aim at increasing the level of training of unskilled or semi-skilled workers. The returning workers may be caught in a serious dilemma, by the seemingly simple fact, that they do not possess the necessary training certificate. As a result, their acquired qualifications remain unrecognized (Primorac, 1982).

In this regard, two things should be kept in mind. The society which the migrant has left has not remained static. Various changes have been occurring, even though the sending countries to which they are returning, have not been developing at the rapid pace that was originally envisioned. The "traditional" society, for example, may have become much more consumer-oriented in the meantime. Thus, it is necessary to separate the changes in attitudes and behavior of the migrants which are a result of their migration experience, from overall changes which have been taking place in their society. Even the remotest villages can be affected through mass media information, such as radios.

Secondly, monolithic cultural and behavioral generalizations have a tendency to overlook the particular social groupings within the society. The attitudes and behavior, as well as the social framework, of a subsistence farmer will be different from that of a wage earner in an urban environment. Thus, the adaptations, behavior, psychology may vary quite considerably depending on the particular social group and milieu from which the migrant workers originate and to which they return.

Concluding remarks

Systematic studies have been attempted since Ravenstein formulated his famous "Laws of Migration" (Ravenstein, 1885). Today, almost one hundred years later, the orientation of migration studies still tends to emphasize only discrete units of the migration phenomenon.

Migration has multiple causes and the relevance of certain factors, or a configuration of factors, may play a dominant or subordinate role at a certain period of time. Return migration is just one part of the whole migration process, which is interlinked to much larger transnational processes.

It is therefore necessary to understand the articulation, and perhaps even more importantly, the disarticulation between the various·levels in producing the causes and effects of migration and return migration. For example, if basic economic structural changes are occurring in the highly industrialized receiving countries, this will have an effect not only on the scope but also on the direction of migration. The resulting change in the set of conditions in the receiving countries, e.g. relocation of industry to other countries, rationalization measures, growing unemployment together with growing discrimination against the foreign workers can bring about their forced or voluntary return home. Subsequently, the whole general direction of migration may change, i.e. a shift of migration flows from the highly industrialized countries of North-western Europe to the Gulf states.

The effects that migration, including return migration, can have on the sending countries must be understood within the relationship these societies have to the highly industrialized receiving countries. The migrant sending countries are regulated in different ways vis-à-vis the receiving countries. Specifically, this is manifested through bilateral agreements regarding workers. More generally, the strategies of development of the sending countries may be geared towards greater economic integration and consequent dependence on foreign financial and technical support of their own native industries — the export of products and labor being an integral part of this strategy. Consequently, this affects not only socio-economic and political developments within the sending country, but also different regions and communities. An analysis of trends and changes within a larger integrated framework can help our understanding of the various possible alternatives, adaptations and behavior of the returning migrants themselves.

GEOGRAPHY OF
RETURN MIGRATION

Joseph Velikonja

Geographers utilize theories and models applicable to the problems of return migration that have been generated by other disciplines. A recent call for migration theories by and for geographers is related to the emergence of behavioral concerns that focus on individual and aggregate behavior, and on space and time concerns. Three conceptual frames are being used 1) Return migration is seen as linear transfer of assets, be it physical as well as human, social and cultural between two locations. The return migration occurs when place utility reverses the relative positions of origin and destination locations. 2) Circular migration reflects the relationship between pairs of locations on a cyclical or circular line pathway. Return migration in this context is a segment of the process and incorporates the vector and the location or the movement and the arrival within an integrated circuit rather than being a segment of a linear relationship. 3) The time parameter allows emphasis to be placed on the linkages through time, where various locations represent stations in the journey of a person or of a group. In this framework, the return migration is the return of an individual or a group to a previously established station. The time related assessment and the territorial impact of return migration reflects the impact of separation either by time or by spatial distance. The probability of interaction declines with time or space distance and the impact of separation similarly increases with either time or space interval. The return migration is affected by spatial distance but is nevertheless often facilitated by a greater ability of participants to overcome the cost and effort that is required to overcome distance. It is similarly affected by time which has produced changes in the behavior of potential returning migrants.

Geographical studies of return migration offer an interpretation of migration as a system of interacting parts requiring an assessment of components and their linkages, including feedback flows. Many studies of migration focus on a one time event in which the origin and destination linkage is explored and analyzed. Migration consists of a circular process, however, in which the move itself is preceded by the information flow between the potential destination and the place of origin (Johnston, 1977) and is often followed by return migration, labeled as counterstream by Lee (1966).

Return migration can imply trans-humance, seasonal migration, labor migration (Poinard, 1979), repatriation, migration of retirees (Cribier, 1975) and even brain drain (Velikonja, 1974) which all include the return journey. Da Vanzo (1981) refers to two central factors that generate return migration: location-specific capital and imperfect information.

Time dimension appears to be a very important variable either as a period of staying away or, as the perception and attitude toward the length of stay. Mechanical measurements of time lapse, such as a month or less than a year from which aggregate data are often obtained, do not account for the perceptual aspect of permanency. Wherever migration is considered temporary, attempts are often made by the migrants themselves, or by the two places that are affected by the migration, to maintain links with the home society to facilitate the return and to ease the reinsertion into the home area. Exposure, experience, acquisition of education, and new skills, and changes in the life cycle, however, make the reinsertion more and more difficult. The specific complementarity demands between the returning migrant and the receiving society are seldom met. Van Amersfoort (1978) refers to such experiences in his study of Moroccan migrants in the Netherlands.

Return migration is preceded by information flow-back. Empirical research has demonstrated that the probability of return is increased if the immigrants retain close links with the home area. Policy implications are then that if the return migration is considered advantageous both for the receiving society and the territory of original departure, efforts should be made to maintain close information linkages between people of the two areas.

Complementarity between the areas of origin and destination has to be specific to facilitate migration and equally enable return migration. While the likelihood of complementarity exists for out-migration flows that involve skilled or unskilled persons, it is less likely present in the case of the return movement. Residence abroad has modified the original migrant, changed his skills and perspectives. The return migrant is not a duplicate of the outgoing migrant; he or she has gained skills and experiences abroad making it unlikely to reintegrate at home. Empirical research has shown that the returning migrants return to the same country, but not to the same location, and much less to the same job. The Yugoslav return migration research has clearly shown it (Baucić, 1972), as did research on returning Turkish and Portuguese workers (Poinard, 1979).

Theories of migration, related to general theories of human spatial behavior and using interacting models or diffusion models benefit by maximization schemes and provide also explanatory and predictive models for return migration flows. The theories are, however, less powerful to interpret and predict individual behavior and the adjustment process and societal benefit that are to be derived from return migration. A number of longitudinal studies of individual migrants were undertaken in less advanced societies: Solomon Islands (Chapman, 1976), New Hebrides (Bedford, 1973), Caribbean (Lowenthal, 1976). In advanced societies such studies were fewer (Bell and Kirwan, 1979; Rikkinen, 1970).

Research in the Pacific (Chapman, 1976), in Africa (Harvey and Riddell, 1975) and in Southeast Asia (Goldstein, 1978) has shown that migration for more than one month, labeled as circular migration, has vastly increased in the postwar period. Circular movement involves two types: frequent, or less than lifetime circular move and lifetime circular migration. Short term circular migration, where the return movement is only one leg of the cycle, is either contract or spontaneous or non-concentrated migration. Its impact on the returning area is less pronounced and the stress on migrant population less severe if the time of absence is short and the cycle is regular.

Migration as an interacting or equilibrating mechanism is less significant for its demographic than for its social consequences. Simple measurements of migration gain significance if placed in the context of the total migration system. Bibliographies (Reeves, 1978; Conaway, 1977) and comprehensive reviews of return migrations have been recently completed (King, 1978; Wiltshire, 1978); numerous other studies have contributed to conceptual and empirical understanding of return migration (Baucić, 1972; Van Amersfoort, 1978; Lowenthal, 1976; Bedford, 1973; Chapman, 1976); others included return migration in studies of general migration systems (Zelinsky, 1971; Mobagunje, 1970; De Jong and Fardner, 1981).

Presently, circular or repeated return moves are enormously affected by the existing level of communication and transportation. Costly and rare in the past, the return to the home location has become a less expensive and more frequent occurrence. Lowenthal (1976) deems the return which is temporary and seasonal as generating disruption in the social and economic fabric of the area. Chapman (1976), on the other hand, on the basis of his observation in the Solomon Islands, points to the social links that exist within the extended family and expands the concept of "home" from one location to numerous locations at which members of the extended family reside. Circulation between these "stations" minimizes the disruption and stress and enables the individual to relocate with less cost and expense.

Contemporary time-geography formulations, initiated by Swedish geographer, Hagerstrand (1969), and vastly expanded in British and American geography (Pred, 1977, 1981), consider migration moves as paths that link discrete stations. In a similar fashion as the daily path incorporates daily return to the home station, the lifetime path often includes return migration as the path to the original home. Return to an intermediate station can be part of return migration as well (King, 1978). Longitudinal data for individual migration behavior are difficult to collect requiring researchers to use surrogate, aggregated, data. Residence is often used as a surrogate for the social neighborhood or surrounding of an individual (Wiltshire, 1978; Zelinsky, 1971). Return migration is therefore a residential movement back to an area that an individual has previously left.

Geographical analyses have yielded some useful conclusions. For instance, distance has been demonstrated to play a smaller role in return migration than in other types of migration (Vanderkamp, 1971). Assuming the concepts of migration streams and counterstreams, the return migration forms a larger proportion of migration counterstreams or reverse flows than in streams of dominant flows (Wiltshire, 1978). Harvey and Riddell (1975) formulated four types of migration processes in a hierarchical system of places on the basis of migration data for Sierra Leone. They postulate that in both developed and developing countries the returning migrant does not move down the hierarchical ratchet, a realization that has important policy implications as well.

ECONOMIC CONSEQUENCES
OF MIGRATION AND RETURN

Elizabeth McLean Petras

Toward the late 1960's and early 1970's, the magnitude of foreign labor in Western Europe was estimated to have been as high as 1 out or every 6 workers, if illegal workers are considered. The sources of large-scale increases in in-migration, and the fluctuations and directions of the migration movements did not correlate directly with labor market conditions among the sending regions. High unemployment and poverty had been acute in these regions before the large-scale movements commenced, and remained severe after out-migration began to recede in the mid-1970's.

As European economic expansion began to level off, the need for foreign labor diminished. States which only a few years earlier had been active in negotiating, facilitating and often supervising the importation of labor took measures to reduce the numbers of foreigners in their own labor markets. The highly elastic supply of foreign labor which had made immigrant workers so attractive in the first place, now became an important factor in attenuating some of the more severe effects of decelerated growth.

In response to the dismantling of the system of labor transfer, some observers and spokesmen for labor-exporting states proposed that the demise of labor immigration be compensated for by European and U.S. investment and relocation of plants to the sending countries (Hiemenz and Schatz, 1979). However, the amount of investment actually directed to former labor exporters has been minor compared to the previous volume of labor supplies which they provided.

To assess whether trends of foreign investment and trade may be linked to recent cross-national flows of labor, we have looked at the period of labor migration from 1960 to 1980, dividing it into two periods: Between 1960 and 1974 both unilateral and mutually agreed upon legislation governing in-migration was established, resulting in a structural dependence on imported workers in Western Europe on one hand and reliance on foreign worker remittances back home on the other. Between 1974 and 1980 deceleration of economic growth depressed labor demand and led to restrictive in-migration policies.

Since 1974, borders of the European labor importing countries have become virtually closed to new labor migrants. A homeward trend also began in that year, although departures have been partially offset by arrivals of family members and births. The composition of in-migration since the mid-

1970's has changed from that of the previous period. In 1970, for example, 68 per cent of the admissions to France were workers. In 1976, only 32 per cent were workers compared to 68 per cent family members (ICMC, 1978).

Labor for the industrial sector in Northwest Europe has generally been drawn from among four sources endogenous to the national labor market: 1) transfers of workers displaced from other sectors, particularly agriculture, but also from artisans or handicraft manufacturers and workers moving from small-scale, less efficient industries; 2) new entrants into the labor force from among young people or women who had not been previous participants; 3) workers available because of general unemployment; or 4) high rates of natural increase. A fifth source, exogenous to national labor, came from in-migration from abroad.

Supplies from the four endogenous sources were not sufficient to meet demands. To illustrate, in 1959, the per cent of total employment in agriculture was only 4 per cent in the United Kingdom, 10 per cent in The Netherland, and 16 per cent in West Germany (Kindleberger, 1967). Germany and France both had gaps among their male population, especially in the 40 to 50 age group. Although there was an increase in the birth rate immediately after World War II, it still did not provide enough new entrants by the mid-1960's. The exceptions were The Netherlands and, perhaps, France. Unemployment rates dropped to 1 per cent in Germany, 1.9 per cent in Sweden, and 2.4 per cent in the United Kingdom; the possibility of easing labor shortages by drawing upon indigenous labor was scant.

There were other grounds for seeking a low-wage labor supplement. With wages increasing between 6 per cent and 10 per cent a year and the unemployment levels ranging between 1 per cent and 2.4 per cent for the United Kingdom, France, Sweden and Germany, workers willing to work for relatively low wages were virtually non-existent among indigenous workers (Kindleberger, 1967). Holding down relative wages in industries such as textiles, shoes, garments, and food processing, was important in order to prevent the cost of goods in these sectors from being priced out of world markets. For this purpose, a low-wage immigrant workforce was considered desirable.

Institutional responses

The receiving countries thus began to revise existing immigration policies to expedite the process of labor transfer. In most instances, the trend was toward greater selectivity aimed at matching emigrants with labor market needs.

In the United Kingdom, the British Nationality Act of 1948 declared colonial subjects to have British citizenship which carried with it the freedom to migrate among any of His Majesty's territories (Rex and Tomlinson, 1979). The United Kingdom entered into government-to-government agreements with Commonwealth countries wherein the latter agreed to recruit, screen, and in the case of Barbados and Jamaica, subsidize, emigration to Britain. This status obtained until the effective closure of Commonwealth immigration in 1962.

In contrast to the free movement from the colonies and ex-colonies encouraged by the United Kingdom, Germany maintained a controlled policy of recruitment, placement and rotation of emigrants. A network of labor recruiting commissions was established abroad, primarily in the Mediterranean basin. Between 1955 and 1964, bilateral agreements were set up with Italy, Spain, Greece, Turkey, and Portugal. Contractual regularization of Tunisians, Moroccans, and Yugoslavs already working in Germany was concluded later (Mehrländer, 1979). German employers were able to control the availability of labor supplies through a stringent selection process, thus guaranteeing industry an adequate labor supply at both the regional and sectoral levels. Moderate wages could be maintained relatively free from the competition of a tight labor market, and regional planners could rid the region of excess workers during recession or declines among activities of industrial sectors (Mehrländer, 1979). In 1973, foreign workers in Germany numbered 2.6 million and their proportion to the native labor force had risen to 12 per cent.

France maintained a more laissez faire policy toward entry requirements. Not only did French industry require manpower for the same reasons as her Western European neighbors but, in addition, French military activities in Algeria had drawn off some portion of the work force to the draft. Consequently, Italian, Spanish, and Portuguese workers were encouraged to enter without restrictions, take up work, and to apply later for legal immigration documents (termed "immigration from within"). Additionally, residents of the former French colonies or territories had *de facto* free movement privileges and were granted residence and work permits once they had secured a job. So free was the movement, that by the end of the 1960's nearly 90 per cent of the more than 50,000 Portuguese in France had regularized their immigrant status from inside the country. No real attempt at restriction or control began until 1972, when state planners realized that "migratory flows (had) a certain autonomy from the very indicators of economic growth which should be guiding them" (Moulier and Tapinos, 1979: 137). In a complete policy turnabout, the government began issuing residence permits contingent on possession of a signed work contract for a job regulated through the Immigration Office. Between 1966 and 1972, the Office National d'Immigration registered 1,194,000 foreign workers and their families in France. The increase of foreign workers in the secondary sectors was 29 per cent compared to 5 per cent rise for French nationals over this period (Moulier and Tapinos, 1979).

Migration patterns

A new international division of labor evolved within the structure of the labor markets during this period in North Europe. Inter-regional integration of labor markets at the global level resulted. Spatially, the linkage was between Southern Europe, the Mediterranean Basin, and Northern Africa, and the industrialized centers of production in Europe. A secondary movement linked the Middle East, South Asia, Asia Minor and the Caribbean to Western Europe. Breaking this movement down by countries, major labor exporters to North Europe were Greece, Turkey, Southern Italy, Spain, Portugal, Yugoslavia, and Algeria. Workers from Ireland, Trinidad, Jamaica, India, Pakistan and Sri Lanka migrated to the United Kingdom. France received laborers from Algeria, Tunisia, and Morocco. Major recipients of this migration were France, West Germany, England, and Switzerland which together absorbed over three-fourths of the movement. Sweden, Luxembourg, and Belgium employed most of the remaining labor with a small percentage employed in The Netherlands, Austria, Norway, and Denmark, and, toward the end of the period, Northern Italy. In Italy, an uneven national development produced both an exodus of migrants from the *Mezzogiorno* and an attraction of in-migrants into the North.

Position of foreign workers in the labor markets

The most commonly cited advantages in the employment of immigrant labor refer to the low wages and labor intensive work in which they were engaged. But this should not obscure their main location in large-scale, complex industries as factory workers. In Germany, for example, nearly four out of five foreign workers were employed in manufacturing particularly in the metallurgical industry. In Swiss factories, as many as 40 per cent of all workers were aliens, approximately 40 per cent of the French Renault workers were immigrants, as were 40 per cent of Ford's Cologne plant workers, and 45 per cent of Volvo's Goteborg workers. Approximately one-third of the immigrants employed in Belgium between 1961 worked in manufacturing, while another 19 per cent were engaged in mining and quarry employment (Mouleart, 1980).

Three functions were served by the movements of surplus labor from the rural or semi-rural economies to the urban industrial centers. Primary was the performance of those less desirable and low-paying jobs in areas of production which have remained labor-intensive and inefficient. By maintaining low, absolute wage levels, employing firms were permitted to expand production without major investment of capital in plant mechanization and automation. That is, the capital to labor ratio could remain low. This was important in production which was not easily mechanized, or where costs of rationalization would have been prohibitive, e.g., construction of the hotel and restaurant industry. Secondly, migrants provided semi-skilled and skilled labor in mecha-

254

nized industries where the inadequacy of local labor pools placed constraints on production capacity. Finally, immigrant workers performed the traditional role of a labor reserve, acting as a depressant on all wages, and thus preventing relative labor costs from cutting too sharply into profits which is always a potential during periods of rapid capital accumulation.

Immigrant labor as a regulator of cyclical unemployment

Initially, at least among several Northwest European countries, the effect of regulation of flows of workers was to maintain artificial control on the supply side of the labor market. The rotation principle served this end in Switzerland and Germany, for example. As noted, when labor markets begame tight in the mid-1970's, foreign workers were encouraged to leave. In the interval between 1974 to 1978 between one million and 1.5 million workers returned to their countries from Northwest Europe. Among the OECD sending countries, i.e., Italy, approximately 600,000 workers returned in 1974-75 alone (OECD, 1978). In France, official entries of new workers fell by 98 per cent between 1973 and 1979 (Lebon and Falchi, 1980).

Between 1974 and 1978, 105,000 previously employed foreign workers were recorded as having departed from Germany. This represented 19.8 per cent of the total foreign workforce within the country. If foreign workers had not returned to their home countries, but had remained within the German labor market, the measured unemployment rate of 4.3 per cent in 1978 would have risen to 6.4 per cent with labor demand constant. Similar departure rates were observed in 1978 in France with 165,700, or 9.2 per cent of the legal immigrant group leaving, in Switzerland where 105,000, or 17.5 per cent of the immigrant population had left, and in Austria where 45,600, or 20.5 per cent of the immigrant population departed (Lebon and Falchi, 1980).

The redundancy of foreign workers was heightened by sharp declines in the economic sector of manufacturing where immigrants were concentrated. This sector was more affected by the cyclical impact of the economic crisis than the economy as a whole (Kuhn, 1978). Throughout the EEC, unemployment was particularly high in the regions where it had previously been low, that is, "in the most economically developed regions, ... thus most prone to changes in the economic climate or most affected by structural changes" (EUROSTAT, 1980: 30-31). Eliminating a share of foreigners in these regional work forces helped offset some of the effects of the economic downturn.

For several of the sending countries, on the other hand, an inversion of migratory movements began. Sharp reductions in emigration emerged for Turkey, Spain, and Portugal around 1973 to 1974. In the case of Greece and Algeria, the decline began somewhat earlier, and for Yugoslavia, there was a slight lag before the number of Yugoslav workers abroad was curtailed. The variation among flow patterns for the sending countries may be accounted for by immigration legislation or recruitment policies within the receiving countries toward which the different flows were directed. Internal political or economic changes within some sending countries may have exerted some influence.

Where the countries had tied their economic policies to labor export, as Turkey and Yugoslavia did, fluctuations in the world economic conditions later created uncertainty within their own economic planning efforts. Thus, a rise in unemployment rates, and a decline in balance of payments as a result of loss of remittances were shaped by economic events external to the labor exporting countries themselves.

Conclusions

Labor migration can have multiple effects on development within countries becoming dependent on labor export. On the one hand, because of the selectivity process which accompanies migratory movements, a loss of skilled manpower and better trained and educated sectors of the work force occurs. The small national supplies of trained professionals and technicians are often depleted. For instance, 39 per cent of the economically active Turkish population had completed primary and secondary school in 1970; among those who emigrated, 77 per cent had attained the same level of schooling (Paine, 1974). This loss of human capital, in which substantial amounts of national capital had been invested, deprived the local economy of their services, while contributing their resources to the growth of the industrialized countries.

With regard to reduction of the high levels of unemployment which plague most sending countries, the importance of out-emigration ranged from substantial to negligible.

Finally, there is the question of remittances. Clearly, the loss of remittances as a source of foreign exchange without the development of substitute earnings sources was bound to have critical effects on several sending countries. It is this factor, probably more than any other, which motivated representatives of labor-exporting countries to call for direct foreign investment in the form of relocation or productive facilities abroad as a substitute for the export of labor.

Regional aggregates of nations from which large-scale emigration took place were frequently drained of trained, skilled labor, technicians, and professionals through out-migration. Sometimes this occurred in the midst of a general labor surplus. To the degree that this "skimming" effect left the labor-exporting countries with less well-trained labor forces, they were often short of valuable human resources necessary to carry out development programs. At the same time, migrant remittances which brought a rapid increase in spending on housing, land, and consumer items, sometimes tended to create inflationary pressures for the non-migrating population. Many of these countries were subsequently confronted with an expansion of unemployment brought about by the halt to further immigration abroad, and by the return of out-migrants in the late 1970's. In some cases, this process was accompanied by a large-scale shift of population from rural to urban regions and the associated disruption of agricultural activities accompanied by further increases in urban land prices.

RETURN IN THE MEDITERRANEAN
LITTORAL: POLICY AGENDAS

Demetrios G. Papademetriou

Labor migration was initially expected to be an unmitigated benefit to both sending and receiving societies. Its exponential and almost uncontrolled growth during the late 1960's and early 1970's, however, prompted a fundamental reassessment with a sobering effect on all the principals in the migration chain. This reassessment has now led to the conclusion that migration has failed to resolve or substantially ameliorate the structural conditions known to fuel migration.

The less-developed countries along the Mediterranean littoral are now faced with the return of their nationals making obvious the rather marginal socioeconomic gains from the skills and remittances of former emigrants. Fundamental to developing contingency plans for return migration is the recognition that return is a crucial public policy and public and private management problem which, although analytically distinct from emigration, is intimately related to it since many of the conditions which would moderate pressures for emigration would also tend to initiate and maintain a return flow. Survey results confirm (Mendez and Moro, 1976; Kennedy, 1978; Widgren, 1976; Adler, 1980, 1981; Unger, 1981; Collaros and Moussourou, 1978; Velzen, 1977; Papademetriou, 1983c) that some of those migrants better equipped to make a strong social, economic and occupational impact on their mother countries have been successful enough abroad so as to be targets of integrationist efforts by the receiving countries making their return unlikely. Regardless of who is attracted to return, however, home countries must realize that many returnees are likely to be interested in engaging in tertiary sector activities. This "preference" cannot be attributed only to the ease of access into that sector or the absence of opportunities in the secondary sector: rather, it must be recognized as one of the most fundamental objectives of emigrants everywhere.

Utilization of remitted
and tranferred savings

If countries of worker origin are to receive more than marginal benefits from emigration, they must commit themselves to a development program which assigns high priority to the role of remitted emigrant funds and channel them toward employment-generating directions which meet the returnees'

259

needs while offering definite dividends to their country by redressing one major component of their socioeconomic predicament: high un — and under — employment. A potentially useful instrument of such a policy can be the channeling of funds into selected existing industrial concerns in return for preference in employment. The advantages of such selectively administered policy can be significant — but only if it is integrated within the country's overall development nexus.

Yugoslavia has been particularly active in this area. Its involvement commenced over a decade ago when it took a step unprecedented in socialist systems: it authorized state enterprises to issue bonds purchaseable only with hard currency in return for preference in employment (Widgren, 1976). Turkey followed a somewhat similar path for a time. This path, however, was in direct violation of the charter of the investment bank formed to assist emigrants to invest their earnings in Turkey (Adler, 1981).

When investment is not directed to existing industries but toward establishing new ones, one of the major emphases can often be on agricultural equipment or agro-industrial enterprises, usually in regions of heavy migrant outflow. Such projects are thought to have continuously compounding benefits as they are likely to begin to stem the decline and deterioration of the countryside by opening new employment opportunities and incentives to remain in agricultural occupations; to economically revitalize regions through industrial decentralization; and to control internal and, subsequently, often international emigration.

These and similar approaches follow the promises of classical economic theories. Accordingly, *human capital, expected income,* and *intersectoral linkage* of economic models serve to explain migration. The first two models are the many variants of the Sjaastad (1962) and Todaro (1976) migration models, which view migration as a rational individual act of income maximization but with the introduction of several nonpecuniary costs and benefits (Rivera-Batiz, 1980). The *intersectoral linkage* model is grounded in the idea that changes in the social and economic structure of one region impact on other regions of that country, as well as on relevant regions of other countries. Such linkages can be of a backward, forward, or final demand nature. For instance, effective rural development programs which substantially raise the standard of living of a given rural area can lead to increased demand for such items as fertilizers, farm implements, machinery and credit, thus increasing economic activity in urban areas and, to the extent that many of these instruments must be imported, in other countries (backward linkages); forward linkages would again benefit urban areas through increased demand for transport and storage facilities for agricultural commodities, agriprocessing facilities, and wholesaling for international distribution; finally, increases in disposable income of rural residents will generate demand for goods and services produced either regionally or abroad, resulting in additional employment (final demand linkages) (Hirschman, 1958).

Leading institutions must thus become actively engaged in assisting migrants with the choice of investment, planning, designing, financing, and managing of such projects. Furthermore, recognizing that the talent and training on which the success of such programs is predicated are areas in which migrants are least adept and prepared, a major effort needs to be undertaken between labor receivers and labor senders to provide for precisely such training to those migrants who show the aptitude for and interest in such programs.

Several prototype programs along these lines exist in Europe. The Federal Republic Germany, for instance, has had such programs with Turkey, Yugoslavia, and Greece; France has attempted several variations of such training programs with Algerians, Spaniards and Portuguese; and The Netherlands offers similar programs to nationals of all of its labor suppliers. The problems, however, have been many and, to a degree, predictable. The funds committed have been small; the total numbers of trainees involved over the last decade have also been small; many "graduates" of such programs often simply refuse to return to their home countries; and inadequate financing has seen very few projects make it from the drawing board to completion. Furthermore, sending country institutions have made only a few good faith efforts in assisting with emigrant-led employment-generating investments. When assistance has been forthcoming, it is usually the exception, rather than the rule. Although the literature is replete with instances of such assistance, they are more in the nature of isolated initiatives rather than integral parts of a comprehensive development strategy. Spain, for instance, reports several bank-led initiatives not only in the housing sector but also in small-scale, labor-intensive enterprises; Yugoslavia and Portugal have emphasized the making of shares in public enterprises available to investors with hard currency, often with preferential treatment in hiring; Turkey has had a long but mixed record with emigrant-financed rural cooperatives and other investment ventures; Greece has recently made some efforts to organize and assist emigrants with the setting-up of emigrant-financed industrial initiatives; and Algeria has had, on balance, a poor record in attracting its nationals to return, in spite of recent massive efforts at infrastructure improvement (especially housing) geared almost entirely to potential returnees (Papademetriou, 1983c; Adler, 1980, 1981; Entzinger, 1978; Van Gendt, 1977; Mendez and Moro, 1976; Widgren, 1976, 1977).

That such migrant-led ventures have had only marginal employment-generating and society-wide developmental impacts can be attributed to many factors, such as the attitudes of migrants both vis-à-vis large-scale enterpreneurial initiatives and overall remittance utilization, and the failure or inability of sending societies to guide and integrate such initiatives into their overall planning schemes. It appears that the modal attitude of the architects of development in countries of worker origin vis-à-vis emigration is one which welcomes remittances almost exclusively as hard currency reserves.

Turkey's mixed record with emigrant initiatives, for instance, can be attributed to official ambivalence toward such initiatives. The Turkish financial community mishandled the issue of foreign worker investments at several key points during its evolution (Adler, 1981). It failed to coordinate them with such key actors as the Ministry of Labor and local governments. DESIYAB, the bank set up to channel remittances, became the object of political football: proposed in 1972, it did not become chartered until 1975 and soon after it began to invest remitted funds in purchasing shares in existing large enterprises instead of investing them in the mandated Turkish Workers' Companies. In addition, the bank's staffing changed with each change in government and thus failed to develop the committed professional cadre necessary to formulate and implement sustained long-term projects. Finally, those activities which were undertaken never became integral parts of regional development initiatives and usually resulted in imbalances and failures (Heopfner and Huber, 1978; Entzinger, 1978).

The labor host countries' record vis-à-vis foreign worker investment initiatives in the workers' countries has been improving, on the other hand. Germany, in reaction to the frequent failures of Turkish workers' enterprises took the initiative in consolidating all such activities into a non-profit umbrella organization (*Verband Tuerkischer Arbeitsnehmergesellschaften*) charged with assisting its members in choosing appropriate investment areas and providing the requisite training facilities, public relations and internal economic information infrastructure. Furthermore, a sister structure was established in Ankara to safeguard the member organizations' interests. Finally, this umbrella organization serves as an important conduit for preparing projects to be funded by the German Development Assistance authorities. The total membership of these *Arbeitsnehmergesellschaften* is nearly 100,000 and the total investment runs into the hundreds of millions of Turkish lira (Adler, 1981; Van Gendt, 1977).

A recently (1981) ratified agreement between Greece and Germany represents the current state-of-the-art in the cooperation between sending and receiving countries. The following brief analysis of that agreement is intended not only to underline the difficulties and opportunities which such cooperation presents but also to place the role of home countries in this process into perspective and document the frustrating gap between promise and performance in this crucial area. The agreement (Greek Ministry of Coordination, 1981) was unmistakably the result of unremitting pressure by the *Verband zur Foerderung Griechischer Arbeitsnehmergesellschaften* (Federation for the Advancement of Greek Worker Companies) in Stuttgart. The Federation, modelled after similar Turkish and Yugoslav organizations, found an able ally in the Ministry of Co-ordination Secretariat for Policy on Inter-European Movements of Greek Labor whose then director, Manolis Deliyannakis, had recently taken the post after long-term residence in the Federal Republic. The agreement codifies procedures which had operated in isolation for many years and took well over two years to negotiate and ratify. Its aim is to assist Greek workers in Germany set up industrial enterprises in Greece. The procedure is as follows: once a group of investors has been formed and an investment idea has been developed (often with the assistance of the Federation), the Federation undertakes preliminary feasibility and market assessment studies in an effort to appraise the prospects for success of the proposed scheme and the likelihood of investor interest from sources other than the Greek workers employed in Germany. If the preliminary analyses prove enouraging, a Federation committee of experts meets to decide whether to recommend the proposed project, taking into account the legal regimes regulating mixed investments in Greece. If the Committee's recommentation is positive, independent consultants are engaged to conduct a full market study; if these findings are also positive, a full feasibility study is authorized and, following its positive results, a corporation is chartered. Following the chartering of a company, the Federation sponsors a series of intensive seminars designed to introduce and train the principals of the corporation and potential investors in the intricacies and principles of investment, management, and related activities. At the same time, there begins a several-month long series of technical regiments covering every aspect of organizing and managing an industrial concern.

Most expenses incurred throughout the course of this process are borne by the German and Greek governments on a 70/30 per cent formula. Of the 30 per cent contribution by the Greek government, one third is an outright grant while the remaining two-thirds are in the form of long-term, low-interest loans with repayment schedules commencing after the company is in actual operation. The cost of technical training is divided among the investors (50 per cent), the German Federal government (35 per cent) and the Greek government (15 per cent) — the latter two contributions being in the form of low-interest loans. The financing of the investment venture, finally, is in accordance with the following terms: the minimum investment by the workers is set at 30 per cent of the total; for the remaining funds, the investors must obtain loans from a variety of quarters, such as commercial sources, preferential-term loans under the provisions of Greece's industrial investment programs, and, in the event that the project is considered a priority under the European Economic Community guidelines, the Community may be asked to participate for up to 40 per cent of the total cost. Finally, up to 20 per cent of the total investment funds can be obtained from special preference loans from a joint Greek-German investment fund supported equally by the two governments.

This elaborate scheme is intended to anticipate and address most of the problems associated with setting up foreign-worker led industrial ventures. Foreign participation, for example, is limited to 40 per cent of each venture so as to preeempt potentially negative local reaction; and a balance is struck between preparing the investment/management/technical team and facilitating the take-off of projects with generous grants and loans yet the investors are asked to carry a financial burden substantial enough to dissuade all but the most serious candidates. Interestingly enough, a conscious effort had been made throughout the course of the delicate negotiations with the Federal Republic to avoid the limelight so as to prevent the premature politicization of the issue (Deliyannakis, 1980).

Although the agreement is very recent, industrial initiatives by Greek workers in the Federal Republic of Germany go back into the mid-1970's and have had an uneven record of assistance by the Greek development authorities. Perhaps as a result of such ambivalent and intermittent assistance, the record is extremely meager. In 1981, only three such companies were in operation, with 122 investors having committed about 0.5 million U.S. dollars and employing a total of 46 workers; two additional companies, with 291 investors and $1.5 million investment had already been chartered; two more companies were in the process of being chartered; finally, seven additional companies were in different stages of preparation (Ministry of Coordination, 1981).

This brief excursus into the details of the Greek-German agreement points to the complexities of assisting foreign workers form their own enterprises and the level of organizational skills which are the *sine qua non* for successful ventures. Yet, even successful projects seem to have only modest employment-generating characteristics.

Occupational skill and the socio-economic re-integration of returnees

Another assumption of labor exporting countries is that the skills of returning migrants will be largely compatible with the economic needs at home. This is usually not the case. The problem reflects the inadeguate attention paid both to assessing the skills of returnees and the employment needs of domestic economies and informing the migrant, while he is still abroad, of such needs, of the availability of jobs, of the level and type of available social services, and, finally, of the opportunities for vocational training (Van Gendt, 1977; Böhning, 1975, 1979; Schiller, 1974).

The logical first step of this process is an accounting of the social, economic, skill, and occupational background, as well as the expectations of emigrants which must then be followed by a concerted effort to match skills and occupational preferences with available job openings. The most efficient way to do that is through a questonnaire (one is already used by Greece and Spain but has experienced serious distribution and collection problems) which will seek answers in the following areas: demographic profiles of respondents (age, sex, marital status, education, region of origin); approximate timing of expected return; vocational qualifications and occupation before emigration and while abroad; occupational and geographic preference upon return; minimum salary requirements (expectations) upon return; and the acceptable levels of social services and infrastructure requirements upon return.

The success of such initiatives will hinge on the labor supplying countries' ability to build a good track record by focusing initially on making only modest claims and carrying them out. The present system denies sending countries a reliable data base. Without such an inventory a return and re-integration policy would be difficult to formulate. The act of matching labor supply with labor demand is the next area fraught with uncertainty and pit-falls, particularly when realizing that return in response to a present labor need may be foolhardy because return is a drawn out process while a labor need is usually immediate.

Naturally, the answer to the operational problems of such efforts are ef-ficiency and commitment. While computerization and formation of a job data bank would be ideal solutions (and have been largely implemented by Italy and Spain), they usually are well beyond the technical and economic resources of most labor senders. Short of this ideal, these countries can focus on developing manpower and employment policies in tune with regional, not just national, development objectives. Such policies, if realistically conceived (perhaps with the assistance of appropriately trained experts from international and regional organizations — OECD or the European Community in the case under discus-sion) and efficiently implemented, can anticipate and direct job creation and, consequently, the placement of returnees. When these efforts become integra-ted with overall schemes of social, cultural, and industrial decentralization and are offered together with incentive structures aimed at attracting potential returnees where they are most needed, they can produce handsome dividends for all concerned. A major stumbling block may be the effective dissemination of such information to one's migrants abroad. It is here that the assistance of receivers can be of incalculable benefit as can the network of the various cul-tural, religious, social, and diplomatic services which are involved in different facets of the migrant's life abroad (Papademetriou, 1978).

There are two main reasons for the frequent failure of the occupational qualifications of returnees to match the skills needed by their countries: first, the migrant's role in the migration process is not to acquire skills. Self-invest-ment in human capital is not his goal and the host countries are simply neither interested in helping him enhance his skills (and thus making him more compe-titive with their own nationals) nor in offering him commensurate occupational advancement; second, the failure to match skills with needs simply reflects a lack in sending country planning. The former problem, of course, is quite dif-ficult to address. To correct the latter problem requires the launching of an aggresive campaign by the sending countries prior to emigration (with language and fundamental skill courses sponsored by the recruiting countries), which would be continued while abroad (aiming at formal or on-the-job vocational training courses followed by equitable occupational advancement). Toward the end of the sojourn, additional training should be geared toward the occu-pational needs of sending countries. A proportion of the cost of these training programs should be borne by the private sectors of the receiving countries, while the sending countries, the prospective ultimate beneficiaries of this training process, should undertake the responsibility of guaranteeing placement for these "elite" returnees (Papademetriou, 1983a, b).

The appeal of transferring capital to labor (both in its investment and production forms) should be the obvious comparative advantage which most senders enjoy over all receivers in certain labor-intensive, low-skill and repetitive production processes. Although any such initiatives would be to the distinct advantage of the investment capital, in the present climate of severe unemployment and general economic and internal political uncertainty this course of action would face almost insurmountable political obstacles.

Of note here is the Dutch REMPLOD (Reintegration of Emigrant Manpower and the Promotion of Local Opportunities for Development), program designed to identify, in cooperation with local research teams, regions and investment strategies specifically intended to impact on areas of high emigration and to induce return migration flows. The project has been dormant since 1977. It invested nearly 30 million Dutch guilders, over 90 per cent of which was expended on general employment creation projects after return migration initiatives proved unsuccessful (Abadan-Unat, 1976; Van Velzen, 1977; Van Gendt, 1976). In this regard, some very interesting, and methodologically ingenious, work has been done in Germany, Switzerland and France. In the first case (Hiemenz and Schatz, 1978), the impact of increasing imports from sending countries as an alternative to foreign labor was analyzed. The authors concluded that almost independently of export expansion, a significant proportion of manufacturing jobs would be lost in the Federal Republic Germany by 1985 and warned of the need for a labor market policy to deal with this contingency. In the Swiss case (Maillat *et al.*, 1976), an effort was made to identify the economic, labor market, social, and political costs involved in the transfer of Swiss industries to the LDC's. The industries identified as the "most transferable" were the textiles, clothing, and metallurgical branches. Finally, a study in France (Tapinos et al., 1978) confirmed the desirability of transferring selected non-competitive industries abroad while pointing out the internal political difficulties which this course of action would encounter.

Conclusion

The Mediterranean Basin countries have still to obtain the promised returns on their emigration "investment". While some relief from unemployment and substantial remittances have been obtained, emigration has failed to provide a discernible developmental impetus in any of the countries. This is not to say that the countries of worker origin have been completely unaffected by emigration. Certainly, the progress of Greece, Spain and, above all, Italy must have been influenced from the vast money transfers which have highlighted the migration process — over eighty billion DM since 1960 from Germany alone (Widgren, 1977; Papademetriou, 1983b). Yet, such transfers have not played a significant and measurable role in the overall development of these countries although they have obviously played a leadership role in the agricultural mechanization so evident in the countrysides of sending countries; and they are responsible for the equally noticeable housing boom, the proliferation of small service establishments, and the growth of tourist-related infrastructure. In short, the process has accomplished at least one important goal: it has significantly improved the economic fortunes of most families whose members have emigrated. Based on this factor alone, one may be likely to conclude that the process has been at least a qualified success.

The areas where public intervention can still allow sending societies to capture some of the promised benefits of migration are remittance utilization and return migration. As countries in the Mediterranean littoral gain a fuller understanding of the forces which impact on the development process, initiatives to integrate remittances and returnees into their economy and society will increase. What is needed, however, is a better understanding of the place of each country in an increasingly interdependent world and the responsibilities which migration imposes on national actors at both ends of the flow. In view of this mutuality of responsibilities, migration becomes a matter virtually impervious to satisfactory solution by unilateral action (Papademetriou and Hopple, 1982).

EXPLAINING RETURN MIGRATION

Anthony H. Richmond

A theory of return migration should be logically derivable as a subset of a more general theory of migration. Unfortunately, the field of migration studies has not generated a generally acceptable theory although there have been various typologies such as that of Petersen (1958). Empirical studies of migration have addressed themselves to major issues, namely the scale and direction of migration flows; the objective characteristics of migrants defined in terms of demographic, economic, social and cultural variables; the motivation for migration and the modes of adaptation and integration of migrants into the receiving society. Studies of return migration have generally been concerned with similar issues, paralleling the above questions.

It is unlikely that any one general theory could encompass all specific empirical foci. However, there are at least three broad philosophic-sociological perspectives that have influenced thinking about migration. They are the functionalist approach; the Marxist or conflict perspective; and the general systems framework, the last endeavouring to incorporate some of the insights derived from both the functionalist and Marxist viewpoints (Pryor, 1981).

Voluntary migration

In an often cited paper, Lee (1966) developed a theory of migration based largely on Ravenstein's original propositions. He examined the concepts of "stream and counterstream" in the context of a model which involves a comparison of positive and negative factors at origin and destination, together with the severity of intervening obstables. His concept of "counterstream" is essentially that of "return migration", overlooking the fact that exchange migration can occur without involving a return movement. Among the factors that he mentions as contributing to return migration are a change of balance of positive and negative factors at origin or destination, consequent, for example, upon an economic depression. He also mentions improved communications and better knowledge of opportunities, together with the fact that not all migrants had an initial intention to stay away permanently.

The common denominator underlying such theories of migration as that of Lee is the essentially voluntary nature of the movement and its responsiveness to changing economic conditions in the sending and receiving areas. It follows that return migration is likely to occur when there is an absolute or relative decline in the gross domestic product per head in the receiving society or an equivalent improvement in the conditions in the sending area. Other factors likely to influence the scale and direction of return migration are the lack of completely successful integration into the receiving society, together with the persistence of social ties and obligations in the sending country, particularly those relating to family relationship. The importance of original intentions in determining the propensity to return come to the fore when the migration has been undertaken because of a desire for travel and adventure, or in order to assist the family in the sending area through remittances. When these short-term goals are achieved this may induce a return to the former country.

Empirical studies of return migration have not succeeded in identifying any consistent pattern with regard to the factors which differentiate between migrants who stay or those who return. Gmelch (1980), reviewing the literature on return migration, concluded that the "pull" factors were strongest in influencing the decision to return, notwithstanding the importance of economic recession in Western European countries. He also noted that the majority of returnees were not "failures" in either economic or social terms, but neither were they necessarily the most successful. In fact, both upward and downward mobility in the receiving society may reduce the propensity to return.

Education too is an important differentiating factor between sedentary and migratory populations. Generally, migrants are somewhat better educated than the average in the source country but are likely to be below the average in the country of destination (Bouvier, Macisco and Zarate, 1976). A logical inference shows returning migrants having a level of education closer to the average for the initial receiving society and above the average for the country of origin and return. This is related to the unwarranted expectations of some that the migrants will receive further education and training in the receiving country which will be a valuable form of human capital when reinvested in the country of origin.

In considering the issue of return migration two questions arise regarding adaptation and integration of migrants. Are those who return more or less "assimilated" than those who stay and, when they return to the country of origin, do returnees face problems of adaptation and have difficulty reintegrating? Until recently, very few studies of return migration have been sufficiently systematic to permit such comparisons.

Cerase (1974) developed a typology of return migration. His work was a study of Italians returning from the United States. He distinguished return migration related to failure to achieve economic goals, return migration governed by a conservative attachment to the values of the sending society, return associated with success in the receiving society and "innovation" on return; finally he refers to the return at time of retirement. It is significant that he observed considerable resistance to attempts by "innovators" to introduce changes in their former communities.

One of the more comprehensive studies of migration and return was that carried out under the auspices of UNITAR and directed by William Glaser (Glaser and Habers, 1974; Glaser, 1978). The study focused on foreign students in a number of western countries. Glaser concluded that when students returned it was because of the pull of family, friends or of patriotic feelings. The ablest students were neither more nor less likely to return than the average, and many of the "stay-ons" were temporary. To increase return, countries must think of the professional's family and welcome foreign spouses (Glaser, 1978: 219). It is interesting to note that members of ethnic minorities in the sending country were less likely to return than those who belong to the majority ethnic group. However, despite pressures to return, some remained in order to obtain on-the-job training or because they saw their career prospects as better in the foreign country.

Involuntary migration

There are a variety of circumstances which give rise to involuntary migration. Forced migration of prisoners both political and criminal, impressment and banishment together with other forms of compulsory relocation, including expulsion, have occurred in quite recent times, often backed by police or military force. Obvious examples are the Uganda Asians or the Indochinese from Vietnam or Kampuchea.Forced migration is clearly the reason for the increasing numbers of refugees in various parts of the world. Many refugees have found temporary asylum in neighbouring countries and have eventually been accepted for longer term settlement elsewhere.

The aspiration to return to the country of origin is rarely absent from any refugee movement and may even persist into the second and subsequent generations. Eastern European refugees in Western Europe, North America and Australia have maintained a strong sense of ethnic identity and have maintained an "ideology of return". From a practical point of view these aspirations may be utopian. Nevertheless, they influence the mode of adaptation of refugee migrants in their new countries, contributing to the propensity to maintain a pluralistic mode of integration, emphasizing language maintenance, ethnic identity and separate institutions.

There is also a coercive element that can be identified even in those migrations that are predominantly economic in character. When individuals appear to be making a free choice it is evident that economic and social conditions create the necessity for choice and constrain the options available. A variety of economic pressures to induce migration are expropriation of land and property, the imposition of taxes or punitive rents, and discriminatory practices against minorities. Each of the sources of coercive or involuntary migration has its equivalent form of return migration. The end of a war or civil strife, the discharge of prisoners and forced labourers, and the repatriation

271

of former refugees are more benign examples. Return migration itself, however, may be coercive when it takes the form of deportation or repatriation, requirements to depart backed by legal sanctions, cancellation of temporary work permits, or the compulsory repatriation of ethnic minorities. Examples of all of these processes can be found in the history of recent international migration movements.

General systems framework:
explanation of migration

A more general systems approach to migration theory is necessary if it is to take into account the complexity of international movements, including return migration. Growing dissatisfaction with static equilibrium models of social systems, and with models of society that were based on analogies with biological and homeostatic processes, led to the development of general systems theories that were much influenced by studies of communications and information feedback as a control mechanism. Social systems are understood to involve continuing ongoing processes, including interchange with other systems and sub-systems. These systems are open, flexible and involve exchanges between boundaries. A continuing process of adaptation occurs in response to internally generated and external sources of conflict. "A central feature of the complex adaptive system is its capacity to persist or develop by changing its own structure, sometimes in fundamental ways" (Buckley, 1967: 206).

For instance, the economic division is recognized to be a world-wide one in which there is an extensive division of labour between countries at varying levels of economic development. There are complex and unequal exchanges between the "core" countries that have established a dominant position and those peripheral and semi-peripheral areas that are maintained in a situation of economic subordination and dependency (Wallerstein, 1974; Petras, 1981). There is a growing consensus on the characteristics of a global system of international migration as well (Richmond and Verma, 1978). The macrotheoretical approach to migration as represented by Hoffmann-Nowotny (1981) focuses on the central concepts of power and legitimation. When these two dimensions of social relations diverge there are consequent "structural tensions". He identifies three types: (a) tension arising from differential rank; (b) disequilibrium tension arising from status inconsistency; (c) incompleteness tension resulting from non-participation in one or more status lines. He argues that structural tensions generate anomy which may be individual, collective or class based. Anomic tensions can be transferred from the level of the unit to that of the system giving rise to inter-institutional anomy. Hoffmann-Nowotny sees emigration as one means of handling anomic tension and balancing status configurations. At the societal level migration may be a policy designed to achieve tension management. Migration is a way of shifting and transforming anomic tension. By the same token immigration may contribute to the building of tension in the receiving society. A tendency in modern mass migration for immigrants to be limited to certain lower levels in the system of stratification he describes as "undercasting" (Unterschichtung). Hoffmann-Nowotny sees this as a "neo-feudal" tendency which could, under certain circumstances, lead to renewed migration. He notes that, to the extent that migration arises from the exploitation of economic development differences between sending and receiving areas, length of residence tends to be short and migration to assume a rotational character.

The latter point is central to the world systems perspective of the neo-Marxist writers. Capital and labour tend to move in opposite directions. Changes in the international division of labour have had consequences for semi-peripheral and peripheral (Third World) countries resulting in a flow of both highly qualified and unskilled workers to the more advanced countries (Glickman and Petras, 1981). The situation is aggravated by the increasing dependence of less developed countries on the fluctuating needs of the more advanced capitalist economies, resulting in some cases in a process of "de-development" (Frank, 1981). In these circumstances, return migration is likely to occur whenever there is an economic recession in the "core" areas and is generally an involuntary response to essentially coercive controls over the international flow of labour. Under these conditions, immigrant labour is seen as a regulator of cyclical problems of the "semi-peripheral" areas. The modern systems approach differs from the earlier Marxist analyses of migration in that it emphasizes global economic interdependence and the changing balance of power between countries within the "core", as well as between the peripheral and semi-peripheral zones.

Immigrant adaptation
and return migration

The general systems approach has also proved fruitful in the study of immigrant adaptation and integration. A multivariate model emphasizes that there are many dimensions to immigrant behavioural adaptation. A high level of acculturation at the cognitive and instrumental levels, accompanied by successful economic integration, does not necessarily lead to identification with the receiving country or permanent residence in it. The multivariate model of immigrant adaptation developed by Goldlust and Richmond (1974) suggested that strong identification with the receiving country, including an intention to settle permanently, was closely associated with length of residence, close family and friendship networks, and with high satisfaction. Low identification and the probability of renewed migration was greatest among the better educated and more highly qualified, together with those whose language and cultural backgrounds were closest to those of the receiving society. This is the opposite of what would be expected if ease of assimilation was a factor in permanent settlement.

Studies of the return migration of Yugoslav immigrants in Germany have also been undertaken using a systems perspective. The general model sees the sending and receiving societies as linked through a suprasystem (Tos, 1976). Immigrants are seen to move from system one to system two in order to change their position in a stratification hierarchy. This involves an understanding of the aspirations and expectations of the migrants. Among the dimensions of the system to be considered are the socialization sub-system, the institutional sub-system and the sub-system of sanctions. Klinar (1976) utilized this theoretical framework in a study of Yugoslav workers in Germany, distinguishing between temporary and permanent migration. He also examined certain "disjunctive" processes which occur when the status aspirations of the immigrant group conflicts with that of the dominant majority and with other ethnic groups. Further studies of return migrants within this systems framework led to the generation of a typology, using a factor analytic program, of the main factors inducing return. The factors were (a) initially low socioeconomic position in the sending society (b) lack of upward mobility in the receiving society (c) strong family ties in the sending country and (d) lack of adaptation in the receiving society (Meznaric and Knap, 1978). Klinar (1978) reviews the evidence from these studies of Yugoslav immigration and return and concludes that the re-migrants did not improve their education or qualifications in system two (i.e., abroad). The income of returnees is lower than it was abroad although most returnees succeed in improving their standard of living, particularly housing conditions, by using their savings (Klinar, 1978).

In his review of return migration, Gmelch (1980) saw no evidence that return migration causes any significant change in the social structure of the sending societies. He quoted Rhoades's (1978, 1979, 1980) view that very few of the benefits for sending societies which proponents of migration anticipated have actually occurred. Gmelch also noted, however, that most of the writings on return migration concern peasants and others returning to developing societies. There is a need to balance this view with more information on the return of middle and upper strata migrants. In this connection the Canadian experience of return migration is particularly relevant.

My own study of British immigrants returning from Canada to the United Kingdom generated certain hypotheses which cast some doubt upon traditional views of the return migration process (Richmond, 1967, 1968, 1969). I coined the term *transilient* to describe immigrants who were highly mobile geographically and often moved from one country to another, returning to the country of origin, often only temporarily before moving on yet again. In my original (1962-63) sample of returnees to Britain, 31 per cent expressed a firm intention of returning to Canada while a further 28 per cent were uncertain of their future plans or expected to move on to a third country. A decade later Motuz (1976) found that almost a third of the returnees (from various countries) intended to return to Canada at some time and over 40 per cent were undecided, or intended to remigrate to another country.

I put forward the hypothesis that return migration would be higher among those who retained approximately the same occupational status and social position and would be low among those who had experienced either upward or downward mobility. Motuz tested this hypothesis and found that one in six of the returning migrants felt that their social position had risen in Canada compared with one in three of the respondents in a control group. Nearly 22 per cent of the returnees felt their social position had declined compared with 18 per cent of the stayers. In other words, 58 per cent of the returnees compared with 47 per cent of those who stayed in Canada up to three years, felt their social position had not changed. The difference between the proportions is related to the question of original intentions. A higher proportion of the intended returners experienced no change in their social position while more intended stayers experienced a decline, leading to the conclusion that not experiencing hoped-for upward mobility is probably associated with changing the original intention to settle and returning to the former country instead.

Conclusions

Migration in advanced industrial and post-industrial societies is largely "exchange migration". High gross rates give rise to only small net differences between sending and receiving areas. Return migration is a part of this exchange process. It does not differ from other types of migration in terms of modes of adaptation. Most migrants do not consider themselves permanently settled in one place. Therefore, complete "assimilation" is unlikely. The dominant mode of adaptation is "transilience". This involves effective economic integration, a high level of cognitive acculturation but low levels of identification with the society or community of residence.

• Return migration is likely to increase (a) when economic conditions improve opportunities for social mobility in the former country or reduce them in the receiving society; (b) when political regimes change or governments of sending or receiving countries offer special inducements to return; (c) receiving countries revoke permits to stay due to internal economic or political conditions. Finally the greater the similarity between the linguistic, cultural or economic characteristics of the sending and receiving areas, and the stronger the communication links between them, the more likely migrants will be to return to place of origin.

RETURN MIGRATION IN COMPARATIVE PERSPECTIVE

Rosemarie Rogers

The major purpose of this paper is to raise critically a number of issues in the study of return migration. The comments offered pertain primarily to migrants whose moves were based on individual decisions (1), and to voluntary rather than forced migrations. They do not pertain to migrants who are in a superordinate position to the host population (conquerors). For systematic overviews of the literature on return migration, see Bovenkerk (1974) and Gmelch (1980).

How should return migration be understood? Must we know a migrant's original intentions in order to evalutate properly the meaning of his return? When is return the fulfillment of an important goal? When is it the result of failure to reach a goal? There is agreement in the literature that migration occurs when individuals or groups experience certain deprivations in their environment and when they expect that their particular need or needs can be better fulfilled elsewhere while the costs will not be inacceptably high. But costs there almost always will be, and why should it therefore be surprising if for some migrants the decision to remain in the host country permanently or to return hangs in the balance for a long time - not only when migrants encounter policies that discourage settlement, but also in classical "im-migration contexts" (Thomas and Znaniecki, 1927)? Or if migrants call their earlier decisions into question and decide all over again, as they and their families go through their life cycles and their needs and preferences change; or as economic or social conditions in the host or sending countries change? Several analyses have suggested that a migrant's return orientation is a powerful factor in determining the degree to which he will become integrated and assimilated in the host society (Kremer and Spangenberg, 1980). Others stress the reverse relationship: return is primarily a dependent variable, one among several possible "regressive" or "anomic" responses to unsuccessful integration and assimilation (Esser, 1980; Hoffmann-Nowotny, 1973). There is no doubt a negative statistical relationship between return intention and degree of as-similation, the causal influence going in both directions as a rule. But it is misleading to stop with the analysis there: as I will try to show below one has a more valid picture of return if the analytical concerns are shifted from the interpretation of central tendencies and correlations to the identification and interpretation of the full pattern of variability in the data.

Another question concerns the validity of certain criticisms of the lack of impact of returning migrants on their home countries' economies. Finally,

I shall ask what the experiences in several migration contexts around the world have to teach us concerning the prospects for success of policies of "temporary" labor migration.

Original intention to settle or return

There is by now a widely recognized pattern in migration: in all "non-immigration" contexts, from South Africa's system of "oscillating migration" to the Middle East with its heavy reliance on "temporary labor" to Western Europe's "rotation principle" of the 1960's, there are smaller or larger residues of permanent migrants, legal or illegal (International Bank for Reconstruction and Development, 1977; Stahl, 1981; Birks and Sinclair, 1980; Serageldin *et al.*, 1983); conversely, there have been considerable return flows from the classical immigration countries (Immigration Commission, 1911, Vol. I; Warren, 1979; Warren and Peck, 1980; Motuz, n.d.).

In Western Europe in the 1960's and early 1970's, when only France and Sweden considered themselves *bona fide* immigration countries, the proportion of migrants who reported that they were migrating or had migrated with the intention to immigrate, never exceeded five per cent (Braun, 1970; Paine, 1975; Gehmacher, 1973). It is obvious that these migrants' initial and even later intentions were strongly influenced by the general norms of temporary migration communicated to them in many ways, including the need to renew work and residence permits on a regular basis. The migrants' statements proved poor predictors of their actual behavior: most stayed on far longer than they had thought they would, because it took them longer than they had expected to reach certain savings targets, because little changed in the economies of their own countries, and because their tastes and aspirations changed once they were abroad. Nevertheless, millions of migrant workers in Europe have in fact returned home (Böhning, 1980). Should we assume that the initial intentions to return were true or that the returns represented overwhelmingly "regressive" or "anomic" behaviors?

Hoffmann-Nowotny (1973) sees the return of Italian labor migrants from Switzerland primarily as a form of anomic adaptation, as an alternative — albeit a healthier one — to "neofeudal distancing". He does grant that return migration need not be anomic by suggesting that non-anomic return of labor migrants is most likely to occur when the host and sending countries' levels of economic development are fairly equal. In the case of certain "target" migrations — when the migrant left his home country in order to solve a specific problem and if no new structural tensions resulted from his migration — non-anomic return can take place as well. From his survey of Italian labor migrants in Switzerland, however, Hoffmann-Nowotny concludes that "the decision to retreat from the immigration context is to be regarded as a consequence of unsuccessful integration" (1973: 265).

278

Hoffmann-Nowotny's conclusions are based on answers to four separate questions concerning the migrants' perceptions of their structural integration, one question on social integration, and one question on how the migrants evaluate their migration experience overall. The answers are cross-tabulated with either one of two questions concerning intention to return vs. to remain in Switzerland (2). The results show that the more integrated the migrant, the less likely he is to say that he will probably return. For example, 43 per cent of the migrants reporting high occupational and financial mobility said that they might return, while 59 per cent of those with low perceived mobility gave this answer. Recalculating the percentages (Table 1), we observe, however, in all instances that there are among the potential returners substantial proportions of respondents who report high integration on that particular variable. But since all we see are bivariate relationships, we cannot ascertain the degree of overlap among high and low integrative responses. Collapsing the responses so that all variables become binary (Table 1), we obtain the following patterns of maximum possible overlap among the high and low integration responses:

— for the "conditional question" on return:
   as many as 41 per cent of the potential returnees could be highly integrated
   as many as 58 per cent of the likely settlers could be highly integrated

   as many as 40 per cent of the potential returnees could be poorly integrated
   as many as 12 per cent of the likely settlers could be poorly integrated

— for the "general question" on return:
   as many as 59 per cent of the potential returnees could be highly integrated
   as many as 72 per cent of the likely settlers could be highly integrated

   as many as 26 per cent of the potential returnees could be poorly integrated
   as many as 4 per cent of the likely settlers could be poorly integrated

   Only a reanalysis of the original data would tell us what the actual patterns are: whether the group of potential returnees shows a bimodal distribution on the combined integration variables — something approximating the hypothetical extreme cases shown above —, or whether there is a much wider spectrum of mixed types. But such an analysis must be done if the potential "unproblematic" (Hoffmann-Nowotny, 1973: 253) returnees are to be given the chance of being discovered, in addition to the well-identified — and perhaps indeed more numerous — potential "anomic" returnees.

   Turning to the classical countries of immigration, we find again important works in the literature that see the migrant who returns essentially as a failure with respect to integration into the host society. Although Esser occasionally (1980: 181, 223) acknowledges that migrants many undertake their

Table 1: Italian labor migrants in Switzerland: six indicators of integration
into the host society by likelihood of return - in per cent, N in ( )

	Potential returners	Likely settlers
	Conditional question on return	
Perceived social discrmination:		
Low	33	67
Medium	27	21
High	40	12
	(N=316)	(N=107)
Perceived reasons of preferential treatment of Swiss:		
Swiss do not receive preferential treatment	24	36
Swiss receive preferential treatment:		
because they are conscientious	23	27
simply because they are Swiss	34	28
to keep the Italians in a lower position	20	10
	(N=330)	(N=104)
Anticipated financial mobility:		
High	41	58
Low	59	42
	(N=343)	(N=109)
Differential frequency of interaction:		
More with Swiss	15	34
Equally frequently with Swiss and Italians	32	43
More with Italians	53	23
	(N=343)	(N=109)
	General question on return	
Perceived occupational and financial mobility		
High	28	46
Medium	31	26
Low	41	29
	(N=229)	(N=191)
Evaluation of emigration		
As good	74	96
As bad	26	4
	(N=220)	(N=185)

Source: Calculated from Hoffmann-Nowotny (1973: 259-263).

Note: The survey, based on a random sample (N=468) of male Italian workers and employees registered with the Zurich employment office, was undertaken in 1969.

Table 1 (cont.)

The first response under the integration variables always indicates highest degree of integration. The conditional question on return and the distribution of responses were as follows: "Assuming that you were offered a job in Italy with the same working conditions and wages as in Switzerland, would you in this case return to Italy or would you remain here?".

Return to Italy	73.3% (343)
Remain in Switzerland	23.3% (109)
DK, NA	3.4% (16)

In the general question on return, the respondents were asked to agree or disagree with the following statement: "I think that in the long run it will be better for me and my children if we stay in Switzerland".

Agree	49.2% (230)
Disagree	41.2% (193)
DK, NA	9.6% (45)

move with full intention of returning (in which case they may choose to become only partially integrated), he nevertheless, throughout most of his literature review as well as in his own general theory, interprets a migrant's desire to return as one among several possible "regressive" responses (1980: 181) to inadequate assimilation. Yet migrants enter also the classical immigration countries with differing intentions as to whether to stay or not to stay for good. Large numbers of migrants have in fact returned home or have moved on to third countries. In these instances is intention to return a good indicator of actual return? And do returnees who are fulfilling their original plans differ with respect to their integration and assimilation from those who planned to stay but then changed their minds? Comparative data for a wide range of countries are not available, but the existing data illustrate clearly that at least in some contexts the migrants' return intentions must be taken seriously. Thus, *a priori* expectations that returns from such contexts are overwhelmingly "regressive" reactions to unsuccessful assimilation are not warranted.

In a study of return migrants from Canada under the auspices of the Canadian Department of Manpower and Immigration (Motuz, n.d.), 11,242 immigrants who had come to Canada between 1969 to 1971 and had been classified as prospective members of the labor market were interviewed six months after their arrival. The survey included a question as to their original intentions to stay or to return which was answered by 11,024 respondents. The answers (Table 2) are strongly related to the migrants' actual situation as of June 1974, that is 3 to 5 years after their coming to Canada. More than nine tenths of those who had planned to settle in Canada were still there in 1974, as compared to only three quarters of those who had planned to move on.

Table 2: Immigrants to Canada: country of residence 3-5 years after entry, by original intention to stay permanently or temporarily - in per cent, N in ( )

Country of residence 3-5 years after entry	Original intention			
	Settle in Canada (N=7623)	Undecided ("came for visit only") (N=387)	Return to country of last residence (N=2500)	Move to third country (N=514)
Canada	92.6	89.4	75.8	74.1
Country of last residence	5.6	8.0	20.4	15.0
Third country	1.8	2.6	3.8	10.9

Source: Calculated from Motuz (n.d., Table I-6, p. 24).

Note: Married women, students, and retired persons were not included in the population to be studied. Of over 16,000 immigrants originally identified as the study sample, 4,009 could no longer be located after six months, and another 1,415 were excluded because they turned out not to be members of the labor market. The sample should be considered as biased against return migrants, since at least some of the immigrants who were not located for the first interview had probably left the country by that time.

Of the 1,043 migrants who had returned to their country of last residence, 699 were reinterviewed. The intended settlers and the intended returners in this group (Table 3) had indeed come to Canada for different reasons. In the first interview more than half of the intended settlers but less than one fifth of the intended returners had given "settlement-oriented reasons". Two reasons for return were mentioned with substantially different frequencies: "work-related reasons", which included having come to Canada on a working holiday or being recalled by one's employer, were mentioned more than three times as frequently by intended returners as by the intended settlers. On the other hand, the most frequently mentioned reason for the intended settlers changing their original plans was lack of employment opportunities.

The intended returners were also more likely than the intended settlers to have worked in the occupations that they had hoped to be working in Canada, had experienced less unemployment and were more likely to report themselves satisfied with employment opportunities and levels of earnings in Canada. Finally, the intended returners also stayed in Canada for a longer time before returning than the intended settlers. Comparing the group of returnees as a whole with the migrants who remained in Canada, Motuz reports that the returnees were more satisfied with the levels of earnings and the cost of living than those who stayed, and that there were no differences between the two groups with respect to their reported satisfaction with housing and educational,

Table 3: Return migrants from Canada: reasons for immigration and reasons for return, by original intention to return or settle - in per cent, N in ( )

	Intended returners (N=338)		Intended settlers (N=361)	
Reason for immigration:				
Adventure, travel	39.6		16.1	
Employer's request	9.5		4.4	
Gain Canadian education, work experience	16.6		10.8	
Working holiday in Canada	9.8		0.8	
Return-oriented reason		*(75.5)*		*(32.1)*
Improve economic situation, standard of living	13.0		41.8	
Be close to relatives, friends	4.1		7.2	
Political situation at home	1.5		7.8	
Settlement-oriented reason		*(18.6)*		*(56.8)*
Other reason		*(5.9)*		*(11.1)*
Reason for Return:				
Lack of Employment Opportunity	19.5		31.9	
Homesickness - Self or Wife	8.0		8.6	
Illness or Death in Family	8.6		11.6	
Other Personal Reasons	19.0		15.2	
Social Life, Climate in Canada	3.3		3.3	
Work-Related Reasons[a]	21.0		6.1	
Other Reasons	20.6		23.3	

Source: Motuz (n.d., Tables III-5, III-6, III-64, pp. 58, 59, 144).

a   Includes: in Canada on working holiday; went home for working holiday; recalled by employer.

health, and cultural facilities. Furthermore, only 3 per cent of the returned migrants (with no difference between the intended returners and the intended settlers) reported that Canadians have been "unfriendly or unhelpful" while, in answer to a somewhat differently worded question, one per cent of those who remained said that they did not feel "accepted" by the Canadian community. While it would be highly desirable to have additional data on other indicators of integration and assimilation, it seems clear that one would not wish to speak about all return migrants from Canada as a single group nor label their return across the board as anomic or regressive.

It should be added that Motuz did find returns to occur more frequently among migrants from countries with levels of development similar to Canada's than among migrants from less developed countries, a finding that she indicates is consistent with the results of the 1961 Canadian census and which also supports one of Hoffmann-Nowotny's hypotheses referred to earlier. Nevertheless, her findings suggest more generally that returns can be planned and *need* not be the result of especially poor integration, and that in any study of return migration it will be worthwhile to seek not only to identify central tendencies, but also to measure and explain the patterns of variability in the data.

Identification with the host country and return

In the studies by Hoffmann-Nowotny and Motuz the indicators of integration or assimilation referred only to *structural* and *social* assimilation. To analyze the full relationship between integration or assimilation and return, it is necessary to measure all dimensions of assimilation, including *cultural* and *identificational* assimilation.

In their study of male immigrants to Metropolitan Toronto, Goldlust and Richmond (1974a, 1974b) identified the "transilient migrant" type, who tends to be well educated and tends to be high on structural and social as well as on cultural (cognitive) assimilation, but low on identificational assimilation. The "transilient" has little commitment to staying in Canada permanently. These findings are consistent with the hypothesis that the process of integration and assimilation tends to proceed in stages, with structural and social assimilation coming first, along with a certain amount of cultural assimilation, and that only when structural and social assimilation are proceeding apace, can full cultural and identificational assimilation follow (Esser, 1980; Hoffmann-Nowotny, 1973; Rogers, 1978). The findings' dissimilarity to the Taft-Richardson results that identificational assimilation precedes cultural assimilation (Taft, 1966; Richardson, 1967, 1974) is only superficial, because the measures of cultural assimilation used in the two sets of investigations are entirely different: the Canadian measure (Goldlust and Richmond) was a strictly cognitive one (factual knowledge about the host country, fluency in the language), whereas the Australian measure (Richardson; Taft) concerned the adoption of norms and values that are modal in the host country. It seems reasonable to assume that cognitive cultural assimilation should occur also without identificational assimilation, but that cultural assimilation in the sense of the internalization of the host population's values should be more likely to follow than to precede it.

Might the stage of identification with the host country be the particular threshold beyond which a migrant's return becomes highly unlikely? After all, once a migrant feels that he has become a Canadian or a German, why should he be thinking of returning to Italy or to Yugoslavia? But what is "identificational assimilation"? Two observations suggest themselves about the great variety of *indicators* used for this variable in different studies. First, it would be analytically preferable to treat some of them as entirely separate and different variables. Second, many of them have a zero-sum quality — more identification with the host country means necessarily less identification with the home country: I suggest that it would enrich our understanding of the relationship between return migration and identification with the host country if in our measurement we were to treat such indicators of identification as "attachment" or "commitment" to the home country. Then we could ask questions such as: are such attachments more salient, overall, to some migrants than to others? What are the sources of the attachments? How do the differing strenghts and sources of attachments interact with other variables to influence decisions to stay or to return? The following are frequently encountered indicators of identificational assimilation.

Return intention itself has been used as an indicator of identificational assimilation (Goldlust and Richmond, 1974a; Esser, 1980); it must of course be treated as a separate variable if we wish to investigate the relationship between differing patterns of assimilation and return.

Another frequently used indicator of identificational assimilation is the desire or past *decision to become a naturalized citizen* of the host country (Goldlust and Richmond, 1974a; Taft, 1966; Esser, 1980). Yet Richmond has concluded elsewhere (1974) that with regard to Canada naturalization is not a valid indicator of identification with the host country: some migrants who identify strongly with Canada do not become citizens, while others become citizens to hold governmental jobs, for instance, without showing strong identification. This finding has a parallel in Finifter and Finifter's (1980) study of American immigrants to Australia who have opted for naturalization.

In Goldlust and Richmond's study, return intention and naturalization were part of a five item "Canadian identification index" designed to measure "commitment to Canada". Their study included also a second, separate measure of identification, an open-ended question asking the respondents how they *identified themselves in ethnic terms* (1974a). The responses to this question turned out to correlate poorly with the Canadian identification index; many respondents who scored high on that index nevertheless did not identify themselves first and foremost as "Canadian" or even "hyphenated Canadian", but rather as "Chinese", "Black", "Jewish", and so forth. This result should not be too surprising, given on the one hand the open-ended formulation of the question and, on the other, the observation that in Canada self-identification in terms other than "Canadian" or "hyphenated Canadian" is not infrequent even among the native born.

What types of indicators of identification with the host country are left, then? More clearcut *national identification* questions were asked in various Australian studies (Taft, 1966; Richardson, 1967). They conceive of the relationship between identification with the host and home countries as clearly zero-sum: the migrant is asked whether he feels himself more Australian than British (Dutch, Italian, etc.) by now or whether he feels that he has not changed very much at all. Kremer and Spangenberg (1980: 151) asked an almost identical question, allowing explicitly also for intermediate (".... in some ways Italian, in some ways German") identifications. Similary, Goldlust and Richmond asked whether the migrant felt that he was "fully a Canadian now" or that he "belonged in (his) old country", and another question on what place the migrant called "home" (1974a: 297; 428-29). Finally, in the Australian and the Canadian studies the migrants were asked which sports team they would cheer for in a match between an Australian (Canadian) team and a team from their former country.

I suggest that one might also ask a variety of questions that tap attachment or commitment to each country separately, without prejudging the relationship between the two responses. For example, to what extent does the migrant "feel at home" in the host country? What does he particularly like about the host country? What does he like less? Which characteristics of the host country make him particularly proud to be there? Which make him not proud? For which sports team would he cheer in a match between a host country team and a third country team? The same questions could then be asked with reference to the home country.

In a pilot study of Yugoslav migrants in Austria, I asked open-ended questions about what the respondents particularly liked or disliked in Austria or Yugoslavia. The answers had two major dimensions, corresponding closely to Kelman's (1969) distinction between two sources of loyalty or attachment to a state system — a "sentimental" and an "instrumental" one — even though Kelman's respondents were not migrants. According to Kelman "..... an individual is sentimentally attached when he sees the system as representing him — as being, in some central way, a reflection and extension of himself. For the sentimentally attached, the system is legitimate and deserving of his loyalty because it is the embodiment of a group in which his personal identity is anchored" (Kelman, 1969: 290). On the other hand, "an individual is instrumentally attached when he sees the system as an effective vehicle for achieving his own ends and the ends of other system members. For the instrumentally attached, the system is legitimate and deserving of his loyalty because it provides the organization of a smoothly running society....." (p. 281).

286

My interviews with Yugoslav migrants in Austria showed attachments to the home and the host country to coexist. With most, though not with all migrants, the attachment to the host country was primarily instrumental, while the attachment to the home country was primarily sentimental. Many migrants appreciated Austria for the jobs it offered, for the opportunity to save and to provide for their families. But some appreciated other dimensions of life in Austria as well, for instance, relationships with supervisors or the reward structure at work, or the amount and opportunities of leisure time, or even the "Austrian way of life".

A few respondents showed hardly any attachment to Austria; others showed some or a good deal; for some the sources of attachment were narrowly circumscribed, for others, they were broad; a few had made a switch and showed only little attachment to their country of origin. But one thing was clear: although finer measurements would almost certainly have demonstrated a negative relationship between degree of attachment to the two countries, this relationship would not have been exceedingly strong, and to have looked at it as the principal finding would have meant glossing over those instances in which the attachments to *both* countries seemed to have been rather weak or rather strong. It remains important to distinguish, theoretically and operationally, between those cases in which the attachment to one or both countries is described as "partial" and those in which one would rather speak of "dual" attachments.

An additional dimension in any comparative view of migration and of return migration is that of *supranational identifications*. When given the option, 36 per cent of Finifter and Finifter's (1980) sample of former Americans who had become Australian citizens preferred to identify themselves as "citizens of the world", the largest response category, while 29 per cent said, that they were "foremost American" and this despite their change in citizenship (1980: 38). Inglehart (1977) found in national samples of European Community populations that the incidence of supranational identifications differed widely among the respondents. The identification was measured by naming "Europe" or "the world as a whole" as either first or second choice for "the geographical unit I belong to first of all" (1977: 335). The supranational identification was higher among the younger and the more educated than among the older and less educated respondents and, as an independent effect, it was higher among the group of "postmaterialists" than among the "materialists" or among the intermediate groups. It follows from Inglehart's hypothesized explanation of the source of "postmaterialist" attitudes that the populations of European labor migrants are unlikely to embrace many individuals of this type, but Richmond's (1969) "transilients" might be more broadly distributed over a "materialism-postmaterialism" scale. It may be the case that to this group national identification is simply less important than it is in other groups. Yet this does not mean that such migrants should not report themselves as "feeling at home" in the host country, and as valuing the country highly.

Reasons for return

Returns may indeed indicate failure to become integrated and assimilated into the host country, but they need not do so. For some migrants they may be "new" decisions, arrived at on the basis of changed personal or societal circumstances. I am proposing eight types of reasons for return according to the types of events that play a role in the return decision.

	Events taking place in or having reference to the home country		Events taking place in or having reference to the host country	
	at the aggregate level	at the individual level	at the aggregate level	at the individual level
Related to the motive for migration	1	5	3	7
Unrelated to the motive for migration	2	6	4	8

1. *Migrants return because they perceive that positive changes have occurred in those situations in their home countries that brought about or contributed to their original migration.* Migrants who left their countries because of political disaffection may decide to return after a change in the regime, as in the case of return migration to Portugal in the latter half of the seventies (Poinard, 1979). Economically motivated migrants may decide to return when they perceive substantial improvement in economic opportunities in the home countries. Examples are return migrants to Puerto Rico in the late 1950's and thereafter, who perceived and took advantage of the increasing job opportunities on the island (Hernandez Alvarez, 1968); the return of Iranians and Iraqis from the Gulf and peninsular States in the 1970's (Birks and Sinclair, 1980): the return of Omanis following political and economic changes in their country in the early 1970's (Birks and Sinclair, 1980); and the higher return rates observed among Italians and Greeks than among, for example, Portuguese and Turks, after the downturn in the Western European economies in the 1970's. Return migration may be unintentionally encouraged by the establishment of public assistance programs that function as alternatives to migration, as, for example, the introduction of the food stamps program in Puerto Rico in 1974 (Stockton, 1978).

2. *Migrants return because events in their home countries unrelated to their original migratory intentions necessitate, in their view, their presence in the country.* Saloutos (1956) reports the return from the United States of considerable numbers of Greek men to fight against Turkey in 1897, and again in the First Balkan War of 1912-13.

3. *Migrants return because the host country no longer satisfies the needs that they came to satisfy, or satisfies them less well than earlier.* Economically motivated migrants may decide to return when opportunities in the host countries decrease in times of economic downturn. Such returns occurred from the United States in 1907 and again in the Depression (Saloutos, 1956), and from Western Europe after 1973. At the same time when well established Puerto Rican migrants returned because of increased opportunities in Puerto Rico, others returned because they had lost their jobs in the process of the industrial displacement occurring on the mainland as a result of increased automation (Hernandez Alvarez, 1968).

4. *Migrants return because events in the host countries unrelated to their motives for migration make it less desirable for them to remain there than it had been before.* The host country may undergo certain social or political or other changes that affect the native population as well as the migrants, and that may also make out-migration more desirable for some of the native-born. There also may be changes that specifically affect foreign migrants, such as a deterioration in the "climate" of acceptance of foreign migrants by the host population, which may occur during periods of economic difficulties or as a reaction to perceived "over-foreignization" (Hoffmann-Nowotny and Killias, 1979).

5. *Migrants return because they have satisfied the goals that they or their families had set for them or, if they had no specific targets, because they feel that they can now change their original situation in the home country.* Examples of "target migrants" are the man from Swaziland who works in the South African mines to secure a bride-price (de Vletter, 1981), the migrant from the Mediterranean working in Western Europe to save money for the construction of a house or the purchase of an apartment or of agricultural machinery, the migrant to Canada who comes there for a working holiday or to gain work experience (Motuz, n.d.), or the Mexican working in the United States who seeks to accumulate funds to become a small proprietor or businessman, which will give him access to credit from private Mexican banking institutions (Diez-Cañedo, 1977).
    Included here are also those migrants who return because they feel that they can now create a different life for themselves at home, regardless of changes at the macro level (see ad 1). These may be economic migrants who perceive that they can now establish themselves in their home countries by opening a restaurant or a transport service, or who return home to retire. Or

the migrant who had left because of personal problems (de Vletter, 1981) and who returns when he feels that these have been solved or forgotten.

6. *Migrants return because their families at home need them and they agree to follow their call.* A migrant may inherit a business or a farm that he is expected to take charge of (t'Hart, 1981), or there may be an illness in the family or, if he is alone abroad, his wife or parents may feel that they are no longer able to bring up his children without him. Hernandez Alvarez (1976) found returns because of illness or death of family members especially among those Puerto Rican returnees who tended to be rather less successful upon their return.

7. *Migrants return because they had erred in their assessment that the needs that motivated their migration could be satisfied better in the host country than at home.* Such returns often occur soon after the migration (Motuz, n.d.). Examples include economically motivated migrants who are unable to obtain work in the host country or who find the cost of living much higher than they had expected and the chances for saving therefore lower. Among the returnees to Puerto Rico in the late fifties, Hernandez Alvarez (1976) identified a group of mostly young migrants with very low education and skills who had never found regular jobs on the mainland. Another example is that of migrants who expect that their cultural or religious or political values will find fuller expression in the host country than in their home country, but who discover upon arrival that they were mistaken; this was the case of many Armenians who left France or the United States after World War II to settle in their "homeland" in the Soviet Union, but, disappointed, returned as soon as it became possible for them to do so.

8. *Migrants return because, although the specific needs that motivated their migration are fulfilled in the host country, they feel that the costs involved are too high.* The economically motivated migrant may obtain work and be able to save, but he may miss many aspects of life in his country or encounter in certain spheres prejudice or discrimination that he is not willing to live with. Or he may return because his spouse cannot adjust to living abroad, or, having migrated alone, because he does not wish to live separated from his family. Hernandez Alvarez (1976) identified returnees to Puerto Rico who had been economically successful in the United States but who had returned because they preferred to bring up their children on the island. He also identified a group of less successful returnees who had left in order to escape their conditions of dependency on family members in the United States. Another example is the migrant who had sought out a host country for cultural or religious reasons and had found his expectations fulfilled in these respects, but who found the long-term economic costs of the move too high; this is the situation of some American Jews migrating to Israel.

290

It hardly needs to be stressed that the eight categories of return are over-simplified for several reasons. For one, just as a migrant often has more than one reason for migration, so there may also be multiple reasons for return. More importantly, several among the types of reasons enumerated will not always be easily distinguishable empirically. I am referring especially to the distinction between events occurring at the aggregate and the individual levels. In a sense there is no distinction: the societal-structural influences work them-selves out through the perceptions and decisions of individuals: it is the *individual* migrant or migrant family who perceive the new opportunities in the home country (categories 1 and 5) or who feel that they are not welcome in the host country (categories 4 and 8). Migrants may be more or less aware of changes occurring on the systemic level. On the other hand, return movements should be predictable, in the aggregate sense, when factors 1 and 4 are at work, but not with factors 5 and 8; and it is also the case that factors 1 and 4 could lead migrants to decide to return simply on the basis of general expectations, even in the absence of actual changes in their current personal situations. In some instances reasons involving the same levels of analysis may also be diffi-cult to separate. For example, a migrant may return because he is needed at home, say to take over a family business (category 6), and this may or may not represent at the same time a change in the situation that had earlier led him to migrate (category 5).

My motivation for this exercise of enumerating several types of possible reasons for return has been twofold. One is that it highlights, I hope, the fact that at the same point in time different members of a return migrant stream may be motivated by quite different reasons for return. These differences will be related to differences in the socio-demographic characteristics of the returnees such as age, education, occupation, and so forth. But this in turn means that observations about return populations being "positively" or "nega-tively" selected from among migrant populations or citizens of a home country really give us only rather little information and can even be misleading in their implications. Second, we should again be reminded not to be fully satisfied with statements such as there exists a negative relationship between degree of integration and assimilation to the host country and incidence of return. We should rather be encouraged to analyze the full range of cases, in order to ascertain the specific patterns of assimilation and return, and the frequency with which they occur.

Hernandez Alvarez' study (1976) of return migrants to Puerto Rico illus-trates these points especially well. The study was based on 1960 census data as well as on a supplementary survey. Puerto Rican migrants were positively se-lected with regard to education and occupation both from among the island population and from the Puerto Rican migrants on the mainland; they re-sembled most closely the general U.S. population (see also Sandis, 1970). But these summary measures really comprised three types of migrants, with very different reasons for return as well as different histories of success or failure before and after their return: one eighth of the returnees had an income that bordered on that of the island's elite; they tended to enter, upon their return, the higher occupational strata in the Puerto Rican cities and towns and to suffer little unemployment; they were often middle-aged parents with small families. At the other end of the spectrum, among the quarter of the returnees that are found in the lowest income group, the young, unskilled, illiterate, those living in unstable family situations (separated from their spouses, divorced, living in consensual marriages), those who had returned to their birthplaces within Puerto Rico, and the unemployed, were over-represented. Finally, the more than three fifths who comprised the middle income group tended to be married, with young children, better educated than the unsuccessful migrants but resembling them in occupational distribution, less likely to have suffered unemployment after their return, and less likely to return to their (rural) places of origin. These three groups differed considerably in how successful they had been in the United States as well as in their reasons for return. Taken together, the three groups illustrate nearly all the enumerated reasons for return. Similar results were also obtained in a study of return migration to Portugal (Poinard, 1979).

Migration, return and development

The failure of migrants, and especially of returning migrants, to contribute to their home countries' economic development has been asserted sometimes emphatically in the current literature on return migration, including in that on returns to Southern Europe. Some of these assertions are certainly valid, but others suffer from one or more of three types of methodological inadequacies, which deserve brief comment.

1. *Inadequate analysis.* One example of too shallow an argument is the frequent criticism of migrants' expenditures on housing in the home countries. One researcher (King, 1977) speaks of the "feverish concern of returning migrants to improve their housing standard" (1977: 245). Specific criticisms refer to the fact that some of the houses built are ostentatious, that some were built in poorly chosen locations, that housing construction has contributed to inflation, and that investments in housing are "unproductive". But several important considerations have been omitted from these analyses. One is the fact that the housing stock in the sending countries has indeed been significantly enlarged and improved thanks to the migrants, whose families and who themselves upon return live more comfortably and where desired, more independently from their families of orientation. Second, some migrants derive an income from rentals of apartments or houses, especially in coastal areas, where such housing attracts increased numbers of tourists, creating additional jobs and which to build his house, one must ask how the seller uses his capital gains,

rather than simply accusing the migrant of spending his savings unproductively and driving up the land prices.

Another example of inadequate analyses concerns the utilization of agricultural land. Some studies find such land use diminishing in villages of heavy out-migration, whereas others report on land purchases by migrants combined with improvements in land use (Helweg, forthcoming). However, the necessary contextual analyses that would allow judgments concerning the economic rationality of both types of decisions, and concerning their overall effects on the regional economies, are often missing, especially in those cases in which reductions in land use are reported.

2. *Inadequate sampling.* Many studies that stress the conservative nature of the returning migrant and the absence of developmental impacts of return migration suffer from lack of adequate representativeness. Rhoades (1979) was careful to point out that his research was conducted only in one rural area of Spain. He concludes, as did Cerase (1974) concerning Southern Italy, that the returnees to the countryside tend not to be innovators. But the designs of these studies preclude any estimates of the proportions of returnees of rural origin who upon their return settle in the home countries' towns and cities. Rhoades notes that only one group of migrants — the older, married ones — tended to return permanently to the Andalusian village he studied; many of the young, single as well as married migrants went on to the cities and the coast. But while he did not generalize beyond his data, some of those who cite him (King and Strachan, 1980, for example) make much of his conclusions concerning the conservatism of one group of returnees, without keeping his findings in perspective. To realize how misleading such generalizations can be, recall that Hernandez Alvarez' group of unsuccessful returnees to Puerto Rico had by far the highest incidence of returns to the countryside, whereas the most successful returnees had settled primarily in San Juan and other cities.

Sampling problems abound in research on return migration. Among older examples concerning Italy are Vigorelli (1969), Zingaro (1969), and Sanjust (1969). A more recent monograph on Greece (Collarou and Moussourou, 1978) exemplifies the problem particularly clearly. Of a carefully drawn random sample from a list of 1000 individual addresses of returnees from Germany to Macedonia, only one half of that number was located. The authors assumed that the other 500 returnees had since remigrated to Germany, migrated within Greece, or moved within their own towns or villages. Of the 500 returnees who were interviewed, 11 per cent said that they did not wish to remain in Greece; two thirds said that they would be willing to go to Germany to be trained for a job in Greece, and 43 per cent said that they would be willing to move to another part of Greece to take up such a job after training. Nevertheless, the authors concluded that ".... migrants are far from 'drifters' — in fact, one is surprised to find how little they name changed occupations and employers either in Greece or in Germany and how unwilling they are to move to another part of Greece in order to find a job" (Collarou and Moussourou, 1978: 203). With half of the carefully drawn random sample never located, and given the respondents' above-cited answers concerning their willingness to move, this is a surprising conclusion indeed!

Another example concerns employment generation in the tertiary sector. It has been much discussed in anecdotal terms: there are many references to a surfeit of taxi services, coffee shops, or shoe stores started up by migrants that imply that most of these businesses must be economically marginal. Yet there is also agreement that in many sending countries along the Mediterranean the economically most successful returnees are those who returned to become self-employed. It is clear that broadly based, systematic studies are needed.

3. *Evaluation against which norm?* Finally, some of the negative judgments concerning developmental impacts of returning migrants are simply a function of the analysts' normative expectations. Why should migrants who left their homes to escape economic hardships — in some cases to escape extreme poverty — become the agents who succeeded in turning around the local and regional economies? Why should individuals who lack economic and management training, and who often have only little general education, become industrial entrepreneurs? Why should the results of individual actions necessarily add up to common social benefits? Yet, this is what was expected of the migrants and reiterated many times in academic and policy discussions, in preambles to recruiting agreements between countries, and so forth (3).

Even if the actual developmental effects were by now fully documented and analyzed, to measure them against the standards defined by official expectations would be to answer a set of questions quite different from more neutral ones such as: what would the sending communities, and what would the lives of the migrants be like, had there been no migration? What proportion of the returnees have succeeded in improving their own and their families' economic situations, not only temporarily but in the long run as well? What developmental impacts have indeed occurred? And how do they differ from one migration context to another, and why?

"Temporary" migration

What types of policies have been used by host and sending countries, at the level of policy formulation, to seek to ensure that labor migration be temporary, when it was in one or both countries' interest that it be so? The observed policies range from strictly enforced departure requirements to offers of return incentives.

In the first case, migrants are permitted to enter the host country only with labor contracts, either individually or as members of a group, and there are limitations on the frequency with which contracts may be renewed, if at all, without an intervening departure. Variations on such systems of labor migration exist today, at least formally, as "oscillating migration" in South Africa, as some of the labor migration to the Middle East, as seasonal workers in Europe, and as the H-2 (temporary work visa) program in the United States.

In a second, intermediate case there is no *a priori* limitation on the number of times that residence or work permits may be renewed without intervening departures, but settlement is discouraged by the existence and enforcement of regulations that restrict the migrants' freedom of action in many ways. For instance, there are requirements that work or residence permits be renewed at frequent intervals and renewals can be refused by administrative decision; work permits may be tied to particular employers or economic sectors; migrants' residence permits may be restricted to certain areas; there may be limitations on family reunification and lack of access to education for the migrants' children; the type of accomodations available to migrants may be circumscribed; and there may be restrictions on owning property. Such restrictions are more common in the Middle East today, but many of them were present in the European host countries not too long ago.

In the third case, countries of origin which desire the return of their citizens from abroad, particularly of occupationally qualified workers, have offered return incentives. Among the countries that have experimented with such policies are Israel, Algeria, Colombia, and India (Rogers, 1981). More rarely, host countries have also offered return incentives in order to try to induce migrants to leave. A recent example is France (Lebon, 1979).

The rate of success in ensuring that migration will in fact be temporary differs, of course, considerably in each case. It is incomplete even in the first case, in which *de iure* the host country retains absolute control of the situation. All these situations, in which a temporary stay is the only option given to migrants, are inherently unstable. Ultimately many migrants do return, but there are pressures for permanence; sooner or later either some liberalization of the restrictions for foreigners does occur, or the host country decides to reduce its reliance on the system, or both. It is not surprising that there are tensions in all situations in which *bona fide* immigration is ruled out as an option, for the in-migrant is viewed unidimensionally as a provider of brawn or brain, but not also as the member of a family, as someone who needs a living space of his own, as someone who can and will decide for himself where and for whom to work, as a *homo politicus.*

As the effects of temporary worker policies unfold, these policies' political or economic wisdom and/or their social morality are brought into question. Who does the questioning and how it is done depends on the particular migration context. Employers have to reconcile the frequent turnover of workers with their need for a skilled and experienced work force; some have to pay transportation costs; there are insecurity and potential costs when the availability of future labor supplies cannot be predicted; and the governments have to bear the costs of enforcing strict systems of temporary migration. The

South African mines with their system of "oscillating labor" have experienced all these tensions (Böhning, 1981; Curtin, 1978; Wilson, 1976; Hance, 1970). They have long employed various systems of reemployment guaranteees and bonuses, to encourage foreign migrants to return to their previous jobs after their enforced several months of residence at home (Elkan, 1978). After difficulties in the 1970's (among them compound confrontations, abrupt departures of migrants before expiry of their contracts, and Malawi's recruitment stop; Wilson; 1976; Stahl, 1981), South Africa decided to diversify her sources of foreign labor and, above all, to reduce the number of foreign miners by employing more native workers. The proportion of foreign workers in the country's mine labor force consequently was reduced from 80 per cent in the early 1970's to about 50 per cent toward the end of the decade (International Bank for Reconstruction and Development, 1977; Böhning, 1977).

The types of pressures that result in the easing of restrictions designed to curb a permanent stay are many. In times of economic prosperity an important one is competition among employers. This was pointed out for Europe by Kindleberger (1967) with reference to policies on housing, community facilities, and social security provisions for the migrants, and by Zolberg (1978) concerning Germany's and Switzerland's policies on family reunification. Family reunification policies are also being liberalized today in the United Arab Emirates, in this case out of concern over their negative effects on the host societies: several cases of rape and attempted rape of local women by South Asian workers who were living separated from their families brought an outcry from the native communities; the crimes were directly linked to the migrants' family circumstances. Since then, exceptions have been made in the application of the law restricting family reunion to workers at the highest salary levels (The Hindustan Times, 1981).

Concern over civil liberties as well as over the policies' potential undesirable social consequences led Germany to rescind several restrictive policies of the 1970's, among them the ceiling on the degree of concentration of foreigners in cities and administrative districts of the country and the policy of combining family reunification with restrictions on the newly arrived family members' access to the labor market. In Europe and increasingly also in the Arab Middle East the schooling of foreign children has been receiving attention.

In Europe the majority of "guestworkers" were being admitted on an annual basis. However, the existing policy instrumens (the requirement that work and residence permits be renewed on a yearly basis) were never systematically used to enforce returns (Lohrmann and Manfrass, 1974; Böhning, 1981). In addition, all European host countries have legislation that confers upon migrants an increasingly protected status once they have been in the country for several years. Thus at the time of the economic downturn in 1973-74, many "temporary" migrants were already long-term or permanent residents. At the same time the host countries did not hesitate to declare recruitment stops: it is for easier to keep out *new* "temporary" migrants than it is to remove those who are already in the country.

Incentive schemes for return formulated by host countries have encountered opposition on moral grounds as well as for reasons of cost and effectiveness. Such proposals have been voted down in the Netherlands and in the Federal Republic of Germany. The French scheme, which was operational for four years, was severely attacked from many sides and finally abolished on the grounds of unconstitutionality (Lebon, 1979). Furthermore, studies have shown that the schemes tend to be utilized primarily by migrants who had been planning to return in any case; they are much less effective in bringing about the return of those not already intending to leave.

The result of these forces is in all cases the permanence or quasi-permanence of a proportion of the "temporary workers". In cases in which the legislation and its enforcement remains most restrictive, as in South Africa, this outcome manifests itself primarily in the presence of considerable numbers of illegal migrants (International Bank for Reconstruction and Development, 1977; Böhning, 1977). Europe also has its illegals (Houdaille and Sauvy, 1974), and there are substantial numbers of illegal migrants in the Middle East (Birks and Sinclair, 1980). In the United States it has been argued that the number of illegal migrants increased after the "bracero program" was terminated in 1966. There is disagreement on how much of the illegal migration to the U.S. today (Johnson and Williams, 1981) is intended temporary migration or "shuttle" migration (Diez-Cañedo, 1977).

The indicators of permanence and quasi-permanence among legal migrants are many: economic activity ratios; sex ratios; length of stay in the host countries; numbers of regular returns among those who leave periodically; the proportion of the members of migrant communities born in the host countries; the growth in the numbers of institutions serving individual migrant groups — schools, churches, clubs, mass media —; the proportion of migrants making use of various social institutions in the host countries; the migrants' increased penetration of diverse economic sectors; their increased role of consumers as well as of producers; the numbers of naturalizations.

The data on Europe are well known. The focus there has become the integration of children and grandchildren of the "temporary" workers. Available data on the Arab host countries are not all as extensive, but those that exist are again striking. In Kuwait, for example, where Jordanians and Palestinians make up more than half of the Arab population and more than two-fifths of the total foreign population in the country, these migrants are there as families; a full 45 per cent of the Jordanians and Palestinians living in Kuwait have already been born there (Birks and Sinclair, 1980). The same type of settling process is going on in all Arab labor importing countries with all nationalities except the South Asians (Serageldin *et al.*, 1983).

Concluding remarks

There are other issues in return migration, not discussed in this paper that need further study. Some of them are *lacunae* in the study of migration generally. For one, I believe that we should look at return migration in a broader comparative perspective than we have up to now. How does return migration relate to the different forms of circular migration? One could begin with a systematic analysis of the migrant's relationship to his family at home and the economic institutions in his home community. Is there no relationship at all? Is the relationship a purely social one, including at most the sending of occasional remittances? Does his migration serve to maintain the family at home? Or, finally, does the migrant himself have one foot in each of two economies, as can be said in the case of "circular migration"? If the latter, how stable is this situation? And is it his voluntary decision (as in the case of Portuguese seasonal migrants who could have become year-round migrants but chose not to; Poinard, 1979), or is this the only way for him to obtain work in the host country?

Second, if reasons for migration help us understand reasons for return, we should also, I believe, include in our analysis of out-migration a more rigorous consideration of the alternatives that had been open to the migrant. Did he merely choose between going abroad and staying put? Or was it a choice between going abroad and staying and accepting the *status quo*; staying and working for change; staying in the home country but undertaking an internal migration? There are many interesting questions here that could be more fully developed and the answers to these would enhance also our understanding of return migration.

(1) Arthur W. Helweg, sees an individualistic bias in much of the literature that I refer to as well as in my own arguments. He notes that in India (Helweg, 1979, 1982, forthcoming), the assumption of primarily individually based decisions to migrate would be quite misleading. There these decisions are usually taken by the extended family, which "finances the emigrants, decides who is the most capable and likely to succeed, and whether the migration will enhance the family or not (not only economically, but also in the prestige realm)....." (written communication, June 10, 1983). Helweg hypothesizes that the individualistic bias in the literature results primarily from an imbalance in the methodologies employed: too many studies are based on surveys conducted at only one point in time, and too few rely on long-term, intensive case studies of families and larger communities viewed as networks located in specific cultures. I accept his criticism as valid. Nevertheless, there certainly are also objective differences from one migration context to another (individual decisions on migration occurring more frequently, say, in Yugoslavia than in India); however, such differences can only be satisfactorily demonstrated when comparable research designs are employed. I am grateful to Professor Helweg for his helpful comments.

(2) Hoffmann-Nowotny uses the term "integration" to refer to what Esser (1980) calls "structural assimilation" (having the same chances as the host population to work, to obtain housing, etc.) and "social assimilation" (contacts with the host population), and he reserves the term "assimilation" for what Esser calls "cognitive assimilation" and others refer to as "cultural assimilation" (the learning of information and skills that allow participation in the host country culture). He argues that, although there is a reciprocal relationship between integration and assimilation, the causal link from structure to culture is stronger than that in the opposite direction. Esser adds the dimension of "identificational assimilation" (definitions of ethnic group membership, retention of ethnic customs, etc.) (see also Kremer and Spangenberg, 1980; Rogers, 1978). Esser uses the term "integration" in a quite different sense from Hoffmann-Nowotny; I shall use it here interchangeably with "structural" and "social assimilation". The Zurich survey was undertaken at a single point in time: questions on intentions to return at the time of the survey were used to divide the sample into a group that was almost certain to remain in Switzerland and another containing most of those who would eventually return.

(3) There are impressive examples of migrants' willingness, while abroad and after their return, to contribute financially to their home communities' development, without expecting individual return. In Yugoslavia, for example, migrants in several communities voted in favor of levies on themselves, to be collected toward the building of local roads, sewer systems, schools, and so forth. Similarly, the prime motivation of some Turkish migrants in buying shares in Turkish workers companies seems to have been simply to help create better opportunities for future generations in their home regions (Penninx and van Renselaar, 1978). The funds involved in such contributions were, of course, only a small fraction of the migrants' savings, most of which were spent on satisfying their own and their families' needs in ways that they perceived to be best. What is indeed disappointing is that the Turkish workers' companies as well as later Yugoslav experiments with pooling more substantial portions of migrants' savings for job creation in the industrial sector were relatively unsuccessful, although there are some exceptions (Penninx and van Renselaar, 1978; Werth and Yalçintas, 1978; Vedris, 1978; Rogers, 1981, 1982). Experiments along similar lines are now taking place in Greece (Fakiolas, 1980).

CUMULATIVE BIBLIOGRAPHY

Abadan Unat, N.
1964 *Bati Almanya 'daki Türk Iscileri ve Sorunlari* (Turkish workers in Germany and their problems). Ankara: State Planning Organisation.

——

1973 "La migration turque et la mobilité sociale", *Studi Emigrazione*, 30: 236-253.

——

1976a *Turkish workers in Europe: 1960-75*. Leiden: E.J. Brill.

——

1976b *Migration and development: a study of effects of international labor migration on Bogazliyan District*, Ankara: Ajans-Türk.

Abou Sada, G. and Jacob, P.
1976 *La condition de la seconde génération d'immigrés*. Lille: CRESGE.

Abou Sada, G. and Tricart, J.P.
1982 *Tunisian migration and return migration policies*. Lille: CRESGE.

Adler, S.
1980 "'Swallows' children: emigration and development in Algeria". Geneva: International Labour Organization, World Employment Programme, Migration for Employment Project, WEP 2-26/WP 46.

——

1981 "A Turkish conundrum: emigration, politics and development, 1961-80". Geneva: International Labour Organization, World Employment Programme, Migration for Employment Project, WEP 2-26/WP 52.

Akerman, S.
1976 "Theories and methods of migration research". In *From Sweden to America. A History of the Migration*. Edited by H. Rundblom and H. Norman. Minneapolis, Minn. and Uppsala: University of Minnesota Press and Uppsala University.

Alapuro, R.
1980 "Finland: An interface periphery". University of Helsinki. Research Group for Comparative Sociology. Research Reports No. 25.

Allardt, E.
1979 "Implications of the ethnic revival in modern, industrialized society", *Commentationes Scientiarum Socialium 12*. Helsinki-Helsingfors: Societas Scientiarum Fennica.

303

1979 *Amtliche Nachrichten* der Bundesanstalt für Arbeit. Nürberg.

Appleyard, R. T.
1962 "Determinants of return migration. A socio-economic study of United Kingdom migrants who returned from Australia, *The Economic Record*, 38 (83): 352-368.

Augenti, A. *et al.*
1982 "Il reinserimento scolastico degli alunni rientrati dai Paesi di emigratione". In *La scuola italiana e gli alunni migranti*. Roma: Ministero della Pubblica Istruzione - Istituto della Enciclopedia Italiana.

Autain, F.
1981 "Press conference". July, 23, Paris.

Badas, R., Milesi, E., and Sanna, A.
1977 *Cagliari: la questione delle abitazioni*. Cagliari: Edes.

Baduel, P.R.
1977 *The social consequences of temporary migration to Europe on the native region's life. The case of the Kebili's delegation (South Tunisia)*. 3e cycle thèse, Sociologie, Paris.

Bagchi, A. K.
1982 *The political economy of underdevelopment*. Cambridge: Cambridge University Press.

Bahadir, S. A.
1978 "Vor- und Nachteile der Wanderung von Arbeitskräften für die türkische Volkswirtschaft". Mitteilungen aus der Arbeitsmarktund Berufsforschung, 11. Jg.

Banco do Portugal
1979-1980 *Relatório anual*. Lisboa.

Baran, P.
1957 *The political economy of growth*. New York: Monthly Review Press.

Barre, R.
1978 "Interview" in *La Croix*. November 17.

Baucić, I.
1972 *The effects of emigration from Yugoslavia and the problems of returning emigrant workers*. The Hague: Nijhoff.

Baucić, I.
1974a "Die Auswirkungen der Arbeitskraftewanderung in Jugoslawien". In *Ausländerbeschaftigung und internationale Politik*, Edited by P. Lohrmann and K. Manfrass. München-Wien: Oldenburg Verlag.

—
1974b "Migration temporaire ou définitive: le dilemme des migrations et les politiques de migration", *Studi Emigrazione*, 33: 121-134.

—
1975 "Co-operation with migrant-receiving countries in the creation and realisation of the job-opening schemes in the underdeveloped and high-emigration regions of Yugoslavia". Yugoslav National Team for Co-operation in the Joint Activity of the OECD Pilot Schemes for Employment Creation of High Emigration Areas (mimeo).

—
1976 "The social aspects of external migration and the Yugoslav experience related to the social welfare of migrants", *DOM*, 24.

—
1978 "Jugolawien". In *Ausländerpolitik im Konflikt*. Edited by E. Gehmacher *et al.* Neue Gesellschaft GmbH.

Baucić, I. and Maravić, Z.
1971 *Vránje i zaposĺjavanje vanjskih Migranata iz SR Hrvatske.* Zagreb: Center of Migration Studies.

Bedford, R. D.
1973a "New Hebridean mobility: a study of circular migration". Canberra: Australian National University. Research School of Pacific Studies, Department of Human Geography, Publication HG/9.

—
1973b "A transition in circular mobility: population movement in the New Hebrides, 1800-1970. In *The Pacific in Transition*. Edited by H. Brookfield. New York: St. Martin's Press.

Bell, D.N.F., and Kirwan, F.X.
1979 "Return migration in Scottish context". *Regional Studies*, 13: 101-111.

—
1981 "Further thoughts on return migration: a rejoinder to Gordon", *Regional Studies*, 15: 63-66.

Benhadji, A.
1976 "Retour et réinstallation des travailleurs migrants dans leurs pays d'origine". *Bulletin de l'Institut International d'Etudes sur le Travail*, 12. O.I.T.

Benouamer, R. and Hemman, A.
1976 *La réinsertion des travailleurs émigrés et la politique de l'émigration dans la stratégie de développement algérien.* Alger: Institut des sciences économiques.

Ben Sassi, T.
1968 "The Tunisian workers in the Parisian Region". *Hommes et Migrations*, Study n. 109.

Berós, M.
1975 "Policies, measures and instruments for the attraction and utilization of savings". In *Yugoslav Report for the OECD Joint Project Services for Returning Migrant Workers.* Zagreb: Center for Migration Studies (mimeo).

Berrocal, L.
1981a "La euroemigración española: un ensayo de interpretación", *Studi Emigrazione*, 18(62): 177-205.

— —
1981b *Marché du travail et mouvements migratoires*, Bruxelles (mimeo).

Bhagwati, J. N.
1977 "The brain drain" in *Rasprave o migracijama, Discussions on Migration, DOM,* 36.

Birks, J.S., and Sinclair, C.A.
1980 *International labor migration and development in the Arab Region.* Geneva: International Labor Office.

Bock, C., and Tiedt, F.
1978 *Befragung jugoslawischer Haushalte in der Bundesrepublik Deutschland.* Bonn: Institut für Sozialarbeit und Sozialpädagogik.

Böhning, W. R.
1972a *The migration of workers in the United Kingdom and the European Community.* London: Oxford University Press.

Böhning, W.R.

1972b ''The social and occupational apprenticeship of Mediterranean workers in West Germany''. In *The demographic and social pattern of emigration plan the South Countries*. Edited by Livi Bacci. Firenze. Dipartimento statistico matematico della Università - CISP.

— —

1975a "Return migrants' contribution to the development process - The issue involved". Geneva: International Labour Office, World Employment Programme, Migration for Employment Project, WEP 2-26/WP 2.

— —

1975b "Some thoughts on emigration from the Mediterranean Basin'', *International Labour Review*, 3(3): 251-277.

— —

1976 "Migration from developing to high income countries". In ILO, *Tripartite World Conference on Employment, Income Distribution and Social Progress and the International Division of Labour*. Geneva: Background papers, vol. II.

— —

1977 "Black migration to South Africa: what are the issues?''. Geneva: International Labour Office, World Employment Programme, Migration for Employment Project, Working Paper, No. 13.

— —

1979 "International migration in Western Europe: reflections on the past five years", International Labour Review, 118(4): 401-14. July/August.

— —

1980 "Guest worker employment, with special reference to the Federal Republic of Germany, France and Switzerland - Lessons for the United States?", Geneva: International Labour Office, World Employment Programme Research, Working Paper, No. 47.

— —

1981 *Black migration to South Africa: a selection of policy-oriented research*. Geneva: International Labour Office.

Borgegard, L. E.

1976 *Return migration from Sweden to Finland after the Second World War. A methodological study.* Forskningsprojektet Migrationen Finland-Sverige. Forskningsrapport 8 B. Stockholm: Nordiska Museet (mimeo).

Bouvier, L. F., *et al.*
1976 "Towards a framework for the analysis of differential migration: The case of education". In A.H. Richmond and D. Kubat, *Internal migration: The New World and the Third World*. Beverly Hills, California: Sage Sage Publications, Inc.

Bovenkerk, F.
1974a *Migration du travail, retour au pays et coopération au développement.* La Haye: IMWO-NUFFIC.

——
1974b *The sociology of return migration. A bibliographic essay.* The Hague: Nijhoff.

Boyd Caroli, B.
1973 *Italian repatriation from the United States, 1900-1914.* New York: Center for Migration Studies.

Braun, R.
1970 *Sozio-kulturelle Probleme der Eingliederung italienischer Arbeitskräfte in der Schweiz.* Erlenbach-Zürich: Eugen Rentsch.

Brettel, C. B.
1979 "Emigrar para voltar: a Portuguese ideology of return migration", *Papers in Anthropology*, 20, 1:1-20.

Briot, F., and Verbunt, G.
1981 *Immigrés dans la crise.* Paris: Editions ouvrières.

Brozek, A.
1977 *Polonia amerykańska.* Warszawa: Interpress.

Buckley, W.
1967 *Sociology and modern systems theory.* Englewood Cliffs, New Jersey: Prentice-Hall, Inc.

Bundesrepublik Deutschland
1980 "Weiterentwicklung der Ausländerpolitik". Beschlüsse der Bundesregierung vom 10. März 1980. Bonn (mimeo).

Bundesanstalt für Arbeit
1973 *Repräsentativ-Untersuchung, 1972.* Nürnberg.

308

Camilleri, C.
1979 *Quelques facteurs psychologiques de la représentation du retour dans le pays d'origine chez les jeunes migrants maghrébins de la seconde géné-ration.* Paris: IRAP.

Campagnac, E.
1978 "Mobilité et transformations des modes de vie ouvriers", *Annales de la Recherche Urbaine,* Paris: Automne.

Carballo, R. and Temprano, A.
1981 *Crecimiento económico y crisis estructural en España, 1959-1980.* Madrid: Akal.

Cardelus, J. and Pascual, A.
1979 *Movimientos migratorios y organización social.* Barcelona: Península.

Caro, L.
1907 *Statystyka emigracji polskiej i austro-wegierskiej do Stanów Zjednoc-zonych Ameryki Pólnocnej.* Krakow.

——

1914 *Emigracja i polityka emigracyina ze szczególnym uwzglednieniem ziem polskich.* Poznań.

Castillo Castillo, J.
1980 *La emigración española en la encrucijada.* Madrid: Centro de Investiga-ciones Sociologicas.

Castles, S. and Kosack, G.
1973 *Immigrant workers and class structure in Western Europe.* London: Oxford University Press.

Cavaco, C.
1980 "Agricultura e tempo parcial em Portugal", *Estudos de Geografia Huma-na e Regional,* INIC. BE, Lisboa.

Cavallaro, R.
1980 "Educazione, cultura, socializzazione degli emigrati. Attività e proposte del Consiglio d'Europa". *Studi Emigrazione/Etudes Migrations,* 57: 61-68.

Cella, G.
1974 "Industrializzazione ed emigrazione: il caso del Mezzogiorno nel decen-nio 1961-1971", *Rassegna Economica,* 38(4): 1067-1088. July-August.

CENSIS
1973 *Indagine campionaria sul potenziale migratorio in Italia*, Roma, mimeo.

Cerase, F. P.
1970 "The return to Italy. Nostalgia or disenchantment: considerations on return migration". In *The Italian experience in the United States*. Edited by Silvano M. Tomasi and Madeline H. Engel. New York: Center for Migration Studies.

—
1971 *L'emigrazione di ritorno: innovazione o reazione?* Roma: Università di Roma, Istituto di statistica e ricerca sociale "C. Cini".

—
1974 "Expectations and reality: a case study of return migration from the United States to Southern Italy". *International Migration Review*, 8: 245-62.

Chabbi Majeri, M.
1976 *20 years of Tunisian migration to France. The ideological, political and economic ground of migration. 3e cycle thèse, Paris V.*

Chaker, R.
1979 "Problématique de la réinsertion des travailleurs. Quel avenir pour l'émigration algérienne?", *Hommes et Migrations*, 968, 15: 3-20.

Chapman, M.
1976 "Tribal mobility as circulation: a Solomon Islands example of micro/macro linkages". In *Population at Microscale*. Edited by L.A. Kosinski and John W. Webb. New Zealand Geographical Society.

Chazalette, A.
1977 "Etude relative à la deuxième génération d'immigrants dans la région Rhône-Alpes". GSU.

—
1979 "Le retour au pays des familles de travailleurs immigrés". GSU.

Chinoy, E.
1955 *Automobile workers and the American dream*. Garden City, N.Y.: Doubleday.

Chirot, D.
1977 *Social change in the Twentieth Century*. New York: Harcourt Brace Jovanovich, Inc.

C.I.E.M.
1980 "Les négociations franco-algériennes". Revue de presse September 18-
    24, 1980. *Presse et immigrés en France*, série "Problèmes et évène-
    ments. Points de vue" 12, 12 p. Paris: CIEM.

Cifrić, I.
1981 *Revolucija i seljastvo u Jugoslaviji*. Zagreb: Centar za Kulturnu djelatnost
    SSO.

Cole, John W.
1977 "Anthropology comes part-way home: community studies in Europe".
    Annual Review of Anthropology, 10: 349-378.

Collarou, T.A. and Moussourou, L.M.
1978 *The return home: socio-economic aspects of re-integration of Greek
    migrant workers returning from Germany*. Athens: Re-integration
    Center for Migrant Workers, Enimerosi 2.

Commissioner General of Immigration to the Secretary of Labor
1909-1919 Annual Report. Fiscal Years 1908-1919, Washington, D.C.: Go-
    vernment Printing Office, 1909-1919.

Conaway, M. E.
1977 *Circular migration: a summary and bibliography*. Council of Planning
    Librarians. Exchange Bibliography. No. 1250.

Cordeiro, A.
1981 *Porquoi l'immigration en France?* Créteil: Office municipal des migrants
    de Créteil.

Cordeiro, A. and Guffond, J.L.
1979 *Les Algériens de France; ceux qui partent et ceux qui restent*. Grenoble:
    IREP.

Cornelisen, A.
1980 *Strangers and pilgrims: the last Italian migration*. New York: Holt,
    Rinehart and Winston.

Corsini, S.A. and Sonnino, E.
1972 "The CISP survey on the families of Italian emigrants abroad". In *The
    demographic and social pattern of emigration from the Southern Euro-
    pean Countries*. Edited by M. Livi Bacci. Firenze: Dipartimento stati-
    stico - CISP.

CRES

1977 *Movimenti migratori in Friuli-Venezia Giulia. 1960-1976 Un'indagine orientativa.* Udine: Regione Autonoma Friuli-Venezia Giulia.

——

1979 *Indagine sulle caratteristiche dei lavoratori che rimpatriano dopo un periodo all'estero. Atti della Seconda Conferenza Regionale sull'emigrazione.* Udine: Regione Autonoma Friuli-Venezia Giulia.

——

1981 *Indagine sul reinserimento professionale, sociale e abitativo dei lavoratori rimpatriati negli ultimi dieci anni..* Udine: Regione Autonoma Friuli-Venezia Giulia.

Cribier, F.
1975 "Retirement migration in France". In *People on the Move.* Edited by L.S. Kosinski and M. Prothero. London: Methuen.

Curtin, P. D.
1978 "Postwar migrations in Sub-Saharan Africa". In *Human migration; Patterns and policies.* Edited by W. H. McNeill and R. S. Adams. Bloomington, Indiana: Indiana University Press.

Da Vanzo, J. S. and Morrison, P. A.
1981 "Return and other sequences of migration in the United States". *Demography*, 18: 85-101.

De Jong, G. F. and Gardner, R. W.
1981 *Migration decision making. Multidisciplinary approaches to microlevel studies in developed and developing countries.* New York: Pergamon Press.

Deliyannakis, M.
1980 *Interview.* Greek Ministry of Coordination. Summer.

Department of National Economy (Tunis)
1980 *The VIth Plan preparation 1982-1986. Orientation report about the industrial sector.* October.

Deutsches Institut für Wirtschaftsfroschung
1978 "Entwicklung der deutschen und der ausländischen Wohnbevölkerung in der Bundesrepublik Deutschland. Vorausberecnungen bis zum Jahr 2000". *DIW Wochenbericht*, 45 Jg., No. 50.

de Vletter, F.
1981 "Labour migration in Swaziland". In *Black Migration to South Africa: A selection of policy-oriented research*. Edited by W.R. Böhning. Geneva: International Labour Office.

Diez-Cañedo
1977 "Mexican migration to the United States". Paper prepared for the Workshop on Comparative Labor Movements, Harvard University Center for European Studies, Cambridge, Massachusetts, October 14-16.

Dijoud, P.
1977 *La nouvelle politique de l'immigration*. Paris: Ministère du Travail. Secrétariat d'Etat aux travailleurs immigrés.

Dohse, K.
1981a *Ausländische Arbeiter und bürgerlicher Staat. Genese und Funktion von staatlichem Ausländerrecht*. Königstein/Taunus: Anton Hain.

——
1981b *Ausländerpolitik und betriebliche Ausländerdiskriminierung*. Berlin: Wissenschaftszentrum.

DOXA
1973 *Indagine sui lavoratori italiani all'estero*. Roma (mimeo).

EEC
1974 *The factual description of the situation of migrant workers within the community and the most important economic, juridical and social aspects*. Bruxelles, mimeo, July.

Elich, J. H. and Blauw, P. W.
1981 *En toch terug..... (Return migration from Australia, Canada and New Zeland)*. Rotterdam: Erasmus Universiteit.

Elkan, W.
1978 "Labour migration from Botswana, Lesotho and Swaziland". *African Perspectives*, 1: 145-156.

El Moudjahid, September 14, 1980.

Engelberg, R.
1944 *Suomi ja Amerikan suomalaiset. Keskinäinen yhteys ja sen rakentaminen*. Helsinki: Suomi-Seura.

Entzinger, H.
1978 "Return migration from West European to Mediterranean countries".
Geneva: International Labor Office, World Employment Programme,
Migration for Employment Project, Wep-2-26/WP 23.

Esser, H.
1980 *Aspekte der Wanderungssoziologie: Assimilation und Integration von
Wanderern, ethnischen Gruppen und Minderheiten.* Darmstadt: Luch-
terhand.

EUROSTAT
1980 *Regional statistics, main regional indicators.* Luxembourg: Statistical
Office of the European Communities.

Ewenczyck, P. *et al.*
1978 *"Retour et développement: l'exemple espagnol, 1960-1978".* Paris:
FNSP-SEAE, (mimeo).

Faina, P.
1980 "Identità della seconda generazione degli emigrati e problemi di inte-
grazione". *Studi Emigrazione/Etudes Migrations,* 57: 8-43.

Fakiolas, R.
1980 "Problems and opportunities of the Greek migrants returning from
Western Europe". Athens: Centre of Planning and Economic Research.

Falala, M.
1979 "Déclaration au journal *Le Monde",* November, 19-20.

Falcinelli Di Matteo, F. and Marcuccini, A. M.
1980 "La politica dei paesi europei in materia di formazione scolastica dei figli degli emigrati". *Studi Emigrazione/Etudes Migrations,* 57: 44-60.

Favero L.
1980 "Situazione scolastica dei figli dei lavoratori rimpatriati". *Studi Emi-
grazione/Etudes Migrations,* 57: 134-151.

——
1981 "Revisione della politica scolastica europea per i migranti". *Dossier
Europa Emigrazione,* 12: 3-5.

Favero, L. and Rosoli, G.
1975 "I lavoratori emarginati", *Studi Emigrazione,* 12(38-39): 155-329.

Ferenczi, I. ed.
1929 *International migration.* Vol. I. *Statistics.* Compiled on behalf of the International Labour Office. New York: National Bureau of Economic Research.

Ferreira, E.S.
1976 *Origens e formas da emigração.* Lisboa.

Finifter, A.W., and Finifter, B. M.
1980 "Citizenship decision-making: durability and change of national allegiance and identification among American migrants in Australia". Paper prepared for the Annual Meeting of the American Political Science Association, Washington, D.C.: August 28-31.

1980 "Finlandssvenska emigranter i Sverige. En intervju-undersökning". *Bilaga till svenska emigrationskommittens betänkande 1980:24.*

Finnäs, F.
1981 "Befolkningsutvecklingen i Svensk-Finland 1950-70. Effecten av sprakbyten och dess bakgrund". *Ethnicity and Mobility,* Research Report No. 9.

1905-1931 "Finnish Official Statistics (Suomen Virallinen Tilasto)", 28. *Siirtolaisuustilasto,* 1-21. Helsinki.

Foester, R. F.
1919 *The Italian emigration of our times.* Cambridge, Mass.: Harvard University Press.

Forschungsverbund (ed.)
1979 *Probleme der Ausländerbeschäftigung.*

Frank, A. G.
1981 *Crisis: in the Third World.* New York: Holmes and Meier.

Friganović, M. *et al.*
1972 *Iz Jugoslavja na rad u Fruncusku,* Zagreb: Center for Migration Studies.

Gehmacher, E.
1973 *Gastarbeiter: Wirtschaftsfaktor und soziale Herausforderung.* Wien: Europa Verlags-AG.

Gentileschi, M. L.
1980 "Il bilancio migratorio". In *Atlante della Sardegna.* Edited by R. Pracchi e A. Terrosu Asole, 2. Roma: Kappa.

Gitmez, A. S.
1977 "Return migration of Turkish workers: effects and implications", Research Report. Ankara: METU

——

1980 "Die Rückwanderung der Gastarbeiter". Research Report. Ankara: METU.

Glaser W.
1978 *The brain drain: emigration and return.* Oxford: Pergamon Press.

Glaser, W. and Habers, G. G.
1974 "The migration and return of professionals". *International Migration Review*, 8: 227-44.

Glickman, N. J. and Petras, E. M.
1981 "International capital and international labor flows: implications for public policy". Working Paper 53. Philadelphia: University of Pennsylvania.

Gmelch, G.
1980 "Return migration". *Annual Review of Anthropology*, 9: 135-59.

Gökdere, A. Y.
1978 *Yabanci Ulkelere Isgücü Akimi ve Türk Ekonomisi Uzerindeki Etkileri. (Labor Migration and its Effects on Turkish Economy).* Ankara: Is Bankasi Publ.

Golab, C.
1977 *Immigrant destinations.* Philadelphia: Temple University Press.

Goldey, P.
1980 "Agricultural Cooperatives in Portugal", *Year Book of Agricultural Cooperation.* Oxford: The Plunkett Foundation.

Goldlust, J. and Richmond, A. H.
1974a "Multivariate analysis of immigrant adaptation". Mimeographed report of the Ethnic Research Programme, Institute for Behavioural Research, York University.

——

1974b "A multivariate model of immigrant adaptation", *International Migration Review*, 8,2: 193-225.

Goldstein, S.
1978 "Circulation in the context of total mobility in Southeast Asia". Honolulu, Hawaii: East-West Center, Papers of the East—West Population Institute, No. 53.

Gordon, I.
1981 "Balance and stability in return migration: a comment on Bell and Kirwan's (1979) Scottish study", *Regional Studies*, 15: 57-61.

Gould, J. D.
1980 "European intercontinental migration. The road home: return migration from the USA". *Journal of European Economic History*, 9: 41-111.

Greek Ministry of Coordination
1981 "Agreement between the Governments of Greece and the Federal Republic of Germany for the assistance of initiatives by Greek workers in the FRG who wish to be occupationally reintegrated into the Greek economy" (in Greek). Athens.

Günce, M. E.
1978 "Turkey-Turkish Worker's Companies". Forschungsinstitut der Friedrich-Ebert-Stiftung, Arbeiten aus der Abteilung Entwicklungsländerforschung, No. 71, Bonn.

Haatanen, P.
1965 *Suhteellisen liikaväestön ongelma Suomen maataloudessa.* Helsinki: Unpubl. MA thesis at the University of Helsinki.

Hägerstrand, T.
1969 "On the definition of migration", *Scandinavian Population Studies*, v. 1: 63-72. Reprinted in *Readings in Social Geography*. Edited by E. Jones. London: Oxford University Press, 1975.

Haicault, M.
1978 "Le travail domestique dans la famille capitaliste". *Critique de l'Economie Politique*, 3, Paris.

Hamberg, E.M. and Hammar, T. eds.
1981 *Invandringen och framtiden (Immigration and the Future).* Stockholm: Liber.

Hance, W. A.
1970 *Population, migration and urbanization in Africa.* New York: Columbia University Press.

Handlin, O.
1969 *Boston's immigrants 1790-1880: a study in acculturation.* New York: Atheneum.

t'Hart, M.
1981 "Heading for Paddy's Green Shamrock Shore: the returned emigrants in Nineteenth Century Ireland". M.A. Thesis in Social and Economic History, University of Gröningen.

Harvey, M. E. and Riddell, J. B.
1975 "Development, urbanization and migration: a test of a hypothesis in the Third World". In *People on the Move.* Edited by L. A. Kosinski and R. M. Prothero. London: Methuen.

Harvey, S.
1980 *Dutch return migration. North Brabant farmers' sons. A case study of settler loss.* Melbourne: La Trobe University.

Hecker, U. and Schmidt-Hackenberg, D.
1980 *Bildungs- und Beschäftigungssituation ausländischer Jugendlicher in Bundesrepublik Deutschland, Part I: Grunddaten der Befragung.* Ed.: Bundesinstitut für Berufsbildung, Berlin: Berichte zur beruflichen Bildung, Heft 3o.

Heikkinen, S. L.
1974 "Ruotsista palanneet". *Siirtolaisuustutkimuksia (Migration studies) 5.* Helsinki: Ministry of Labour.

Hell, W.
1976 "Amerikanisch-deutsche Rückwanderung". In *"... nach Amerika!" Auswanderung in die Vereinigten Staaten. Ausstellung aus Anlass der Unabhängigkeitserklärung der Vereinigten Staaten von Amerika am 4. Juli 1776.* Hamburg: Museum für Hamburgische Geschichte.

Helweg, A. W.
1979 *Sikhs in England: the development of a migrant community.* New Delhi: Oxford University Press.

——
1982 "Emigration from Gujarat: the effects". *India International Centre Quarterly,* 9, 1: 30-36.

——
"Emigrant remittances: their nature and impact on a Punjabi village", in a book edited by M.S.A. Rao (Forthcoming).

Hernandez A. J.
1967 *Return migration to Puerto Rico*, Westport, Conn.: Greenwood.

Hesse-Biber, S. J.
1981 *Migrant as actor*. New York: Irvington.

Hiemenz, U. and Schatz, K. W.
1978 *Trade in place of migration: an employment-oriented study with special reference to the FRG, Spain, and Turkey*. Geneva: ILO, WEP.

——
1979 *Trade in place of migration*. Geneva: ILO.

Hirschman, A. O.
1958 *The strategy of economic development*. New Haven, Conn.: Yale University Press.

Hoepfner, K. H. and Huber, M.
1978 "Regulating international migration in the interest of the developing countries: with particular reference to Mediterranean countries". Geneva: International Labour Organization, World Employment Programme, Migration for Employment Project, WEP 2-26/WP 21.

Hoffmann-Nowotny, H. J.
1973 *Soziologie des Fremdarbeiterproblems: Eine theoretische und empirische Analyse am Beispiel der Schweiz*. Stuttgart: Ferdinand Enke.

——
1978 "European migration after World War II". In *Human Migration*. Edited by McNeil and Adams.

——
1981 "A sociological approach toward a general theory of migration". In *Global trends in migration: theory and research on international populations movements*. Edited by M. M. Kritz *et al.* Staten Island, N.Y.: Center for Migration Studies.

Hoffmann-Nowotny, H. J. and Killias, M.
1979 "Switzerland". In *The politics of migration policies*. Edited by Daniel Kubat *et al.* New York: Center for Migration Studies.

Hofstede, B. P.
1964 *Thwarted exodus, postwar overseas migration from the Netherlands*. The Hague: Martinus Nijhoff.

Houdaille, J. and Sauvy, A.
1974 "L'immigration clandestine dans le monde". *Population*, 29, 4-5: 725-41.

Hvidt, K.
1971 *Flugten til Amerika eller drivkraefter i masseudvandringen fra Danmark 1868-1914.* Odense: Jysk Selskab for Historie.

ICMC
1978 *Migration News*, No. 1 (January-March).

Immigration Commission (The Dillingham Commission)
1911 *Abstracts of Reports of the Immigration Commission.* U.S. Senate, 61st Congress, 3rd Session. Document No. 747. 2 vols. Washington, D.C.: U.S. Government Printing Office.

Inglehart, R.
1977 *The silent revolution: changing values and political styles among Western publics.* Princeton, N. J.: Princeton University.

Institut für empirische Sozialforschung
1980 *Befragung deutscher und ausländischer Haushalte zur Ausländerintegration in Berlin*, ed.: Der Regierende Bürgermeister von Berlin, Senatskanzlei-Planungsstelle.

Instituto de Estudos para o Desenvolvimento (IED)
1981 *Problemas relacionados com a adesao de Portugal à CEE - Estratégias e conceitos*, Lisboa: IED.

Instituto Espanol de Emigración
1980 *Emigración Española Asistida*, Madrid.

International Bank for Reconstruction and Development (IBRD)
1977 "Migration from Botswana, Lesotho and Swaziland". Washington Report No. 1688-EA.

International Labour Office (ILO) - UNDP - Tunisian Planning Department
1974 *For an employment policy in Tunisia: contribution to the study of the problem and elements for a strategy.*

International Labour Office
1976a "Migration of workers as an element in employment policy". In *L'emigrazione dal Bacino Mediterraneo verso l'Europa industrializzata*. Edited by Istituto di Demografia dell'Università di Roma. Milano: F. Angeli.

International Labour Office
1976b *Tripartite world conference on Employment, income distribution and social progress and the international division of labour.* Geneva: Background papers, vol. II.

ISFOL
1976 "Formazione linguistica e professionale dei lavoratori migranti. Indagine sui bisogni formativi dei lavoratori italiani in Germania". *Quaderni di formazione ISFOL*, 31:32.

ISTAT
1962 I *Censimento generale dell'agricoltura.* Roma.

——
1970 "Indagine speciale su alcuni aspetti socio-professionali del movimento migratorio con l'estero nel periodo 1962-68", *Annuario di statistiche del lavoro e dell'emigrazione*, vol. XI. Roma.

——
1972 II *Censimento generale dell'agricoltura.* Roma.

Istituto di Demografia dell'Università di Roma, ed.
1976 *L'emigrazione dal Bacino Mediterraneo verso l'Europa industrializzata.* Milano: F. Angeli.

ISVI
1976 *L'emigrazione meridionale nelle zone di esodo.* Edited by E. Reyneri. Catania.

——
1979 *Emigrazione di ritorno e professionalità.* Edited by E. Reyneri. Catania.

ISVI, FORMEZ
1976 *L'emigrazione meridionale nelle zone di esodo*, vol. I-II. Catania (mimeo).

Jackson, J. A.
1967 *Ireland. Supplement report OECD seminar on emigrants returning to their home country.* Paris: OECD.

Janson, F. E.
1931 *The background of Swedish immigration 1840-1930.* Chicago, Ill.: University of Chicago Press.

Johnson, K. F. and Williams, M. W.
1981 *Illegal aliens in the Western hemisphere: political and economic factors.*
New York: Praeger.

Johnston, J. A.
1977 "Information and emigration: the image making process", *New Zealand Geographer*, 33: 60-67.

Jones, M. A.
1960 *American immigration.* Chicago, Ill.: University of Chicago Press.

Jurecka, P., and Werth, M.
1980 *Mobilität und Reintegration. Analyse der wirtschaftlichen, sozialen und entwicklungspolitischen Effekte der Migration von ausländischen Arbeitnehmern, untersucht am Beispiel der Rückwanderung in die Türkei,* Saarbrücken: ISOPLAN.

Jutikkala, E.
1953 *Uudenajan taloushistoria.* Helsinki: WSOY.

Kallweit, H. and Kudat, A.
1976 *Rückwanderung ausländischer Arbeiter: zwangsweise oder freiwilling.* Berlin: Wissenschaftszentrum Berlin.

Kayser, B.
1971 *Manpower movements and labour markets.* Paris: OECD.

——
1972a *Cyclical determined homeward flows of migrant workers and the effects of emigration.* Paris: OECD.

——
1972b *Les retours conjoncturels des travailleurs migrants.* Paris: OCDE.

Kelman H. C.
1969 "Patterns of personal involvement in the national system: a social-psychological analysis of political legitimacy". In *International politics and foreign policy: a reader in research and theory.* Edited by J. N. Rosenau. New York: The Free Press.

Kennedy, C.
1978 *Policy implications of recent migration research.* Paris: OECD Development Center, CD/R (78).

Kero, R.
1974 *Migration from Finland to North America in the years between the United States Civil War and the First World War.* Turku: University of Turku.

Kindleberger, C. P.
1967 *European post-war growth: The role of labor supply.* Cambridge, Mass., Harvard University Press.

King, R.
1977 "Problems of return migration: a case study of Italians returning from Britain". *Tijdschrift voor Economische en Sociale Geografie*, 68: 241-246.

—— 1978 "Return migration: A neglected aspect of population geography". *Area*, 10: 175-182.

—— 1979a "Return migration: review of some case studies from Southern Europe". *Mediterranean Studies*, 1: 3-30.

—— 1976b "The Maltese migration cycle: an Archival Survey". *Area*, 11: 245-249.

—— 1980 *The Maltese migration cycle: perspectives on return.* Oxford: Oxford Polytechnic Discussion Papers in Geography, No. 13.

King, R. and Strachan, A.
1980 "The effects of return migration on a Gozitan Village". *Human Organization*, 39: 175-179.

Klinar, P.
1976 "Yugoslavia workers in the Federal Republic of Germany. The theoretical models for empirical sociological research of international migration". In *International Migration and Adaptation in the Modern World.* Edited by A.H. Richmond. Toronto: I.S.A. Research Committee on Migration.

—— 1978 *Remigrants from the underdeveloped areas of emigrant society and the problems of their reintegration.* Uppsala: IX World Congress of Sociology.

Koelstra, R. W. and Van Dijck, P.J.C.
1978 *Working in the periphery. A rescuing for the less developed regions in Tunisia.* The Hague: IMWOO Remplod.

Koelstra, R. W. and Tieleman, H. J.
1977 *Development or migration. A survey about the possibilities of employment promotion in less developed regions of Tunisia.* The Hague: IMWOO Remplod.

1925 *Kongres Wychodźstwa Polskiego w Ameryce.* Odezwy, mowy, referaty, rezolucje, uchwaly oraz urzedowy protokól odbyty w dniach 21-23 maja 1925. Chicago, Ill.: Druk. Zwiawkowa Zgoda.

Korkiasaari, J.
1981 *Preliminary data from a study on return migration.* Unpublished.

Körner, H.
1978 "Die Integration der ausländischen Judendlichen". *Wirtschaftsdienst,* 58.

——

1981a "Adjustment of changing international conditions". *Intereconomics.*

——

1981b "Zusammenfassender Bericht über die Abschlussdiskussion zum Thema Probleme der Rückwanderungs- und Reintegrationspolitik". In *Rückwanderung und Reintegration von ausländischen Arbeitnehmern in Europa.* Edited by H. Körner and M. Werth. Saarbrücken.

Korte, H.
1980 "Einbürgerung oder Rückwanderung? Ergebnisse und Interpretationen sozialwissenschaftlicher Froschung". In *Gastarbeiter.* Edited by W. Slim Freund. Neustadt: Weinstrasse.

Krane, R. E. ed.
1975a *Manpower mobility across cultural boundaries. Social, economic and legal aspects. The case of Turkey and West Germany.* Leiden: E.J. Brill.

——

1975b "Effects of international migration upon occupational mobility, acculturation and the labour market in Turkey". In *Manpower mobility across cultural boundaries. Social, economic and legal aspects. The case of Turkey and West Germany.* Edited by R. Krane. Leiden: E.J. Brill.

Kremer, M. and Spangenberg, H.
1980 *Assimilation ausländischer Arbeitnehmer in der Bundsrepublik Deutschland*. Königstein/Ts: Hantein.

Kruiter, H.
1981 *Inpakken en wegwezen? Een onderzoek naar kenmerken en motieven van emigranten naar Australië, Canada en Nieuw-Zeeland*. The Hague: Ministerie van Sociale Zaken.

Kubat, D. ed.
1979 *The politics of migration policies*. New York: Center for Migration Studies.

Kubiak, H.
1979 "Polozenie spoleczne i ewolucja świademości narodowej ludności polskiej w USA w latach 1900-1919". In *Polonia wobec niepodległości Polski w czasie I wojny światowej*. Edited by H. Florkowska-Francić, *et al.*, Wroclaw-Warszawa-Krakow: Ossolineum.

Kudat, A.
1974 *International labour migration: A description of the preliminary findings of the West Berlin migrant worker survey*, Berlin: Wissenschaftszentrum Berlin.

Kuhn, W. E.
1978 "Guest workers as an automatic stabilizer of cyclical unemployment in Switzerland and Germany". *International Labor Review*, 12,2: 210-222.

Külewind, G.
1974 "The employment of foreign workers in the FRG and their family and living conditions. On the 1972 sample survey by the Federal Institution of Labour". *The German Economic Review*, 4: 359-361.

Lebon, A.
1978 "Présentation d'un travail collective: les migrations externes". *Revue Française des Affaires Sociales*, N. spécial. April-June.

——
1979a" L'aide au retour des travailleurs étrangers", *Economie et Statistique*, 113: 37-46.

——
1979b "Un bilan des retours au pays d'origine des travailleurs immigrés". *Problèmes économiques*, 1631: 27-29. July.

Lebon, A. and Falchi, G.
1980 "New developments in intra-European migration since 1974". *International Migration Review*, XIV: 4, 539-579. Winter.

Lee, E. S.
1966 "A theory of migration". *Demography*, 1: 47-57.

Le Garrec, J. and Perraudeau, J.
1980 "Les socialistes et l'immigration. Rapport présenté au Comité directeur du Parti Socialiste". *Hommes et Migration*, N. 1002. December 15.

Leguina, J. *et al.*
1976 "Les migrations intérieures en Espagne". In ISA, Research Committee on Sociology of Regional and Urban - Development, *Convegno internazionale sui problemi sociali dello sviluppo urbano e regionale*. Messina-Reggio Calabria (mimeo).

Lento, R.
1951 *Maassamuutto ja siihen vaikuttaneet tekijät Suomessa vuosina 1978-1939*. Helsinki: Wäestöpoliittinen tutkimuslaitos.

Levi Strauss, C. ed.
1977 "L'identité". Seminaire interdisciplinaire 1974-75. Paris: Col. Grasset.

Lind, J.
1977 "Ruotsinsuomalaisten paluualttius ja paluun esteet". *Siirtolaisuustutkimuksia (Migration studies)*, No. 13. Helsinki: Ministry of Labour.

Lindberg, J. S.
1930 *The background of Swedish emigration to the United States. An economic and sociological study in the dynamics of migration*. Minneapolis: University of Minnesota Press.

Linz, J. J. and de Miguel, A.
1966 "Within-nation differences and comparisons: the eight Spains". In *Comparing nations. The use of quantitative data in cross-national ressearch*. Edited by R. L. Merritt and S. Rokkan. New Haven and London: Yale University Press.

Livi Bacci, M.
1972 "The Countries of Emigration". In *The demographic and social pattern of emigration from the Southern European countries*. Edited by M. Livi Bacci. Firenze: Dipartimento statistico-matematico dell'Università-CISP.

Lohrmann, R. and Manfrass, K. eds.
1974 *Ausländerbeschäftigung und internationale Politik.* Münich: Oldenbourg.

Lowenthal, D.
1976 "The return of the non-native: new life for depopulated areas". In *Population at Microscale.* Edited by L. A. Kosinski and J. W. Webb. New Zealand Geographical Society and the Population Commission of the International Geographical Union.

MacDonald, J., and MacDonald, B.
1964 "Chain migration, ethnic neighborhood formation and social networks". *Milbank Memorial Fund Quarterly*, 42: 82-97.

Maillat, D. *et al.*
1976 "Transfert d'emplois vers les pays qui disposent d'un surplus de main-d'oeuvre comme alternative aux migrations internationales: le cas de la Suisse, I, II". Geneva: International Labour Office, World Employment Programme, Migration for Employment Project, 2-26/WP-5, 8.

Mangalam, J. J.
1968 *Human migration.* Lexington: University of Kentucky Press.

Manganara, J.
1977 "Some social aspects of the return migration of Greek migrant workers from West Germany to rural Greece". *Review of Social Research*, 29.

Markoff, J.
1977 "The world as a social system". *Peasant Studies*, 1(VI): 2.

Marshall, A.
1973 *The import of labour: the case of the Netherlands.* Rotterdam University Press.

Mayer, J., and Lebon, A.
1979 "Mesure de la présence étrangère en France". *Pour une politique du travail*, 13. Paris: Ministère du Travail et de la Participation.

Mehrländer, U.
1978 "Bundesrepublik Deutschland'. In *Ausländerpolitik im Konflikt. Konzepte der Aufnahme- und Entsendeländer.* Edited by E. Gehmacher *et al.* Bonn.

——

1979 "The Federal Republic of Germany". In *The politics of migration policies.* Edited by D. Kubat. New York: Center for Migration Studies.

Mehrländer, U. *et al.*
1981 *Situation der ausländischen Arbeitnehmer und ihrer Familienangehörigen in der Bundesrepublik Deutschland. Repräsentativuntersuchung 1980.* Bonn: Forschungsinstitut der Friedrich-Ebert-Stiftung. Forschungsbericht im Auftrage des Bundesministers für Arbeit und Sozialordnung. Bonn.

Mendez, J.E.C. and Moro, O. E.
1976 "The relation between migration policy and economic development". *International Migration*, 14(1/2): 134-61.

Merico, F.
1978 "Il difficile ritorno: indagine sul rientro degli emigrati in alcune comunità del Mezzogiorno". *Studi Emigrazione*, 50: 179-212.

Michaud, G. ed.
1978 "Identités collectives et relations interculturelles". Paris: Complexe.

Ministère du Travail
1981 "Allocution de M. le Secrétaire d'Etat chargé des immigrés, sur la politique du gouvernement à l'égard de la population immigrés et des réfugiés. In *Migrations Informations*, 37. Paris: Ministère du Travail.

Miracle, M. P. and Berry, S. S.
1970 "Migrant labour and economic development". *Oxford Economic Papers,* 22: 86-108.

Mobagunje, A. L.
1970 "System approach to a theory of rural-urban migration". *Geographical Analysis*, 2: 1-18.

Monson, T. D.
1975 "Differences in industrial learning behaviour of Turkish workers at home and abroad: causes and consequences". In *Manpower mobility across cultural boundaries. Social economic legal aspects. The case of Turkey and West Germany.* Edited by R. E. Krane. Leiden: E. J. Brill.

Moral Santin, J. A.
1981 "El capitalismo español y la crisis". In *Crecimiento económico y crisis estructural en España, 1959-1980.* Edited by R. Carballo and A. Temprano. Madrid: Akal.

Morokvašić, M.
1973 "Jugoslovenski radnici u inostranstvu: klasna svest; borba radnickeklase u

zemljana imigracije (Yugoslav workers abroad: class consciousness and the workers' struggle in the immigration countries". *Sociologija*, 2: 273-288.

—— 1975 "L'émigration yougoslave". *Revue française d'études politiques méditerranéennes*, juin, 90-106.

—— 1980 *Yugoslav women in France, the Federal Republic of Germany and Sweden.* Paris: Centre National de la Recherche Scientifique, 642 (mimeo).

—— 1981 "Les Yougoslaves". In *L'argent des immigrés*. Paris: Presses Universitaires de France, INED, Cahier No. 94: 267-299.

Morokvašić, M. and Rogers, R.
1982 *Return migration to Yugoslavia, innovative return migrants and prospects for economic development*, unpublished research report.

Motuz, C.
n.d. "Return migration: an analysis of return migration from Canada: 1969-1974". Mimeographed report of the research projects group (Project R-22). Ottawa: Department of Manpower and Immigration.

Mouleart, F.
1980 "The immigration policy of the Belgium Government (1961-1979)". Paper presented at the International Regional Science Association, Cambridge, Mass., June 14-15.

Moulier, J. and Tapinos, G.
1979 "France". In *The politics of migration policies*. Edited by D. Kubat. New York: Center for Migration Studies.

Munter, A., ed.
1979 "Ruotsin muuton ongelmat". *Siirtolaisuustutkimuksia A7*. Turku: Institute of Migration.

Munter, A.
1980 "Julkisen työnvälityksen merkitys Ruotsin muutossa ja siirtolaisten työhönsijoittaminen vuonna 1978". *Siirtolaisuustutkimuksia* (Migration Studies), 15. Helsinki: Ministry of Labour.

Nett, R.
1971 "Civil rights we are not ready for: the right of free movement of people on the face of the earth". *Ethics*, 81: 212-27.

Ney, J. W. and Eberle, D. K.
1975 *A selected bibliography on bilingual-bicultural education*. Washington-Arlington: ERIC Clearinghouse on Languages and Linguistics, Center for Applied Linguistics.

OECD
1967 *Emigrant workers returning to their home country. Final report*. Paris: OECD.

——
1978a *La chaine migratoire*. Paris: OCDE.

——
1978b *Migration, growth and development*. Paris: OECD.

——
1980 *The migratory chain*. Paris: OECD.

OECD-SOPEMI
1973-1981 *Continuous Reporting System on Migration*. Paris: OECD.

——
1981 *L'immigration en France en 1980 et premiers mois de 1981*. Paris: OCDE.

Paci, M.
1973 *Mercato del lavoro e classi sociali in Italia*. Bologna: Il Mulino.

Paine, S.
1974 *Exporting workers: the Turkish case*. London: Cambridge University Press.

Pamietniki
1977 *Pamietniki emigrantów. Stany Zjednoczone*, vol. 1. Warszawa: Ksiazka i Wiedza.

Papademetriou, D. G.
1978 "European labor migration: consequences for the countries of workers origin". *International Studies Quarterly*, 22(3): 377-408.

Papademetriou, D. G.

1983a "Rethinking international migration: a review and critique". *Comparative Political Studies*, 15,4: 469-98.

—

1983b "A retrospective look at Mediterranean labor migration to Europe". In *The Contemporary Mediterranean World*. Edited by C. F. Pinkele and A. Pollis. New York: Praeger.

—

1983c *The impact of international migration on the development of the countries of worker origin: the case of Greece.* (Forthcoming).

Papademetriou, D. G. and Hopple, G. W.

1982 "Causal modelling in international migration research: a methodological prolegomenon". *Quality and Quantity*, 16: 369-402.

1980 "Paro y políticas de empleo". *Papeles de Economía*, No. 8, Madrid.

Penninx, R. and van Renselaar, H.

1978 *A fortune in small change. A study of migrant workers attempts to invest savings productively through joint stock corporations and village development co-operatives in Turkey.* The Hague.

Petersen, W.

1958 "A general typology of migration". *American Sociological Review,* 23: 256-66.

Petonnet, C.

1979 *On est tous dans le brouillard.* Paris: Col. Galilée.

Petras, E. Mc Lean

1981 "The global labor market in the modern world economy". In *Global trends in migration: Theory and research on international movements.* Edited by M. M. Kritz *et al.* Staten Island, New York: Center for Migration Studies.

Pienkos, A. and Pienkos, D.

1981 "Badania nad zachowaniami politycznymi Amerykanów polskiego pochodzenia". *Przeglad Polonijny*, No. 1.

Pilch, A.

1976 "Odpowiedź refentów". In *Mechanizmy polskich migracji zarobkowych.* Edited by G. Bobińska. Warszawa: Ksiazka i Wiedza.

Poinard, M.
1979a *Le retour des travailleurs portugais,* Collection Migrations et Sociétés. Paris: La Documentation Française.

——
1979b "Le million des immigrés. Analyse de l'utilisation de l'aide au retour per les travailleurs portugais en France". *Revue Geographique des Pyrénées et du Sud-Ouest,* 50: 511-539.

Pred, A.
1977 "The choreography of existence: comments on Hägerstrand's time-geography and its usefulness". *Economic Geography,* 53: 207-221.

——
1981 "Social reproduction and the time-geography of everyday life". *Geografiska Annaler,* 63B: 5-22.

Price, C. and Martin, J.
1976 *Australian immigration, a bibliography and digest, no. 3 part. 1.* Canberra: The Australian National University Press.

Primorac-Davidović, M.
1976 "Radnici na privremenom radu u inostranstvu: Mit o sticanju kvalifikacija". *Dometi,* 7: 41-49.

——
1982 "O povratku nasih radnika iz inostranstva". *Socioloski Pregled,* 1-2 (XVI): 5-43.

Radlović, O.
Normativno reguliranje privremeno g zaposljavanja jugoslavenskih gradjana u inozemstvu (Normative regulation of temporary employment of Yugoslav workers abroad). *Rasprave o migracijama* (Discussion on Migration). Zagreb, No. 31.

Raivio, Y.
1975 *Kanadan suomalaisten historia I.* Copper Cliff, Ontario: Finnish-Canadian Historical Society.

Ravenstein, E.G.
1885 "The laws of migration". *Journal of Royal Statistical Society,* 48: 167-227.

Reeves, P.
1978 "Retirement migration: A bibliography, Council of Planning Librarians". *Exchange Bibliography*, No. 1510.

Rex, J. and Tomlinson, S.
1979 *Colonial immigrants in a British city.* London: Routledge and Paul Kegan.

Reyneri, E.
1979 *La catena migratoria.* Bologna: Il Mulino.

——

1980 "Emigration and sending area as a subsidized system in Sicily". *Mediterranean Studies*, 1: 90-113.

Rhoades, R. E.
1977 "Rasgos estructurales del empleo y paro en la formación social española". *Información Comercial Española*, 553: 64-90.

——

1978 "Intra-European return migration and rural development: lessons from the Spanish case", *Human Organization*, 37 (2): 137-48.

——

1979a "From caves to main street: return migration and the transformation of a Spanish village". *Papers in anthropology*, 20 (1): 57-74.

——

1979b "Toward an anthropology of return migration". *Popular Anthropology*, 20: 1-111.

——

1980 "European cyclical migration and economic development: The case of Southern Spain. The return of urban migrants to their rural homes and their impact there". In *Urban life*. Edited by G. Gmelch *et al.* New York: St. Martin's Press.

Richardson, A.
1967 "A theory and a method for the psychological study of assimilation". *International Migration Review*, 2, 3: 3-29.

——

1968 "A shipboard study of some British born immigrants returning to the United Kingdom from Australia". *International Migration*, 6: 221-238.

Richardson, A.
1974 *British immigrants and Australia: a psychosocial inquiry*. Canberra: Australian National University Press.

Richmond, A. H.
1967 *Post-war immigrants in Canada*. Toronto: University of Toronto Press.

——
1968 "Return Migration from Canada to Britain". *Population Studies*, 22(2): 263-271.

——
1969 "Sociology of migration in industrial and post-industrial societies". *Migration*. Edited by J. A. Jackson. London: Cambridge University Press.

——
1974 "Aspects of the absorption and adaptation of immigrants". *Canadian Immigration and Population Study*. Ottawa: Information Canada.

——
1978 "The economic adaptation of immigrants: a new theoretical perspective". *International Migration Review*, 12: 3-38.

Rikkinen, K.
1970 "A circular model of interprovincial migration in Finland". Fennia Helsinki, 99:8.

Ringen, A. ed.
1980 *Migration to and within the Nordic countries. Report from the Vth Nordic Conference on Labour Migration research*. Oslo: Nordic Council on Ministeries and Institute of Applied Social Research.

Rivera-Batiz, F. L.
1980 "A demand-pull model of labor migration". Bloomington: Department of Economics Discussion Paper No. 80-2, Indiana University.

Rogers, R.
1978 *On the process of international migrants' integration into host societies: a hypothesis and comments*. Cambridge, Mass.: M.I.T. Center for International Studies monograph C/78-16.

——
1981 "Incentives to return: patterns of policies and migrants' responses". In *Global trends in migration: theory and research on International populat-*

ion movements. Edited by M. M. Kritz *et al*. New York: Center for Migration Studies.

Rogers, R.
1982 "Employment creation through migrants' loans to enterprises in Yugoslavia". In *Return migration to Yugoslavia: policies, the innovative return migrant, and prospects for economic development*, final report submitted by M. Morokvasić and R. Rogers to the Rockefeller-Ford Research Program on Population and Development Policy.

Rosenlew-Cremieux, A.
1982 "Vara svenska invandrare". En studie av aterflyttarbarn i den svenska skolan i Björneborg. SLS: s nämnd för samhällsfroskning. Forskningsrapport No. 41.

Rosoli, G.
1977 "L'emigrazione di ritorno: alla ricerca di una impostazione". *Studi Emigrazione/Etudes Migrations*, 47: 235-246.

——
1980 "La scolarizzazione dei figli degli emigrati: analisi e indicazioni". *Studi Emigrazione/Etudes Migrations*, 57: 3-8.

Rubenstein, H.
1979 "The return ideology in West Indian migration", *Papers in Anthropology*, 20(1): 21-38.

Rudas, N.
1974 *L'emigrazione sarda*. Roma: Centro Studi Emigrazione.

Saloutos, T.
1956 *They remember America: the story of the repatriated Greek-Americans*. Berkeley: University of California Press.

——
1974 "Exodus USA". In *Divided society. The ethnic experience in America*. Edited by G. Greer. New York: Basic Books Inc.

Sandis, E. E.
1970 "Characteristics of Puerto Rican migrants to and from the United States", *International Migration Review*, 6,2: 22-42.

Sandlund, T.
1980 "Ethnicity and mobility. Description of a project", *Ethnicity and Mobility*. Research Reports No. 1.

Sandlund, T.

1981 "Geografisk förändring bland finlandssvenskarna 1950-1975", *Ethnicity and Mobility*. Research Reports No. 7.

——

1982 "Social Structure and Social mobility. A study of the Swedish population in Finland 1950-1975", *Ethnicity and Mobility*, Research Reports No. 10.

Sanjust, A. M.

1969 "Reintegration of returnees in Sardinia", *Migration News*, 18,2: 14-18.

Saraceno, E.

1978 *An analysis of the three main types of reentry in Udine and Pordenone from 1970 to 1977*. Udine: OECD.

——

1980 *Migrazioni e mercato del lavoro. Il caso del Friuli-Venezia Giulia (Italia). OECD, Réunion d'experts sur migration et marché du travail. Examen d'expériences concrètes au plan régional à partir du cas de la région Frioul-Venetie Julienne''*. Marina di Aurisina, Trieste. (In collaborazione con Roberto Grandinetti).

——

1981 *Emigrazione e rientri. Il Friuli-Venezia Giulia nel secondo dopoguerra.* Udine: Cooperativa editoriale Il Campo.

Schierup, C. U.

1983 "Imigranti i Kriza", *Nase Teme*, 1-2 (XXVII): 48-68.

Schiller, B.

1974 "Channeling migration: a review of policy", *International Labour Review*, 111: 335-55. April.

——

"Utilisation of migrant workers' savings, with particular reference to their use for job creation in the home country", OECD: MS/M/404/467 (mimeo).

Schlag, W.

1961 "A survey of Austrian emigration to the US". In *Osterrich und die Angelsach siche Welt.* Edited by O. Hietsch. Wien: Wilhelm Braumüller.

Schneider, J. and Schneider, P.
1976 *Culture and political economy in Western Sicily*. New York: Academic Press.

Seferagić, D.
1977 "Scientific work in Yugoslavia on migrant returnees and their impact on the mother country". *International Migration Review*, 11: 363-374.

Semmingsen, I.
1950 *Veien mot vest. Annen del. Utvandringen fra Norge 1865-1915*. Oslo: Aschehoug.

Serageldin, I. *et al.*
1983 *Manpower and international labor migration in the Middle East and North Africa*. New York: Oxford University Press.

Serrano, A. and Malo de Molina, J. L.
1979 *Salarios y mercado de trabajo en España*. Madrid: H. Blume.

Signorelli, A. *et al.*
1977 *Scelte senza potere. Il ritorno degli emigranti nelle zone di esodo*. Roma: Officina Edizioni.

Simon, G.
1977 *Situation and perspectives of Tunisian migration. Planning Department and International Labour Office Report*. Tunis.

Sjaastad, L. A.
1962 "The costs and returns of human migration", *Journal of Political Economy*, 70(5): 80-93. October.

Smith, C. A.
1976 "Analyzing regional social systems". In *Regional Analysis, Volume II: Social Systems*. Edited by C. A. Smith. New York: Academic Press.

Solé, C.
1981 *La integración sociocultural de los immigrantes en Cataluña*. Madrid: Centro de Investigaciones Sociológicas.

Stahl, C. W.
1981 "Migrant labour supplies, past, present and future; with special reference to the gold-mining industry". In *Black migration to South Africa. A selection of policy-oriented research*. Edited by W. R. Böhning. Geneva: International Labour Office.

337

Stahl, C. W.
1982 "International labour migration and international development". Geneva: ILO. International Migration for employment, Working Papert, No. 1.

Stasik, F.
1973 *Polska emigracja polityczna w Stanach Zjednoczonych Ameryki. 1831-1864.* Warszawa: Państwowe Wydawnictwo Naukowe.

Statistiska Centralbyran (SCB)
1977 *Population changes,* Part 3. Stockholm: Official Statistics of Sweden (SOS).

——
1981 *Facts about Swedish immigrants, living conditions,* Report No. 26. Stockholm: Official Statistics of Sweden (SOS).

Stockton, W.
1978 "The Puerto Ricans' new migration", *The New York Times Magazine,* November 12: 20-22, 88-93.

Stillwell, J. C. H.
1980 "Theoretical and empirical analysis of internal migration: a research bibliography". University of Leeds, School of Geography, Working Paper 284.

Svenska emigrationskommittens betänkande
1980 *Kommittebetänkande 1980: 24.* Helsingfors: Statens tryckericentral.

Swanberg, V.
1980 *Medelklassrealism.* Stockholm: Gidlunds.

Swanson, J.
1979 "The consequences of return migration for economic development: a review of the literature", *Papers in Anthropology,* 20(1): 39-56.

Swindell, K. and Ford, R. G.
1975 "Places, migrants and organisation: some observations on population mobility", *Geografiska Annaler,* 57B: 68-76.

Szentes, T.
1976 *The political economy of underdevelopment.* Budapest: Akadémiai Kiadó.

Taamallah, K.
1976 *The Tunisian migration to France. The social and demographic aspects and the coming back problems involved.* 3e cycle thèse, Paris I.

Taft, R.
1966 *From stranger to citizen: a survey of studies of immigrant assimilation in Western Australia.* London: Tavistock Publications.

Tajfes, H.
1973 *Social identity, social categorisation and social comparison in intergroup behaviour.* Bristol: University of Bristol.

Talamo, M.
1967 "L'émigration de retour dans le cadre des mouvements migratoires". In *Les Travailleurs émigrés retournant dans leur pays.* Paris: OCDE.

Tap, P.
"Identités collectives et changements sociaux". Colloque International, Université TOULOUSE-Le-MIRAIL. Toulouse: Ed. Privat.

Tapinos, G.
1974 *L'économie des migrations internationales.* Paris: A. Colin.

Tapinos, G. *et al.*
1978 "Possibilité de transfert d'emplois vers les pays d'émigration en tant qu' alternative aux migrations internationales des travailleurs: le cas français, I, II, III". Geneva: International Labour Office, World Employment Programme, Migration for Employment Project, 2-26/WP-24, 25, 26.

Tassello, G. and Favero, L.
1979 *La problematica del ritorno degli emigrati e del loro reinserimento in Italia. Rapporto curato dal CSER su commissione del CIEM.* Roma: CSER.

Tedebrand, L. G.
1976 "Remigration from America to Sweden". In *From Sweden to America. A history of the Migration.* Edited by H. Runblom and H. Norman. Minneapolis, Minn. and Uppsala: University of Minnesota Press and Uppsala University.

Temprano, A. G.
1981 "Cambios demográficos y crecimiento económico en la España desarrollista". In *Crecimiento económico y crisis estructural en España, 1959-1980.* Edited by R. Carballo and A. Temprano. Madrid: Akal.

Thomas, W. I. and Znaniecki, F.
(1918) 1927 *The Polish peasant in Europe and America*. 2 vols. New York: Alfred A. Knopf.

Todaro, M. P.
1976 *Internal migration in developing countries: a review of theory, evidence, methodology, and research priorities*. Geneva: ILO.

Toivoven, A. L.
1963 *Etelä-Pohjanmaan valtamerentakainen siirtolaisuus 1867-1930*. Helsinki: Finnish Historical Society.

Tos, N.
1976 "A systems model for migration research. (Yugoslav workers in Federal Republic of Germany". In *International migration and adaptation in the modern world*. Edited by A. H. Richmond. Toronto: I.S.A. Research Committee on Migration.

Trebous, M.
1970 *Migrations et développement. Le cas de l'Algérie*. Paris: OCDE.

Tuna, O.
1967 *Yurda Dönen Iscilerin Intibak Sorunlari* (Readaptation of Returning Workers), SPO Research Report, Ankara.

Unger, K.
1980 *Ausländerpolitik in der Bundesrepublik Deutschland*. Saarbrücken.

——
1981 "Greek emigration and return: structural factors and characteristics of the immigrants". Athens July 1981.

——
1983 *Die Rueckkehr der Arbeitsemigranten: eine Studie zur Remigration nach Griechenland*. Saarbrücken: Breitenbach.

United Nations
1979 *Trends and characteristics of international migration since 1950*. New York: United Nations (E. 78. XIII. 5).

Valkonen, T. *et al.*
1980 *Suomalaiset. Yhteiskunnan rakenne teollistumisen aikana*. Juva: WSOY.

Van Amersfoort, J. M. M.
1978 "Migrant workers, circular migration and development", *Tijdschrift voor Econ. en Soc. Geografie*, 69: 17-26.

Vandercamp, J.
1971 "Migration flows, their determinants and the effects of return migration", *Journal of Political Economy*, 79: 1012-1032.

van Dijk, P. J. C. and Penninx, R.
1976 *The Remplod Project, a Dutch experiment of policy and research in the field of migration and development*. The Hague: REMPLOD.

Van Gendt, R.
1977 *Return migration and reintegration services*. Paris: OECD.

Van Velzen, L.
1977 *Peripheral production in Kayseri Turkey*. Ankara: Ajans-Turk Press.

Vedriś, M.
1975 "The utilisation of migrant workers. Hard currency savings in productive economic activities". In *Yugoslav Report for the OECD Joint Project*, Services for Returning Migrant Workers'. Zagreb: Center for Migration Studies (mimeo).

——

1977a "Investment of external migrants' savings in the public sector of the economy", *DOM*, 33.

——

1977b "The inclusion of external migrants in the economic and societal life of SR Croatia", *Ekonomski pregled* ("The Economic Survey", ES), 3-4.

——

1978a "From foreign currency savings to a workplace in homeland", *DOM*, 46.

——

1978b "The establishment of labour relationship with citizens giving their resources to basic organisations of associated labour (i.e. enterprises) for job creation". *Propisi i praksa* ("Regulations and Practice"), 10.

——

1978c "Contemporary external migration from Yugoslavia to the countries of West Europe", *ES*, 9.

Vedriś, M.
1978d "The transfer of technology and international labour migration", *Migracije* ("Migration"), 2.

Velikonja, J.
1974 "Some geographical implications of the brain drain". In *Regional Studies, Methods and Analyses*. Edited by I. Bencze and G. Bora. Budapest: Hungarian Academy of Sciences.

Verhaeren, R. E.
1980 "Immigration and crisis", *International Migration Review*, XII: 2, 210-235.

Vigorelli, P.
1969 "Returning migrants reemployed in Italian industry", *Migration News*, 18,2: 3-13.

Villey, O.
1981 "Le redéploiment actuel de la main d'oeuvre étrangère passé le premier choc de la crise", *Travail et Emploi*, 8: 47-55. April-June.

Virtanen, K.
1979 *Settlement or return: Finnish emigrants (1860-1930) in the international overseas return migration movement.* Helsinki: Finnish Historical Society.

Wallerstein, I.
1974 *The modern world-system: capitalist agriculture and the origins of the European world-economy in the Sixteenth Century.* New York: Academic Press.

Walsh, J. A.
1979 "Immigration into the Republic of Ireland", *Irish Geography*, 12: 104-110.

Warren, R.
1979 "Alien Emigration from the United States: 1963 to 1974". Paper prepared for the Annual Meeting of the Population Association of America, Philadelphia, April 27.

Warren, R. and Marks Peck, J.
1980 "Foreign-born emigration from the United States: 1960 to 1970", *Demography*, 17,1: 71-84.

Weichdacher, A.
1981 *Ausländische Arbeiterfamilien, Kinder und Jugendliche: Situations-analyse und Massnahmen.* München: Deutsches Jugendinstitut.

Werth, M.
1981 "Anmerkunger zur Wirksamkeit deutscher Reintegrationsprogramme für türkische Arbeitnehmer". In *Rückwanderung und Reintegration von ausländischen Arbeitnehmem in Europa.* Edited by H. Körner and M. Wert. Saarbrücken.

Werth, M. and Yalcintas, N.
1978 "Migration and reintegration: transferability of the Turkish model of return migration and self-help organisations to other Mediterranean labour-exporting countries". Geneva: International Labor Office. World Employment Programme, Migration for Employment Project Working Paper No. 29.

Wester, H.
1977 *Innovationer i befolkningsrörligheten. En studie av spridningsförlopp i befolkningsrörligheten utgaende fran Petalax socken i Osterbotten.* Uppsala: Uppsala University.

Widgren, J.
1977 *The migratory chain.* Paris: OECD.

——
1981 "Invandrarpolitik och langsiktsplanering". In *Invandringen och framti-den.* Edited by T. Hammar and E. Hamberg. Stockholm.

——
1982 *SOPEMI 1981. Reports in new trends in Swedish and European migrat-ion.* Stockholm: Commission on Immigration Research (EIFO).

Wiest, R.
1979 "Anthropological perspectives on return migration: a critical commen-tary". *Papers in Anthropology,* 20(1): 167-88.

Wihtol de Wenden, C.
1980 "Le retour des travailleurs immigrés en France dans leurs pays d'origine", *Die Dritte Welt,* 3-4: 291-305.

——
1981 "Les orientations récentes de la politique française de retour: 1980-1981", *Crises en Europe et émigration maghrébine,* Alger: CREA.

343

Willcox, W. F. ed.
1929 *International migrations*. Vol. I. New York: National Bureau of Economic Research.

Wilpert, C.
1980 *Die Zukunft der Zweiten Generation - Erwartungen und Verhaltensmöglicjkeiten ausländischer Kinder*. Königstein/Taunus: Anton Hain.

—— 1983 "Zukunftsperspektiven von Migrantenfamilien", *Soziologische Forschungen*, Technische Universität Berlin, Institut für Soziologie.

Wilson, F.
1976 "International migration in Southern Africa". Geneva: International Labor Office. World Employment Programme, Migration for Employment Project Working Paper No. 3.

Wiltshire, R.
1978 "Return migration to lagging regions: a bibliographic survey with special reference to North America and Europe", The Science Report of the Tohoku University, *Geography*, 28: 87-99.

Woodward, S. L.
(forth.) "Political changes in the European Mediterranean arena: an overview of considerations for policy-markers". In *Stability and change in the contemporary Mediterranean World*. Edited by A. Pollis and C. Pinkele. New York: Praeger.

Yasa, I.
1978 *Yurda Dönen Isciler ve Toplumsal Degisme*. Ankara: TODAIE Publ.

Zampaglione, A.
1977 "I giovani in agricoltura tra esodo e sottoccupazione", *Rivista di economia agraria*, 3: 612-33.

Zelinsky, W.
1971 "The hypothesis of the mobility transition", *Geographical Review*, 61: 219-249.

Zingaro, R.
1969 "Reintegration of returnees in Andria", *Migration News*, 18,2: 19-22.

Zolberg, A. R.

1981 "International migrations in political perspective". In *Global trends in migration: theory and research on international population movements.* Edited by M. M. Kritz *et al.* Staten Island, New York: Center for Migration Studies.

NAME INDEX

349

SUBJECT INDEX

PROGRAM

The First European Conference
on International Return Migration

Rome, November 11-14, 1981

Consiglio Nazionale delle Ricerche

Sponsored by the
Research Committee on Migration, International Sociological Association
(ISA)

with the Cooperation of the
Centro Studi Emigrazione - Roma

and the Support of the
Consiglio Nazionale delle Ricerche
Presidenza del Consiglio dei Ministri
Ministero degli Affari Esteri
UNESCO
Ford Foundation
Volkswagen Foundation

Local Organizing Committee
Chairman, G. Rosoli, Centro Studi Emigrazione
Via Calandrelli 11 - 00153 Roma
F. P. Cerase, Representative of the Board of the Research Committee on
Migration - ISA

Wednesday, November 11

FIRST PLENARY SESSION

Return Migration to Italy

Chair: F. P. Cerase, University of Rome

M. Brutti - C, Calvaruso, CENSIS, Rome
Return Migration to Italy and Labour Market

E. Reyneri, ISVI, University of Catania
Return Migration, Economic Stagnation and Potentials in Departure Areas

L. Favero - G. Tassello, CSER, Rome
Return Migration With Particular Reference to Educational Problems

I. Musillo, ILO, Geneva,
Return and Employment in the Italian "Mezzogiorno"

Research Projects in Friuli, Campania, Puglia, Sicily, Sardinia

Thursday, November 12

FIRST WORKSHOP

Return Migration to the Mediterranean Basin West:
Research Findings

Chair: M. B. Rocha-Trindade, Ministry of Foreign Affairs, Lisbon

E. de Sousa Ferreira, Instituto Superior de Economia
Some Socio-economic Considerations on Reintegration of Migrants: the
Portuguese Case

E. Serra-Santana, Université de Toulouse-Le Mirail
Return: Realization of a Project or End of a Dream?
The Case of Returning Migrants to Bragança

G. Abou-Sada, C.N.R.S., Lille
Tunisian Migration and Return Migration Policies

C. Solé, Universidad de Barcelona
Return of Immigrants - Integration in Catalonia

SECOND WORKSHOP

Return Migration to the Mediterranean Basin East:
Research Findings

Chair: K. Kassimati, National Centre of Social Research, Athens

358

K. Unger, Universität Bielefeld
Determinants of the Occupational Composition of Returning Migrants in Urban Greece

R. Fakiolas, Centre of Planning and Economic Research, Athens
Size, Structure and Socio-economic Effects of Return Migration in Greece

S. Meznaric, Confederation of Trade Unions of Slovenia, Ljubljana
How Policies Fit the Reality? Some Recent Research Findings on Returning Migration and Policies in Yugoslavia

M. Morokvasić, C.N.R.S., Paris
Intended Return and Job Creation: the Case of Yugoslav Migrant Workers in France and Germany

A. Gitmez, Middle East Technical University, Ankara
Resettlement and Re-adaptation of Returning Turkish Migrants

SECOND PLENARY SESSION

Impact of Out-migration (Return) on Populous Countries in Europe: Comparison between the Federal Republic of Germany and France

Chair: U. Mehrländer, Friedrich-Ebert-Stiftung, Bonn

H. Körner, Technische Hochschule Darmstadt
The Case of Federal Republic of Germany

A. Lebon, Ministère du Travail et de la Participation, Paris
The Case of France

Discussant: H. Korte, Ruhr-Universität Bochum

Friday, November 13

THIRD WORKSHOP

Return Migration to the Mediterranean Basin: Policies

Chair: S. Tomasi, Editor International Migration Review, New York

J. Aveling, OECD, Paris
The OECD Views on Return Migration

C.W. de Wenden, C.N.R.S., Paris
French Policy on Return Migration in the Context of the Franco-Algerian Agreement of 1980

J.P. Garson, Université de Paris
Return Migration in Algerian Economic Development in the 1980's

J. Cazorla, Universidad de Granada
Return Migration Policies in the Iberian Peninsula

I. Baucić, Centre for Migration Studies, Zagreb
Ten-year Experience in the Realisation of Yugoslav Policy of Return Migration

M. Vedris, Centre for Migration Studies, Zagreb
Activities concerning the Return and the Work Re-integration of Yugoslav Migrant Workers

FOURTH WORKSHOP

Return Migration to Europe from Overseas

Chair: E. McLean Petras, University of Pennsylvania

M. C. t'Hart
Returning Emigrants in the XIXth Century

S. Sassen-Koob, Brooklyn College
Causes and Consequences of Labor Migration in Europe: the Case of Greece

P.W. Blauw, Erasmus University, Rotterdam
Return Migration to the Netherlands from Canada, Australia and New Zealand

A. Walaszek, University of Krakow
Return Migration from the USA to Poland and Evolution of Consciousness of Polish Immigrants in the USA

THIRD PLENARY SESSION

*Impact of Out-migration (Return)
on Less Populous Countries in Europe*

Chair: H. J. Hoffmann-Nowotny, University of Zürich

K. Virtanen, University of Turku
Return Migration as a Factor of Finnish Overseas Migration

T. Hammar, EIFO, Stockholm
Dilemmas of Swedish Immigration Policy: They Were Invited to Stay Permanently - Do They Want to Return?

T. Sandlung, EIFO, Stockholm
Finnish Emigration to Sweden, with Special Emphasis on Re-emigration

Saturday, November 14

FIFTH WORKSHOP

Return Migration of Long Term Migrants

Chair: D. Kubat, University of Waterloo

A. H. Richmond, York University
Theories of Return Migration and the Variable of the Length of Stay

D.D. Gregory, ICMD, Hanover, USA
The Effects of Long Term Stay Abroad on Migrants: the Spanish and the Portuguese

E. McLean Petras, University of Pennsylvania
International Return Migration and International Capital: Policy Implications

R. Rogers, Tufts University
Return Migration in Comparative Perspective

ABOUT THE AUTHORS

GEORGES ABOU SADA is a researcher with the Centre national de la recherche scientifique in France. He is currently working with OMINOR (Observatoire des migrations internationales dans la région du Nord-Pas-de-Calais).
Address: OMINOR, 1 rue François Baës - 59046 Lille, France.

IVO BAUCIC is director of the Centre for Migration Studies, Zagreb, at the University of Zagreb. He is author of many books and essays on Yugoslav emigration in Europe.
Address: Centre for Migration Studies, Krcka 1, Flajpanova 1 P.O. Box 88 - 41001 Zagreb, Yugoslavia.

LUCIANO BERROCAL is professor at the Université Libre de Bruxelles. His most recent book is entitled *Marché du travail et mouvements migratoires* (1983).
Address: Université Libre de Bruxelles, Institut d'Etudes Européennes, Ave. F.D. Roosevelt 39 - 1050 Bruxelles, Belgium.

P. WIM BLAUW, associate professor of sociology at Erasmus University in Rotterdam, dealt with questions of migration and urbanization in his two latest books: *Soort bij Soort* (1980) and *Emigreren* (1983).
Address: Erasmus Universiteit Rotterdam, Faculteit der Economische Wetenschappen, P.O. Box 1738 - 3000 DR Rotterdam, Netherlands.

CLAUDIO CALVARUSO, sociologist, head of the social department of the CENSIS Foundation is author of many essays on Italian emigration, among them: *Sottoproletariato in Svizzera* (Roma, 1971); *Emigrazione e sindacati* (Roma, 1974).
Address: CENSIS, Piazza di Novella 2 - 00199 Roma, Italy.

FRANCESCO P. CERASE is professor of Sociology at the University of Rome. Secretary-Treasurer of the Research Committee on Migration, ISA. His main works include *L'emigrazione di ritorno: innovazione o reazione?* (Rome, 1971), *Sotto il dominio dei borghesi. Sottosviluppo ed emigrazione nell'Italia meridionale* (Roma, 1976). He is lately interested in the politics of migration.
Address: Research Committee on Migration, Via Aquileia 15 - 00198 Roma, Italy.

RITA L. CHEPULIS is a doctoral candidate in the Department of Anthropology at Yale University, in the United States. Between 1980 and 1983, holding an IREX grant, she conducted migration research on Croatian workers in Yugoslavia.

Address: Posilovićeva 4 - 41000 Zagreb, Yugoslavia.

JOED H. ELICH is currently research assistant at the Centre for the Study of Social Conflicts, University of Leiden, in the Netherlands. He is co-author, with Blauw, of *Emigreren*.
Address: Klieverink 178 - 1104 KD Amsterdam, Netherlands.

ROSS FAKIOLAS, trained at the London School of Economics, is Professor of Economics at the Technical University in Athens. His books deal principally with issues of the labor market and migration of Greek workers.
Address: Centre of Planning and Economic Research, 66 Heroon Polytechnion St. - Athens, Greece.

LUIGI FAVERO is the editor of the monthly review *Dossier Europa-Emigrazione* and supervises the research projects carried out by the Centro Studi Emigrazione-Roma. Author of many essays on migration.
Address: Via Dandolo 58 - 00153 Roma, Italy.

JEAN-PIERRE GARSON teaches economics at the Université Paris-Sud. His special interests are in Algerian-French migration. His latest book, co-edited with Georges Tapinos, is *L'argent des émigrés* (1980).
Address: 20 Avenue des Cottages - 92340 Bourg La Reine, France.

MARIA LUISA GENTILESCHI is professor of Geography at the University of Cagliari in Sardinia. She is member of the International Geographical Union, Commission on Population Geography.
Address: Università di Cagliari, Istituto di Geografia, Piazza D'Armi - 09100 Cagliari, Italy.

ALI S. GITMEZ is presently associate professor of Social Psychology at the Middle East Technical University in Ankara. His most recent studies deal with returnees to Turkey.
Address: Middle East Technical University, Department of Management, Inonu Bulvari - Ankara, Turkey.

PATRICIA GOLDEY is a researcher with the Agricultural Extension and Rural Development Centre at the University of Reading.
Address: Agricultural Extension and Rural Development Centre the University of Reading, London Road - Reading RG1 5AQ, Great Britain.

TOMAS HAMMAR is the director of the Center for Research in International Migration and Ethnicity, the University of Stockholm. Recently, he has edited *European Immigration Policy* (1984). Professor Hammar is Executive Secretary of the Swedish Commission on Immigration Research (EIFO).

Address: Center for Research in International Migration and Ethnicity, Freds-gatan 2 - 111 52 Stockholm, Sweden.

HANS-JOACHIM HOFFMANN-NOWOTNY is professor of Sociology and Director of the Sociological Institute at the University of Zürich. His work in migration, in addition to his writings on theory, includes a study of Italian migrants in Zürich.
Address: Soziologisches Institut, Universität Zürich, Wiesenstr. 9 - 8008 Zürich, Switzerland.

KOULA KASSIMATI is member of the National Centre of Social Research, Athens.
Address: The National Centre of Social Research, 1 Sophocleous St. - 122 Athens, Greece.

RUSSELL KING teaches geography at the University of Leicester. His migra-tion research project, briefly reported on here, will be published in book form in the near future.
Address: The University of Leicester, Department of Geography - Leicester LE1 7RH, Great Britain.

PETER KLINAR is a senior professor at the University of Ljubljana. His work in the area of migration is reported in Yugoslav publications and frequently presented before international conferences as well.
Address: University of Ljubljana - 61100 Ljubljana, Yugoslavia.

HEIKO KÖRNER is professor of Economics at the Technische Hochschule Darmstadt. His publications are in the area of macro economics.
Address: Technische Hochschule Darmstadt, Residenz Schloss - 6100 Darms-tadt, W. Germany.

HERMANN KORTE is professor at Ruhr-Universität.
Address: Steinweg 18 - 484 Rheda, W. Germany.

ANDRE' LEBON is senior advisor to the statistical data collection on labor force at the Ministère du Travail, France. His many publications offer a de-tailed analysis of foreign labor in France and the second generation migrants.
Address: Ministère des Affaires Sociales et de la Solidarité Nationale, Direction de la Population et des Migrations, 1 Place de Fontenoy - 75700 Paris, France.

JOSE' J.R. LEITE PEREIRA is professor of Economics at the University of Lisbon.
Address: Instituto Superior de Economia da Universidade Tecnica de Lisboa, Rua Miguel Lupi - 1200 Lisboa, Portugal.

URSULA MEHRLÄNDER is senior researcher with the Friedrich Ebert Stiftung in Bonn. Her doctorate is from the University of Bielefeld; she is well known for her survey work on the situation of foreign youth in the Federal Republic.
Address: Friedrich-Ebert-Stiftung, Godesberger Allee 149 - 5300 Bonn 2, W. Germany.

SILVA MEZNARIC is a political scientist holding a faculty position at the University of Ljubljana, where she also works at the Center for Migration Studies.
Address: Center for Selfmanagement Studies , Miklosiceva 36 - 61100 Ljubljana, Yugoslavia.

MIRJANA MOROKVASIC is research sociologist with Centre National de la Recherche Scientifique in France. Dr. Morokvasić specialty is sex roles and development. She spent one year as visiting researcher at the University of Berlin, in 1982-83.
Address: CNRS, Groupe d'Etude des roles des sexes, de la famille et du développement humain, 82 rue Cardinet - 75017 Paris, France.

JILL MORTIMER is a geographer at the University of Leicester. She works closely with Professor Russel on migration in Italy.
Address: The University of Leicester, Department of Geography - Leicester LE1 7RH, Great Britain.

ITALO MUSILLO, former assistant at the ILO, is presently working at CREDIS.
Address: CREDIS, 22 route Chapelle - 1227 Grand-Lancy, Switzerland.

DEMETRIOS G. PAPADEMETRIOU, PhD, is president of Population Associates International, a research firm in New York City. A trained political scientist, Dr. Papademetriou has written a number of overview papers dealing with worker migrations in Europe and elsewhere.
Address: Population Associates International, 33 Alan Loop - Staten Island, N.Y., 10304, USA.

ELISABETH MCLEAN PETRAS is professor of Regional Science at the University of Pennsylvania. She is best known for her interpretation of capital transfers in lieu of migration, documented in many papers she has authored. Professor Petras is currently spending a research leave in Athens (1983-84).
Address: Department of Regional Science, University of Pennsylvania - Philadelphia, Penn. 19104, USA.

EMILIO REYNERI is professor of Political Science at the University of Catania. He is author of *La catena migratoria* (Bologna, 1979).
Address: Università di Catania, Facoltà di Scienze Politiche, Via Beato Bernardo 5 - 95100 Catania, Italy.

ANTHONY RICHMOND is professor of Sociology at York University in Canada. His latest book is a study of immigrants in Canada and Australia, co-authored respectively with Professors Warren Kalbach and George Zubrzycki. (1982).
Address: York University, 4700 Keele St. - Downsview, Ont. M3J 1P3, Canada.

MARIA BEATRIZ ROCHA-TRINDADE, professor of Sociology at the Universidade Libre de Lisboa, former Secretary of State to Emigration and Portuguese Communities Abroad.
Address: Nucleo de Estudos das Migrações, Praça do Arreeiro 11 - 1000 Lisboa, Portugal.

ROSEMARIE ROGERS is professor of Political Science at The Fletcher School of Law and Diplomacy, Tufts University.
Address: Tuft University, The Fletcher School of Law and Diplomacy - Medford, Mass. 02155, USA.

GIANFAUSTO ROSOLI is editor of *Studi Emigrazione*, member of the Centro Studi Emigrazione in Rome, author of many essays on migration, and editor of *Un secolo di emigrazione italiana: 1876-1976* (Roma, 1978).
Address: Centro Studi Emigrazione, Via Dandolo 58 - 00153 Roma, Italy.

TOM SANDLUND is professor of Sociology at Abo University in Turku.
Address: Department of Sociology, Abo Academy - SF 20540 Turku, Finland.

ELENA SARACENO has been working since 1976 at CRES, a regional research center in Udine. Her work deals mainly with migration as relating to regional development: *Emigrazione e rientri. Il Friuli-Venezia Giulia nel secondo dopoguerra* (Udine, 1981).
Address: CRES, Via Palladio 8/1 - 33100 Udine, Italy.

SASKIA SASSEN-KOOB is associate professor of Sociology at Queens College, New York, City University of New York.
Address: 110 Green St. 9F - New York, N.Y. 10012, USA.

EMA SERRA-SANTANA, native of Chile, has been in France since 1973 as professor of Sociology at the Institut de sciences sociales at the Université de Toulouse-Le Mirail.
Address: Université de Toulouse-le-Mirail, 39 rue de la Concorde - 31000 Toulouse, France.

CARLOTA SOLE' is professor of Sociology at the University of Barcelona.
Address: Departamento de Sociologia, Facultad de Ciencias Económicas, Universidad de Barcelona, Pedralbes - Barcelona 34, Spain.

EDUARDO DE SOUSA FERREIRA is professor of Economics and Director of the Centro de Estudos de Dependencia at the Universidade Technica in Lisbon. His recent work deals with questions of migration in Portugal.
Address: Centro de Estudos da Dependencia - Instituto Superior de Economia da Universidade Técnica de Lisboa, Rua Miguel Lupi - 1200 Lisboa, Portugal.

ALAN STRACHAN is a researcher-geographer affiliated with the University of Leicester.
Address: The University of Leiceter, Department of Geography - Leicester LEI 7RH, Great Britain.

GRAZIANO TASSELLO is a sociologist, coordinates the activities at the Centro Studi Emigrazione-Rome and collaborates with the journal *Studi Emigrazione*.
Address: Via Dandolo 58 - 00153 Roma, Italy.

SILVANO TOMASI, president of the Center for Migration Studies, editor of the *International Migration Review* is author of many books and essays in the field of migration. Co-author of *Global trends in migration* (New York, 1981).
Address: Center for Migration Studies, 209 Flagg Place - Staten Island, N.Y. 10304, USA.

NIKO TOS is a sociologist at the Center for Migration Studies in Ljubljana.
Address: University of Ljubljana - 61100 Ljubljana, Yugoslavia.

KLAUS UNGER works at the Department of Sociology, University of Bielefeld, Federal Republic of Germany, where the Center for Development is located. His dissertation has been published under the title *Die Rückkehr der Arbeitsemigranten*, 1983.
Address: Universität Bielefeld, P.O. Box 8640 - 4800 Bielefeld 1, W. Germany.

MLADEN VEDRIS is a researcher with the Center for Migration Studies in Zagreb, where his numerous research reports on international migration of Yugoslav workers are published.
Address: Centre for Migration Studies, Flajpanova 1, P.O. Box 88 - 41001 Zagreb, Yugoslavia.

JOSEPH VELIKONJA is professor of Geography at the University of Washington in Seattle. His doctorate is from the University of Rome. His interest in international migration between Europe and North America centers on Italian and Yugoslav migrants.

Address: University of Washington, Department of Geography, 408A Smith Hall - Seattle, Wash. 98195, USA.

KEIJO VIRTANEN is professor of History of Civilization at the University of Turku. His latest book is *Settlement or return. Finnish emigrants between (1860-1930) in the international overseas return migration movement* (1979). *Address*: Institute of History of Civilization, University of Turku - 20500 Turku 50, Finland.

ROBERT VIVOLO is a researcher at Columbia University. *Address*: 417 West 118 St. - New York, N.Y. 10027, USA.

ADAM WALASZEK, graduate of the Jagiellonian University in Cracow, is on the Staff of the History Institute there. One of his recent publications is a book on *Return Migration from the United States to Poland after WWI*. *Address*: Polonia Research Institute, Jagiellonian University Rynek Gl. 34 - 31010 Krakow, Poland.

CATHERINE WIHTOL DE WENDEN-DIDIER is researcher with the Centre National de la Recherche Scientifique in Paris. Her current interests lie in the field of illegal migration. She is also the editor of the Newsletter of the Research Committee on Migration, ISA, which appears in the *International Migration Review*. *Address*: CNRS - Equipe de recherches sur les migrations internationales, 82 rue Cardinet - 75017 Paris, France.

CZARINA WILPERT is affiliated with the Institut für Soziologie at the Technische Hochschule, Berlin. Her work is primarily in the area of second generation in-migrants and their ways of cultural adjustment. *Address*: Technische Universität Berlin, Institut für Soziologie, Doverstrasse 1 - 1000 Berlin 10, W. Germany.

FRANC ZIZEK is migration researcher and economist at the Center for Migration Studies in Ljubljana. *Address*: University of Ljubljana - 61100 Ljubljana, Yugoslavia.

The Centro Studi Emigrazione-Roma (CSER), is a cultural institute founded in 1963 to study the historical, sociological, economic, legislative and pastoral aspects of Italian and international migration movements. The Center publishes books and journals dealing with human migration and refugee movements.

Periodicals

Studi Emigrazione/Etudes Migrations (quarterly)

Subscription rates	one-year	Italy	L.	24.000
"		Foreign	L.	28.000

Dossier Europa-Emigrazione (monthly)

Subscription rates	one-year	Italy	L.	18.000
"		Foreign	L.	20.000

Publications

A. Perotti (ed.) *La società italiana di fronte alle prime migrazioni di massa,* 1968, 511 p. L. 25.000.

Migrazioni-Migrations. Catalogo della Biblioteca CSER-Catalogue of the CSER Library, 1972, 806 p. L. 20.000 - Vol. II, L. 10.000.

AA.VV., *L'emigrazione italiana negli anni settanta,* 1975, 270 p. L. 13.000.

U. Marin, *Italiani in Gran Bretagna,* 1975, 205 p. L. 11.000.

G.F. Rosoli (ed.), *Un secolo di emigrazione italiana: 1876-1976,* 1978, 385 p. L. 25.000.

R. Cavallaro, *Storie senza storia. Indagine sull'emigrazione calabrese in Gran Bretagna,* 1981, 262 p. L. 16.000.

G. Rovere, *Il discorso omiletico,* 1982, 432 p. L. 19.000.

P. Borzomati (ed.), *L'emigrazione calabrese dall'Unità ad oggi,* 1982, 308 p. L. 18.000.

D. Kubat, *The politics of return. International return migration in Europe,* 1984, xii-369 p. L. 19.000.

CSER — Via Dandolo 58 - 00153 ROMA

The Center for Migration Studies is an educational, nonprofit institute founded in New York in 1964, committed to encourage and facilitate the study of socio-demographic, economic, political, historical, legislative and pastoral aspects of human migration and refugee movements.

Periodicals

International Migration Review   Subscription Rates: 1 year   25.00

Migration Today   ,,   ,,   ,,   ,,   19.00

Publications

Italian repatriation from the United States (1900-1914). By Betty Boyd Caroli 1977. Pp. 160. $ 9.95.

The assimilation of ethnic groups: the Italian case. By James A. Crispino, 1980. Pp. 205. $ 14.95 (cloth).

Images. A pictorial history of Italian Americans. 1981. Pp. 300. $ 29.95.

The immigrants speak. The Italian Americans tell their story. By Salvatore J. LaGumina, 1979. Pp. 209. $ 14.95 (cloth).

The Italian in America. The progressive view (1891-1914). Edited by Lydio F. Tomasi, 1978. Pp. xvi-309. $ 9.95.

The Italian experience in the United States. Edited by Silvano M. Tomasi and M.H. Engel. 1976. Pp. x-239. $ 9.95.

The Italians of Greenwich Village. By Donald Tricarico, 1984. Pp. 190. $ 17.50 (cloth).

Global trends in migration: theory and research in international population movements. Edited by Mary M. Kritz, Charles B. Keely and S.M. Tomasi, 1981. Pp. 532. $ 14.95 (cloth), $ 9.95 (paper).

In defense of the alien. Volumes I, II, III, IV, V, and VI. Proceedings of the 1978, 1979, 1980, 1981, 1982, 1983, Annual Legal Conferences on the Representation of Aliens. Edited by Austin T. Fragomen, Jr. and Lydio F. Tomasi, $ 60.

Italian Americans and religion. An annotated bibliography. By Silvano M. Tomasi and Edward Stibili, 1978. Pp. 225. $ 14.95 (cloth).

Piety and power. The role of Italian Parishes in the New York Metropolitan Area (1880-1930). By Silvano M. Tomasi, 1975. Pp. xi-201. $ 14.95 (cloth).

4069 - TIPOGRAFIA CITTÀ NUOVA DELLA PAMOM - 20 - 3 - 1984
00165 ROMA - LARGO CRISTINA DI SVEZIA, 17 - TEL. 5813475/82